Sport and Society

Series Editors
Benjamin G. Rader
Randy Roberts

Books in the Series Sport and Society

BEYOND THE RING

Jeffrey T. Sammons

BEYOND THE RING

The Role of Boxing in American Society

University of Illinois Press
Urbana and Chicago

Publication of this work was supported in part by a grant from
Rutgers, The State University of New Jersey, Camden Campus.

© 1988 by the Board of Trustees of the University of Illinois
Manufactured in the United States of America
C 5 4 3 2 1

This book is printed on acid-free paper.

Library of Congress Cataloging-in-Publication Data

Sammons, Jeffrey T. (Jeffrey Thomas), 1949–
   Beyond the ring.

   (Sport and society)
   Bibliography: p.
   Includes index.
   1. Boxing—United States. 2. Boxing—Social
aspects—United States.   I. Title.   II. Series.
GV1125.S26   1988   796.8'3'0973   87-19041
ISBN 0-252-01473-1 (alk. paper)

To Agnes, Oscar, and Mabel
—loving mother, stepfather,
and grandmother

It's like being in love with a woman. She can be faithful, she can be mean, she can be cruel, but it doesn't matter. If you love her, you want her, even though she can do you all kinds of harm. It's the same with me and boxing. It can do me all kinds of harm, but I love it.

Floyd Patterson

Contents

Preface

It is not a common occurrence for an academic historian to write about prizefighting, a sport that has made more people turn up their noses than reach for a pen, so I would like to share with you this book's origin. As both an only child and a product of the post–World War II baby boom, television was often my babysitter and my companion. My grandmother still fondly recalls my endless fascination with the "picture box." I cut my teeth on cartoons, Superman, Davy Crockett, Roy Rogers, and space adventures, but as I grew, sport soon became my passion. My likes and dislikes were often determined by household opinion and our close proximity to Philadelphia—home of the "stinkin' Phillies." After the "Whiz Kids" era the local team had neither quality nor racial enlightenment to recommend it, and while the Dodgers stood tall in our house because of Jackie Robinson, his trade and retirement soured the family on the team and on baseball in general. High school football, in our town of 20,000, meant more than the collegiate or professional variety, and basketball was for city kids. Consequently, boxing and wrestling held sway. Because I detected fakery in the latter at an early age, prizefighting became a favorite with me.

Although Joe Louis had retired before I was old enough to appreciate his greatness, the stories my folks told me convinced me of his impact on the sport. When I asked about Rocky Marciano, my grandfather dismissed him as a usurper who would not have stood a chance against Louis in his prime. The Brown Bomber's demise was a disappointment to my family, as it was to most blacks. His late-career losses, rather inglorious comeback, business failures, and tax problems angered black Americans who had looked to him as a source of pride. I could sense even then that Joe Louis was more than a boxer and that boxing's influence extended beyond the ring.

I never saw Louis fight, but I did witness the next best thing, Sugar Ray Robinson, whose handsome looks, processed hair, kingly entourage, and reputation for lovely ladies made me aware of yet another side of the sport. He was a little old for a fighter when I began to closely follow the game, and much of his flash and grace had been diminished, yet he engaged in terrible, bloody, and brutal wars with Carmen Basillio, Gene Fullmer, and Paul Pender. My grandmother was rarely pleased with Robinson's performances against these men. She frequently commented that when two black men were in the ring they tried to kill each other, but in mixed-race bouts blacks were far less aggressive. I attributed Robinson's performances to his age. Interestingly, Randy Roberts has documented the phenomenon of blacks employing defensive styles against white fighters in *Papa Jack*.

For all his greatness, Sugar Ray Robinson never captured my heart. I needed a hero from my generation, someone in step with the times. Along came a brash young Kentuckian named Cassius Clay who happened to fit my own outrageous, obnoxious sport profile (I imitated Elgin Baylor, nervous twitch and all; and I batted like Rocky Nelson, with my front foot pointing directly at the pitcher). When "Brassius Cassius" penned his poems and called himself the greatest, I defended him from scorn with my own poems. Never had an athlete been more right for me.

Before the "Louisville Lip" had completely cast his spell over me, however, a tragic event opened my eyes to an ugly and sorrowful side of boxing. Human misery and death came into our living room when Emile Griffith battered a helpless Benny "Kid" Paret into erect but unconscious submission as a stunned referee, Ruby Goldstein, looked on zombielike. I remember my grandmother screaming at the TV, "He's killing him," and she was right. Paret lapsed into a coma and never regained consciousness, dying of massive brain damage. The public placed most, if not all, of the blame on the poor referee. I did not turn my back on the sport, however, because I, like other fans, was led to believe that Paret's death was a freak accident. In fact, poor medical supervision, greedy managers, and bad blood between Griffith and Paret had produced a macho death struggle. Rumors circulated widely that Griffith had intended to make Paret pay for calling him *"maricon,"* a derogatory Spanish term for "gay."

When featherweight champion Davey Moore was killed a year later, the antics and ring artistry of Cassius Clay diverted my attention and society's from the tragedy. With his stunning technical knockout of Sonny Liston in 1964, even Clay's detractors had to agree that the loud-mouthed kid was doing more to elevate boxing to its mythical status as a "sweet science" than anyone ever had. He was the embodiment of grace, beauty, and skill. Then came his conversion to the Nation of Islam. As Cassius X and then Muhammad Ali, his nonconformist words became nonconformist deeds, and his association with Malcolm X, a black separatist and chief spokesman for the Black Muslims, made boxing fans anxious and government officials suspicious. I was not concerned, however, perhaps because I doubted his sincerity. To me he was still flamboyant, playful, and "crazy." The Black Muslim thing had to be a publicity stunt.

Ali's reaction to the reclassification of his draft status soon disabused me of that notion: the staunchly committed Black Muslim refused induction and sacrificed his boxing crown and his career for his religious beliefs. For three years Ali lived in legal and professional limbo as lawyers worked feverishly to restore his right to earn a living and ultimately ward off a possible lengthy prison term. No longer boxing's heavyweight champion, he became the people's champion—hero of the dispossessed and the antiestablishment crowd. His fights were not against another boxer but against an unjust system. When he returned to the ring, his was already one of the most recognizable faces in the world. Yet in the end, as with so many greats, Ali stayed in the game too long. With his decline my interest in boxing waned.

When I entered the University of North Carolina in 1975, sport history was the farthest thing from my mind. After an unfruitful search for a dissertation topic, however, I seized the opportunity to join this growing field and decided that boxing had the most potential for historical treatment, despite its rather unseemly image. From my perspective, no sport could provide more insight into human thought, actions, and relations than the ancient and nearly universal activity known as pugilism.

Certainly, other scholars have successfully treated boxing in a historical context. A host of well-written and amply documented biographies have added immensely to our understanding of the sport and, more important, to American social history. Among these works are Alexander Young's *Joe Louis as Symbol, 1935–49* (1968); Anthony Edmonds's *Joe Louis* (1973); Al-Tony Gilmore's *Bad Nigger: The Historical Impact of Jack Johnson* (1975); Randy Roberts's *Jack Dempsey: The Manassa Mauler* (1979) and *Papa Jack: Jack Johnson in the Era of White Hopes* (1983); and Chris Mead's *Champion—Joe Louis: Black Hero in White America* (1985). Although valuable contributions, each has a built-in limitation; namely, the public careers of boxers are very brief and rarely extend beyond their days in the ring. Boxing biographies are subject to an

extremely short time frame, and by isolating and emphasizing the contributions of one individual, they tend to understate the importance of
events, institutions, and societal change in the course of history.

Thus, I set out to write a sustained history of boxing, an approach
that would admittedly sacrifice depth for the sake of a broader perspective.
Whole books could be written on many of the subjects or themes that I
touch on, and if that happens I will feel vindicated, for I want to show
the possibilities for scholarship in the history of boxing.

A meeting with Elliot Gorn (*The Manly Art*) in 1978 helped me
establish my limits. Since Gorn had already staked his claim to the
eighteenth, nineteenth, and early twentieth centuries, I was left with the
period 1930–80. Fifty years of boxing was still a lot to handle, and
additional limits were necessary. Some individuals suggested that I concentrate on race and boxing, but I rejected that advice because of my
belief that such a focus would force me to neglect too many important
aspects of boxing history, thus limiting the work's perspective, outreach,
and impact. Ultimately, I decided to concentrate on the heavyweight
division of professional boxing, whose big men provide the sport's most
notable symbolism. Yet there were exceptions—Sugar Ray Robinson,
Rocky Graziano, and Jake La Motta, to name a few. Each man was able
to overcome the handicap of size and generate enormous fan interest
and support for himself and the game; and, more important for my
purposes, each man's career had considerable social and historical
significance. Robinson's attitudes toward race, business, and boxing
were as critical to his impact as his skill in the ring. Graziano and La
Motta reflected the ethnic elements of boxing and symbolized the
influence of crime, monopoly, and television on the sport and, to some
degree, the larger society. Since my purpose was to focus on contact
points between boxing and societal developments, I could not ignore the
International Boxing Club (monopoly), the broadcasting networks (television), or Frankie Carbo (organized crime), even though they are not
always closely tied to the heavyweight division.

Although the bulk of my original and primary research is from the
period after 1930, I was not comfortable with the starting date, for I
realized that boxing's development could not be understood without
giving considerable attention to the sport in the late nineteenth and
early twentieth centuries. Thus, I backtracked to include a discussion of
boxing through its transition from illegal activity to sanctioned sport.
Not coincidentally, this development occurred within the context of the
transformation of American society from a preindustrial to a modern
industrial nation. Yet I do not hang boxing on some prepackaged modernization construct; rather, I let the sources dictate the storyline. The

process reveals that boxing *is* history. It reflects societal trends and developments. It is a microcosm of the larger society and, as such, can isolate, magnify, and amplify conditions that are easily lost or difficult to discern in the larger society.

Acknowledgments

Although much of the work of historians is a solitary endeavor, the finished product is almost always a communal enterprise. I have many people to thank for making this book possible, yet there are too many to recognize in the space allotted and too many to remember after all these years. To those whose names do not appear below, please understand that I do appreciate your help.

Among those who lent a hand, six individuals stand above all others in the depth, length, and importance of their contributions. The idea for a comprehensive book on boxing and society would have never come without the insistence of Roger W. Lotchin, my dissertation advisor and later friend, that I start anew and think broadly. When others pushed for a narrower focus he helped me resist. The incentive to complete what appeared to be an endless dissertation process came from James Kirby Martin, who hired me on faith, gave me time to write, provided a thorough critique of the thesis, and introduced me to a university press editor. That editor, Lawrence Malley, with Job-like patience, tolerated my petulance, soothed my frequently injured pride, and skillfully guided me through the difficult journey of writing a book. Randy Roberts, the Buddy Ryan of editors, alternated between the carrot and the stick in moving me along. While his sometimes caustic comments occasionally produced more heat than light, I know that this work is much better for them.

Although he came late to the project, I am extremely thankful for the thorough and constructive critique of Anthony Edmonds. Other scholars who read parts or all of the manuscript and provided helpful suggestions include Steven Mintz, Susan Kellogg, Raymond Gavins, Humbert Nelli, Ian Phimister, Martin Melosi, Marilyn Young, and Donald Spivey. My greatest debt of gratitude, however, is owed to Elliot Gorn, who could have been a rival but instead became a critic, mentor, confidence-builder, and, most of all, friend. From our meeting in 1978 to the present, no one has given more to this project than he, and all because he wanted to.

I am indebted to the many pleasant and helpful archivists who aided me in uncovering primary sources at the National Archives, the Library of Congress, the Massachusetts Archives, the Texas Archives, the Louisiana Archives, the Senate Judiciary Committee, many House committees, the Barker Collection at the University of Texas, the University of New Orleans, and the Amistad Collection in New Orleans, where I was once literally locked in. I would be remiss in not singling out Ms. Debra Newman, formerly of the National Archives and now of the Library of Congress, for her generous assistance over the years. The same applies to Don Heinrich Tolzmann of the University of Cincinnati Library.

Allow me to thank Melvin Adelman for providing a very valuable document obtained under the most difficult circumstances. Thanks also go to David Theis, whose editorial comments greatly enhanced the manuscript. The readibility of this work owes much to Theresa Sears, a superbly thorough and able copy editor, who made important contributions to style, grammar, and fact. She has earned my sincerest appreciation and respect. I am grateful to Leroy Bellamy, Lloyd Wells, Robert Hart, Patricia McWhorter, the Reverend Ray Martin, and Roy Foreman for the fine photographs they made available to me. Unsung heroes of the project, those who read through and typed the dreadful handwritten drafts, are Donna Smith, Twyla Friloux, Monica Mau, Darla Selman, and Mahmudul Huque.

Of course, research is not possible without fiscal support. I gratefully acknowledge the Whitney M. Young, Jr., Foundation, the Southern Fellowships Fund, the National Endowment for the Humanities Summer Stipend, and the University of Houston Office of Sponsored Programs, where Mary Morse, Barbara Fiorella, and Susan Rhodes lent much assistance. James Pipkin of the College of Humanities and Fine Arts at the University of Houston stands out for his support and direction.

Ben Rader, a series editor, is much appreciated for his gentle encouragement and advice. Special mention is also in order for Mrs. Russell Black, widow of Julian Black, who trusted me with priceless photographs and documents. I have recognized others for their time and effort by telling their stories.

Finally, please allow me to thank my wife, Mariam, for putting up with me and my unpublished-manuscript-induced mood swings. She has been both a tower of strength and a source of inspiration.

Introduction

Beyond the Ring tries to capture the fits and starts, the detours and digressions of human experience and its accompanying societal developments. Notwithstanding the basically chronological organization, this book is not a straight-line history. Several steps backward are often necessary to make forward movement more understandable and meaningful. Where major themes arise I try to provide adequate background and context.

In Chapter 1 prizefighting emerges not only as a contest pitting one man against another but as a struggle against the impersonal forces of a changing society. John L. Sullivan was as much a transitional historical figure as a prizefighter. Boxing was often an arena in which law, order, and social growth were tested. It was also, at times, the target of Progressive reform initiatives and a scapegoat for antiforeign and racist sentiments.

The career of Jack Johnson (chapter 2) reflected the racism, nationalism, xenophobia, and petty jealousies that were part of the Progressive movement. The floodgates of boxing reform that opened in Johnson's wake were indicative of a heightened morality and society's uneasiness with the changing world. The reaction to Johnson was also part of some people's struggle to maintain, retain, and/or regain status and prestige. As both a man and a symbol he posed a threat to society because of his alleged immorality/amorality and because he violated the sacred code of conformity.

Chapter 3 traces boxing's role in the uncertain and turbulent 1920s. As a compensatory activity, prizefighting reached unprecedented heights in popularity and prestige, yet there was far more to the sport than that which took place in and around the ring. By carefully observing the growth and development of boxing, one can learn much about the changing status of women; for example, women's war for liberation was fought in the world of sport as well as in the larger society. Events in and related to boxing also reveal the bitter battles being fought by the forces of modernity and tradition, so often manifested in the rural-urban split. World War I, the Bolshevik Revolution, and the volatile economy helped produce a "Nervous Generation" that aggressively sought stability in the midst of rapid change. Prohibition symbolized the rift, but so did state control of prizefighting. Each initiative represented a turning point in the tug-of-war between individual liberty and state welfare. A boxer named Robert Fitzsimmons personified the dilemma.

In Chapter 4 we see how war and technology have made the world a much smaller place, and how developments in boxing reflected the importance of America in world affairs. Boxing became a barometer of the national mood, as xenophobia gave way to profit margins. English and American cultural differences surfaced over fight rules, and Nazi intolerance came through loud and clear in a succession of boxing-related incidents. The participation of Jews in the sport and the attendant departure from their culture revealed the pressures to blend in at all costs. Some observers have suggested that America got the boxing champion it deserved at this period in history; more often it got the champion it needed. James J. Braddock's rise from relief to fame and purported fortune coincided perfectly with F.D.R.'s New Deal.

When Braddock fell short on the inspirational level, Joe Louis (the focus of chapter 5) excelled. Domestically, Louis countered the Great Depression; internationally, he helped expose Nazi racial hatred and evil intentions. Directly and indirectly he also exposed some of America's own shortcomings, especially in matters of race. The no-win dilemma of cooperation or noncooperation that followed Louis affected every black in the country. He showed that regardless of the degree of whitewash, total assimilation for blacks was impossible. The dearth of black social and intellectual accomplishment was evident in that black America's greatest hero was a prizefighter. Louis gave blacks and most Americans a tremendous psychic lift.

After the depression and World War II, America found itself confronted by a host of new opportunities and problems. In Chapter 6 I describe how television, with boxing as its experimental subject, informed and entertained, but also preoccupied, the American people. In many ways, however, television revealed the negative side of technology; we could see firsthand that not only was America becoming more sophisticated but so were its criminals. Technological developments and corporate structures greatly enhanced the ability of crime figures to exercise greater control over larger areas, within the legitimate sector as well as the illegitimate. And all of this—organized crime, big business, and television—came together through a mutual acquaintance: boxing. Of course, one cannot treat crime without looking at law enforcement and the way politics and personalities often hampered the judicial process on a local, statewide, and even national level. In raising the issue of monopoly, for example, crime's relationship with boxing also reveals the subjective, if not capricious, actions and decisions of our leaders.

In Chapter 7 I discuss the civil rights movement, which erupted with an unprecedented fervor just as our concern with criminal infiltration of American society had peaked. A new activism, sparked by Rosa Parks's historic act of civil disobedience, forced America to inspect its conscience and to make some effort to live up to its principles. The "successful" desegregation of sport by blacks helped to reinforce prevailing notions about the proper path to progress, peace, and harmony. Yet, not all blacks were satisfied with the prescribed formula. The brash young boxer named Cassius Clay, who renounced Christianity for the Nation of Islam, became a powerful symbol of the conflicts brewing in American society. In Ali and the reaction to him, one finds the elements of the complex spectrum of black thought and action. He exposed the shifting tides of public tolerance with regard to racial issues and American involvement in Vietnam. Contrary to what most observers have concluded, Muhammad Ali changed very little over time; what did change was the country's reaction to him and what he represented.

Yet boxing remains, despite its history, a primitive, dangerous sport, nothing more nor less than two men hitting each another. Why does it still exist? And what does boxing's existence say about its advocates, participants, and the larger society? I examine these issues in the Conclusion, deviating from both the heavyweights and the well-known fighters on whom I concentrate throughout the book. Why young men choose the profession and their willingness to face overwhelming odds and tremendous risks for a chance at glory says much about boxing and American society. In the end I hope to show that sport, specifically boxing, has a usable past, one that will enable us to better understand ourselves and our place in society. Historians must accept the challenge to place sport in its proper context, as a reflection of the society that fostered it.

BEYOND THE RING

1

Crime or Sport?
The Development of Modern Prizefighting

Most people's familiarity with boxing is directly related to their age and personal identification with the top fighters, yet neither criterion provides an accurate perspective. Indeed, both points of reference often facilitate natural but misleading urges by which individuals tend to relate to the heroes of their youth. To wax nostalgic about these heroes is an affliction common to us all; to deny their glory would, in a sense, be to deny one's own worth. The exception is the pioneer and the trailblazer. Here, history and legend combine to preserve greatness. If the title "Father of" is also bestowed, then immortality is assured.

When we consider the origins of modern American prizefighting, one name comes to mind before all others—John Lawrence Sullivan, a.k.a. the "Great John L." and the "Boston Strongboy." In an age of youth worship, "star wars" technology, and mass computerization, this basic, physical man still stands for the potential of the individual and the survival of the fittest. He is the embodiment of the American Dream, in which the lowliest individuals rise to the top by their own initiative and perseverance. The elusiveness of that dream is immaterial; the meaning of the dream is in its acceptance, not its fulfillment.

Unfortunately, in the tendency to focus on the outstanding individual, important trends, events, and mass movements are often ignored, distorted, or obscured. Although few people would argue Sullivan's heroic stature or his contribution to a sport desperately in need of prestige and acceptability, he must be viewed carefully in the context of his times. To overemphasize the individual is to overlook basic elements in the social milieu as well as to discount influences from abroad that facilitated this extraordinary man's personal popularity and the acceptance of his profession.

The Cultural and Legal Setting

Like so many American cultural, social, political, and intellectual institutions, boxing originated in England. In the late 1700s, when the sport in America existed only in its crudest form, prizefighting in Britain had assumed an air of sophistication and acceptability. The English looked upon most American institutions, especially the sporting kind, as crude. Their perceptions were, for the most part, accurate. The prevailing opinion among colonial Americans had held amusements counterproductive and threatening to survival, and during the revolutionary period Puritans and Republicans, especially in the North, associated game playing with the decadent and oppressive monarchies of Europe. Later, evangelical Protestants pressed for limits on sport, citing strict Sabbatarian rules against gambling, "riotous" amusements, and drinking. Yet the forces for change gathered strength, and economic prosperity introduced a leisure ethic that increasingly threatened the American work ethic.[1]

The 1820s and 1830s were marked by increased urbanization and industrialization, which stimulated a need for new and accessible diversions. The mood of society at large was captured by Phineas T. Barnum in his classic line, "Men, women, and children who cannot live on gravity alone, need something to satisfy their lighter moods and hours."[2] As the cities attracted more and more immigrants who were unaccustomed to restrictions upon amusements and games, leisure's opponents lost further ground.

By 1850 sport had found a very unlikely proponent—New England clerics. Henry Ward Beecher, son of the famous Calvinist minister Lyman Beecher, along with Thomas Wentworth Higginson and Edward Everett, developed and promoted a positive sporting ideology that justified the playing of certain sports as healthful, an alternative to vices, and a proper training tool for young children.[3] Their opinions reflected to a large degree the emerging spirit of English "muscular Christianity," with its reconciling of a robust physical life and Christian morality and duty. This new social gospel even maintained that physical strength built character and righteousness, making the believer fit for God's work and, implicitly, the nation's. By the second half of the nineteenth century the novels of Thomas Hughes, especially *Tom Brown's Schooldays at Rugby College,* and Charles Kingsley's *Two Years Ago* had solidly established muscular Christianity in the United States and England.[4]

Nationalism soon joined religion as an ally of sport. Political groups such as the Loco Focos, the Barnburners, and the Know Nothings pointed to a strong strain of nativism by the 1840s. And as America continued to grow and become aware of itself as a nation, "distinct, different, and superior" to the "corrupt monarchies" of Europe, Americans strove to improve, if not perfect, the young republic's institutions and individuals.[5] Foreign critics wasted few words in condemning the physical health of Americans. According to one English critic, "To roll balls in a tenpin alley by gaslight, or to ride a fast trotting horse in a light wagon along a very bad and very dusty road, seemed the Alpha and Omega of sport in the United States." American critics chimed in with examples of the ordinary citizen, "a pasty-faced, narrow-chested, spindle-shanked dwarfed race—a mere walking manikin to advertise the last cut of the fashionable tailor."[6]

Such talk worried many Americans. Essayist and editor N. Parker Willis openly deplored America's athletic ineptitude. "It [physical condition] is the only attribute of power in which they [Americans] are losing ground," he wrote. Foreseeing an impending struggle between England and America for world supremacy, he warned, "America could doubtless afford at some cost of order and staid propriety to purchase an enthusiasm for physical culture and masculine vigor and beauty."[7] Willis suggested that boxing might help, and oddly enough he found support from clerics. One such man, Thomas Wentworth Higginson, believed that the sport was brutal but confessed, nonetheless, that a limited knowledge would improve the manliness of any youth. He agreed with Dr. Oliver Wendell Holmes that "anything is better than this white-blooded degeneration to which we all tend."[8] Himself a puny, asthmatic fellow, Holmes openly admired and frequented the training camp of the U.S. heavyweight champion John Camel Heenan, commonly called the "Benicia Boy."[9]

The movement for wholesome sports and outdoor recreation met with considerable resistance. Puritan insistence that austerity and unattractiveness were evidence of duty proved formidable. Boxing's task was the toughest of all, for pugilism suffered from legal as well as religious opposition. According to English law, as laid down in *Blackstone's Commentaries 183,* "a tilt or tournament, the martial diversion of our ancestors is an unlawful act: and so are boxing and sword playing, the succeeding amusements of their posterity."[10] Perceived by the courts as a throwback to a less civilized past, prizefighting was classified as an affray, an assault, and a riot. Despite considerable disagreement with judicial rulings by the legal community and widespread public support for prizefighting in England, the dominant force of American judicial opinion, especially in the North, consistently ruled boxing to be illegal.[11]

Throughout the early 1800s the devotees of the sport bribed and dodged police, sneaking off to some anchored barge, wooded glade, or barn to witness a fight but keeping ever alert to a possible raid by authorities.[12] Not only were these fights considered brutal, but the competitors had difficulty confining their pugilistic pursuits to the ring. Moreover, the character of many fight enthusiasts was objectionable, and gambling frequently led to riots among the spectators.[13]

As the frequency of prizefights increased, various states moved beyond general and sometimes vague statutes to pass legislation that expressly forbade fistfights. Massachusetts courts, still clinging to their Puritan heritage, led the way in upholding convictions for violations of the state's 1849 prizefight statutes. In an 1876 case, *Commonwealth v. Colberg,* the state supreme court confirmed its intention to maintain a lawful and ordered society—one in which prizefighting had no place: "Prize fighting, boxing matches, and encounters of that kind serve no useful purpose, tend to breaches of the peace, and are unlawful even when entered into by agreement and without anger or ill will."[14] The decision devastated the sport in Massachusetts and closed every legal loophole, including the fiction that boxing and allegedly scientific sparring contests, often characterized by the use of gloves, differed from prizefighting.

Like a migratory flock in search of favorable conditions, prizefighting moved southward. In what some egocentric Americans, including Senator Robert C. Byrd of West Virginia, still consider the first world's heavyweight championship bout, Paddy Ryan and Joe Goss fought in ostensible secrecy at Colliers, West Virginia.[15] Organizers chose the tiny Brooks County town for its proximity to the Ohio and Pennsylvania state lines: if raided by hostile law officers, participants and followers could scatter across the borders to escape arrest.[16]

Although most early championship fights took place in rural, secluded locations, boxing grew increasingly more attractive to overworked and overwhelmed city dwellers. According to historian Dale Somers, "As the tempo of industrialization and urbanization accelerated, America became a mass society composed of people whose lives were governed increasingly by the machine and the time clock."[17] In the process, individual accomplishments gave way to the impersonality of collective progress. Boxing symbolically countered that trend by putting the individual at center stage and thus gave the illusion that we had returned, at least temporarily, to our "rightful place" among all things.[18]

There were more practical reasons as well for the sport's hold on urbanites: then as today, many viewed prizefighting as an opportunity to rise above poverty and discrimination. Also, publicity and advertising not only elevated boxing's importance but extended its outreach. Moreover, profit-seeking promoters made significant contributions to the growth of the "manly art."

Richard Kyle Fox, an Irish immigrant who rose from impoverished newspaper employee to owner of the *National Police Gazette* in two years, significantly contributed to the growing interest in boxing. He took the financially troubled scandal sheet—a nineteenth-century *National Enquirer*—and added a sports section, which appealed to leisure-craving, exploited urbanites. Reporting on sport was not enough, however; Fox actually promoted sporting events as a way of providing a steady fare for fans to experience and his paper to cover.[19] These contests resembled the televised "trash sports" of the 1970s and 1980s. Oyster-opening, one-legged dancing, and steeple-climbing captured his readers' fancies as well as their pennies, making Fox a millionaire by his mid-thirties. In the process, he made himself the P. T. Barnum of the world of sport.

One fateful evening in the spring of 1881, while at Harry Hill's Dance Hall and Boxing Emporium on New York's East Side, Richard Fox found a man who was neither easily impressed nor bullied—John L. Sullivan, then known as the Boston Strongboy.[20] Sullivan's reputation preceded him, a result of his touring the vaudeville circuit offering fifty dollars to anyone who could last four rounds with him in the ring. From these illegal encounters, veneered as "sparring exhibitions," allegedly originated his famous challenge, "I can lick any sonofabitch in the house."[21] Fox invited the brash fighter to his table for a business talk, which Sullivan impolitely declined, gaining Fox's hatred.

The Father of American Prizefighting

On February 7, 1882, without Fox's involvement, Sullivan wrested the heavyweight title from Paddy Ryan in ten minutes and thirty seconds. Fox was furious and vowed to break Sullivan as well as control the crown. He did neither; Sullivan beat all comers, including a few Fox hopefuls. Nonetheless, Sullivan's success was good for Fox because it was good for boxing.

By 1887 the Boston Strongboy had become the Great John L., an international figure who had risen through the ranks without looking down on others. Sullivan did more than build a personal following, however; he helped to elevate the sport of boxing. The prize ring now spanned the gulf between lower and upper classes, for which John L. Sullivan was as responsible as anyone. Despite the fact that he defended his title three times with bare knuckles under London Prize Ring Rules, he popularized the glove contest and the Marquess of Queensberry

Rules, which he preferred.[22] As such, he modernized the "manly art,"
sanitized and conventionalized the apparent brutality, and "made it
possible to decide championships before athletic clubs under the best
auspices, before classes of people who formerly took little interest in the
sport."[23] None of Fox's fighters possessed the qualities to achieve these
ends.

Boxing's progress was gradual yet steady, as evidenced by the
geographic locations of fights, the followers, the press coverage, and the
legal attitudes toward prizefighting. For example, the Sullivan-Ryan
bout in Mississippi City, Mississippi, attracted coverage from many of
the nation's leading newspapers, including the *New York Herald,* the
New York Sun, and the *Boston Globe.* It also appealed to criminals like
Red O'Leary, a bank robber, and Frank and Jesse James, and to a less
notorious but well-known group that included Nat Goodman, the actor;
Dan O'Leary, the pedestrian (runner); and Harry Hill, owner of the
pugilistic saloon where Fox and Sullivan had met. Prominent among the
spectators, according to one observer, were merchants, educators, and
professional men—"No more orderly crowd ever started for a Sunday
School picnic."[24] Law enforcement agencies were not convinced of the
social value and orderly nature of the event, however. Before 1882
neither Mississippi nor Louisiana had laws prohibiting prizefighting per
se. But the Ryan-Sullivan fight clearly exposed the ineffectiveness of
applicable statutes against unlawful assembly and riot, which should
have prevented the encounter, and as a result the lawmakers of both
states passed legislation calling for the imprisonment of persons convicted
of prizefighting. The new law lay in wait for Sullivan.[25]

In 1887 the Great John L. rejected an offer from Fox to fight his
favorite charge, Jake Kilrain, a six-foot, 190-pound Irish-American from
Baltimore. Sullivan had the undisputed world title on his mind and left
for France to fight England's Charlie Mitchell, who strangely enough
was not his country's official champion. The fight went on for three
hours and thirty-nine minutes before officials called it a draw, leaving
considerable doubt as to Sullivan's ability and America's claim to the
world championship. The fact that Mitchell weighed only 160 pounds to
Sullivan's 210 aroused suspicion about the latter's courage. But, Sullivan,
although many other things, was no coward. Like so many champions
after him, he simply wanted to hold the title as long as possible without
unduly risking it.[26]

When Sullivan earlier expressed his intention of not accepting
Kilrain's challenge, "court intrigue" replaced ring skill as a means of
succession, and Fox declared that Sullivan had forfeited his title. True to
a sport in which language made a shambles of logic, where battles were

fought in four-cornered rings, or squared circles, Kilrain was crowned champion with a special diamond-studded, silver *National Police Gazette* championship belt. The move initiated a popular referendum of sorts, which eventually established Sullivan as the first "peoples' champion."

According to James Cox, in his fascinating article "The Great Fight: 'Mr. Jake' vs. John L. Sullivan," loyal Boston admirers of Sullivan, perhaps spurred on by his manager, Pat Sheedy, solicited contributions "for a tribute that would make Fox look like a piker."[27] The result was something certainly fit for a king: "the $10,000 Belt" had a base of flat gold, fifty inches long and twelve inches wide, with a center panel consisting of Sullivan's name spelled out in diamonds; eight other frames contained his likeness, the United States Seal, and various American eagles and Irish harps; an additional 397 diamonds studded the symbolic ornament. Cox speculates that when the Great John L. received the belt before some 3,500 fans at the old Boston Theater on August 8, 1887, he uttered one of his many memorable lines, "I wouldn't put Fox's belt around the neck of a goddamn dog!" To some, Sullivan's lack of humility seemed to invite an unkind fate; later, he would pawn the belt for $175, having pried out all the diamonds.[28]

John L. Sullivan could no longer ignore his fans' demands to quiet Fox and win back the working man's crown from the rich usurper. But he was grossly out of shape, subject to bouts of excessive drinking, and suffering from unknown illnesses, which raised doubts even in the minds of his unflinchingly loyal followers that he had the will or the ability to carry out his boasts.[29] The well-known physical culturist, body builder, and wrestler William Muldoon was called on to get Sullivan into shape for the fight of his life against a younger and apparently better conditioned Jake Kilrain. Despite executive orders against the fight by Governors Francis T. Nicholls of Louisiana and Robert Lowry of Mississippi, interest in the event increased as the country's major newspapers reported at length on the fighters' training activities. The prefight coverage represented a significant step in the sport's movement toward acceptance; not long before, the nation's leading papers had condemned boxing as a brutal and barbaric activity not fit for modern society.[30] Now, out-of-town and out-of-state fight fans flocked to New Orleans for the match, and ladies talked about it freely "in places which had never heard pugilism mentioned before."[31]

The day before the monumental encounter, which would judge the worth of the common folk as much as the two men's fighting skills, three special trains left New Orleans for the secret fight location in Richburg, Mississippi. Two to three thousand spectators paid anywhere from fifteen dollars for "chained circle" seats to nothing at all for Aunt Mattie's perch on the lower branches of a large oak tree.[32]

The fight began at 10:30 in the morning, on July 8, 1889, and before it ended the temperature had soared to well over 100 degrees. Under London Prize Ring (bare knuckle) rules, the two men wrestled, clinched, and threw one another to the ground between occasional punches. "First blood" came from Sullivan in the seventh round as a result of a Kilrain right to his ear, and much money changed hands. Blood flowed from the champion again when a spiked shoe, used for traction in the earthen ring, pierced his foot, and when he vomited in the forty-fourth round the crowd took that as a sign that his stomach was gone. Instead, Sullivan regained his strength. After the seventy-fifth round Kilrain's manager, Mike Donovan, "threw up the sponge." According to the *New Orleans Picayune,* "he did not wish to be a party to murder."[33]

The Great John L. stood triumphant, the undisputed champion in America and hero to the common folk. The fight fixed the sport in the national consciousness and promoted it to glory, for it represented survival of the fittest reduced to its most understandable terms. Even the anti-prizefight *New York Times* admitted that the event had aroused widespread enthusiasm, more so than any presidential election. Dale Somers's characterization of the champion captures the essence of the man, the significance of his epic struggle, and the changing tastes of a nation: "If his personal conduct left much to be desired, Sullivan's bearing in the ring was gradually and inexorably helping to make professional boxing a sport that drew support from all ranks."[34]

Heroes and the Law

Immediate postfight events reveal a different side of the status of heroes and their professions. Contrary to popular belief, special treatment of athletes is not a contemporary phenomenon. When modern athletes who commit serious crimes are merely slapped on the wrist, there is a tendency to decry the present pampering of sports heroes. Such thinking fails to recognize the historical nature of this phenomenon. John L. Sullivan could very well be the most important, if not the first, example of the athletic hero who stood above the law.

The authorities who watched over the Sullivan-Kilrain fight dutifully restrained themselves until it had reached its conclusion. Perhaps they too were enjoying it; or perhaps they were waiting for one or both boxers to die. By law, such an end would have elevated the crime from prizefighting to murder. As no one died, the authorities had to settle for violation of the state's prizefight statute.[35] Both Sullivan and Kilrain were arrested, but they were charged and arraigned separately. The grand jurors of the Mississippi Circuit Court for the Second Judicial District of Marion County, at a special August term in 1889, handed down the following indictment: "John L. Sullivan . . . , by and in pursuance of a previous appointment and arrangement made to meet and engage in a prize-fight with another person, to wit, with Jake Kilrain, did then and there, for a large sum of money . . . , unlawfully engage in a prize-fight with the said Jake Kilrain, to wit, did then and there enter a ring, commonly called a 'prize-ring,' and did . . . beat, strike, and bruise the said Jake Kilrain, against the peace and diginity of the state of Mississippi. Jas. H. Neville, Dist. Atty."[36] The first count of the indictment was for violation of the 1882 statute, a misdemeanor; the second was for assault and battery, a felony. The jury convicted Sullivan on the first count and acquitted him on the more serious second count. Facing a one-year prison sentence, the champion engaged the law firm of Calhoun and Green, which appealed on behalf of the beleaguered warrior. The state of Mississippi, or at least Marion County, did not seem impressed with the heavyweight championship or its holder.

The Mississippi Supreme Court accepted the appeal, and on March 17, 1890, Judge S. H. Terrel probably shocked the state and its attorney general, T. M. Miller, by overturning the conviction on the basis of a faulty indictment, sending the case back to the Marion County Court.[37] He reasoned, based on a motley yet related set of precedents that ranged from a slave accused of burning a house to the seizing of French brandy, that the statute under which the arrest had been made neither defined the offense of prizefighting nor identified what action constituted a violation of its provisions. Judge Terrel apparently was not convinced that prizefighting per se constituted a crime. His concern, which many English jurists shared, was whether the fight threatened to disturb the peace, and the indictment did not convince him of such. *State* v. *Burnham* (1884) clearly defined a prizefight, but it was never cited. In the end, the justice ruled that the indictment failed because it excluded the fact that Kilrain had also fought.[38]

According to legal scholar Elmer Million, the Mississippi statute contained many errors, as decisions before and after have shown. In this instance the judge's exercise in verbal gymnastics of the highest order obscured the crime. At the retrial, Sullivan pleaded guilty to the misdemeanor and paid a $500 fine. The county had gained time to reflect upon this living legend and had decided it did not want to punish him so much as avoid totally undermining the law; hence the plea bargain, though that term surely was not used at the time. In any case, Sullivan's increasing popularity would have made obtaining another conviction difficult.

In April 1893, for example, the Texas Court of Criminal Appeals reversed an earlier conviction against Sullivan for his failure to procure a license to fight Bob McGhee on January 12, 1893, in Dallas County. The court held that the 1891 statute that made prizefighting a felony repealed an 1889 law by implication. Strangely enough, the felony crime carried only a misdemeanor penalty of a $500–$1,000 fine and a sixty-day minimum to one-year maximum jail term. The 1891 law itself was ambivalent about preventing prizefights and punishing participants. In fact, Sullivan had been kept out of Texas in 1889 by Governor Lawrence S. Ross, who voiced his opposition to prizefighting despite the legislature's decision to allow prizefighting at that time.[39] Texas's confusion on the issue would come back to haunt the state in the not too distant future.

Boxing Comes of Age

No greater proof of John L. Sullivan's contributions to the game can be offered than the reaction to him and prizefighting in New Orleans. Professional promoters lost no chance to exploit the sport's growing popularity by staging regular bouts, which was to be expected. Surprisingly, however, members of the elite Young Men's Gymnastic Club and the Southern Athletic Club took up the sport on an amateur basis. Before long the two clubs began to sponsor self-proclaimed "clean and decorous" professional fights, promoted by officers of the clubs or their agents in an effort to reduce the influence of gamblers and avoid the disgraceful "tactics of money-making professions."[40] The bouts were fought with gloves, under the Marquess of Queensbury rules.

Alarmed by the boxing mania in New Orleans, reform-minded citizens appealed to city and state officials to enforce the 1882 law against "personal combat with fists." Mayor Joseph A. Shakespeare failed in his attempt to tie the promoters' hands by refusing permits for "glove contests." By January 1890 influential supporters of the ring, including Captain Bat Galvin of the police department, forced city council members to permit sparring exhibitions; then, in March the council permitted all regularly chartered athletic clubs to stage glove contests. This action implied a distinction between sparring exhibitions and glove contests, on the one hand, and prizefights, on the other. The *Picayune* recognized the council's ploy and asked Governor Francis T. Nicholls to intervene, because "every time a prize fight takes place it will always be given by a so-called athletic club."[41] The governor responded by asking the legislature to strengthen the 1882 statute, which it did, but the sport's allies left a loophole by inserting a section that permitted glove contests, clearly a euphemism for prizefights, in chartered clubs.

An angry Nicholls allowed the law to take effect without his signature.[42] Soon, clubs throughout New Orleans staged prizefights and newly chartered athletic organizations came into existence in response to the legalization of glove contests. The New Orleans Athletic Club, in 1889, and the West End Athletic, Columbia Athletic, and Metropolitan clubs, in 1890, all took advantage of the hospitable legal climate.[43]

These clubs helped to change the nature of boxing by introducing the sport to Gilded Age economics. During the thirty-year period following the Civil War, America had undergone a transformation and become a tightly structured society with new hierarchies of control. There was a tremendous increase in the influence of business in America. Despite the Rockefeller, Carnegie, and Morgan legends, this era, characterized as the Age of Incorporation, represented the beginning of the faceless, nameless "corporation man," something the public did not readily perceive. According to historian Alan Trachtenberg, "The prominence of such names indicated that business was still thought of as a field of personal competition, of heroic endeavors, and not of corporate manipulation."[44] Obviously, corporate life was too unfamiliar for most Americans to understand or acknowledge it.[45] Yet by 1904, close to three hundred industrial corporations had won control over more than two-fifths of the nation's industries.

While individual fighters might still have retained the freedom associated with artisans, who were rapidly losing ground to industrialization, the promotion of boxing matches took on a corporate concept. Through much of the 1880s managers of fighters, or middlemen like Richard Fox, arranged contests, and the fighters earned their keep largely through side bets, as gate receipts rarely produced significant revenue. But when athletic associations began to promote fights, they offered increasingly larger purses in an all-out bid to win the right to stage certain bouts. By the mid-1890s top pugilists at various clubs and in a variety of divisions fought for thousands of dollars, frequently on a winner-take-all basis.[46]

New Orleans's clubs competed among themselves and also bid against prestigious athletic associations in the East and West. By 1890 the Crescent City had become the showcase of American prizefighting, its reputation built on such fights as Jake Kilrain versus James J. Corbett, which thrust the latter man into the boxing spotlight. Future middleweight, light-heavyweight, and heavyweight champion of the world "Ruby" Robert Fitzsimmons, from Australia, fought his second American-based contest at the Audubon Athletic Association, in New Orleans.[47] Greater attractions would follow.

The old Olympic Club, founded in 1883 as an athletic association for young men in New Orleans's Third District, had by 1890 entered the field of boxing promotion, leasing some prime city land and erecting an enclosed arena. With this modern facility, equipped with electric lights and canvas mat, and a $12,000 purse, it successfully outbid three other clubs, including the prestigious Puritan Athletic Club of Long Island, for the right to host the Jack Dempsey–Robert Fitzsimmons match for the middleweight championship of the world. This Jack Dempsey ("Nonpareil"), whose first name the not-yet-born William Harrison Dempsey would later borrow, was the greatest middleweight fighter of his time, having held the championship since 1884. The title changed hands after a prizefight that was as brutal as, if not more so, than any bare-knuckle fight. When Fitzsimmons finally knocked out his opponent in the thirteenth round, Dempsey's eyes were cut, his nose and mouth were bloodied and swollen, and the skin around his neck and upper anterior ribs was raw from the challenger's relentless blows. Blood covered his body.[48]

Boosted into national prominence by this match, the Olympic Club was acclaimed America's prizefight center. Yet legal proscriptions against prizefighting in New Orleans and Louisiana loomed large in the minds of those intent on increasing publicity to maximize profits from what were obviously not legally sanctioned sparring matches and glove contests. According to Dale Somers, the club decided to test the state law by openly advertising a fight between Ed McCarthy and Tommy Warren on September 22, 1891. Authorities arrested the two fighters, who stood trial and were found not guilty after closing arguments and five minutes' deliberation by the jury.[49]

After a series of other top-notch contests, the Olympic Club felt it was free to pursue the ultimate plum of the prizefight game: the services of the Great John L. Sullivan. He agreed to fight any and all challengers—except blacks—for a purse of $25,000 and a side bet of $10,000, winner take all. James J. Corbett, who had made a reputation for himself in a sixty-one-round draw with a black Australian national, Peter Jackson, and who had met Sullivan in an 1891 exhibition, welcomed the offer. Not satisfied with just a heavyweight championship match, the Olympic Club organized an 1890s-style triple-main-event fight card—"The Carnival of Champions."[50] For three consecutive days, beginning on September 5, 1892, the club presented a lightweight championship fight between Jack McAuliffe and Billy Myer, a featherweight championship fight featuring George "Little Chocolate" Dixon against Jack Skelly, and, of course, the grand finale pitting the Great John L. against "Gentleman Jim" Corbett.

The same kind of enthusiasm and interest generated for the Kilrain-Sullivan fight manifested itself for these fights, but on a higher level and across a broader spectrum of society, so much so that they overshadowed the presidential race. Conspicuously present at the first fight were members of the Boston Club, seated in mahogany chairs as they watched their fighter, Jack McAuliffe, successfully defend his crown.[51] The second fight proved to be a crowd-pleasing, bloody spectacle. Unfortunately, it had assumed serious racial implications as a result of negative press coverage and marked the beginning of the end of interracial fights in New Orleans, despite the fans' apparent acceptance of Dixon's victory. A newspaper article that appeared before the fight, intimated that fans might react hostilely to a "colored boy" beating a white man. When no such reaction occurred, the press nonetheless felt obligated to inform the public of the implications of interracial prizefights, especially when they ended in a white's defeat. Both the *Daily Picayune* and the *Times Democrat* voiced their objections and pressured the Olympic Club to declare that it would no longer stage such matches.[52]

On September 7 the long-awaited "clash of the Titans" materialized. At age thirty-four, the flabby and boxing-old Sullivan proved no match for his quick, bright, younger opponent.[53] After waging a gallant fight for twenty rounds, a battered and weary John L. took the count in round twenty-one and America had a new heavyweight champion. An orderly and proper succession had taken place, and while Americans would mourn the past, they realized that boxing's future was secure. As Sullivan admitted later, "if I had to get licked I'm glad it was by an American."[54]

In New York, San Francisco, Boston, Washington, and other major cities, thousands of interested fans made their way to bulletin boards for printed, round-by-round descriptions of the fight and to major hotels for telegraphic reports. While opinions as to how Corbett won varied as much as did feelings about the outcome, one thing was certain: prizefighting had a firm hold on the public. Seemingly, boxing had come a long way from the barbaric eye-gouging spectacles of the frontier and the clandestine backwoods brawls of the 1870s.[55] Now, the fighters wore gloves; they fought three-minute rounds and rested one minute; and they fought on canvas in front of some of the best people society had to offer. Prizefighting had also arrived as a commercial enterprise. After expenses for the three fights, the Olympic Club recorded a profit of more than $50,000; moreover, the bouts attracted thousands of tourist dollars to New Orleans.[56]

Reform Backlash

When the spirit of boxing reform swept the East in the 1890s and early 1900s, those states that did not have specific laws preventing prizefighting enacted them and those that already had them became more vigilant about their enforcement. This "Purity Crusade" to harness and control society's baser instincts reflected a generation-long debate between Spencerian and reform Darwinists. William Graham Sumner, the American proponent of Spencerian Darwinism, maintained that stateways could not change folkways. He claimed that a society with "no-holds-barred" business competition was in consonance with scientific law; and boxing was the reduction of the Darwinian principle of "survival of the fittest" to its simplest and most tangible terms. On the other side stood Harvard President Charles W. Eliot, who believed that evolution had taken the individual out of the jungle and that civilization had a higher goal than the use of physical force and warfare.[57] Boxing's continued success thus depended not only upon adherence to the letter of the law but also on the outcome of debates concerning the nature of the individual and society.

Prizefighting in New Orleans came under heavy fire from its critics. Reverend Clarence Greeley, the general agent of the International Law and Order League, pleaded with the press to condemn and destroy the sport. He argued that if northern newspapers could run the lottery business out of Louisiana, they could do the same for prizefighting. Greeley and others correctly believed that until prizefighting could be stopped in New Orleans, the sport would continue to be attractive to Americans everywhere. When New York authorities refused a match, New Orleans was eager to accept it.[58]

Nearly everyone knew that the fights taking place at the Olympic Club were clearly not sparring exhibitions, and Louisiana finally recognized this fact in November 1893 when Attorney General Milton J. Cunningham, with the full support of the new governor, Murphy J. Foster, brought suit against the Olympic Club for violating both its charter and the 1890 law.[59] The state hit hard at the fashionable and respected club, arguing that it had "fostered, encouraged, and maintained exhibitions" commonly known as prizefights, which were witnessed by large assemblies composed of, to a great degree, "noted thugs, confidence men, and criminal characters." The attorney general charged that the fights not only forced contestants to commit assault and battery upon each other but endangered the public and threatened life and property. Worst of all, what went on at the Olympic Club set bad "examples to the young [and] discouraged honest industry by disproportionately rewarding sanguinary exhibitions of brute force."[60] Attorney General Cunningham seized upon the opportunity to exploit recent events that might make prizefighting and the athletic clubs in general vulnerable to attack, the most notable being the murder of the Olympic Club president by members of the board during a directors' meeting.[61]

In what appeared to be an open-and-shut case, the prosecution apprised the court that between the fall of 1890 and October 1893, some seventeen encounters had taken place at the Olympic Club, with prize money totaling $95,200, of which $86,050 went to the winners and $9,150 to the losers. Yet the Olympic Club maintained that it promoted and staged only exhibitions.[62] Despite clear evidence that the contests were indeed prizefights in which the victors were rewarded, in which blood was drawn, in which participants fought to the finish, the jury ruled that they were merely sparring matches and therefore legal. It had been convinced by the city's most respected citizens that these were scientific and skillful exhibitions, notwithstanding the fact that championships had changed hands.[63]

The background and community standing of the witnesses might help to explain what seemed an inexplicable decision. Defense witnesses included a college president, the New Orleans chief of police, a prominent lawyer, and a host of other reputable citizens. The defense lawyer ostensibly admitted he selected the college president because he was "a typical representative of the conservative element of this community." Crediting himself with witnessing "all the principal contests we have had here from the beginning to end," the man testified to having seen blood but never serious injury.[64] Published descriptions of the Dixon-Skelly fight question his memory, eyesight, or veracity: "What with bruises, lacerations, and coagulated blood, Skelly's nose, mouth and eye presented a horrible spectacle, and as the poor fellow staggered about almost helpless, even some of the most blasé at the ringside were heard to shudder and some even turned away at that face already disfigured past recognition and heard the ugly half-splashing sound as his blood-soaked gloves again and again visited the bleeding wounds that had drenched them."[65]

The next two witnesses, a lawyer and a city official, gave similar testimony, including a comparison of Sullivan's fights against Paddy Ryan and Jake Kilrain, in which London Prize Ring rules operated. These witnesses recalled little of the clinching, thumping, and gouging characteristic of those fights. The police commissioner, whose men were entrusted with supervising the fights, considered the Sullivan contest one of the greatest fights that ever took place, based on skill and science. The jury obviously paid little heed to the hard evidence presented by the prosecution of illegal liquor sales and gambling on the premises, which these same law enforcers had allowed.

The defense then had a leading New Orleans lawyer comment on the atmosphere and the spectators during an Olympic Club bout. He maintained that the people who attended these contests were orderly and well-behaved, and he further ventured that these people, in regard to personal respectability and behavior, stood above the average of ordinary political assemblies.[66] Speaking to the trend toward exciting combative activity among the populace, a school board member claimed: "Compared with that popular game nowadays known as football, which I think the American people have gone crazy about, the contests that I have seen at the Olympic Club are superior in every respect and in point of humanity and as appealing to the aesthetic senses."[67] This invidious comparison continued well into the twentieth century, as boxing interests frequently cited the injuries and deaths from football to justify the continuance of pugilism.

Such testimony apparently convinced the jury that the Olympic Club had not violated the 1890 law. Determined to end prizefighting in Louisiana and punish the Olympic Club, the attorney general filed an appeal with the state supreme court. Yet, after considering all the evidence, including a contract that detailed a prizefight in every respect but used the words "glove contest,"[68] the justices ruled that the prosecution had not proved these contests violated state law; and further, if the state sought remedy it should do so through the legislature. Moreover, it dealt what seemed to be a final blow to the prosecution's case by agreeing with the lower court that expert testimony as to the differences between a prizefight and a glove contest was permissible. Attorney General Cunningham refused to give up and asked for a rehearing on the question of inadmissible testimony. Evidently aided by Justice C. J. Nicholls, who had dissented on the testimony question, Cunningham succeeded in convincing the state supreme court that such testimony had been improperly admitted, and on May 7, 1894, the court ordered a new trial, although it did not interfere with the Olympic Club's right to stage a "boxing exhibition."[69] Taking advantage of its legal victories, the Olympic Club opportunistically planned another triple event for the prizefight-hungry fans of New Orleans. Only one fight took place, however, and it hastened the end for New Orleans boxing.

During the fight, George "Kid" Lavigne knocked out hometown hero and suspected mulatto Andy Bowen, who fought as a white.[70] As Bowen fell, his head hit the hard ring surface; he died the following morning. Bowen's death produced a flood of controversy and turned the tide against prizefighting in the Crescent City and elsewhere. Louisiana

Governor Murphy J. Foster's determination to end prizefighting escalated, and within a few months of Andy Bowen's tragic demise, with that memory fresh in the minds of many Louisianans, the case against the Olympic Club came before the court one more time. Persistence paid off for the state as Justice Samuel D. McEnery, speaking for the court, ruled: "Fighting in the arena of the Club . . . is prize fighting, and no other description can be given to it."[71] The decision effectively killed prizefighting in Louisiana. Efforts to revive the sport proved futile as city, parish, and state officials strictly applied and enforced the law.[72]

Although New Orleans was not the exclusive preserve of boxing, as Steven A. Riess proves in his fine article on boxing in New York, and although the city's preeminence was relatively shortlived, historians Dale Somers and William Adams provide convincing evidence for New Orleans's role in the modernization of prizefighting.[73] Both credit the transformation, in large part, to the support of the elite athletic clubs, whose members gave the sport increased respectability through their interest and involvement. The requiring of Marquess of Queensberry rules, the increased authority of the referee, and the limiting of rounds, all of which came with club control, were evidence of the conventionalization and modernization of the game.

Athletic organizations also facilitated equalization of competition through the insistence on rigid adherence to weight classifications. Allen Guttmann, in his important study on sport, recognizes equality of competition (in conditions) as one of the seven distinguishing characteristics of modern sport. Before the Civil War and for a short period following it, fighters were either lightweights or heavyweights. The entry of athletic clubs into boxing ushered in four additional categories (bantamweight, featherweight, welterweight, and middleweight).[74] These clubs are credited as well with modernizing the business side of boxing. Matchmaking replaced the challenge system, and club officials competed for fights by guaranteeing large purses and by sending agents to negotiate with fighters and their managers. Dale Somers is convinced that "by the turn of the century, the mechanics of promotion had been fully developed by athletic clubs."[75]

A Rocky Trail West

With its decline and virtual disappearance in New Orleans, prizefighting turned—or more accurately, returned—to the West. Although the sport was not restricted to that region, it seemed to find a more conducive environment in the newer and less hidebound territories and states of the American frontier. Boxing's first stop was Texas, where it encountered a variety of conflicting signals. As the earlier case involving John L. Sullivan had revealed, Texans were not sure how they felt about prizefighting—the reaction of a state that was somewhere between the Bible Belt and the wide-open West.

The prizefight issue came to a head in the summer of 1895 as Gentleman Jim Corbett prepared to meet Robert Fitzsimmons for the heavyweight championship in Dallas. Before the contest could be held, lawyers for the promoters had to wage a legal battle against the state. The point of attack was an 1891 statute, which they maintained was invalid for a variety of reasons, including its punishment of a felony crime with a misdemeanor sentence. The disparity between crime and punishment was not unusual, although in this instance the law probably reflected the state's ambivalence toward prizefighting. The real and more difficult question was whether the legislature actually sanctioned prizefights through a legal technicality.

An 1889 tax statute permitted prizefighting under certain licensing and taxing procedures, but in 1891 the legislature enacted an anti-prizefight statute that did not repeal the earlier statute and provided only weak penalties for violation. Attempts to significantly strengthen the newer law and to correct its defects failed. In 1895 a revised penal code was passed with the old prizefight statutes intact, as was a new civil statute with the 1889 prizefight provision.[76] Both bills became law without Governor Charles A. Culbertson's signature. Since the penal code reached his desk on April 25 and the civil code on April 29, the proboxing faction maintained that the latter repealed the former. As the Corbett-Fitzsimmons bout was scheduled for Dallas, the county attorney there appealed to Attorney General Crane, who, in a lengthy document, argued that the 1891 statute was valid and still in force; the order in which the bills arrived on the governor's desk was irrelevant—the date on which the Senate passed the bills was the determining factor. On this basis, Crane ruled, the penal code became effective one day later than the civil code, and prizefighting was therefore illegal.[77]

Crane's opinion neither satisfied nor thwarted the backers of the fight. Governor Culbertson then entered the fray as the leader of the forces arguing against the validity of the penal code; whether he did so for legal reasons or because of a personal conflict with members of the Dallas sporting fraternity is not clear.[78] In any event, as an apparent test of the prizefight statute a boxer named Jess Clark was charged with violating the law. To avoid imprisonment, Clark brought a writ of habeas corpus before the Court of Criminal Appeals. Without the aid of his associates, who were on summer recess, Judge J. M. Hurt ruled that the

1891 statute had been invalidated by the revised civil code of 1895 and that Clark had not violated the law.[79]

Hurt's decision shook the reform elements in Dallas and the state. Now Corbett, who had objected to fighting in violation of the law, readied to defend his crown. Governor Culbertson threatened to ignore the judge's decision and, if necessary, use the military to stop the fight. Not sure as to the proper course of action, the governor first called for a full court to hear the case and then summoned a special session of the legislature. That body wasted no time in passing an anti-prizefight act, which differed from the 1891 law in two extremely important ways—it provided for a prison sentence of no less than two years and no more than five years, and it included a clause repealing all conflicting laws. Reform elements in Texas had finally succeeded; not even a hero like Corbett could thwart the opposition.[80]

Although denied a Texas venue, Corbett's handlers remained undaunted. With the shrewd impresario William A. Brady at the helm, the combatants sought a stage in the Indian Territory. The attorney general of the United States said no. Then they tried Arkansas, a state that was historically hostile to prizefighting. When Sullivan had signed to fight Kilrain in 1889, for example, governors across the nation had prepared to block the proceedings, including Arkansas Governor James P. Eagle, who declared that, if necessary, he would use all lawful means to stop the illegal event.[81] His resolve was not tested, but six years later William Brady put new leaders of that state's government to the test.

Having learned from his misadventures in Texas and Indian Territory, Brady replaced a frontal assault with subterfuge. He organized an athletic club in Little Rock, Arkansas, which was granted a corporate license by municipal authorities, to stage boxing exhibitions by and for club members. The Corbett-Fitzsimmons match would be staged under the auspices of the new club. Brady's machinations and the city's compliance prompted an immediate response from the attorney general's office. Not only was there concern about a violation of Arkansas law but also about the city's collusion in the matter. One observer noted, "Mr. Brady and his conferes, having secured an arrangement with the municipal authorities, thought they had the state by the throat."[82] The state sought an injunction and was granted one by Chancellor Martin of the Chancery Court of Pulaski County, Arkansas. Martin decided that the bout posed a threat to public safety and that Little Rock's complicity conflicted with the idea of state sovereignty.

Not until March 1897 did Brady and company find a suitable and hospitable site in Carson City, Nevada, with its free and easy approach to drinking, gambling, and boxing. A new heavyweight champion was crowned, as the strong, skillful, and durable Fitzsimmons knocked out the younger but less fit Corbett in the fourteenth round.[83] The venue proved to be more historically significant than the fight's results, however, for big-time prizefighting had returned to the West. New York, in an effort to attract boxing matches to the East, passed the Horton Law in 1896, which legalized "pugilism under the polite name of 'boxing bouts'." But as there was generally no control over the promotion of bouts, gamblers, corrupt officials, and crooked managers dominated the sport. An apparently fraudulent fight between Jim Corbett and Kid McCoy in August 1900 led to the repeal of the Horton Law. A quick replacement, the Lewis Law, which allowed the staging of boxing tournaments only for members of properly constituted clubs, did little to prevent championship prizefighting from returning to the West.[84]

Prizefighting Western Style

The western railway camps, which allegedly "sprouted as fast as spikes were driven," in the late 1860s became the sites of saloons, gambling houses, dance halls, and brothels. The regular Sunday morning amusement for the roadbed workers in the Wyoming hills was a prizefight between representatives of two camps. The men fought barefisted under London Prize Ring rules and the winner took the fifty-dollar purse (half of which had been donated by each camp). Oddly enough, the best-known name from mining camp fighting was not a boxing champion but a referee—Wyatt Earp, the oil baron, horse racer, gunfighter, and U.S. marshal in Arizona.[85]

A skillful amateur boxer and keen student of the game, Earp began his refereeing career in 1868, at the age of twenty, in an important bout between two Chrisman mining camp bullies. According to biographer Stuart Lake, before long Earp had become a regular on the Sunday mining camp circuit. He oversaw a Fourth of July bout between the professional Mike Donovan and unknown John Shanssey that was witnessed by a crowd of nearly three thousand men, and he had the added responsibility of handling the big betting pool. Donovan beat Shanssey so badly that the latter gave up boxing and eventually made a name for himself as a mail carrier and mayor of Yuma, Arizona. What should be remembered about these camp fights is that they represented a more orderly and controlled environment than most people associate with the Old West. Personal disputes as well as intercamp rivalries were settled by organized, supervised prizefights using established boxing rules, with tightly controlled gambling pools. The corporate structure that would soon dominate the West seemed to have influenced even the most basic and primitive of sports. Indeed, Earp, who is better remembered as a law agent and gunfighter, may have mediated more fistfights than shootouts.[86]

One fight to which Wyatt Earp's name will always be linked took place between Robert Fitzsimmons and Tom Sharkey at Mechanics Pavilion in San Francisco on December 2, 1896. Although tainted by controversy, the bout foreshadowed the emergence of championship boxing in California. The Olympic Club, the Golden Gate Club, and the California Athletic Club all had stellar reputations for the quality of their prizefights. According to sport historian David Wiggins, the California Athletic Club might have been the first organization to stage regular contests under the Marquess of Queensberry rules.[87] Yet despite their influence and affluence, neither the California Athletic Club nor any other club in the state had been able to land *the* prestige event—the heavyweight boxing championship of the world.

In the fall of 1896 California seemed on the verge of a breakthrough. The most talked-about event in the boxing world was the upcoming Fitzsimmons-Sharkey contest, to be refereed by Earp, who had returned to California from Texas. Quite the sportsman, he had raced horses and made a name for himself among men who lived free and easy. When promoters for the championship contest could not agree on a referee, chance and reputation brought Earp and them together. With rumors of a fix prejudicing the crowd, on the day of the fight Earp felt compelled to announce his intentions to "call things as I see them, not as someone else may want them called." He asked for the crowd's approval, received it, and stripped off his coat and vest and went to work.[88]

Fitzsimmons, who weighed only 156 pounds, was a powerful puncher and a master tactician. His strategy for the awkward Sharkey called for a right uppercut to the jaw followed by a crushing blow to his opponent's exposed solar plexus. Fitzsimmons's relentless body assault included questionable blows near the belt area, which Earp warned him about; in fact, the referee nearly stopped the fight, but Sharkey pleaded for its continuance. In the eighth round Fitzsimmons's left hook found Sharkey's jaw and was followed by a body punch; as Sharkey fell forward he caught a wicked blow to the groin. He lay writhing in pain and reflexively clutching himself as his seconds rushed into the ring, whereupon he fainted and was removed from the scene while still unconscious. Few spectators had seen the low blow, but an examination by physicians confirmed that a foul had been committed. Earp had no choice but to award the $10,000 winner's check to Sharkey's manager.

Martin Julian, Fitzsimmons's manager, obtained an injunction preventing payment and charged that Earp's decision had been deter-

mined in advance, which provoked an international controversy thanks
to the San Francisco newspaper that published Julian's charges. The
owner of that paper had allegedly lost $20,000 on Fitzsimmons and was
determined to destroy Earp. When a team of six physicians established
conclusively that Sharkey had suffered genital trauma, the newspaper
owner backed down. In the end, Sharkey probably gained the least. He
continued to box against the sport's best but was never able to capture
the coveted title. In 1898 he won a match against former champion Jim
Corbett as a result of a foul, but his greatest moment came in 1899 when
he lasted an entire twenty-five rounds against the invincible James J.
Jeffries. Sharkey suffered two broken ribs in that fight and never seriously
contended for the title again.[89] Earp won back his reputation and
became a U.S. marshal, and a legend in his own time. Fitzsimmons
shortly thereafter captured the heavyweight championship and still ranks
among the all-time greats of boxing. And California, within a few years
of the 1896 debacle, could rightfully proclaim itself "Boxing Capital of
the World," even if circumstance, more than planning, had made the
designation appropriate.

As eastern, midwestern, and southern states turned against prizefighting, the newer, wilder, and somewhat lawless mining states of Nevada
and California became havens for the sport, especially major championship fights, even though the activity was technically illegal. As so aptly
put by Randy Roberts, "it was a law honored more in the breach than in
the observance."[90] According to David Pivar, the Purity Crusade was an
eastern development with little or no appeal to westerners. Indeed, the
licensing "policies, previously applied to the sale of alcohol in the West,
were also applied to prize fighting when Nevada licensed it [prizefighting]
in 1897." Purity Crusaders called the act the "Nevada Disgrace."[91]

The East's Last Gasp: Progressivism in Microcosm

The success of prizefighting in the mining boomtowns of the West
made eastern promoters and fans envious. As previously indicated, the
Horton Law was an attempt by New Yorkers to fill the void left by
prizefighting's exodus, as well as a preemptive measure against western
competition. For a short time the strategy worked. James J. Jeffries won
the heavyweight championship from Robert Fitzsimmons in 1899 on
Coney Island and defended his title twice in New York before shifting
permanently to the West; all four of Jeffries's title defenses after 1900
took place in San Francisco. And there was one fight that never took
place but probably revealed more about prizefighting and its relationship to the larger society than all of Jeffries's previous fights combined.

John C. Heenan, known as the "Benicia Boy," fought Tom Sayers of England in April 1860 for the world's heavyweight championship. The fight ended in the thirty-seventh round when the ropes were mysteriously cut and police rushed in to halt the contest before one man could emerge victorious. Charging conspiracy, the American press declared Heenan the winner; its British counterpart defended Sayers's claims to victory. From a wood engraving in *Momus,* May 19, 1860. (Library of Congress)

An 1883 J. G. Hyde lithograph of the top heavyweights and their haunts. John L. Sullivan's primacy reflects American ethnocentricity more than it does pugilistic achievement. (Library of Congress)

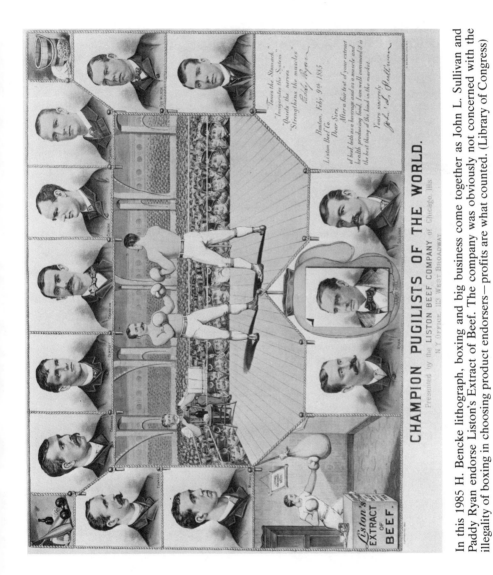

In this 1985 H. Bencke lithograph, boxing and big business come together as John L. Sullivan and Paddy Ryan endorse Liston's Extract of Beef. The company was obviously not concerned with the illegality of boxing in choosing product endorsers—profits are what counted. (Library of Congress)

Opponents of nineteenth-century prizefighting often cited the effect of the activity on the spectators. This George Cruikshank painting strongly suggests that boxing was a threat to public order since more action occurred in the gallery than in the ring. (Library of Congress)

Boxing proponents maintained that fight crowds were orderly and mannerly, as in this artist's rendition of a "gentlemanly" audience watching a fight at the Olympic Club in New Orleans in 1893. (Louisiana Collection, Tulane University Library, New Orleans)

George "Little Chocolate" Dixon, bantamweight champion, as he appeared in 1893 before his historic fight with Jack Skelly. (Louisiana Collection, Tulane University Library, New Orleans)

Professor John Duffy, proprietor of "Duffy's Arena" in New Orleans and one of the country's leading referees in the late 1800s. Duffy was known for his proficiency, honesty, and impartiality. (Louisiana Collection, Tulane University Library, New Orleans)

James J. Corbett's defeat of England's Charles Mitchell made the young American the undisputed champion of the world. He is shown here, with promoter and manager William A. Brady, in the company of European heads of state. By the Strobridge Lithographic Company, of Cincinnati and New York, 1894. (Library of Congress)

Despite recent failures, many businessmen, public officials, and promoters continued to devise evasive schemes for the purpose of staging prizefights—and with good reason. Although opposition to prizefighting went virtually unchallenged in rural areas, overworked, overregulated, and underentertained urbanites needed "wholesome entertainment." Cincinnati, for one, had a large potential clientele and an abundance of opportunistic men ready to exploit them. To that end, on December 8, 1900, a contingent of that city's outstanding business and civic leaders executed a contract for a championship boxing match between James J. Jeffries and Gus Ruhlin (a.k.a. "The Akron Giant").[92] The circumstances that led to Cincinnati's involvement and the series of events that prevented the fight from taking place put boxing directly in the middle of a controversy involving nativism, state sovereignty, personal greed, and public welfare. The episode, which had deep roots in the city's troubled past, convincingly shows that far more than morality fueled the opposition to prizefighting and a host of other so-called vices.

Founded in 1794, Cincinnati grew rapidly in the first half of the nineteenth century. With its strategic location in the Ohio Valley and along the Ohio River, it attracted a cosmopolitan population composed of large numbers of Germans, Irish, and blacks. However, ethnic differences and sharply defined residential areas eventually fostered disorder and conflict. The growing unrest reached crisis proportions in the spring of 1884, when a controversial jury verdict in a murder trial resulted in three nights of bloodshed, which left 54 people dead and 200 wounded.[93] In 1886 the ripple effect of the Chicago Haymarket upheaval touched Cincinnati, and while the city escaped the crisis without bloodshed, a certain uneasiness hovered over it for decades. The alcohol question, which had intense ethnic implications, was also a source of disorder.

In 1886 Sabbatarian agitation against the "continental Sunday," which called more for conviviality than worship and rest, touched off a countermove by a predominantly German group of citizens, the Bund fur Freiheit und Recht. The dispute over observance of the Sabbath represented only one of the many conflicts that divided immigrants from natives. Sunday drinking, rampant crime, and labor agitation were all linked to immigrants, especially the Germans. Reformers not only intended to restore the Sabbath to a day of rest and worship, they also hoped to neutralize the rising influence of the relative newcomers.[94]

Germans and their music and song had become a part of Cincinnati by 1800. Singing clubs and societies proliferated, and soon the river city became a musical center for German singers. In 1849 Cincinnati hosted the first German musical convention and festival—the Saengerfest. Out of the festival came the Associated Saenger Societies of the United

States, or the Saengerbund. In 1870 and 1879 Cincinnati hosted the annual Saengerfest, which was characterized by much feasting and conviviality.[95] Naturally, the city became the logical choice for the fiftieth anniversary celebration of the Saengerbund, scheduled for 1899.

Thirty-one of the city's most outstanding citizens, led by Leopold Kleybolte, Frank A. Lee, Fenton Lawson, William N. Hobart, and George Guckenberger, were entrusted with planning the anniversary festival. Their major task was to secure a building large enough to accommodate 4,000 singers and additional thousands in the audience. They had one built, but it proved unsafe and necessitated a virtual reconstruction at a cost of $100,000—an overrun of $65,000.[96] The building was not ready until the day after the opening of the festival, which undermined the public's confidence in the planners. Attendance fell far below expectations, as did revenues, and the festival created a $70,000 deficit for the thirty-one men who had guaranteed payment. Not willing to cover the loss, the festival's backers decided that since they had acted out of civic duty, the citizens of Cincinnati should bear the financial burden.[97] When the request for voluntary contributions—mixed with cajolery and threats—evoked a weak response from the citizenry, the promoters tried an appeal to greed: they would conduct a lottery, with the Saengerfest Building or $10,000 cash as a prize. Pressure by legal authorities forced them to abandon the unlawful scheme.[98]

Shortly thereafter the group authored a revealing proposal to stage a "boxing contest" in the Saengerfest Building. Where attempts to stir civic duty and greed had failed, the scheming thirty-one believed that an appeal to baser instincts would surely arouse the public. The proposal read: "Cincinnati is not a Puritan city. There are no Blue Laws here. We are pleasure loving and admire a perfect physique and the manly art of self-defense. The state may be straight-laced, but even it excepts boxing contests before authentic athletic clubs from the crime of prize-fighting, and we have a liberal young mayor to interpret the words."[99] With some degree of pressure and coercion, the thirty-one backers thus convinced Mayor Julius Fleischmann, a prosperous distiller and businessman, that a boxing contest would be good for the city and for him personally. The first man of Jewish extraction to hold the mayoral post and a man who considered himself a reformer, Fleischmann had no time for those who wished to restrict Cincinnati's leisure activities. After his assurance that a fight permit for a duly constituted athletic club would be issued, the debtors sent an emissary to New York to interview William Brady for the purpose of arranging a bout to eliminate the Saengerfest debt.

On December 8, 1900, the two sides reached an agreement: a preliminary contest would feature two black boxers, and the principal contest would pit heavyweight champion James J. Jeffries against Gus Ruhlin of Akron, Ohio. No one who read the contract or related newspaper accounts doubted that both contests were actually prizefights; the latter was to determine the heavyweight champion of the world. Jeffries and Ruhlin would receive 55 percent of the gross receipts, with 75 percent of that amount going to the winner.[100] To comply with the law, however, the Cincinnati backers formed the Saengerfest Athletic Association, and Mayor Fleischmann issued the necessary permit. He acted despite warnings from the city's attorney and the sound arguments of fifteen prominent lawyers, as well as the pleas of a committee of citizens who wished to save the city from shame.[101]

Opponents of the fight saw little hope in persuading local officials to stop it, so they sought intervention from the state capitol in Columbus. Despite a petition from 1,000 business institutions requesting that Governor George K. Nash stay out of the dispute, the governor saw through the subterfuge and expressed his determination to halt what was obviously going to be a prizefight. As plans proceeded and as anticipation heightened, Governor Nash urged Attorney General J. M. Sheets to take action, which he did on January 29, 1901, asking for an injunction to prevent the proposed exhibition. Although questions of order, morals, public welfare, and legality arose, Nash viewed the issue primarily as one of sovereignty. He wanted to prove that, as the state constitution stated, "the supreme executive power of this state shall be vested in a Governor."[102]

Under the direction of Judge Howard Hollister, the state court had to decide three critical issues: Was the proposed contest an exhibition or an illegal prizefight? Was the municipality or the state the proper authority? Was an injunction the proper remedy?[103] Judge Hollister did not doubt that the contest would be "a most animal and brutal" struggle for mastery. He emotionally recalled the contest in which Jim Corbett received his "quietus" and a tragic Ohio contest between David Seville and Arthur Majesty, in which Majesty died. With money and a title at stake, the judge felt that humane or sentimental consideration among the contestants would play no part. Moreover, he believed the potential for harm extended far beyond the ring. In his mind the complainant had shown conclusively that the proposed affair was likely to injure public and private morals, subvert common right, and threaten the "welfare, safety, comfort, peace, morals and happiness of her citizens, and the honor and dignity of the state."[104] In *Plessy* v. *Ferguson* (1896), the U.S. Supreme Court had clearly established the states' police powers; thus, Judge Hollister had no doubt of the governor's authority. The only question to be decided as far as he was concerned was the remedy.

Citing a list of pertinent precedents from other states, including the aforementioned Texas, Arkansas, and Louisiana cases, in addition to the similar case of *The Columbian Athletic Club* v. *State* (Indiana), Judge Hollister ruled that to enjoin the contest was the only suitable remedy. Convinced that irreparable mischief would flow, he concluded that the threatened wrong had to be prevented. His final statement read, "Let a perpetual injunction issue as prayed for in the petition."[105]

Although the local reformers had won a major battle, Governor Nash benefited even more. On the heels of this legal victory he was able to push through a constitutional amendment that conferred a limited veto power upon the governor. Moreover, the change brought many municipal governments under the control of the governor and his appointees, a development that undoubtedly affected the Cincinnati election of 1905, when a Democratic reform candidate, Edward J. Dempsey, succeeded the Boss Cox–backed Fleischmann as mayor. As for the guarantors of the Golden Jubilee of the Associated Saenger Societies of the United States, their debt remained outstanding. On March 31, 1901, the *Court Index* posted a daily notice that a subscription paper was available, in the Law Library of the courthouse, for the convenience of lawyers who might wish to contribute any sum for the payment of the balance due by the thirty-one original investors.[106]

William Brady received $5,000 from the Cincinnati promoters for his troubles, as had been previously agreed. He and the boxing fraternity also learned a valuable lesson—to leave the East and its reform initiatives alone. Boxing would no longer serve as a fall guy for progressives, not when the West willingly offered its hospitality and good faith. However, everyone seemed to realize that for boxing to reach its full potential, eventually it would have to return to the East, to the country's centers of wealth and population. The West would be only a temporary haven until the reformist cloud blew over. In the meantime, prizefighting would have to do all that it could to establish itself as a legitimate sporting and business activity, thus recommending itself to America's finest.

Brady took his charge to California, where Jeffries engaged in several exhibitions before meeting Gus Ruhlin in San Francisco for the heavyweight championship,[107] a title Jeffries retained with a fifth-round knockout. California had staged its first heavyweight championship fight and in the process became the undisputed boxing capital of the world.[108] The West had opened itself to another gold rush, as young men, called by the chance for adventure, fame, and fortune, prospected with gloves rather than picks and shovels, in boxing rings instead of mine shafts. One of the young men who went west in search of his fortune was Arthur John "Jack" Johnson, who would alter the sport of prizefighting and, in the process, leave his mark on American history.

2

Total Onslaught
Racism and Reform

When Jack Johnson moved west to gain fame and fortune in the prizefight game, no one, perhaps not even he, could have imagined that an obscure black man with little education but innate intelligence would eventually turn the boxing world—and, almost, America itself—upside down. After all, Johnson's most notable boxing contest to date was one in which he lost to an aging Joe Choynski. Throughout his career Johnson had trouble with smaller opponents, and after the beating he took from the hardluck San Franciscan, Johnson noted, "He hit the bulb [eye] so hard I couldn't close it." That one punch was enough to make the future great concede defeat. Then, as if that were not bad enough, both men were jailed after the fight and treated like common criminals. Johnson complained later that "a man in jail for murdering his wife got out two days quicker than [I] did." After twenty-four days behind bars the two fighters posted bond, and within a month Johnson was fighting regularly in Galveston. According to Randy Roberts, however, his matches "were as much ignored by the newspapers as they were enjoyed by the spectators."[1] The flood of 1900 had set back Galveston's progress as a boomtown, and the Johnson-Choynski affair apparently destroyed it as a fight town. Johnson had no choice but to stake his claim in the West.

Johnson's successes sparked a wholesale onslaught against boxing that subsided only with his defeat in 1915. Until then the sport remained on the defensive against groups with motives ranging from religion to racism, who were united in their goal to destroy or limit the evils of the "ignoble art." Johnson's impact and the race obsession that nearly consumed prizefighting can only be understood in the context of history and the larger society.

Racism and Sport

Very few issues in the history of the United States have been so obtrusive, persistent, and volatile as relations between whites and blacks. In fact, this nation's character is, in part, a product of its race relations. Ostensibly "conceived in liberty and dedicated to the proposition that all men are created equal," America has not applied that guiding principle to the treatment of its largest racial minority.[2] Racism remains a vexing and perplexing problem, even a mysterious one, largely because its existence has been denied, obscured, or ignored. Moreover, it has often been distorted by economic issues that exacerbate or alleviate its effects. With the abolition of slavery, for example, historian Pierre L. Van der Berghe has observed that, since race no longer clearly established vocational and social limits, whites demanded laws that would ensure physical separation and black subordination. Thus, once lovable, childlike, unthreatening blacks became "beasts" and "menaces" to civilization.[3] This anxiety and hatred spread naturally to the world of sport. Whites no longer wanted to watch blacks perform on the baseball diamond, and they certainly resented and feared black dominance in the ring.[4] Instead of serving as a haven from an unequal and unfair society, the realm of sport has closely followed patterns established by the larger society, including the pervasive myth that humans are judged solely by performance.[5]

Since prizefighting has been characterized by some as a true test of skill, courage, intelligence, and manhood, boxing champions have traditionally stood as symbols of national and racial superiority. Consequently, black challengers to white American champions have been perceived as threats to white and national superiority. If football was "the expression of the strength of the Anglo-Saxon . . . the dominant spirit of a dominant race," then boxing reduced this expression to individual terms. Indeed, the Progressive Era's concern with "racial betterment" was often tested in the world of sport.[6]

Although there is debate on the subject, most written accounts indicate that the first black boxers were slaves. Owners allegedly pitted their finest physical specimens against one another in "no-holds-barred" matches for the glory of the plantation and sizable wagers. Boxing historian Elliot Gorn maintains this practice was rare because it violated sound business sense; he argues that it was mostly the stuff of myth, more likely to have occurred in novels, like *Mandingo* and *Drum,* than in reality. However, Frederick Douglass described boxing and wrestling, along with drinking and other merriments during holiday periods, as "among the most effective means in the hands of the slaveholder in

keeping down the spirit of insurrection." Recent experiences add considerable weight to Douglass's remarkable conclusion that sport has a
historical application as a form of social control.[7]

Exploitation and brutality were facts of slave life, and as historian
John Blassingame points out, slave masters ran the gamut from the
benevolent to the cruel, from the rational to the insane.[8] Paul Magriel, a
boxing historian, maintains that slaves did box but believes that these
pugilists received little for their services at the risk of life and limb. On
rare occasions an extraordinary male slave would transcend his lowly
position in life, by strength of character and body, to reach the highest
level of boxing, only to find there a lack of recognition and constant
scorn.[9]

Tom Molineaux was said to have been such a person. A former
slave, in 1809 Molineaux became the second American to attain status
as an international challenger and the first black to fight for the heavyweight championship. Despite these accomplishments, the American
press, certainly aware of his epic and heroic encounters with British
champion Tom Cribb, virtually ignored Molineaux.[10] Even less known
and less publicized was the fact that the first American prizefighter of
international repute was also black. Bill Richmond, known as "The
Black Terror," mauled the best British boxers in the late 1700s and early
1800s, losing only to Cribb in 1805 after a grueling bout that lasted one
hour and thirty minutes.[11] Although Magriel's conclusion that the near
absence of coverage resulted from an editorial conspiracy is unsupported
by the evidence, racial considerations surely could have combined with
disinterest to produce the "blackout."[12]

The first black heavyweight of note to fight white opponents in the
United States was the West Indian–born Australian Peter Jackson.
Interestingly, his career reflected the changing patterns of race relations.
Jackson had once fought the great Jim Corbett to a sixty-one-round draw
in 1891, but he failed in many attempts after that date to obtain matches
with Corbett or John L. Sullivan.[13] Jackson himself realized that Corbett's
refusal to fight him again was more than a boxing matter, and he took his
plight to the public, eloquently presenting his boxing skills as well as his
personal qualifications. Never once mentioning race, Jackson calmly
offered, "I have never challenged Corbett and I never will." He maintained
that he had never challenged any man but, like the mythical reluctant
political candidate, "always stood ready to battle any recognized champion who wanted to 'go'."[14] While holding out false hope that the boxing
fraternity operated on merit, Jackson, according to biographer David
Wiggins, "developed a sadness and intimacy with misery" that character-

ized not only black athletes but many blacks who confronted the oppressive and humbling racial discrimination of the age.[15]

Jackson never did fight for the heavyweight championship of the world. He died on July 13, 1901, at the age of forty; the official cause of death was listed as tuberculosis, though Wiggins believed that a broken heart contributed mightily to the fighter's rapid downfall. Not only had the boxing world shut him out but so had the society. His rejection by management at the well-known Baldwin Hotel in 1897, where he had frequently stayed in the past, symbolized his plight and that of all blacks in America.[16]

Unfortunately, Jackson had not understood the importance of race. By the 1880s the heavyweight boxing championship symbolized, to some extent, America's rise to world power at the expense of declining British influence. In this context, the holder of the title stood as a shining example of American strength and racial superiority. More important, during this time attitudes toward blacks hardened dramatically, compared with the 1840s through 1870s, when abolitionist fervor and radical Republican legislation had, among other things, helped blacks to reach a high-water mark in achievement and status. But from 1880 to 1900 blacks fell to the depths in prestige and condition. At the time it was not unusual to hear northern liberals and former abolitionists professing blacks' inferiority and lack of fitness to participate fully in white society.

Actions backed up these words and feelings. In fact, the mostly northern, Republican-dominated U.S. Supreme Court issued a succession of rulings against civil rights between 1873 and 1898, culminating in *Plessy* v. *Ferguson* (1896).[17] Called by some the worst decision since the Dred Scott case, the ruling guaranteed second-class citizenship for blacks by institutionalizing "separate but equal" status.[18] In the South this stiffening occurred because of the distinct threat of blacks to white supremacy; in the North it represented a desire to reconcile with the South, at the expense of blacks, who no longer seemed necessary to the Republican power base and who stood in the way of economic progress. While the changing attitudes and laws brought about black disfranchisement, segregation, and economic hardship, they also reversed black gains in the sporting arena. In the 1870s and 1880s blacks had participated in integrated baseball, horse racing, and even golf, but by 1900 they had virtually disappeared from white-dominated sport.[19]

Although Peter Jackson was denied the opportunity to fight for the heavyweight title, boxing practices in some ways stood as an exception to the exclusionary tendencies of other sports and the larger society. George Dixon held the bantamweight title from 1890 to 1892 and the featherweight title from 1892 to 1900. Despite an ugly reaction to his brutal victory over Jack Skelly in New Orleans in 1892, one that, as has been shown, effectively ended interracial fights there, Dixon went on to fight other whites and to beat them. Another black, Joe Walcott, won the welterweight title in 1901 and held it for five years. The great Joe Gans held the lightweight title from 1902 to 1908. Yet most of the fights after 1892 took place in the West or North, a shift that reflected legal and racial changes in the game and in society.[20]

On the basis of these interracial fights, boxing seemed egalitarian compared to the larger society. Black boxers were apparently spared the denigration of their less fortunate brethren, as prizefighting provided an apparent escape from discrimination and racism. Appearances were misleading, however. Boxing is, and always has been, a sport of confrontation and combat, a weaponless war, individualized; thus, fighting between blacks and whites did not indicate comradeship or social acceptance. Furthermore, Dixon, Gans, and Walcott all fought in the lighter weight classifications, and though their battles against whites may have been disturbing to many whites, their size was a mitigating factor; they did not symbolize the nation or their race, since the biggest fighting men have always had that burden. Thus, while those smaller black men still fought white opponents, their bigger brethren had to battle in the shadows, mostly against fighters of their own color and never for the championship.[21]

Jack Johnson, the "Black Menace"

After the 1905 retirement of the legendary James J. Jeffries, a huge man with a granite jaw, the heavyweight division deteriorated and so did fan interest. An inconsistent and uninspiring Marvin Hart took the vacated title in an elimination bout against former light heavyweight champion Jack Root. Seven months later, in his first defense of the title, Hart lost to the little-known and less than spectacular Tommy Burns, a German-Canadian whose real name was Noah Brusso. Burns proved to be a little more active than Hart, defeating an assortment of opponents from the near great to the virtually unknown between 1906 and 1908; among the better fighters were "Fireman Jim" Flynn and "Philadelphia Jack" O'Brien. As champion, however, Burns had little drawing power, and poor gates combined with relentless fan pressure to weaken society's insistence on a color barrier.[22]

Lurking in the shadows was Jack Johnson. In 1907 he destroyed the forty-two-year-old but still dangerous Robert Fitzsimmons, a victory that enhanced Johnson's image and his confidence—both in the ring and the bedroom. According to biographer Randy Roberts, "subconsciously, if not consciously, victories over white boxers stimulated Johnson's relationships with white women. He would celebrate every major victory in his career in the arms of one or more white females."[23] Eventually this affinity for white women, which met with overwhelming public resentment and hostility, combined with Johnson's ring prowess and antics to make him the most controversial and perhaps the most courageous boxer of all time.

Not long after his second-round knockout of Fitzsimmons, Johnson took on the unsportsmanlike but able Fireman Jim Flynn in a fight that would determine the next leading contender.[24] Flynn is best remembered as the only man who ever knocked out Jack Dempsey. Despite Flynn's dirty tactics, Johnson finished off his opponent in the eleventh round. The bout that Flynn had hoped would guarantee him a rematch with Burns, the champion, resulted in a black man's moving to the threshold of the boxing throne. Johnson did not hesitate to assert his rights as a challenger, and sportswriters agreed that the American credo of fair play should not be held captive by bigotry. Like soldiers without a war, sportswriters seemed to hunger for the excitement of battle and the chance to cover a good fight, if not to wage it themselves. Whether Johnson was bad news or good news did not matter to them; he was news, and that sold papers and built reputations.

A complex set of factors operated to make writers of all sorts support the idea of equal opportunity in sport when black athletes in general suffered discrimination and when Johnson himself had been treated unfairly throughout his career. Some sportswriters believed then, as many do now, that sport was sacred, isolated from the larger society. Sport provided an escape from a world dominated by politics, by unfair competition, by impersonal and uncontrollable forces. Implicit in this assumption was the view that the affairs of sport would remain confined to sport. The argument followed that, if immune to the forces outside, boxing was also powerless to influence the external world. Moreover, those writers with racial concerns were buoyed in their confidence that white physical and intellectual superiority would prevail. But should Tommy Burns, who was a lackluster, unpopular foreigner, lose, boxing would gain, for a black champion would bring back interest and money to the game, his reign would surely be temporary, and his ultimate defeat would symbolically reaffirm white racial supremacy. Destruction of the insolent, defiant Johnson, a usurper of a white privilege, in a morality event of good versus evil, would serve as a lesson akin to a public lynching for blacks who did not know their place in American society.

Burns, although not American, did not rush to break the local tradition started by John L. Sullivan, but market forces and pressure from Johnson and some sportswriters, as well as the shrewd and determined efforts of Sam Fitzpatrick, wore him down. In 1906, following years of mixed success as his own manager, Johnson formed a mutually beneficial alliance with Fitzpatrick, who had the ability to arrange matches that other managers and promoters believed impossible. If anybody could help Johnson penetrate the color barrier it was Fitzpatrick. No admirer of Johnson's personal life, this perceptive judge of talent saw in his fighter a man of enormous money-making potential.[25] Wary of trusting any manager, Johnson nonetheless appreciated Fitzpatrick's eye for talent and his ability to make matches. Their relationship showed signs of paying early dividends when Fitzpatrick nearly closed a deal for a fight at the National Sporting Club in London. The offer of 500 pounds to the winner, with each side bearing its own expenses, appealed to neither man.[26] If guaranteed $30,000, however, Burns agreed to fight Johnson anytime, anywhere.

When Burns left England for Australia, Johnson was not far behind. Afforded a hero's welcome, Burns stimulated considerable interest in boxing-mad Australia. Wherever he went, though, he had to answer questions about meeting a black opponent, to which Burns repeatedly responded that only money separated Johnson and him. Burns defeated two Australian challengers, Bill Squires and Bill Lang, before large crowds, to the delight of promoter Hugh D. McIntosh. This slick promoter, also known as "Huge Deal," had bigger plans, however. Even before Johnson arrived in Australia, a deal had been struck for a fight between Burns and the black challenger. McIntosh would not only promote the fight, he would referee it as well.[27]

Jack Johnson was wary of the racist Australian atmosphere and dissatisfied with the arrangements for the fight, which included a pro-Burns referee (McIntosh). The prospects for a fair encounter seemed poor. The Australian press portrayed Johnson as a threatening black menace; American writers reacted with relative calm. American whites remained convinced that blacks lacked strategy, intelligence, courage, and skill, critical elements to boxing success; therefore, they had nothing to fear from black boxers. Concern that "equal opportunity in the ring would erupt into other areas of American society" would be alleviated by a match that would "set to rest for all time the matter of fistic supremacy . . . between white race and colored."[28]

The black challenger overcame his concerns and the hostile conditions to knock out the courageous Burns in the fourteenth round. More ominous to whites than his victory, however, was the manner in which Johnson conducted himself. With almost every punch he delivered a taunt, a devastating combination designed to fluster and belittle his white opponent while elevating himself. If Johnson did not look upon the defeat of Burns as a "racial triumph," he certainly wanted to prove his own superiority as a man.[29] In doing so, Johnson sought the greatest white prerogative—supremacy over all others—for himself.

Australia took the defeat far more seriously than did America. Both white and black America seemed rather unmoved by the event until novelist Jack London sounded the call for Jim Jeffries to come back and "remove the golden smile from Jack Johnson's face."[30] Others did not share his sense of urgency, but Johnson soon changed their opinions.[31] Within a year the black champion had successfully defended his heavyweight title five times against the likes of Philadelphia Jack O'Brien, Al Kaufman, and the great middleweight Stanley Ketchel. Almost as alarming to whites was the success of another great black heavyweight boxer, Joe Jeannette. Together Johnson and Jeannette seemed to spell doom for white superiority in boxing. Following a devastating Jeannette victory over a white boxer in New York shortly after Johnson won his title, serious-faced men discussed the situation in fearful voices. Johnson was dominating the heavyweight division and Jeannette seemed capable of defeating the best white boxers available. To certain people this portended a disaster.[32]

In addition to Johnson and Jeannette, the black heavyweight boxing brigade included Sam McVey and Sam Langford, which made an extended black reign entirely possible. Sam Langford was especially memorable. From runaway child and later athletic club janitor, Langford would become, by age eighteen, one of the most formidable fighters of his time. A natural welterweight, the "Boston Tar Baby" was able to whip men who dwarfed him in both height and weight. It was said that he had to fight far heavier opponents because men his own size refused to take him on.[33]

A black champion or champions should not have precipitated a national crisis, yet hatred and hysteria did just that. By the end of 1909 cries for a fight between Johnson and former champion James J. Jeffries had reached fever pitch. In December, Jeffries succumbed to his imploring fans, visions of sporting immortality, and the lucrative financial rewards. The former champion maintained that he was responding to "that portion of the white race that has been looking to me to defend its athletic superiority."[34] Tex Rickard, a man known for his money-making genius and lack of conscience, promoted the spectacle. Sensing that large monetary gains could be had by exploiting race issues, Rickard employed the regrettable theme of black versus white in his highly professional publicity campaign. Al-Tony Gilmore, another Johnson biographer, believes that Rickard's "approach played hand-in-hand with the deeply entrenched racial fear and hostilities of Americans and soon the stories of Rickard worked their way from the sports pages into the front pages of the American press."[35]

This time Rickard's greed, insensitivity, and flair for the spectacular backfired. He had blown the fight out of proportion, almost to the level of a second revolution. Newspapers disparaged Johnson and his race, one likening him to a barbarian against Caesar; another called him a coward who would lose once he looked the champion in the eye, "for Jeffries had Runnymede and Agincourt behind him, while Johnson had nothing but the jungle."[36] A song written by Dorothy Forrester captured the essence of the chauvinism, racism, and hatred that poisoned so many minds. In a paean of praise for the great "white hope," entitled "Jim-a-da-Jeff," she instructed Jeffries to:

> Commence right away to get into condish,
> An' you punch-a da bag-a day and night,
> An'-a din pretty soon, when you meet-a da coon,
> You knock-a him clear-a out-a sight.
> Chorus: Who's dat man wid-a hand like da bunch-a banan!
> It's da Jim-a-de-Jeff, oh! da Jim-a-da-Jeff,
>
>   . . . .
>
> Who give-a da Jack Jonce one-a little-a tap?
> Who make-a him take-a one big-a long nap?
> Who wipe-a da Africa off-a da map?
> It's da Jim-a-da-Jeff.[37]

This rhythmically light, simple song, written in the popular vaudeville Italian-style dialect, reflected not only racism but also the refusal to acknowledge blacks as Americans. In beating Johnson, Jeffries would reaffirm both the inferiority of Africans and the white desire to exterminate these barbarians. Unfortunately for the followers of Jeffries, it would be Johnson's fans who sang victory songs. In the end, however, funeral dirges would have been more appropriate, for all of America suffered greatly. Few could have imagined that newspaper stories and symbolic war songs would be able to generate such hatred or that the Jeffries-Johnson fight would send shock waves throughout the nation.

Whites were not alone in casting the fight into the largest of symbolic terms, for blacks reacted to the racist statements and sentiments with defiant and proud messages of their own.[38] The *Chicago Defender* declared emphatically that Johnson would also be fighting "Race Hatred," "Prejudice," and "Negro Persecution." Reverend Reverdy Ransom, a black Chicago leader, agreed that "what Jack Johnson seeks to do to Jeffries in the roped arena will be more the ambition of Negroes in every domain of human endeavor."[39] Others took a higher ground and asserted that Johnson stood for black elevation if not salvation.[40]

According to legend, when Johnson and Jeffries met in a San Francisco saloon five years before their historic bout, Johnson challenged the reigning champion. Jeffries allegedly replied, "I won't meet you in the ring because you've got no name. . . . But I'll go downstairs to the cellar with you and lock the door from the inside. The one who comes out with the key will be the champ." Johnson, a raw, unknown boxer, backed down.[41] Now he had worldwide fame and his boxing skills had been honed to perfection. Jeffries was a beardless Santa Claus, content with farming, fishing, drinking, and eating; his skills resided in his memory. Although he trained hard for the fight and lost over seventy pounds, he was too old and too ring-rusty for his strong, artful opponent.

On that most sacred of American holidays, July 4, 1910, the two men prepared for battle before an angry and anxious crowd of greats, near greats, and common folk in Reno, Nevada. The fight was over before it started. The superhuman Jeffries was no more; the hope of an ethnocentric, chauvinistic, sports-mad society had succumbed to age. Johnson later wrote, "Hardly had a blow been struck when I knew that I was Jeff's master."[42] Jeffries must have suspected as much, for he told his own corner, "My arms won't work, but just give me time and I'll be allright."[43] Johnson was not willing to give him time without exacting a heavy price. "Package being delivered Mister Jeff," was Johnson's way of punishing his opponent with words as well as punches. He also verbally assaulted former champion Jim Corbett, who was in Jeffries's corner. Jeffries's fans, sensing he could not respond to the embarrassing treatment, called for official intervention before their hero fell to a humiliating defeat, a fate too cruel for proud whites to bear. But intercession did not come and Johnson finished what he had started with a knockout in the fifteenth round.[44]

That afternoon and evening following the fight there were many deaths and injuries from racial conflicts throughout the country. Defiant words and demonstrations of pride from blacks led to retribution from angry and threatened whites. According to Randy Roberts, "never before had a single event caused such widespread rioting. Not until the assassination of Martin Luther King, Jr., would another event elicit a similar reaction."[45] Although Johnson's victories in the ring were grating on the white American public and stimulating to the nation's blacks, his character was also a central issue. His fondness for fast cars, fancy clothes, glib talk, and, most of all, white women, had alienated both whites and elitist blacks while endearing him to the increasingly militant and assertive black urban masses. In a brilliant account of black culture and consciousness, historian Lawrence Levine maintains that "Johnson ruptured role after role set aside for Negroes in American society." Moreover, "the very extent of white anger and fustration made Johnson's victory sweeter."[46] Johnson was not just a fighter but a symbol. His defeats of whites were victories for the black race. This excerpt from a street song indicates Johnson's effect upon his fans:

> The Yankees hold the play
> The white man pulls the trigger;
> But it makes no difference what the white man say
> The world champion's still a nigger.[47]

When black pride and the white reaction to it resulted in belligerent displays and riotous acts, boxing and society clashed as never before. Those associated with prizefighting knew that Johnson had brought unprecedented negative attention to this vulnerable sport, yet his name filled arenas and sold newspapers. Some observers counseled patience: soon the "right" man would surface to redeem the white race. They were convinced that the only way Johnson and his legacy could be erased was for him to be beaten fairly and squarely. Others believed that was impossible. To them Johnson represented a serious threat to the social order. Thus, an odd alliance of racists, reformers, and public officials formed to reduce the presence of boxing in American society.

Rearguard Attacks

Johnson's inactivity in 1911 and his subsequent defeat of all challengers frustrated boxing promoters and angered the American public. The search for the great "white hope" had extended even to South Africa and yielded nothing but "great white jokes."[48] As boxing's popularity declined, its opponents seized the opportunity to prey upon a weakened beast. The United Society of Christian Endeavor, the Anti-Saloon League of America, and the California Women's clubs all used Johnson as a scapegoat in an attempt to destroy a sport they believed was immoral, corrupting, and bestial. The anti-prizefight groups were not only armed with the power of indignation, they were also able to appeal to patriotism and racism. The latter, often bolstered by paternalism, helped put boxing on the defensive.[49]

The first significant victory in this attack was the banning of the Johnson-Jeffries fight film. In 1910 William Shaw, general secretary of the United Society of Christian Endeavor, which boasted some four million members, sent out an urgent plea that governors prevent the film from being shown in their states. The racial climate in many areas strengthened the plea. Racial tensions ran so high in Cincinnati, for example, that Mayor Louis Schwab had banned the film by executive order, for fear it would set off a race riot.[50]

Racial violence was fresh in everyone's memory. Only two years earlier, on the heels of a horrible riot in Springfield, Illinois, concerned whites and blacks came together to organize the National Association for the Advancement of Colored People, to stem the tide of racist poison from overflowing the nation. William Walling, a reporter for a Springfield newspaper and a Georgian by birth and rearing, whose liberal views on race and socialism had forced him out of the South by the time of the riot, wrote, "Either the spirit of the abolitionists of Lincoln and Lovejoy must be revived and we must come to treat the black man on a plane of absolute political and social equality or Vardaman and Tillman will soon have transferred the Race War to the North."[51] The Springfield riot presaged a terrible trend in American race relations, and Walling's prophecy found fulfillment. In 1919 alone race riots occurred in twenty-five cities and towns across the nation. At least 120 people died and hundreds more were injured as black aspirations to full citizenship and equality clashed with white supremacy and the economic status quo in a hysterical postwar America. In this atmosphere of xenophobia and red baiting, blacks became the inner enemy.[52]

Shaw and his supporters got results. Even England and South Africa agreed not to show the Johnson-Jeffries film, and at least fifteen states and the District of Columbia passed legislation forbidding its exhibition.[53] The victory was even bigger than Shaw could have imagined, however. The state legislatures did not specifically prohibit the showing of the Johnson-Jeffries film, for the assumption was that there would be other fights featuring Johnson that they would also have to act upon. Thus, they banned the showing of all prizefight films, which left the sport stunned. Moving pictures had provided tremendous exposure and increased revenues for boxing, and while the sport itself remained illegal in most states, the showing of films had not previously been an issue. Now, the new legislation would severely limit the profit-making capacity of prizefighting. The ban on boxing films had tremendous implications for the success of the sport for years to come and also led to continuous court challenges and ingenious attempts to circumvent the law.

Anti-boxing groups did not rest on their laurels. Although purity reformers had pressured Congress since 1896 for a national law prohibiting fight films, they now had the support of diehard racist congressmen, like Representative Seaborn A. Rodenberry of Georgia and Senator Furnifold Simmons of North Carolina. In late May–early June of 1912, the two men introduced bills into Congress calling for a prohibition on the interstate transportation of fight films. Johnson's victory over Fireman Jim Flynn on July 4, 1912, and the ugly national mood reinforced the sense of urgency. By July 31, 1912, the transportation of prizefight films in interstate commerce for purposes of public exhibition was a federal offense.[54] This blanket approach to a specific problem took on far-reaching importance and led to court tests involving congressional intent, states' rights, and interstate commerce. Ironically, it also later denied many Americans the opportunity to see the "redemption" of the white race in the Johnson-Willard fight of 1915.

Enemies of the black race used the Johnson example to press for racist legislation. Rodenberry, having tasted victory on the film issue, pressed for national legislation to prohibit interracial marriage. Johnson's flaunting of his relationships with white women stirred the passions of hatred and envy among ministers, the press, and politicians, and Rodenberry exploited that mood. His demagoguery must have made diehards like Theodore Bilbo, James K. Vardaman, and "Pitchfork Ben" Tillman proud. However, despite Rodenberry's predictions that the habits of Jack Johnson, if followed by other blacks, could lead to a race war bloodier than the great North-South conflict, his measure failed to gain the necessary support. While many legislators shared his abhorrence of miscegenation, few thought Johnson worth the trouble of demeaning the Constitution with such regressive legislation.[55]

While Jack Johnson was clearly a source of pride to many blacks, and to some an alter ego, a man many blacks wished they could be—reckless, independent, bold, and superior in the face of whites—to other blacks he was a source of embarrassment and resentment. Many middle-class, upwardly mobile blacks tended to accuse their less-refined, less-reserved, and less-cultured brethren of casting aspersions on their race. When southern blacks migrated to northern cities after 1900 in unprecedented numbers, social relations were often as strained between older black residents and the newcomers as they were with whites. Even when the more-established blacks tried to help their rural and southern brothers and sisters, their manner was often paternalistic and condescending.[56] Johnson, in many ways, represented the "bad nigger" whites were so willing to parade as an example of why blacks must be kept in "their place." W. E. B. Du Bois opposed Johnson's marriages and affairs outside his race for reasons involving black pride and strategy. Du Bois felt that racial pride and love of oneself were essential to the uplift of black people, and to alienate whites over something so unnecessary as seeking white women was a deterrent to racial progress. Yet, like most black leaders and regardless of personal feelings about miscegenation,

A young Jack Johnson in an uncharacteristic bare-knuckle pose. (Library of Congress)

Harry Wills of New Orleans, one of the many great black boxers who did not fight for the heavyweight championship. Neither Jack Johnson nor his white successors Jess Willard and Jack Dempsey would fight the dangerous Wills. (The Historic New Orleans Collection, Museum/Research Center, acc. no. 1974.25.2.52)

Du Bois opposed legislation preventing intermarriage. Such legislation would entrench black inferiority by implying "that black blood is a physical taint."[57]

While ambivalence best characterized the black community's opinion of Johnson, most whites viewed him as a menace to the established social order and to Anglo-Saxon civilization, and they were intent upon his destruction as a powerful symbol. Attempts to legislate him out of society mostly failed, but the United States government was quietly using existing laws to build a case against him that would remove Johnson from circulation and make him an example to all blacks who strayed off the established course.

In 1913, after a lengthy investigation and occasional harassment, the Bureau of Investigation, forerunner of the F.B.I., announced an eleven-count indictment against Jack Johnson, with charges ranging from aiding prostitution and debauchery to unlawful sexual intercourse and sodomy. His arrest was made possible by the White Slave Traffic Act of 1910, better known as the Mann Act, named for James Robert Mann, a moralistic Republican congressman. Although most convictions under the act involved commercialized sexual vice, the law was so worded that any man who crossed a state line with a woman other than his wife and had sex with her could be prosecuted. Johnson must have violated the law since he had made many trips with a woman named Belle Schreiber between Chicago and Pittsburgh. An all-white jury convicted Johnson despite hard evidence and sentenced him to one year in prison and a $1,000 fine.[58] In this instance concern for racial order had exceeded concern for law and the doctrine of reasonable doubt.

Johnson escaped from the authorities while on bond and made his way through Canada to Europe. Although his escape made the authorities look very foolish, one major objective had been accomplished: Johnson had been removed from American society. An unfair, racist system had done what no individual could—remove that golden smile from Jack Johnson's face. There was only one thing still to be done: wrest the heavyweight championship away from the black titleholder.

After two years in Europe, fighting anyone for a few dollars, a broke and depressed Johnson agreed to fight big, white Jess Willard in Havana, Cuba. The black champion could not return to the States without risking certain arrest, but the neighboring island assured adequate spectators and press coverage. Willard took the match seriously and worked his enormous body into incredible condition; Johnson, by contrast, trained irregularly and entered the contest overweight and out of shape. When Willard knocked out Johnson in the twenty-sixth round, a prostrate Johnson raised his hands to protect his eyes from the torrid tropical sun. Was it a reflex reaction or a voluntary, controlled act? Johnson maintained he lost the fight on purpose so as to receive a light prison sentence upon his return to the States and pointed to his eye-shielding as proof. Randy Roberts maintains that Johnson, unable to make a deal, bet $2,500 on himself to win.[59] It is safe to say that only Jack Johnson knew what really happened. Whatever the circumstances, most white Americans rejoiced in the return of the heavyweight crown to their race. Willard became an instant hero, one who brought renewed confidence to the physical and moral strength of white America. Yet Johnson's legacy haunted boxing and America for years to come.

One of the most perplexing problems Johnson caused the sport concerned the anti–fight film law, and the protracted conflict that ensued perhaps reflected concerns with technology as much as with race or prize-fighting. A fighter could only be in one place at one time, yet motion pictures enabled him and his influence to be widespread and uncontrollable. The use of film showed our ingenuity but also complicated the ability to exercise control over boxing and undesirable events and people.

Fight over Films

T. Lawrence Weber, who had little interest in the racial implica-tions of the Johnson-Willard fight but who sensed its money-making potential, tried to distribute a film of the fight for widespread exhibition. To his surprise, customs officials confiscated the film at Newark, New Jersey. Weber, a well-known film distributor, decided to challenge the anti–fight film law, which he believed had had one purpose—to reduce the negative influence of Jack Johnson. Weber's legal counsel understood, however, that victory could be secured only by disproving the act's constitutionality and establishing the intent of Congress.[60] Arguing that Congress had "exceeded its powers under the commerce clause and was exercising police powers reserved in the state," Weber and his lawyers took the case all the way to the Supreme Court of the United States. There Weber's contention was set aside with finality. The justices held that since the power of Congress over foreign commerce was already recognized and enforced by the courts, its authority to prohibit the introduction of foreign articles went without question.[61] Weber's argu-ment that the law purported to prevent the showing of the films and not to prevent their importation or transportation was dismissed with equal ease: the motives of Congress could not be used as an excuse for not recognizing the laws it enacted.[62] The government permanently impounded Weber's film of the Johnson-Willard fight.

Still, money-hungry promoters were determined to enrich themselves while satisfying the desires of boxing fans, anti-Johnson elements, and entertainment seekers by showing the Johnson-Willard film. They seemed willing to try anything to evade the law, and one approach in particular proved quite ingenious. In April 1916 New York authorities uncovered a scheme by which negatives of the fight film were developed into positives without physically importing the film into the United States.[63] The process merits description. A movie camera was set up on the American side eight inches from the New York–Canada border, with the lens directed to the north. At approximately the same distance on the Canadian side rested a box with an electric light; through this was run an original positive film taken from the negative film made in Havana. Unexposed film was moved along a reel and through the camera on the American side; the two reels were connected in a way that allowed both to turn simultaneously, and thus a negative reproduction was made in America of the positive film in Canada. Pantomimic Corporation then rephotographed from the secondary negative and prepared to distribute positives of the contraband film.[64]

Upon threats of confiscation by the collector of the Port of New York, the Pantomimic Corporation filed suit. Two U.S. courts rejected Pantomimic's complaint on the ground that although the letter of the law had not been violated, the spirit had. While only rays of light had been brought in, the higher court held that the actions of the parties to transfer a prohibited picture from Canada to New York constituted the conducting of foreign commerce and violated the law against the importation of prizefight films.

For a few years the ruling effectively halted such subterfuges, but by 1922 the anti-fight film law had been widely violated.[65] As a result, Congress attempted to strengthen the original act. One proposal called for the seizure and destruction of such films. Another, in 1924, was an effort to clear up the intent of the original statute by punishing those in possession or control of such films.[66] Neither bill made much headway. With Jack Johnson gone, the problem was not so pressing; and more important, by 1922 prizefighting had gained added respectability and even legality in some states.[67] Although justification for and enforcement of the law proved increasingly difficult, calls for repeal got no further than did attempts to strengthen the measure. Resolution appeared distant, and Congress seemed content to let the courts carry the burden. In doing so, it exacerbated the problems of enforcement.

While authorities were willing to halt the technological reproduction of potentially dangerous and barbaric activities, they were far less willing to deal with the sport of boxing itself. The actions of Congress, perhaps as much as anything, reflected the nation's ambivalence and

uneasiness with modernizing society. To halt boxing would be to limit
the individual's baser instincts—to deprive people of their natural selves,
their competitive drive, and their centrality in the order of things. If
boxing was out of control, the sport was not at fault, for it was essentially
noble. The blame had to fall on undesirable elements, in this instance
Jack Johnson and an uncontrollable medium, film. All too often human
attempts to control the environment through invention result in a reduction of our own importance and an increase in depersonalization. Motion
pictures had this effect.

Jack Johnson's Legacy

With Johnson out of the heavyweight championship picture, the
boxing world believed that the major obstacle to respectability had
disappeared. It was probably correct. But those who believed that Johnson's
removal from his position of influence would ease racial tensions and
deter black aspirations were mistaken. Johnson was a forerunner of,
and a critical ingredient in, a new social movement. Because he was
the first black champion and such a controversial one, he left an indelible
mark upon the sport and the larger society. Indeed, long after the
Willard fight, tales of Johnson's physical prowess, his great speed, his
predictions on fights, and, moreover, his ability to humble his white
opponents and anger the American public, still circulated among blacks.[68]
To many, Johnson was the long-sought liberator, "the deliverer and
uplifter of their persecuted race."[69] To others, his reign as champion was
the most satisfying event since the end of slavery.[70]

Jack Johnson foreshadowed, and in some ways helped to create, the
"New Negro"—a more militant black who was disillusioned with southern segregation, northern de facto discrimination, and the undelivered
promises of the American creed. The riots and other exhibitions of
restlessness, frustration, dissatisfaction, and pride that followed Johnson's
victories, had, by the end of World War I, come with more frequency
and purpose. Black soldiers returning from the war found unemployment,
broken promises, and discrimination, which they had fought to overcome.
Those blacks who pressed openly and militantly for their rights found
harsh treatment in both the North and the South. Leading black historian John Hope Franklin calls the post–World War I era "the greatest
period of interracial strife the nation had ever witnessed."[71] Writing
about this same period, C. Vann Woodward adds "that the Southern way
was spreading as the American way in race relations," thus confirming
William Walling's earlier prediction.[72] The war caused a reactionary tide
in society and in prizefighting, and the color line in the heavyweight

division grew wider. Few whites wanted to see another black as champion, especially someone like Johnson, who would stand indefinitely as the negative standard by which all black boxers would be measured. With Johnson out of the way and the other current black boxers neutralized, the sport's promoters could once again concentrate on the pursuit of legitimacy and acceptance.

3

The Troubled Twenties
A Time for Heroes

In the aftermath of World War I, expected opportunities for racial equality failed to materialize in the larger society, and, not unexpectedly, the heavyweight division of the boxing world proved equally unpromising for blacks. Yet the war had a remarkable, salutary effect on the sport itself. The great conflict legitimated the martial arts and fused boxing with patriotism. Other social, political, and economic forces, both related and unrelated to the war, would eventually lift prizefighting and its practitioners to unprecedented levels of respectability and profitability.

Martial Spirit

Before the "war to end all wars," men had struggled mightily to clarify the concept of manliness in a rapidly changing society. Owen Wister's *The Virginian* represented one notable outlet for men's virile fantasies, something urbanizing America had virtually precluded. Zane Grey's and Clarence Mulford's westerns, and even Edgar Rice Burroughs's *Tarzan,* ministered to the same psychological need. Yet reading about adventure was not good enough. The tremendous growth of organized sports in the late nineteenth century gave those men who were not satisfied with vicarious adventure the opportunity to act out their aggressions, prove their virility, and emerge victorious. It also allowed spectators to identify closely with, and even share, this experience. The Boy Scouts of America, founded in 1910 by Ernest Thompson Seton, author of popular nature books, served a similar purpose.[1]

Even so, historian Peter Filene indicates, men needed a more thorough challenge to prove their masculinity than books, sports, or scouting could provide. The First World War seemed to be the answer. After all, as one soldier's father put it, "You have gone over to demonstrate the right kind of manhood, for it is that which weighs in a fight and wins it."[2] When Congress declared war on Germany at President Woodrow Wilson's urging, the war became not only a crusade for freedom, democracy, safety, and peace but a proving ground on which American middle-class men could act out and reclaim the manliness that modernizing America denied them. Distinction in battle represented a chance to restore the Victorian ideals of pure, strenuous manhood as a counterpoint to fragile femininity. Of course, manliness meant more than physical courage; it included the intangible element of character. To recapture these qualities would benefit the doughboys and would redound to the credit of all Americans.[3]

Americans won the war but at enormous cost. It was a long (relative to expectations), brutal, and impersonal military conflict, and it disappointed those in search of their manhood. Less a proving ground for individual heroism and courage, it had become a testing arena for technological weaponry. The war generally lacked heroism and heroes, at least in the public mind. Other than Sergeant York and General Pershing, few names stood out; the best-known soldier, ironically, was the so-called Unknown Soldier.[4] American men longed for some kind of reassurance, for reaffirmation of their own self-worth and manhood. Historian Roderick Nash describes the people and their age as the "Nervous Generation," noting that "the spectacle of war and the frustrations of the peace did leave many citizens bewildered and shaken."[5] Adding to fears of bolshevism and worldwide revolution were the transformations wrought by population growth, urbanization, economic change, and black militancy. Americans were caught in a web of ambivalence; they welcomed these developments as steps in the direction of progress, but they also cursed them as evidence of "the passing of frontier conditions, the loss of national vigor, and the eclipse of the individual in a mass society."[6]

Sport benefited greatly from this frame of mind. It became a surrogate frontier, where individuals "confronted tangible obstacles and overcame them with talent and determination."[7] Baseball held on as the national pastime, and collegiate football became a national passion;[8] yet boxing benefited most directly. As Nash explains, "Modern man had largely transcended direct physical struggle, but the need for it persisted in the human psyche."[9] Prizefights became one form of mock struggle "that satisfied the urge to conquer."[10] They allowed for idle dreams about an era in which battles were fought one-on-one and hand-to-hand. After the horrors of mustard gas, bombs, mortars, and machine guns, boxing represented a more simple and noble past, with men in control of their destiny. Indeed, the barbarism of real war made boxing seem dignified, if not dainty.

Theodore Roosevelt, who presided over our nation during its emergence as a world power, was himself a fitness buff and a zealous pugilist. He viewed boxing as patriotic, in the national interest, and important in military training. During preparations for World War I, Roosevelt's beliefs were put into practice as professional boxers led the way to military fitness, higher troop morale, and public confidence in the boys "over there."[11]

Mike Gibbons of the fighting Gibbons brothers was the premier physical fitness specialist of World War I. Films showing him whipping the doughboys into shape did as much for recruiting and morale building as for physical training. Demonstrating how bare hands could beat bayonets, Gibbons passed on the know-how and allegedly developed so much confidence among the recruits that army spokesmen bragged, "Nothing could ever rattle a man after this type of education."[12] Boxing was also the most popular recreational activity among the troops. General John J. "Black Jack" Pershing, supreme commander of the United States Expeditionary Forces, speaking to an inter–Allied Forces boxing champion, noted, "This game of yours is what makes the American Army the greatest in the world."[13] A nation of good boxers surely had to be a nation of fighting soldiers.[14] With such praise from military leaders and the endorsement of returning veterans, the sport gained added prestige and unprecedented public attention in the postwar years.

Journalist H. W. Whicker believed that boxing substituted for war and provided the means for releasing aggression in a tense society.[15] He maintained that the war not only enhanced the popularity of the sport but changed its style. According to Whicker, before World War I life in America had proceeded "in a more leisurely fashion; we had no place to go, we went there slowly—the water in our emotional boilers was lukewarm."[16] This is clearly an overstatement of prewar tranquility, yet there is little doubt that the years immediately following the war were among the most hysteria-ridden in our nation's history. Urban race riots, extreme labor unrest, and unprecedented levels of xenophobia characterized the postwar era—all of which convinced Whicker that change in the social and political climate influenced the public's attitudes toward the type of boxing it desired. He believed that the war had inflamed the public's collective mind, making the blood hot, the pulse race, until the "killer part became the rage."[17] Once content with the scientific and skillful exhibitions of a Gentleman Jim Corbett, in which contestants "ebbed and flowed like the shifting tide," by 1917 boxing fans were demanding "one lethal punch and a man prone on the canvas."[18] Although a difficult issue about which to generalize, Whicker's point seemed to be supported by the changing tastes of baseball fans as well. Initially captivated by brainy, strategic, defensive baseball, fans in the twenties identified most with George Herman "Babe" Ruth, whose frequent and titanic blasts, aided by the new "live" ball, were baseball's answer to the knockout punch.

The Killer Became the Rage

Jess Willard proved to be an extremely disappointing champion. His size and strength could not compensate for his lack of agility, punching power, and, most of all, charisma. His boring title defense in March 1916 against an inept boxer named Frank Moran ended in a "no-decision" finish, although the newspapers gave the win to Willard. No one wanted to promote a bout with him as champion; and, no longer able to make a decent living from the sport, Willard traded on his past deeds and reputation, touring with "The 101 Ranch" Wild West Show. He did not defend his title for another three years.[19]

Under normal circumstances Willard would have been forced to fight or lose his title; but no white challengers could be found, and promoters did not want to risk backing another black champion. Sam Langford, despite his loss to Fred Fulton and the fact that he was nearly blind, still might have been the best black boxer around. Sam McVey, Bill Tate, Joe Jeannette, and the young Harry Wills also stood at the top of their profession; but as blacks they had no chance of fighting for the championship. White America would rather have the crown placed in mothballs than worn by a black man.[20] Then a most unlikely hero emerged: William Harrison (better known as Jack) Dempsey, a former hobo, at home on the rods and in the ring. After a rough start in boxing, which featured barroom challengers, a knockout loss to Fireman Jim Flynn, a humiliating defeat at the hands of black boxer John Lester Johnson (although Dempsey was a decided underdog, losing to a black man was never emotionally easy in the current racial climate), and his refusal to fight Joe Jeannette, Dempsey catapulted himself into the top contending position with defeats of Carl Morris, "Gunboat" Smith, and Fred Fulton. All past their prime, these fighters still represented the cream of the crop among white boxers in America.[21]

Under the expert guidance of promoter George L. "Tex" Rickard, Dempsey prepared to challenge for the heavyweight crown. Although his fighter was virtually unknown to the public, Rickard planned to capitalize on the champion's lackluster ring performances and his reputation for unfriendliness and miserliness. Moreover, according to Randy Roberts, "Rickard was willing to bet his own money that the public would pay a great deal to boo the heavyweight champion who had ignored America's war effort"[22] (though he could not exploit this weakness too much, for Dempsey had also avoided the call to duty). Mainly, the promoter saw an opportunity to tap America's love of the underdog. Taking a page from *Jack and the Beanstalk,* the unknown Dempsey would become "Jack the Giant Killer."[23]

Rickard made Willard a respectable offer to come out of semi-retirement, and after a difficult search for a site, which included Rickard's attempt to bribe Ohio Governor James M. Cox, arrangements were made to hold the title bout in Toledo on July 4, 1919.[24] Although opposition came from ministers and reformers on moral grounds, and from politicians and service groups on patriotic ones, the fight was never seriously threatened. The public viewed boxing's revival as a positive outcome of the war. The sport's ever-growing mass of supporters was firmly convinced that boxing had shed its undesirable features and followers and represented pure and simple entertainment.[25] Boxing had made a giant leap toward respectability.

Under a blazing Toledo sun, Jack Dempsey put aside the obligatory "feeling-out period" and stormed out of his corner to floor his towering opponent five times. Saved by the bell, a battered, swollen, and bloodied Willard withstood two more rounds of brutal punishment before conceding defeat. Dempsey's shocking performance immediately captured the public's attention and imagination. He fulfilled the need that H. W. Whicker earlier had sensed in the American public for demonstrations of all-conquering power and lethalness. Despite his past, Dempsey would go on to become one of America's greatest compensatory sport heroes. According to historian Benjamin Rader, promotion, publicity, and careful selection of opponents made the man far more successful than his ability warranted. Indeed, "Dempsey's reputation as a peerless slugger rested as much on myth as fact."[26] His knockout percentage of .613 was not exceptional, falling far below later champions Rocky Marciano (.877) and Joe Louis (.760);[27] and Dempsey defended his title a mere six times in seven years, compared to twenty-five times in twelve years (four of which were spent in military service) for Louis.[28] Only one opponent, Gene Tunney, was a high-quality boxer, and Dempsey lost to him twice.

Yet no amount of hyperbole or false advertising could have won over the American public so effectively and completely. Rader believes that what made Dempsey a hero was a deep-seated need in the American people to produce and sustain the "dazzling galaxy of sports idols," which placed Dempsey and Ruth at the top. He explains the process: "The athletes as public heroes served a compensatory cultural function. They assisted the public in compensating for the passing of the traditional dream of success, the erosion of Victorian values and feelings of individual powerlessness. As the society became more complicated and systematized and as success had to be won increasingly in bureaucracies, the need for heroes who leaped to fame and fortune outside the rules of the system seemed to grow. No longer were the heroes the lone business tycoon or the statesmen, but the 'stars'—from the movies and sports."[29] The irony, of course, was that the public felt this way toward Dempsey, Ruth, and Red Grange at the very time that the sports themselves— boxing, baseball, and football—were becoming increasingly regulated and business-oriented. While the fans lifted their own spirits on psychic compensation, sports officials, promoters, and the press reaped unprecedented fiscal compensation. The Golden Age of Sport seemed more descriptive of the profits earned than the performances given.

Worthy or not, boxing was a popular attraction. If not loved, "Jack the Giant Killer" or the soon-to-be "Manassa Mauler" nonetheless stimulated interest and excitement. Tex Rickard saw in Dempsey the opportunity to reap unprecedented monetary rewards, but he knew this could not be fully realized without legalization of the sport. If he could make boxing appeal to as broad an audience as possible, he would increase its chances for widespread acceptability. Never a man to let principle stand in the way of profits, Rickard openly courted women for their presence at and support of prizefights. If charity could cover a multitude of boxing sins, then Rickard assumed that women could sweeten the air around the ring. But just as boxing used women for a boost in prestige and fortune, opportunistic females sought returns for themselves and their sex. The relationship of women to boxing in the 1920s reveals a remarkable and important, yet little discussed, moment in the history of women.

Petticoats and Legitimacy

Once forbidden to work outside the home and unable to vote nationally until 1920, women have long suffered as second-class citizens in American society. The attitudes among men that work against women in the larger society were, and often still are, even more pronounced in the realm of sport. The Dutch philosopher Johann Huizinga wrote that play was once identical to ritual, and the witnessing of play or ritual by a female in some primitive societies could result in her death.[30] In American society death has been replaced by the loss of reputation or femininity.

The male response to female invasion of the sacrosanct athletic world is deeply rooted in male insecurity and ambivalent self-identification. Historian Henry May observes that to some American males "it was disquieting in itself to find the weaker sex taking on the roles of athlete, professional, or political agitator."[31] Thus, if sport was, as Peter Filene argues, a male sanctuary for protecting manliness in uncertain times, women could not enter.[32]

Perhaps no sport has been more confined to the realm of men than boxing. An activity alleged to foster healthy psychological and physical development in a man—strength, agility, aggressiveness, independence, and courage—could only be viewed as unhealthy and unnatural for women.[33] Moreover, boxing has always been associated with an unsavory subculture; it is part and parcel of America's underbelly. Uncertain about their own morality, men wanted to keep women out of this environment, because only pure women could keep men away from total profligacy. This male double standard demanded that women be more circumspect than men.[34] Not to be overlooked was the notion of boxing as the "single contest" or individualized war. And if war was a "vestige of male sanctity," then women had to be kept at a distance from its gunless analogue.

The early prizefights were no place for ladies, or, for that matter, gentlemen. Characterized by bloody spectacles in the ring, more real dangers probably existed outside it. Rioting, pickpocketing, gambling, drinking, and fighting, among other ills, frequently accompanied the fight scene.[35] The anti-boxing laws that society demanded existed more to protect the public from corruption and violence than to protect the participants.

Although historical records reveal at least one case of a boxing match between women in the 1880s, the contest was an anomaly and must have been that period's answer to contemporary, voyeuristic mud wrestling.[36] With few exceptions, in the late nineteenth and early twentieth centuries women were not allowed to attend prizefights, or they did so at the risk of their reputation. Rumors circulated freely about society girls attending the spectacles dressed as men, but reportedly the first woman to openly break the barrier was Mrs. Robert Fitzsimmons.[37] In the beginning, even she had to resort to clandestine methods to watch her husband fight. For example, when he fought Tom Sharkey in San Francisco in 1896, social sanction forced Mrs. Fitzsimmons to hide in a lumber room adjoining the arena, from which she could view the contest through a peephole. At the time, men in dinner jackets had begun to attend prizefights, so there was hope that women in dresses might not be far behind.[38]

History was made in 1897 when Robert Fitzsimmons fought Gentle-man Jim Corbett for the heavyweight title. It was the first championship match ever filmed and the first to be staged in a specially built, open-air arena in America.[39] It was also the first for which a woman could be seen in a fighter's corner. The following day, according to Albert Payson Terhune, leading newspapers chronicled and editorialized Mrs. Fitz-simmons's presence at the contest. Ministers preached about it. To many observers her actions came to symbolize American decadence, and they believed it boded ill for the family. These widespread fears of change were not without foundation, for as historian John Higham describes the 1890s, this was an era of intangible master impulses characterized by aggressive and burgeoning nationalism. Higham also points to important and "analogous ferments in other spheres," among them "a boom in sports and recreation and the unsettling condition of women."[40] The same forces that were transforming boxing touched women. Urbanization, industrialization, and increasingly modern transportation fostered social change which in turn led to the "New Woman," whose "salient traits were boldness and radiant vigor."[41]

As boxing moved East again and into the country's urban centers, women took advantage of the significant deterioration of external con-trols over morality and attended prizefights in increasing numbers. World War I played a direct role in their association with the sport. Before legalization, public bouts took place in New York for various war charities under the auspices of women like Anne Morgan, the philanthropic sister of J. Pierpont Morgan. The women who attended these bouts entered in a hitherto solely masculine amusement.[42] And as the war-induced impetus pushed boxing ever closer to the realm of respectability, those promoting the sport encouraged the attendance of women to increase the sport's appeal to the more "refined" elements of society. They saw in women and in genteel men the ultimate goal—the complete legalization of prizefighting.

Mindful of this, when Dempsey fought Willard in Toledo, Tex Rickard made special arrangements for women spectators—a "Jenny Wren" section. To the surprise and perhaps dismay of many, women seemed able to handle the brutality. They did not, as men predicted, run "in search of smelling salts" but rather enjoyed the action.[43] Rickard liked what he saw and often boasted, "Women have given us insurance for the future of boxing . . . here in the Garden [Madison Square]; we do not think much of a fight unless it draws women."[44]

Although women were good for the sport, many observers did not appreciate their attendance at prizefights, even during the Roaring Twenties. Journalist Charles W. Wilcox, in his description of an incident following Tiger Flower's close win over Harry Greb in 1926, seemed intent on showing that some women could not handle their newfound "privilege." According to Wilcox, the decision for Flowers provoked two ladies, fans of Greb, to rush "screaming down an aisle, as each, grabbing a chair" violently assaulted a reporter they had mistaken for a boxing judge. Reportedly, the combined efforts of six police were necessary to subdue the women.[45] In their actions the reporter saw a frenzied, hysterical partisanship, not thought possible in women, which when coupled with their physical violence led him implicitly to indict them for assuming masculine physical qualities.

By attending prizefights women thus found themselves in something of a dilemma. On the one hand, their reaction showed that, contrary to common belief, they differed little from men emotionally, as least as far as boxing was concerned. On the other hand, women suffered from the hardened male notion that they lost something when they took on male prerogatives. This issue of whether women differed from men and, if so, whether they should remain different prompted considerable debate among females in the 1920s. Some interesting opinions emerged from the context of women analyzing themselves as prizefight fans.

The Ring as a Platform

By the 1920s women had reached unprecedented heights in the sporting world, and their involvement in boxing set certain standards for future generations of spectators. To some extent the First World War had helped to liberalize attitudes toward physical activity for women: the fact that they had assumed heavy industrial jobs during the war was not lost on the public.[46] When men answered the call to military duty, opportunities also arose for women in journalism,[47] and the female participation in sport led to coverage of women's events.

While there were no female boxers to write about, women journalists did cover the prizefight scene, for the attendance of women at prizefights had become a subject of great social interest. The fact that the sport had become chic excited the boxing establishment and the press. Boxing matches became unofficial fashion shows, the place where the "glamorous people" could be seen, and female writers were expected to cover such affairs. However, the women who wrote about prizefighting also seized a rare opportunity to make strong social statements for and about women. Some employed boxing to underscore the differences between the sexes; others highlighted the similarities. Each, in her own way, tried to show the nobility and value of women.

Two outstanding articles capture the essence of the debate. An anonymous writer for *Atlantic Monthly* gave away her position in the revealing title "Women Aren't Fans." Through a tongue-in-cheek analysis of fan reaction to a prizefight, she masterfully demonstrated that women were not men's equals but their superiors. When she admitted differences, they only raised the stock of women.[48] To her the "stuff that fans are made of—frenzied, hysterical, pleading, shouting, swearing fans—is not of the same piece as the patterns from which women are cut."[49] Why? Because men insisted upon vicariously reliving their childhood aspirations of athletic glory by closely, if not dangerously, associating with athletes and their exploits. Men were victims or captives, as the "child is father to the fan." While "girls grow up, definite and finally, . . . boys never do, quite. And when you're grown up you can't lose your self-consciousness in a game."[50]

While feeling that women did not belong at prizefights, she insightfully explained their attendance and their willingness to subject themselves to being "strangers in a strange land." First, women went to boxing matches because it was "the thing to do." Socialites wore evening gowns to the fights and hobnobbed with prizefighters, thrilled to be part of this newest fad. Women also went along in an effort to share in their husbands interests. Attending a prizefight was not, to this anonymous writer's mind, a political statement, and she denied that her own attendance defied convention and broke any rules. However, women's active participation in such sports as tennis and golf, where intelligence, not emotions, was the key spoke volumes for their progress, as these sports involved "none of that fighting frenzy which demands victory in a professional and clean struggle, which women do not and cannot understand or share, but which is the breath of life to true sports fans."[51]

At sporting events of the past, it was not uncommon for supporters of the victorious team or individual to toss their hats aimlessly into the air. If recovered, these items often bore no resemblance to the original. The anonymous writer recalled men tossing their hats at a fight, and she wryly concluded that while plenty of men might sacrifice headgear to the greater glory of the moment, it seemed unimaginable that the outcome of a contest would mean more to a woman than a hat.[52] Although the reader could take this opinion literally—that women were more fashion-conscious and probably understood the value of a dollar better than men—I think the author intended to convey something more. Metaphorically, the hat represented the head, the mind, and to lose one's hat was to lose one's senses. In other words, excitability, a trait so negatively associated with women, might more appropriately fit men who toss their hats.

Katharine Fullerton Gerould, who covered the first Jack Dempsey-

Gene Tunney fight in 1926 for *Harper's,* purposely avoided drawing distinctions between men and women. Instead, through a skillful account of a "great" event, she showed that a woman could write and observe in an analytic manner, guided not by sex but by a detached imagination within the context of a unique moment. Clear throughout her writing is an unmistakable assertion that women could deal with the gore, the blood, the violence, and more. However, Mrs. Gerould strained credulity to make her points; her efforts were marred by overcompensation and apology.[53]

Gerould's hyperbolic description of the fight scene, in which "to half close the eyes was enough to imagine that we were all the guests of Julius Caesar," may have been an attempt to make her male counterparts Damon Runyon and Paul Gallico envious. Although, she had heard prizefighting described in the context of "brutal halls of bloodlust" associated with "sordid treacheries of dope and fouls and 'framing,' in furtive sports clubs," she clearly felt that a "cloud of governors, a bevy of millionaires, the Pennsylvania Boxing Commission and the Liberty Bell" would guarantee "that the air would blow clean on the fight."[54] In comparing the fight crowd to a football crowd, Gerould found none of the "rowdiness, drunkenness, bad manners, maudlin emotionalism" associated with the latter. In her mind and by her description boxing had arrived as both a sport and a spectator event. As blows were given and taken, she refused to retreat from her position that what she had witnessed represented a Greek tragedy with the participants being both artists and works of art. What some observers thought of as brutality and barbarism, Gerould depicted as a "sweet science" with "plastic beauty" in which the participants "dance, they spar, they clinch . . . and every instant reveals to the eye some new aspect of art or strength."[55] Unlike the anonymous female writer, who seemed determined not to let boxing get in the way of women's issues, Gerould often took attention away from what a woman could do and transferred it to what a prizefight could be.

Gerould's statement about the strength and calm of women did come through in her contemplated response to the criticism she expected would follow her attendance at a boxing match. She had planned to escape guilt by falsely admitting she had become "quite sick" as a result of the fight. But on second thought, she decided on evasive crudity. In response to a woman friend's question about how she could stomach the blood and gore, Gerould casually explained that they "wash 'em off" between rounds.[56] No greater proof could she offer of women's ability to be like men than to observe a prizefight, in all its aspects, with imagination, skill, calm, reason, and, most of all, callousness.

Neither writer answered the question of whether women should strive for distinctiveness from or similarity to men. Nonetheless, both women clearly revealed that there was much to be learned about the feelings, abilities, and roles of women from a careful analysis of institutions that have tended to exclude them, especially the sporting kind.

From the above accounts there can be no doubt that boxing had arrived, and women played no small part in helping to transform its image to the point that government officials had become some of its most ardent supporters. Indeed, by the time of the first Dempsey-Tunney fight, the legal sanction of prizefighting by state laws and local option was commonplace. State control of prizefighting changed the nature of the game and represented the last hurdle toward respectability; even more, the removal of sanctions opened the door to unimaginable profits. With legalization, boxing became entertainment on a grand scale. It also became big business. And with commercialization came new problems, such as rigged fights and the fleecing of the public, which led honest critics to again question the integrity of the sport.

The Purity Crusade Continued

State sanctioning of prizefighting signaled the changing relationship between modern government and the rights of the individual. On a more general scale it represented the conflict between the forces of tradition and modernity. The timing of the Volstead Act, perhaps the most blatant attempt to control individual morality and preference, and the legalization of boxing provide an instructive contrast and comparison of state action and the clash of opposing social value systems.

Concern over drinking was evident during colonial times, with opposition largely confined to religious groups. Following the Revolutionary War, a spirit of republicanism took hold of the new nation, and the consumption of alcohol, especially when excessive, posed a threat in the minds of many to achieving a virtuous republic. Liquor, like so many other luxuries, was associated with the decadent monarchies of Europe. Yet drinking was acceptable to most Americans, and abolitionists and temperance groups were not very effective.[57]

Incredible social change overtook the country in the first two decades of the nineteenth century. Many people left the East in search of increased personal freedom on the frontier. Jeffersonianism seemed to offer a democratic ideology stressing unfettered individualism rather than the communal ideals of traditional republicanism. Moreover, the arrival of immigrants, the expansion of industry, and the growth of cities created optimism among many for an open society. Yet these changes also produced uncertainty, even anxiety, about the future.[58] Long-established American families feared a loss of status and position; many others, especially staunchly anti-urban, anti-immigrant farmers, associated drinking with the unwashed hordes from southern and eastern Europe who were overrunning America's cities and spreading themselves, their ideas, and their corruptness across the countryside. Prohibition had its roots in status anxiety, rural-urban conflict, bigotry, and, probably least of all, morality; as these forces ebbed and flowed, so did the prohibition and temperance movements.[59]

The Purity Crusade of the late 1880s and 1890s became intensely concerned with the rampant social and political disorder of post–Civil War America.[60] Cutthroat competition in the business world, deplorable and unsafe working conditions, the machine politics of the burgeoning cities, disgustingly overcrowded, disease-ridden slums, and rising crime attracted the attention of reformers, many of whom believed that intemperance stood at the center of most of these problems. These new reformers, who also sought the virtuous republic, stressed a broad-based reform effort. For example, the Women's Christian Temperance Union, under the leadership of Frances Willard, concentrated on temperance activities but also dealt with crime, suffrage for women, and a host of other social and political issues. The abolition of boxing remained an important objective of these reformers.[61]

According to Mark Lender and James Kirby Martin, the authors of *Drinking in America,* by the 1890s temperance had become a national policy issue for a majority of Americans.[62] Fringe groups were joined by mainstream politicians in promoting temperance as a means to reduce poverty, corruption, and disease. The press and even many industrialists, concerned about productivity and work-related accidents, supported the movement. But the major push for prohibition came from farming regions, with their large number of persuasive proponents. Don Kirschner, in *City and Country,* argues that the modern form of this movement to foster rural values in everyday thought, action, and law probably dated from 1895 and the founding of the Anti-Saloon League.[63]

Soon after the formation of the ASL, the prohibition movement was able to broker with both political parties for support in return for votes. With Wayne B. Wheeler of Ohio in charge of the national legislative effort, the league soon overwhelmed powerful "wet" supporters. By 1903 over one-third of the nation's population, about thirty-five million people, lived under some type of antiliquor law; by 1913 the figure had risen to forty-six million, approximately half the populace. Congress took on an increasingly "dry" look, and by 1916 temperance-minded legislators could assure that action would be taken on a prohibition amendment to the Constitution. In Kirschner's opinion, "what intensified this development from a series of localized tremors into a national earthquake was [World War I]." With patriotism on their side and German brewers on the other, the "drys" had little problem with the nation's lawmakers.[64]

The Eighteenth Amendment was quickly passed in both the House and Senate in December 1917, and thirty-six states had ratified it by January 1919, officially voting prohibition into the Constitution. The enabling legislation, formally called the National Prohibition Act, was better known as the Volstead Act, after Representative Andrew Volstead of Minnesota. Volstead and his supporters believed the act would control national morality; opponents of prohibition argued that the measure would increase the crime rate, irreparably damage the economy, and impede the integration of immigrants into American society.[65] Although alcohol consumption rates dropped from 50 to 33 percent during prohibition, the amendment caused as many, if not more, problems than it solved. First, prohibition made available an almost unparalleled opportunity for the illegal and steady earning of large sums of money. Second, it stimulated the growth of real organized crime; it was "a crucible for eliminating the various social and cultural distinctions which had previously distinguished the various ethnic groups of the underworld from one another." Third, problems of enforcement frustrated government officials and supporters of the legislation.[66]

By the mid- to late twenties the reform spirit had lost its edge. Big business seemed less threatening and more beneficial than it had in the 1880s and 1890s; also, immigration quotas limited the influx of foreigners, and the postwar threat of bolshevism had given way to euphoria over the deceptively bullish economy. Kirschner accurately concludes that "the cultural grievances of the countryside were beginning to recede because they were slowly being drained of substance." In the end, the farmers' commitment to the cause of temperance was overpowered by their attraction to the better things in life that the new society had to offer.[67] Moreover, many Americans came to question the role of government in controlling individual morality. By 1929 enforcement difficulties and a changing social context heralded the eventual demise of the Volstead Act. Seen as a source of disorder rather than order, prohibition suffered under the attacks of businessmen who had once supported the measure but who now lashed out against it. With the election of Franklin Delano Roosevelt in 1932, the "wets" had a friend in the White House. In 1933 the Twenty-first Amendment to the Constitution repealed the Eighteenth Amendment.[68]

The long and hotly contested drinking debate had preoccupied much of the nation for years while draining the energy of the combatants.

Although reformers in the city and country often included boxing among their targets, they were rarely able to muster the same unity and strength that had carried them to a temporary victory over alcohol. Prohibition was *the* cause; it was the nationwide symbol, for the Purity Crusade and its rural allies, of everything that was wrong in America.[69] Boxing proved to be a different story.

The pro-boxing movement, bolstered by the war and its aftermath, struggled mightily to erase the negative image of prizefighting and convince opponents of its benefits to both the men who boxed and the larger society. Proponents of legalized pugilism adorned their proposals with provisions that banned Sunday matches, made the use of liquor illegal (before ratification of the Eighteenth Amendment), prohibited gambling at or on the matches, and levied penalties for fraudulent matches.[70] Promises of contributions to the states' coffers through tax revenues also enhanced the sport's appeal. While a few predominantly rural states continued to resist the pressure for legalization, the public appeared ready.[71]

By the second decade of the twentieth century much of the populace, the courts, and the government seemed convinced that prizefighting, in and of itself, was not a social ill. Its role in World War I had left many with the impression that the sport, if conducted under proper conditions, lent itself to the development of skill and courage. Furthermore, the success of prizefighting in the West greatly influenced opinion in the East, and the public's desire to see similar encounters led eastern states to reconsider boxing prohibitions. There remained, however, the problem of permitting something the public wanted while exposing that same public to the unwholesome influences of gamblers, criminals, and other disreputable types who stood on the fringes of the ring.[72] While the temperance movement had adopted the abolitionists' conclusion that only prohibition could solve the liquor problem, boxing's reformers decided that a moderate course of action seemed best suited to solving their problem. State regulation became a middle ground between outright prohibition and the unfettered legalization of prizefighting. The application of Jeffersonian ideals of a libertarian state was diminishing in direct proportion to the increasing complexity of society. Although government officials knew that the regulation of the sport would not end the gambling and rioting often associated with it, regulation might "insure a measure of decorum."[73]

The eastern movement toward state control resumed in New York in 1911, with the enactment of the Frawley Law. Under Chapter 779 of the Laws of 1911, the New York State Athletic Commission came into existence, and boxing or sparring matches, as opposed to prizefights, were placed within the commission's purview.[74] However, little was done to clean up the sport, and there was endless confusion and controversy over the distinctions between illegal prizefighting and legal boxing or sparring. The Frawley Law was repealed in 1917, and in 1920 the State Assembly, at the direction of James J. Walker, Tammany Hall politician and future New York City mayor, modified the controversial existing act such that "the anti-prize fight provisions of section 1710 of the Penal Law shall not apply to any boxing, sparring, or wrestling match or exhibition, conducted, held or given pursuant to the provision of this act, nor to any boxing, sparring, or wrestling match or exhibition in which all the contestants are amateurs."[75] The state made no distinction between prizefighting and boxing; thus, legality or illegality was determined not by the nature of the fight but by its auspices: prizefights that took place outside the commission's control were illegal. Interestingly, the state's disinterest in amateur boxing seemed to indicate that money represented the primary source of evil. As other states followed, the enormous burden of control fell upon newly empowered and expanded athletic commissions which would execute the laws, assure compliance with the legislative mandates, and oversee the sport. Many people who were close to the game held the opinion that as long as these commissions remained vigilant, boxing had nothing to fear from racketeers.[76]

The wily governor of New York, Al Smith, thought differently and resisted signing the new law, which would serve as a model for other states, until he was convinced by letters from a hundred clergymen that respectable elements of society supported it. He knew all too well of the alliance between Tammany Hall and the unsavory men who controlled boxing.[77] James Walker would later be accused of personally accepting over $1,000,000 in "beneficences" from firms doing business with the city. When the Seabury Commission, established in 1930 to investigate corruption in New York City, uncovered widespread graft, the dapper playboy fled the country rather than face a court of law.[78]

With its foundation in partisan, sometimes corrupt politics, state control of prizefighting was not an effective way to clean up the sport and in some cases made boxing more attractive to criminals. Legalization brought with it widespread acceptance and increasing revenues, which added stability to gambling. Nothing could change the nature of those "full blooded patrons" who always had and always would bet heavily on boxing contests.[79] There was something in this sport, according to one observer, that appealed to fans whose lives were devoid of opportunities and motives to exhibit courage, endurance, and the ability to withstand physical punishment; legal or not, they would continue to find a way to bet their goods and feelings on professional gladiators who embodied these elusive characteristics.[80]

In fact, prizefighting became so lucrative that those with a vested interest in it sometimes did anything they could to promote the sport. States and their athletic commissions became rivals for bouts and often refused to cooperate with one another in preventing illegal, unethical, or unsafe activities. Moreover, the media took a bigger and more active role in promoting fights once the sport was legally sanctioned. In doing so, of course, they became a party to gambling and in many instances helped to perpetrate frauds on the public. Even the boxer sometimes put himself above the law. Corrupt promoters and commission officials found ready accomplices in many heavyweight champions whose services meant far more to states and localities in terms of revenue than did scrupulous enforcement of legal codes.

Whatever the specific effects of state control on prizefighting, the legalization of the sport was a significant event in the game's history. It was further evidence of the expanding role of government and its influence over individual lives and actions. Governmental control of prizefighting not only ensured the involvement of politics and law in the realm of sport, it made the regulation of prizefighting part and parcel of the bureaucracy of the modern state. A case involving one of the greatest and most tragic prizefighters of all times, Robert Fitzsimmons, illustrates the point, for he truly belonged to another era. At the individual level he represented the clash between the forces of tradition and modernity.

Man against the State

In 1914 Robert Fitzsimmons, the legendary middleweight, light heavyweight, and heavyweight champion of the world, found himself at age fifty-one waging his toughest battle ever—for the right to fight and to earn a living. His case proved to be a most difficult one for the New York State Athletic Commission, the prosecution, and the courts, because the man had been so successful as a boxer at an age when most fighters had long since hung up their gloves. Fitzsimmons was thirty-five years old when he defeated James Corbett for the heavyweight championship. More than a year later he lost the title to James Jeffries, thirteen years younger and thirty pounds heavier. In a return match, when nearly forty, Fitzsimmons gave Jeffries one of the worst beatings ever witnessed but lost the fight after he broke both hands against "Jeffries' granite jaw and steel-shod skull."[81] Then in 1902, at age forty, he won the light heavyweight championship, which he held until 1905.

Having boxed since his teens, Fitzsimmons epitomized the fighter who knew nothing outside the ring. For all his athletic glory he had not a penny to show; he literally fought to eat, participating in some 370 ring contests in all. Because of the number of fights he had been part of, and on the advice of a physician, NYSAC ruled that Fitzsimmons was "incapacitated by reason of his age and physical condition from competing in a boxing contest."[82] The order of December 30, 1913, read: "The State Athletic Commission after discussing the question of Bob Fitzsimmons appearing, in its various angles, have [sic] decided unanimously it is for the best interests of the boxing game that he should not be permitted to box in this state."[83] The catch-all phrase "best interests of the game" was used and abused often by this and other boxing authorities. When not applied arbitrarily, capriciously, and politically, it implied that the concern of the state was not so much the individual as the preservation of the sport.[84]

Fitzsimmons filed suit in an attempt to have the ruling set aside. His lawyer focused on questions of state credibility, individual liberty, and governmental authority. He argued that the commission's allegations were controverted by the boxer's physical condition and by the testimony of private physicians who had examined Fitzsimmons; that the commission, with no regard for due process, had deprived his client of the right to pursue a lawful calling; and that in denying Fitzsimmons certain civil liberties, specifically those contained in the Fourteenth Amendment to the U.S. Constitution, NYSAC had exceeded its power.[85]

The court was not persuaded by such reasoning. It justified the commission's existence and explained that NYSAC, of necessity, was compelled to limit individual rights. The state, in choosing between prohibiting prizefights and leaving them untouched by law, had adopted a middle course. While this legislation restricted those who wished to pursue prizefighting as a vocation, the court maintained that it did so in the same sense that other provisions of the penal code restricted the exercise of a personal liberty deemed harmful to the community—for example, suicide, or the practice of medicine.[86] Interestingly, the court made no attempt to perpetuate the legal fiction that prizefighting was different than sparring or boxing; neither did it debate Fitzsimmons's professional (versus amateur) status or the legality of what he did for a living.

In turning its attention to the Fourteenth Amendment and how it related to the interests of the state, the court held that "no matter how comprehensive and elastic the provisions of the Fourteenth Amendment of the Federal Constitution may have been held to be, these provisions do not protect these liberties which civilized states regard as properly subject to regulation by its penal law."[87] So changed was the nature of the state toward its citizens, however, that "liberty" now had a double meaning: in a negative sense it meant freedom from restraint; in a positive sense the state could secure liberty by the imposition of restraints. The court held that it was in the latter, positive sense that the state, through its police powers, ensured the freedom of all its citizens by restricting the actions of certain groups of citizens.[88]

In reaching a decision that reflected the opinion and words of the distinguished English jurist Lord Coleridge, in *Regina* v. *Coney* (1882), the court concurred with NYSAC's judgment that allowing Fitzsimmons to fight meant risking serious injury to the man, the sport, and society. It found no evidence that the commission, in reaching its decision, had acted with less than worthy motives or that it had acted arbitrarily or capriciously. As a result, the court had no choice but to uphold the commission's ruling, thus ending the long and once illustrious career of the great Robert Fitzsimmons.[89]

This case provides some insight into the changing relationship between individual liberty and the state in defining the nature of public welfare at the expense of personal freedom. In establishing a precedent for state action, it went beyond sport and into the realm of states' rights and the Constitution.[90] During this period of time individual states were still reaping the benefits of the Reconstruction backlash to federal authority. Yet whether authority rested in federal or state hands, the individual was losing ground in a more regulated, bureaucratic, and complex American society.[91]

Not All That Glitters Is Gold

With the legalization of prizefighting in New York in 1920, dramatic changes in the complexion of the sport soon followed. Confined to the West for more than two decades, boxing now took firm root in the East, and New York City quickly assumed a place as the capital of pugilism.[92] Sportswriters approached prizefighting from a new perspective and newspapers devoted considerably more space to it. In 1922 gate receipts in New York State alone totaled $5,000,000,[93] as observers noted that prizefighting was "an industry controlled by businessmen, run on business principles, financed by banks, and licensed and supervised by state laws and officials just as banking and insurance."[94] Not everyone appreciated these changes, however. To purists, commercialization represented a corrupting influence, leading them to ask, "[When] enormous sums of money are at stake in a single contest, what chance is there for the really sporting elements?"[95]

This move to commercialize boxing brings us back to Tex Rickard, the master of ballyhoo, who acquired his reputation through an incredible "grasp of the art of space grabbing."[96] Like P. T. Barnum, Rickard had the extraordinary ability to sense the public's needs and then fulfill them. He promoted every heavyweight title bout that resulted in a new champion from Jack Johnson to Gene Tunney (with one notable exception—the Jess Willard victory over Jack Johnson in 1915).[97] Early on, heavyweight fights had been advertised largely through the personal challenges of the contestants. When John L. Sullivan "abused every obscene no good in the bar" or when "Bob Fitzsimmons promised to spit in Jim Corbett's eye," they were building up interest in and excitement for a match in the best way they knew how.[98] Rickard turned these challenges into a carefully orchestrated campaign characterized by slick press-agentry. He made boxing promotion an art form. The Georges Carpentier–Jack Dempsey fight in 1921 ranks as the pièce de résistance of his creations; contemporaries called it the "*chef d'oeuvre* of milking the public."[99] What Rickard did was capitalize on the worldwide popularity of postwar prizefighting by arranging a fight between Dempsey, known as the "Manassa Mauler," and French war hero Georges Carpentier.[100]

Rickard knew that the undersized Carpentier stood little chance against the larger and more powerful Dempsey, but a public caught up in the glories of war and its heroes was blinded to the realities of the situation. Many Americans would pay dearly to see Dempsey, who had avoided military service by claiming to be the sole support of his mother and sibling, put in his place by a real patriot; others would support a fellow American right or wrong. Spectators were also divided along class, sex, and ideological lines. In fact, Rickard made the fight appealing to everyone—except, of course, knowledgeable sportswriters, who doubted Carpentier's chances. Their support was essential for the fight to be a financial success, so a Rickard assistant "leaked" information to the press concerning the Frenchman's "evil eye" and a mysterious punch he was perfecting.[101] As the news spread, ticket sales increased dramatically, as did public interest in the contest. In the end, 80,183 fans paid a total of $1,789,238 to see Dempsey, who was never challenged, knock out Carpentier in the fourth round. Millions more listened to a blow-by-blow radio description of the action.[102]

The sport grew immensely and so did Dempsey's popularity. After the Carpentier fight the public welcomed their new hero, a man who had shunned the military, with "open arms and prodigal purses."[103] Even the Shelby (Montana) American Legion agreed he was a "great slacker."[104] Not everyone appreciated Rickard's successful promotion, however. The fight led some observers to conclude that modern professional boxing occupied "an infinitely lower plane than the heroic contests of classic times or of eighteenth-century England."[105] Romanticizing a past that had never really existed, contemporary boxing experts argued that the fighters of old fought mainly for the love of the sport; Dempsey and his fellow pugilists postured "for the clang of the cash register."[106]

While monetary incentives affected the integrity of this manly art, perhaps a more serious development emerged in the debasing influence that the commercial success of boxing exerted on the media. The evidence clearly indicates that Rickard could not have foisted inferior matches upon the public without media collaboration. Critics noted that sportswriters filled their pages with quarrels and boasts of managers and with betting odds for gamblers. A leading journalist, Heywood Broun, condemned these writers for the discreditable practice of printing stories signed by fighters who had neither written nor even seen them.[107]

The corrupting influence of commercialization on both the boxer and the press found perhaps its greatest expression in the Jack Dempsey–Tommy Gibbons fight in Shelby, Montana, on July 4, 1923. The fight that was to have returned this boomtown to its former glory actually hastened its demise. Elaborate preparations for the event and Dempsey's financial demands tore the town apart and drained its resources. Moreover, the fight itself strained the credibility of the sport and its ally, the press.[108]

Dempsey had refused to sign an agreement to fight Gibbons until promoters had deposited $200,000 in the bank and assured him a lien on the box-office receipts. The fight was a "stinker," going fifteen rounds with precious little action, and to no one's surprise Dempsey was victorious. Some people attributed the champion's poor showing to Gibbons's clever yet awkward style; skeptics cited the guarantees to Dempsey as the real reason for his dismal performance.[109] The press, recognizing its vested interest in the continuation of the Dempsey mystique, seemed willing to sacrifice reportorial accuracy and integrity for financial benefit. Critics condemned the *New York American*'s attempt to one-up its competitors by carrying what it called a "telegraphoto" of the final round. The photograph, contrary to what the name implied, had not traveled by telegraph; nor did it show the Dempsey-Gibbons fight. The fraud indicated to one critic that a "dollar diet" made "an unbalanced ration for both journals and pugs."[110]

A potentially more scandalous set of circumstances surrounded the Jack Dempsey–Luis Firpo fight in September 1923. After this wild and controversial brawl against Argentina's "Wild Bull of the Pampas," most of the attention centered on the unbelievable action and Dempsey's dirty tactics. In the very first round Firpo knocked Dempsey through the ropes; with the assistance of photographers, Dempsey reentered the ring and knocked Firpo down seven times. In the second round, Dempsey finished off his charging, flailing opponent with a devastating combination of punches. According to Randy Roberts, "no fight in the history of boxing ever generated as much disgust and praise, controversy and reform."[111] The most significant reform, of course, was the modification of the neutral corner rule. After every knockdown Dempsey stood over his prone opponent, ready to pounce just as soon as Firpo got to his feet. Each time the challenger rose, the unforgiving Dempsey leveled him. Although a rule existed to prevent this type of action, the referee failed to enforce it. (As a result, New York boxing officials took the decision out of the referee's hands and ruled that the timekeeper could not allow a count to begin until the boxer delivering the knockdown blow had gone to the farthest neutral corner. Many think this rule cost Dempsey the championship in his return bout against Gene Tunney in 1927, when referee Dave "Long Count" Barry, in accordance with the rules, refused to proceed with the count against the downed champion until Dempsey had retreated to the farthest neutral corner. Tunney recovered and went on to retain his title.)

While all the attention focused on the activity in the ring, the real Firpo-Dempsey story probably took place behind the scenes. Allegations of wrongdoing took thirty years to surface, and they did so only because of a seemingly unrelated crime investigation on the New York docks, which had long been controlled by labor racketeers. The unions hired criminals to protect and further their interests, and more often than not employers did the same. When William J. McCormack was called to testify, the line of attack was his apparent involvement in a little-known boxing scandal in 1923.

McCormack's life story sounds like a Horatio Alger novel. He rose from wagon boy to trucking magnate, in 1920 helping to found the United States Trucking Company. In 1927 he sold his interest in that company and entered the sand and gravel business, founding the Penn Stevedoring Company three years later; in 1944 he incorporated and became president of the Morania Oil Company. McCormack became such an important figure on the New York docks that he referred to himself as "the little man's Port Authority."[112] When he was called before an investigating committee in 1953 to establish his role in labor racketeering, he denied knowing anything about the theft, loan-sharking, gambling, union corruption, and other evils associated with the docks, but he was not a particularly credible witness. During the five years prior to 1953, McCormack and members of his family had made payments to unknown parties totaling $984,908, none of which could be accounted for by business receipts or invoices; moreover, his dock employees, although members of the International Longshoreman's Association, earned fifty cents per hour less than other dockworkers. The conclusion was that these payments had gone to labor racketeers.[113]

In the course of the investigation some spectacular and damaging information surfaced from the past. While McCormack was vice president of the United States Trucking Company, Alfred E. Smith became the company's board chairman, an appointment that made good business and political sense, since Smith had powerful ties to Tammany Hall. After Smith's election as governor of New York, McCormack was appointed chairman of the licensing committee of the state athletic commission, whose power has already been demonstrated. McCormack may have abused that power, for on January 30, 1924, not long after his appointment, he resigned under mysterious circumstances. Speculation was that Governor Smith had forced him out. Almost thirty years later allegations surfaced that McCormack had extorted $81,500 from Tex Rickard, the notorious boxing promoter, before he would grant a license for the Jack Dempsey–Luis Firpo fight in New York City. In 1953, under oath, McCormack dismissed the charge as an "alcoholic's dream," alluding to the man who had made the accusation.[114]

Enter former magistrate Francis X. McQuade, a frail, seventy-four-year-old with a clarity of mind and voice that belied his weakened physical state, who presented credible, detailed information of the alleged extortion. In addition to his judgeship, McQuade had been treasurer of the National Exhibition Company, which owned the New York (baseball) Giants from 1919 to 1928; he also held considerable stock in the Polo Grounds Athletic Club, which controlled the team's home field. McQuade testified before the investigating committee that Charles A. Stoneham, president of the Giants, had called him into his office one day and told him that Rickard had been forced to hand over $81,500 to McCormack to ensure the Dempsey-Firpo match and now could not come up with the money to pay for using the Polo Grounds. Stoneham ordered McQuade to demand that McCormack turn over the money to him, which he did. A letter from Stoneham to John J. McGraw, manager of the Giants, on August 24, 1925, supports this scenario: "The $81,500 was duly credited upon the books of the Polo Grounds Athletic Club under date of Feb. 1, 1924. This amount had been carried in 'cash,' but I had an idea that it would be better to have it in the bank to make a true record for income tax requirements."[115]

Although McCormack was never formally charged, his alleged extortion was one of many questionable practices that would plague athletic commissions and the boxing profession, constantly placing the sport in jeopardy and opening it up to infiltration by organized crime.

Clearly, money was at the heart of the problem. Owen White, in a scathing article for *American Mercury* in 1926, attacked prizefighting as a public fraud and directed his venom at Jack Dempsey. Sensing that the American public wanted the truth, he asked the questions he thought they would ask if given the opportunity.[116]

White wondered how "this lout had become so excessively rich without even doing any real work"; his answer was simple: "sucker money."[117] He reasoned that neither promoters nor managers nor the press wanted this "paraffine-padded paragon" (an allusion to Dempsey's plastic surgery) to perform in the ring very often "when all of his *real* fights with managers, janitors, and movie directors were so much more interesting."[118] Sparing no words in exposing an industry he believed preyed upon and misled a gullible public, White spoke of a "flabby era" of "high toned boxers"; what passed for glory he considered "idiotic elegance." He pointed an accusatory finger at his fellow journalists: as conspirators with boxing, it was "not their business to protest so long as the price of Scotch remains high and they have to buy shoes for their children." Prizefighting would continue to flourish so long as it could depend on "the vivid imagination and light literary touch of a sports writer to turn a checker game into a battle of Gettysburg."[119]

In the end, as had so many others, White placed the blame on commercialism. He maintained that money often led boxers to follow the line of least resistance: increasingly larger purses for losers made a fixed contest more satisfying than a real battle, especially when the defeated boxer could "make as much money as a prohibition agent." Future generations might, according to White, associate the crooked figures of boxing with "slouch hats, double-breasted suits, and cigars," but their predecessors were "gentlemen in raccoon coats who were twin brothers to the gentlemen in half masks who sell Florida real estate."[120]

The first Jack Dempsey–Gene Tunney fight, which took place in 1926 during Philadelphia's sesquicentennial celebration, represented everything Owen White deplored. Tex Rickard, never reluctant to repeat a successful formula, saw in the match the same ingredients for a good-versus-evil drama that had proven so profitable in the Carpentier-Dempsey fight. Tunney, a former U.S. marine of impeccable character, stood in stark contrast to the brutish Dempsey, who had "passed up the khaki when the shooting started."[121] Grantland Rice called the spectacle the "Golden Fleece," worth little as a competitive sporting contest but much as a profitable enterprise. It drew 120,757 spectators, the largest fight crowd in history, and reaped a record-breaking $1,895,733,[122] thanks in part to the press, which appeased the reading public's appetite for news, gossip, and speculation about the contest. Dempsey, who had not defended his title in more than three years, was out of shape, but Rickard, his aides, and the press succeeded in concealing this fact from the public, which bet on the champion at preposterous odds. The publicity, according to critics, seemed to represent the systematic "exploitation of the volume and intensity of popular interest in the fight."[123] After his defeat, some observers speculated that Dempsey had been poisoned; others alleged that promoters and gamblers had approached Dempsey and Tunney with offers to follow a three-part scenario—one win each in their first two meetings, with the third fight to be decided by the two men. The fact that Dempsey lost twice in a row rules out such a deal.[124]

Sporadic and insightful criticism of prizefighting continued throughout the so-called Golden Era, but the consensus pronouncements of the sporting press, coupled with the demi-god stature of both Dempsey and Tunney, muffled the critics.[125] Ultimately, responsibility for remedying the situation was placed on the people who paid "cheerfully through the nose for distant glimpses of fighters in action" while failing to demand the standards that reportedly kept other sports clean.[126] Critics reasoned that "one suspicious fight which fell flat financially would do more to eliminate fraud than all of the exposés."[127]

The debate still rages over Dempsey's greatness and the real significance of the era in which he fought. How he and his contemporaries measured up against the pugilists of long ago is a matter of conjecture. One fact remains indisputable, however: black men were denied the opportunity to prove their worth or show their greatness, having been excluded from heavyweight championship bouts since 1915. Commercialization and corruption were only minor corrosive agents wearing away the era's golden veneer compared to racism and discrimination, which were potent acids eating at the core. When Dempsey and Tunney retired, the trappings of regal splendor were removed and the press could no longer hide the fact that some of the best boxers had been denied an opportunity and that the whole sport had suffered for it.

4

Chaos Reigns
Exit of the Champions

When Jack Dempsey won the championship from Jess Willard in 1919, the relatively unknown new champion curried public favor by playing on the race question. Dempsey assured white America, often at Tex Rickard's urging, that under no circumstances would he entertain challenges from blacks. The vow was music to the ears of the dominant white majority, which had been outraged by Jack Johnson, the black champion who had cast a shadow over white superiority.[1]

Few observers doubted that exclusionary racial policies provided a short-term boon to boxing, as the neutralization of "black menaces" brought with it legalization and commercialization. While baseball, which took similar steps at the same time, could hide within its team structure the effects of a diluted talent pool, the one-on-one nature of boxing clearly revealed them. In the long run, the severe limitation of interracial fights and the total prohibition against blacks in heavyweight championship contests undermined the stability, and even the credibility, of the manly art. Boxing's eventual decline confirms the theory that the progress of an institution and, by extension, a society is dependent upon the contribution of all its people. Until the boxing world, like the larger society, passed through this xenophobic, intensely racist stage, black fighters, like their societal counterparts, were backed into a corner.

Institutional Racism

Legitimate heavyweight contenders such as Joe Jeannette, Sam McVey, Sam Langford, and Harry Wills were tripped up by the color line. Although a few interracial bouts took place, black fighters more often than not waged war against each other for meager purses and under dreadful conditions. Jeannette fought Langford at least ten times, and Wills and Langford battled so often that no accurate count exists (estimates range from fourteen to twenty-two).[2] Jack Johnson fought on the "Negro circuit" in his prechampion days, but he never risked his crown, his reputation, his money, or his health on any black boxers. Ironically, his caution not only spoke volumes about these fighters' abilities but served as proof to some observers that black prowess and not white prejudice motivated Jack Dempsey and other white boxers to avoid black challengers. This possibility notwithstanding, the failure of boxing or governmental authorities to facilitate and perhaps force acceptance of a black challenger for a period of twenty-two years indicates institutional racism and conspiracy.

Perhaps no one individual more clearly revealed the legacies of Jack Johnson and racist fears than did "Battling" Siki, whose defeat of Georges Carpentier earned him the light heavyweight championship of the world in 1923. Such was the impact of the black Senegalese boxer's victory that one editor called it "a distinct jolt to the foundation of the world as it is today."[3] While Americans had perceived Jack Johnson as a threat to race relations in the United States, they considered Siki a threat on a global scale, in which the "prestige of the white race [was] in danger now as never before in recent history."[4] The editor of the *Springfield Republican,* while admitting that it was "a preposterous absurdity" that "national or racial prestige should be affected by a bout of fisticuffs," found himself unable to ignore the reality of the situation.[5] Americans no longer deluded themselves about isolation, for European, and even African, developments crossed the Atlantic with regularity. Shaken by the guns of battle, traumatized by an uneasy peace, haunted by red scares and red summers, Americans were determined to quell disruptive influences from abroad and within. Immigration quotas, alien roundups, relaxation of due process, and mass deportation evidenced a society searching for answers and finding scapegoats.

The seemingly irrational American response to Siki's victory contrasted sharply with the reaction of the French, who accepted the defeat of their white hero and "unreservedly transferred [their] admiration and affection to the new champion."[6] Not satisfied with fomenting hysteria at home, Americans tried to convince their former allies of their folly in having allowed the fight to take place and then endorsing a black champion. The American press warned France that its rule over African colonies depended on prestige and not force, and victories like

Siki's might make French colonial subjects "lose their attitudes of respect-ful admiration for white men."[7] The message was not only for the benefit of the French; Siki was also a reminder to those Americans who might have forgotten Jack Johnson.

Although Siki fought as a light heavyweight, he nevertheless loomed as a "dark cloud on the horizon," having defeated the fair, handsome, and suave heavyweight champion of Europe. Only two years earlier, Carpentier had fought Jack Dempsey for the heavyweight championship of the world; now, Siki aroused fears that he might advance to the heavyweight class and challenge for the title. The sporting press did little to improve his image in America, with its stories about him frequenting "dazzling cafés accompanied by a pet lion"; to many readers he became a strange combination of savage and international playboy.[8]

The fact that Siki was also a war hero did not allay fears but instead exacerbated them. Not unlike their black brethren in the United States, black Africans from French colonies fought heroically and bravely, believing that service to their country would hasten the day of their equality and independence. Indeed, the French went far beyond the United States in treating their black soldiers as equals; they did not try to hide them from combat, nor did they force them to fight with a foreign army. Black Africans, Algerians, and Moroccans fought under the French flag, and when France occupied Germany, "colored troops" were used to "humiliate the barbarians." Some critical observers argued that the "servants," who had been "flattered and courted by white women, written up and flattered by the press, jollied and flattered by our politicians," no longer believed their "masters" invincible or even superior.[9] Colonel J. L. A. Linard of the American Expeditionary Force Headquar-ters had to warn French army officers to avoid any intimacy with their black counterparts beyond civil politeness, for to do otherwise would diminish whites in the eyes of the French colonials and spoil the Ameri-can blacks.[10]

Siki as war hero and boxing champion posed a symbolic threat. Should he ever wear the heavyweight crown, with all its symbolism, he could do untold harm to Western society. Fast living and an untimely murder removed Siki from the scene in 1925, yet his legacy was con-firmed more than ten years after his death when writers warned the promising black heavyweight Joe Louis to avoid, at all costs, following the errant ways of Siki. They urged Louis to refute, by words or action, "those extreme advocates of white supremacy who assume that the negro belongs inevitably in a lower walk of life."[11]

Voices of Dissent

While prevailing attitudes militated against a black man challeng-
ing for the heavyweight title, the voices of dissent grew louder as the
instability and anxiety stimulated by World War I diminished. A booming
economy and the roar of the twenties signaled a return to "normalcy,"
which was reflected in the world of sport. Baseball commissioner Kenesaw
Mountain Landis had banned the "fixers" of the 1919 World Series and
restored order to the national pastime, while Babe Ruth's stupendous
feats virtually erased the memory of Joe Jackson and the so-called Black
Sox. Red Grange in football and Bobby Jones in golf gave Americans
much of which to be proud. A sense of trust had finally suffused the
sporting world.

A few writers felt the changing climate might be conducive to
removing the racial barrier from the heavyweight championship. The
prime mover in this initiative was Nat Fleischer, founder and editor of
Ring magazine, then and now the leading boxing publication. Fleischer
was certain that he had found the right black man, Harry Wills, to mount
a challenge. The outspoken editor assured his readers that Wills, who
was bright, able, articulate, and humble, was "a credit to the game and
to his race."[12] Wills himself reinforced that image by downplaying the
significance of race in his quest for the title. He publicly dismissed the
"talk about the menace of colored supremacy" as "all bunk," yet he
knew all too well that racial considerations prevented him from fighting
Jack Dempsey. While some boxers had been able to gain entrance to the
elusive champion's training camp by disguising themselves, Wills showed
he had a good sense of humor and a keen understanding of the situation
by noting that "a colored man can't disguise easily."[13] His glib comment
addressed a serious fact of life for blacks—that skin color branded them
in a prejudiced society. Members of other oppressed and scorned groups
could change their names, speak unaccented English, and assimilate
culturally, but no matter how "white" a black man acted, he was still
black.

Fleischer persisted, using *Ring* to generate some public support for
a Wills-Dempsey championship bout. By 1925 Paddy Mullins, Wills's
manager, had moved his fighter into position as a logical contender, and
on the strength of the black challenger's record and public demands, the
New York State Athletic Commission, by a two-to-one vote, ruled that
Dempsey would have to face the black challenger. Under political
pressure, Commissioner George E. Brower reversed his position and
sided with William Muldoon, an alleged racist. James Farley, a Democrat who was not willing to abandon his Harlem constituency, held fast

and filed a minority report. NYSAC's subsequent majority vote for a Dempsey-Tunney fight doomed Wills and quashed the state's chance to host the "fight of the century."[14]

Politics seemed always to stand in the way of boxing, justice, and business. Legalization of the sport had provided a variety of patronage jobs ranging from clerks to commissioners; it also spawned bitter political rivalries. Although NYSAC had to approve a fight, an independent committee was responsible for issuing licenses to the individual fighters. That committee, under the leadership of Colonel John J. Phelan, conducted independent investigations of Gene Tunney and Jack Dempsey. Tunney received his license, but on August 16, 1926, Phelan announced that until Dempsey agreed to fight Wills, his license would be withheld.[15] Politics and personality differences, more than altruism, likely decided the issue. Tex Rickard had many political enemies in New York, and his arrest and prosecution on morals charges in 1921 further damaged his already shady reputation.[16] Following his bout with Firpo, Jack Dempsey did not have an official fight in New York until July 1927, and by then he no longer held the heavyweight title.

The internal squabble of the "Grand Dukes of New York," as the "pompous, back biting" commissioners were called, allowed Philadelphia to step in and host the Dempsey-Tunney bout.[17] Pennsylvania's ready acceptance certainly indicated little interest in racial or legal considerations. The press hailed Governor Gifford Pinchot's decision to allow the fight and boasted that prizefighting in the Keystone State was a straight business and sporting matter, devoid of politics. Later, an Indiana court would rule, in *Dempsey v. Chicago Coliseum Club* (1928), that Dempsey had a legitimate and binding contract to meet Wills before fighting anyone else.[18] But in 1926, with the "best people of Philadelphia and the state of Pennsylvania" behind him, the Manassa Mauler met Tunney and was rewarded royally.[19] The fight said much about the value of the heavyweight championship and the stature of the titleholder.

Why did Dempsey refuse to meet Wills or any other black man? Was he scared or was he a racist? While many people, including Wills, believed that Dempsey avoided Wills out of fear, Randy Roberts calls such speculation "nonsense," because Dempsey "was fully confident that he could defeat any man in the world."[20] However, Roberts himself describes the occasion when Dempsey ran away from a black boxer because he believed the man would destroy him.[21] Credited by Roberts with the intelligence and instinct to never allow himself to be overmatched,[22] Dempsey was not so readily defended by some of his contemporaries. The venerable trainer Bill Shannon, an avowed "Dempsey phobe," when asked about the fighter's ability, answered with a question:

"Who did Dempsey lick outside of some down-and-outer in a café?"[23]
Although few doubted his courage, there was reason to suspect that the
fear of losing his crown and all that went with it played a major role in
Jack Dempsey's choice of opponents, just as it had for the great John L.
Sullivan and even Jack Johnson.

Despite Dempsey's vow to never cross the color line, racism did
not seem to be a prime motive for his actions. Jim Tully, a boxing writer,
believed that Dempsey had "no racial prejudices,"[24] and Roberts con-
cedes that he was at least flexible on the race issue, a conclusion the
evidence seems to support.[25] Before winning the championship, Dempsey
had fought blacks, and afterward he sparred with and fought exhibitions
against them. Even his criticism of Joe Louis, and his role in the second
great "white hope" episode, seem to have been motivated mostly by
pride and monetary gain. Dempsey was an undeniable opportunist who
broke a contract with Wills—a contract he denied ever having signed—to
accept a $500,000 guarantee to fight Tunney in Philadelphia. Although
he lost his crown, the rewards were grand—and they were even grander
for the rematch in 1927. Dempsey, who was accused of many things, was
never accused of being a fool. It may be, as Randy Roberts argues, that
Dempsey never had much say in the selection of his opponents but
merely abided by Rickard's vow to never again promote a heavyweight
championship involving a black man.[26]

Decline and Near Fall

On September 22, 1927, at Chicago's Soldier Field, before 104,943
fans and for a record gate of $2,658,660, Gene Tunney once again
defeated Jack Dempsey. The fiscal success of the event belied the
troubled future of boxing. Protested on the grounds that Dempsey, who
had evaded military service, somehow desecrated the hallowed memorial in which the fight was staged, tainted by an unforgettably long count,
and won by the less than charismatic Tunney, the contest raised the
obvious question, What next?[27] Without Jack Dempsey boxing was in
trouble. Even though Tunney was the heavyweight champion, he fell flat
as a gate attraction, largely due to an uninspired boxing style and a
lackluster personality. He could not hit with the explosiveness that
crowds had come to expect; and while he was admired for his clean
living and military service, his pseudo-intellectualism and aloofness
worked against him.

Tunney retired in 1928, following a financially disastrous victory
over Tom Heeney of New Zealand.[28] According to Grantland Rice, his
retirement "threw the orderly succession to boxing's throne into a cocked

hat."[29] One writer's sarcastic comments captured the gravity of the situation and the depth of despair: "Kings and Presidents come and go in orderly fashion. But when a heavyweight champion quits unbeaten, a form of baffled bewilderment falls upon civilization, and even the leading impresarios can't quite figure how they can turn out a silk purse from a sow's ear."[30] To find a new heavyweight champion would be easy; to find one who could bring in the fans was another matter. The death of flamboyant promoter Tex Rickard in 1929 only compounded the problem. The current crop of heavyweights was an "uninspiring lot," and many fans begged for the return of the legendary Jack Dempsey, which surely would have been "a stale anti-climax."[31] As John Kieran of the *New York Times* so aptly stated, when Dempsey "went over the hill, the ring lost most of its drama."[32] Now the fans would not be satisfied with anything less than "another Dempsey, a hitter, a man who can put them down and keep them down."[33] Dempsey may not haved knocked out all of his opponents, but he did it convincingly when it counted.

The hope that a mere mortal could replace the Manassa Mauler indicated that public perception had not yet caught up with reality. Dempsey, who was, according to Randy Roberts, the perfect metaphor of the twenties and both of its extremes—"the world of tinsel and the world of bone"[34]—had been transformed from a rough, crude, violent man into a sport and cultural hero. The media had turned brutality into combativeness, sullenness into diffidence, and crudeness into plain innocence. Sport historian Ronald Story writes: "For the masses he was an all-conquering hero: for the 'fast crowd,' a star to rival Ruth or Valentino; for the middle class, a respectable champion who placed boxing at last on a moral plane and got invited to the White House."[35] Even Benjamin Rader, who is critical of Dempsey, and Randy Roberts, one of his more sympathetic biographers, agree that "without the prosperity, inward-directed interests, slackening of moral restraints, and advancements in promotional techniques" of the twenties, "the Dempsey mystique would not have developed."[36] The "Nervous Generation" had moved on, and so had its heroes. A new hero would have to be created to fit the requirements of the new age.

Foreign Liberators?

Not realizing the role of changing times and a new social environment in the making of heroes, leading impresarios searched desperately for a man on whose head the crown would fit.[37] However, their desire to make money while satisfying an impatient public's demands for heroes sent boxing to an all-time low. Mediocre boxers, archaic rules, foreign invaders, a rash of "foul fights," and criminal dealings all came to characterize boxing in the early thirties.

As the nation settled into a period of relative calm, the "war began to fade into the background and our pulse returned to normal," quipped one observer. The boxing world took note and tried to capitalize on the decline of chauvinism and xenophobia. If a foreign boxer could rekindle fan interest, which would in turn increase revenues, so be it. Grantland Rice's outcry in 1929 that "the shade of John L. shudders at the threatened invasion of American ring supremacy by pugilism's foreign legion" was little more than one man's opinion.[38] American heavyweight contenders had proven so uninspiring that Max Schmeling, a German, received widespread support as the most promising boxer anywhere. One writer observed that while boxing supremacy might have appeared to some "an undeniable part of the Anglo-Saxon tradition," a foreigner would do in a pinch. Schmeling's boxing talents remained a matter for speculation, as he fought his way through unknown and untried Europeans. However, the American press and boxing promoters supported this dark, rugged German, touting him as another Jack Dempsey; in so doing they seriously misread both Schmeling and the American public.[39]

Schmeling, who looked a lot like Dempsey, proved himself against a less than brilliant group of fighters in the United States, among them Joe Sekyra, Pietro Corri, Johnny Risko, and Paulino Uzcudun, and his sweep "earned" him a shot at the crown. On June 12, 1930, he faced the very unpopular Joseph Paul Zakauskas (or Cukoschay, or Cukosky), an American of Lithuanian ancestry who was better known as Jack Sharkey, the "Boston Gob," or the "Boston Braggart." Sharkey was an unpredictable fighter of some talent—classy, tough, yet inconsistent, often flashing brilliance against the best but doing almost nothing against inferior opponents. In July 1927, in a fight to determine who would meet the heavyweight champion Gene Tunney, Sharkey had given Jack Dempsey a boxing lesson for seven rounds. But his taunting of Dempsey throughout the fight enraged the hungry and desperate former champion, who proceeded to land what appeared to be a devastating blow to Sharkey's groin. As Sharkey clutched himself and appealed to the referee for relief, Dempsey unloaded a vicious left to Sharkey's unprotected jaw. The Boston Braggart, racked with pain, was dragged to a corner of the ring, where efforts to revive him were begun.[40] He eventually recovered from the beating, but his constant complaining about the outcome of the fight and his less than stellar subsequent performances did not endear him to the American public, who labeled him a "sobbing sailor."[41]

A few press reports claimed that when Sharkey met Schmeling he would be favored over the German by the judges and the referee. Such speculation betrayed an ignorance of both the boxing climate and the machinations of promoters.[42] Sharkey floored Schmeling in the fourth round, but as the German lay on the canvas taking the count, his manager, Joe Jacobs, persuaded officials that Sharkey had struck an obvious low blow. The judges awarded a surprised challenger the championship on a disqualification of Sharkey for hitting below the belt. Max Schmeling had won the crown on the seat of his pants, and even his native Germany could not take much pride in the victory.[43]

Low Blows

While there was hope that Schmeling would inject new life into boxing, winning the championship as he had did the sport little good, for this was the first time the heavyweight championship had been won on a foul. The tainted victory threatened boxing's image and officials concluded that measures to prevent recurrences were necessary. In 1930 alone, eleven fights had ended in punches below the belt. Briton Phil Scott, known as "Fainting or Feinting Phil," had made a living out of feigning injury and winning fights. The existing foul rule, which stated that the recipient of the blow won the fight if he was unable to continue, was easily abused, many observers insisting that the fallen had faked injury. Critics once again pointed an accusatory finger at commercialism, which had allegedly diluted manhood, fair play, sportsmanship, and integrity.[44]

Recognizing the threat to the sport, the New York State Athletic Commission devised a solution some observers felt succumbed more to commercialism than did "foul finishes." The new rule, enacted on July 17, 1930, permitted fighters to wear a special protective device to lessen the risk of groin injuries and established that no boxer in New York State would be awarded a bout on the basis of his having been incapacitated by a low blow. Referees were told to ignore the claim of a felled fighter and begin the count; they were also instructed to note any punch that was obviously below the belt and then penalize the offender with the loss of a round. Incredibly, a low blow that ended in a knockout gave the bout to the puncher, but a low blow that did not end the fight gave the round to the victim. The ruling did not sit well with critics, who mused, "Foul lightly, says the rule and suffer for it; foul hard and be champion."[45] To others it represented the removal of the "last least trace of sportsmanship."[46] Some observers, borrowing from a leading advertising slogan of the day, suggested the rule would lead to "56 varieties of slugging low."[47] Despite the fact that Phil Scott was a leading offender, the British Board of Boxing Control, which had not witnessed the degree of fraud and criminality associated with American prizefighting, refused to accept such a change, decrying it as "a surrender of the rules," a "confession of intolerable conditions," and an "outrage on fair play and sportsmanship."[48] Cynical Americans responded, "Why bring in the rules, fair play, and sportsmanship? In this game they went out with the Chicago fire."[49]

The seemingly trivial conflict pointed to major differences in British and American attitudes toward conventions, traditions, and standards of play, which in turn said much about the countries' divergent approaches to problems in the larger society. For example, Jack Hiller, in an exceptional essay on "Language, Law, and Sport," posits the novel idea that the reactions of a given nation to games and sports are a reflection of the way that nation reacts to law. In support of his premise Hiller points to Britain's respect for law and its preoccupation with playing games by the rules. Indeed, the British public schools have inculcated the notion that gentlemen, the country's future leaders, must guide by example. Thus, adherence to unwritten codes of conduct has had a profound basis in British life, including sport, despite the fact that the ideal of fair play often has succumbed to circumstances and conditions. Accordingly, Hiller could find no American equivalent to the British expression, "That's not cricket." Instead, the American emphasis was on winning, as typified by Leo Durocher's famous admonition, "Nice guys finish last." Hiller sees this attitude carried over into American legal practice, which has been characterized by considerable courtroom chicanery.[50] What he fails to see is that tradition, not government, has dictated the terms of competition more in England than it has in America, where reckless, cutthroat competition has accompanied modernization and required rules to compensate for the lack of convention. British historian Dennis Brailsford believes that the concern in England with fair play signals that sport had to achieve a greater ethical sensitivity in order to justify its place in a modern and morally strict society. Boxing, he concludes, had the most lengthy and difficult journey.[51]

It was not at all surprising that boxing in America took on distinct characteristics as a result of "cultural diffusion" and adaptation to new conditions, as described by sociologists David Riesman and Reuel Denney.[52] The surprising thing was that boxing actually changed so little. American football, for example, was derived from English rugby, but early on Americans had trouble with rugby's subtleties and its demand for honesty on the part of the players. While rugby, played honestly by the aristocracy, served as a message to England's lower classes to have faith in their rightful leaders, America was not so class bound, nor did it see the athletic field as the forum for dissemination of gentlemanly notions. The social Darwinian concept of survival of the fittest, coupled with unfettered business competition, spurred American youth to approach games as if they were life-and-death struggles, as training grounds for the ruthless world of business and politics. Gentlemanly behavior and *code duello* gave way to the overwhelming desire to win. The flying wedge, locked-arm blocking, and brutal line play became characteristic of American football, and the addition of helmets and padded uniforms represented a link with technology; lines of scrimmage and downs represented the American drive toward symmetry and order as elements of a modern bureaucratic society.[53] More than anything, the strict, codified rules of American football most clearly reflected the differences between Britain and the United States. America was aggressive, forward-looking, unbound by tradition, and driven by materialism; Britain, while aggressive in establishing colonies and fostering the Industrial Revolution, had a sense of tradition that served to harness and mollify the reckless, succeed-at-all-costs drive to modernity that characterized its runaway offspring.

Uniquely American circumstances required that boxing in this country have as few unregulated elements as possible. Those observers who admitted that critics had raised many valid points nonetheless believed that NYSAC's "low-blow" rule was necessary to improve present conditions.[54] Three years after its adoption, not one bout had been terminated by a punch below the belt. By 1934 practically all state athletic commissions adopted the rule, and many considered it the most constructive measure ever drawn, benefiting the fighters and the public. Still, the British refused to budge, maintaining as late as 1938 that the rule "struck at the very foundation of boxing."[55]

Rise of the Nazis

Rule changes notwithstanding, Max Schmeling still held the heavyweight title. Developments in the German political situation began to alter the significance of Schmeling's victory, but American boxing promoters who were interested in money, and fans who wanted action, concerned themselves only with the narrowly defined limits of the ring. Strong, but largely ignored, signals of German racial attitudes, chauvinistic intentions, and enlistment of sport as a political weapon had already surfaced through a boxing-related incident in 1929.

Of all the humiliating, punitive measures taken against Germany for its role in World War I, none rankled the proud but battered nation more than the French deployment of colored colonial (Algerian) troops in the occupied western zones. This occupation, which the Germans derisively called the "Black Shame," was used by the National Socialists to turn the British and the Americans against the French and also to help undermine the cause of liberal democracy by discrediting the New German Republic, which had allowed the disgraceful occupation.[56] The "Black Shame" came together with sport, to the delight of the Nazi press, in a May 1929 boxing tournament sponsored by some German municipal athletic clubs. The contests, in which Algerian soldiers met Germans, provoked a vicious war of words by the Nazis against the French, the Algerians, and the major opposition party, which the Nazis blamed for allowing such "travesties." Capitalizing upon an earlier rape of a little girl in Mainz, allegedly committed by an Algerian soldier, the Nazi press invoked the purity of white maidenhood and accused the tournament organizers of betraying their own people, dubbing the matches the *Die Schwarze Schmach des Weissen Mannheim* ("The Black Shame of White Mannheim"). Dan Morrow, in an unpublished study, concludes that the Nazis' reaction indicated an intent to confirm, legitimate, and intensify racial prejudices, all of which culminated in the annihilation of millions of non-Aryans.[57] Their treatment of the incident also confirmed a willingness and ability to use sport to bolster and expand Nazi political and racial programs. Sport became a potential weapon in the international arena. As social historian Allen Guttmann argues, this trend has accelerated: "Western sports have increasingly become vehicles for the inculcation of militarism, nationalism, and imperialism."[58]

By the summer of 1931 the Nazis had made significant gains in the *Reichstag* elections, receiving the support of German industrialists. At the same time the German press did an about-face in its treatment of heavyweight champion Max Schmeling. Not long before it had blasted Schmeling for his inglorious victory over Jack Sharkey and his subsequent avoidance of a rematch. But after the champion's July 3, 1931, lackluster victory over William "Young" Stribling, of Georgia, there was unqualified praise from the German press. The fight convinced American promoters that the uninspiring Schmeling had to go, while in Germany the media, sport officials, and political leaders all made speeches paying tribute to the man who had become "a credit to the Fatherland" and "a shining example of German sportsmanship."[59] Some of the faithful believed that Schmeling's victory could be used to "increase foreign confidence in Germany's inexhaustible energies whereof Schmeling is a brilliant example."[60] All of the rhetoric was intended to convince first the Germans and then anyone else listening that a country that could produce such a champion would not be floored by mere economic problems.[61]

Schmeling's achievements, combined with those of newly crowned Wimbledon tennis champion Fraulein Hilda Krahwinkel, gave political issues stern competition for front-page space as Germany basked in the glory of its athletes' accomplishments. The German newspaper *Leipziger Neueste Nachrichten* offered the following message for domestic and foreign consumption: "We do not desire to overrate the results, but they prove to our great satisfaction that the German folk, although not yet free from the Young Plan and the Versailles Treaty, are not in the slightest thinking of dropping out of world affairs."[62] This exaltation of its athletes signified a larger and more ominous national and racial jingoism, however. The seeds of the Hitler youth movement were being sown, and shortly German athletes would march side-by-side with the führer's storm troopers. Schmeling, willing or not, led the way as German athleticism became the metaphor for a fascist perspective of the world.[63]

Before Hitler rose to power, and before the Nazis could capitalize fully on Schmeling's symbolic importance, boxing officials had maneuvered the reluctant champion into a rematch with Jack Sharkey. Despite the assurances two years earlier of NYSAC Chairman James Farley that the commission would protect "the rights of every fighter regardless of whether he is a native of New York, California, or a foreign country," in 1932 boxing officials robbed the German fighter of his crown. Schmeling outboxed Sharkey for fifteen rounds and left little doubt in most people's minds that he had successfully defended his title; even Sharkey awaited the decision with his head down, arms over the ropes, as defeated fighters so often do. When the announcement was made that Sharkey had won, he was reportedly incredulous and, remarkably, at a loss for words.[64]

Although New York boxing officials had deprived Hitler of a great propaganda tool, they had not been motivated by anti-fascism. Few people fully understood Hitler's intentions, and even fewer dreamed he could carry them out. While Schmeling may have been a symbol of athletic chauvinism in Germany, on this side of the Atlantic he was just another fighter who had failed to live up to the expectations of the New York–controlled boxing industry. Promoters saw him as an uncontrollable, uncharismatic champion and a financial liability as well, and they were delighted to be rid of him. They could not have guessed that four years later Schmeling would make a remarkable comeback and be on the verge of regaining the title just as the Nazis made ready to conquer all of Europe.

The Great Crash

Max Schmeling returned to Germany brokenhearted and angry, uncertain about his future in the American-controlled sport. Promoters were seeking their own answers, for Sharkey's past and his unconvincing victory over Schmeling did not make him a popular champion.[65] The heavyweight division continued on its downward spiral, which had an effect on all the other divisions. Professional wrestling, with all its fakery, had surpassed boxing as an attraction because it provided fans with all the ingredients boxing lacked: drama, action, and glamorous heroes and villains, like "Big Jim" Londos, the heavyweight Americans knew best in the early thirties. Boxing pundits suggested radical solutions, like the abolition of the heavyweight division.[66] However, few popular white newspaper reporters had the nerve to suggest that the solution to boxing's woes might be found in the pool of black fighters. James T. Dawson, not well known for his racial egalitarianism, nevertheless tried to put race aside in the best interests of boxing and promoted a black contender.

In mid-1930 Dawson had glowingly praised Larry Johnson, whom he described as "Chicago's spectacular negro light-heavyweight."[67] Johnson, who possessed tremendous power, had successively knocked out, in stunning fashion, Leo Mitchell, Fred Lanhart, and Joe Sekyra; the latter had gone the distance with Max Schmeling in 1929. Dawson was convinced that this talented black fighter was "one of the most dangerous contenders for the light-heavy title."[68] Although such promotional rhetoric verged on heresy, Dawson evaded censure simply because Johnson was not a heavyweight. Yet on June 18, 1930, when Johnson clearly beat Pete Latzo, he was disqualified for fouling, a decision Dawson called part of a conspiracy to remove Johnson from possible heavyweight contention.[69] Whatever the officials' intent, Johnson virtually disappeared from the prizefight scene. Another black contender, George Godfrey of Philadelphia, also found his heavyweight title aspirations squelched by boxing officials. A farcical fight with Primo Carnera, ending in a foul, cost Godfrey "his boxing license, half his purse, and his status as a heavyweight contender,"[70] and he eventually left the sport and became a wrestler.[71] Neither Dawson nor any other white writers pushed the cause of black boxers further. The time was still not right for a black champion, because boxing had still not exhausted all its white options.

Pathetic Primo

The fortunes of boxing continued to sag, and while aficionados were convinced that Jack Sharkey would never be a popular champion, who could replace him? In 1928, a six-foot six-inch, 260-pound Italian circus strongman was plucked from obscurity and thrown into the lion's den of professional prizefighting. Primo Carnera, led by his French manager, Leon See, found instant success against a string of mediocre-to-poor European fighters. His only tested opponent was Young Stribling; their two fights ended in fouls, with Carnera winning the first and Stribling the second.[72]

Although a relatively agile man, Carnera lacked the skills of a boxer. He could not throw or absorb hard punches, but because of his enormous size he was an immediate gate attraction, something American promoters noted with keen interest. After Carnera's arrival in the United States in 1930, Louis Soreci, Billy Duffy, and Walter Friedman skillfully guided his career. Unfortunately for the naïve boxer, and for the fight game, Duffy and Friedman were front men for mobster Owen "Owney" Madden and "Dutch" Schultz, and they engaged the Italian heavyweight in a series of apparent setups and dives.[73] Few of these fake fights could have occurred without the complicity of boxing commissions and the press, yet in the beginning even the press had serious questions about the skills of Carnera and the legitimacy of his fights. In January 1930 Carnera beat Elziar Rioux in forty-seven seconds in the first round. Rioux went to the canvas six times, and the press reported that the 18,000 fans who had paid $59,625 to attend the fight never saw a blow landed.[74] The Illinois Boxing Commission withheld both fighters' purses, and after an investigation it suspended Rioux and fined him $1,000. The commission imposed no penalty on Carnera, a decision that clearly reflected the tendency of boxing officials to protect leading contenders or champions, regardless of guilt, and penalize the victims.[75]

The desperation of boxing promoters and the press was betrayed by their attempts to manufacture a Dempsey-Carnera battle. By staging a remake of the Willard-Dempsey fight of 1919, they hoped to turn back the hands of time, a senseless and futile gesture. Fortunately Dempsey could not be lured back into the ring. The press nevertheless endeavored to make Carnera into a great fighter and a potential hero. It pointed to his victory over Stribling, a leading heavyweight contender, while downplaying the fact that Carnera had won on a foul. James R. Harrison of the *New York Morning Telegraph* speculated in 1930 that if handled "properly and given the necessary polishing, this marvelous equipment might be turned into a devastating force." He went so far as to predict that Carnera could be the "greatest drawing-card since Jack Dempsey."[76] Even John Kieran, a heretofore outspoken critic of Carnera, altered his opinion of the foreign challenger.[77]

Any objective observer would have concluded from the available evidence that poor Primo Carnera could not fight. In April 1930 the California Athletic Commission revoked the licenses of Carnera and his managers for a "suspicious" victory over Leon Chevalier in Oakland. After reviewing transcripts from the California Commission, the New York State Athletic Commission barred Carnera, sometimes referred to as the "Ambling Alp," for life. Other states, anxious for the prestige and financial rewards that a big-money prizefight could bring them, ignored the California and New York bannings. When Carnera met George Godfrey on June 24, 1930, in Philadelphia, the fight ended in a controversial "foul finish" win for the Italian, and as noted Godfrey, not Carnera, was suspended by the Pennsylvania State Athletic Commission.[78]

Despite Carnera's less than impressive record, the Madison Square Garden Corporation had signed the hapless giant to an exclusive contract on January 13, 1930. As part of the agreement he would fight the winner of the Max Schmeling–Young Stribling match for the heavyweight championship. This move represented a desperate power play by the Garden management, who had witnessed a serious decrease in revenues because of the declining popularity of boxing.[79] On April 27, 1931, NYSAC agreed to reinstate Carnera for a bout against Jack Sharkey at Ebbetts Field. When reminded of the contract between the Garden and Carnera, Commission Chairman James A. Farley dismissed it and went on the offensive, declaring on April 30 that the Carnera-Sharkey fight would be for the heavyweight crown.[80] NYSAC exceeded its bounds by stepping directly into the realm of promotion, an injudicious move that underscored the image of athletic commissions as self-serving, self-interested entities, not regulatory agencies. Recognizing the inherent political problems of state control, sportswriter John Kieran made an urgent plea for a national governing body that could and would enforce its edicts without regard for "partisan politics, financial gain, or local prestige."[81] His call would be repeated by others throughout the years.

The Garden took Farley and the commission to federal court and won an injunction to prevent Carnera from meeting Sharkey.[82] It also tried—but failed—to halt Schmeling's fight against Stribling in Cleveland. The German boxer's victory dashed hopes for according championship status to the Sharkey-Carnera bout, which the Garden now saw no point in stopping. The fight took place at Ebbetts Field on October 12, 1931, and Sharkey won it in fifteen rounds, propelling himself into the leading heavyweight contender's position. He later beat Schmeling as a result of what many observers believed was the worst decision in championship boxing history.[83]

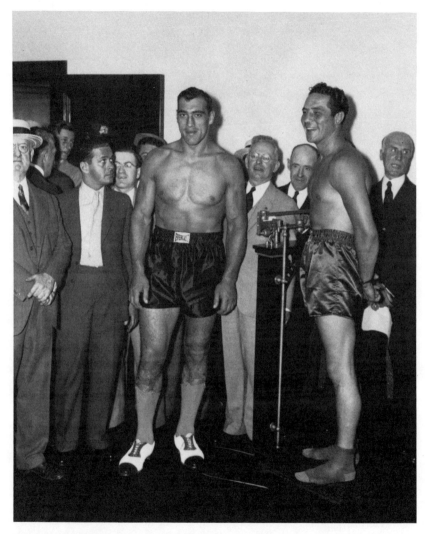

Champion Primo Carnera (left) and challenger Max Baer at the weigh-in before their 1934 fight. The undersized Baer captured the heavyweight title. (UPI/ Bettmann Newsphotos)

Promoters mistakenly thought that as a Jack Dempsey look-alike, Germany's Max Schmeling would capture the imagination and interest of American fans. (Library of Congress)

Carnera nursed his wounds and took on "King" Levinsky and Vittorio Campolo before returning to Europe, where he padded his record, earned money for his backers, and made American fans anxious for his return. Fighting at least two bouts per month, Carnera amassed an incredible number of knockouts, a pattern he continued after his return to the States; in fact, at one point he fought an unbelievable seven times in one month, winning five fights by knockouts.[84] The legitimacy of the fights and the quality of opponents remain in doubt, however, and Carnera had to pass one more test before he could get his long-awaited shot at the title. On February 14, 1933, he met a promising young Boston heavyweight, Ernie Schaaf, at Madison Square Garden. Many observers considered that bout the strangest in prizefight history. Schaaf went to the canvas in the thirteenth round from a punch described as something between a jab and a hook; he rose at the count of nine then sank again to the canvas. The crowd erupted into cries of "fake" and "fraud"; reports had one irate fan cynically, yet innocently, asking, "Why don't you take him to the hospital to make the act look good?"[85] Schaaf remained unconscious for seventy minutes and died three days later. United Press International called it "one of the dullest yet most sensational prize fights in recent fistic history,"[86] a fight that never should have taken place because Schaaf had not been in the best of health.

What had made this fight interesting was an announcement that the winner would meet Jack Sharkey for the heavyweight championship. Considering that Sharkey managed and owned a part of Schaaf, and that NYSAC had been aware of this for some time—even agreeing to Sharkey's presence in Schaaf's corner—led some observers to conclude that Schaaf would lose according to a prearranged plan. Their suspicion found apparent confirmation when Sharkey, one day before the fight, signed to meet Carnera for the championship. W. O. McGeehan, a legendary "gee-whiz" sportswriter for the *Herald Tribune,* declared NYSAC culpable of fraud, "fully warranting the fingers of suspicion" because it had permitted Sharkey "to second a fighter who was supposed to fight him in the event he won." "In permitting that," he argued, "the Boxing Commission was a party to hoodwinking the customers, if the customers could be hoodwinked anymore."[87]

The commission's sins did not end there. Soon after Schaff died, boxing commissioner William Muldoon, while ostensibly acting to prevent such tragedies in the future, suggested that a new weight class be established for oversized competitors, a proposal that had the real effect of boosting Carnera's status. Muldoon, whose experience with the sport went back to the bare-fisted days of the great John L. Sullivan, was astute, well respected, and extremely influential. People listened when a man of his stature concluded: "Carnera is a great athlete from his feet up. He has speed and activity of a middleweight and as far as his punching is concerned, he needs no snap to his blows, a point on which he has been criticized because of his great bulk."[88] Others joined in singing Carnera's praises, including Tommy Loughran, a former light-heavyweight champion who suggested that Carnera be forced to wear larger gloves or be otherwise handicapped—whether that meant tying a hand behind his back or blindfolding him, Loughran did not say.

With all the clamor, an investigation into the Carnera-Schaaf bout was inevitable; and the results were predictable. The investigatory body concluded that Schaaf had been seriously ill prior to the fight and should not have participated. Doctors suggested that he had suffered brain damage in previous fights and that even the slightest blow in his condition could have been fatal. Blame was spread among the handlers, the doctors, the boxing commission, Carnera, and certain criminal elements, but no action was taken.[89] NYSAC belatedly acknowledged the suspect nature of the relationship between Sharkey and Schaff and prohibited boxers from holding financial interest in other boxers.[90] Schaaf's death overshadowed the fact that the commission had really been a party to potential fraud; that it had failed in its duty to protect both the public and the fighters. Unquestionably, its dubious practices had contributed to a man's death.[91]

The supreme irony of the tragedy was that Carnera emerged as a credible fighter with a greatly enhanced public image, which those who stood to gain from his success did not hesitate to exploit. Before the flowers on Ernie Schaaf's grave had time to wither, NYSAC approved and heartily endorsed a Sharkey-Carnera heavyweight championship match, scheduled for June 29, 1933, in New York City. Everything about the fight had a foul smell, including Sharkey's reputation and that of his manager, "Fat John" Buckley. The training camps of both fighters were overrun with mobsters and other toughs, as part of Detroit's notorious Jewish-led Purple Gang hung around like vultures, ready "to muscle in on the concessions and the fight pictures."[92] Sharkey looked awful against his enormous Italian opponent, and after five rounds of negligible action he was knocked out with a "shadow punch" that left Carnera more bewildered than his felled opponent.[93] The normally talkative Sharkey maintained uncharacteristic silence about the fight, and months later one honest observer noted that "Carnera is as underdone as a raw onion." If a worthy opponent were allowed to fight honestly, the new heavyweight champion would be "teed up for a fungo match."[94]

If nothing else Carnera was an active fighter. Within four months of his title victory he faced perpetual challenger Paulino Uzcudun, the "Bounding Basque." Although Carnera was not able to knock out Uzcudun, he did come away with a fifteen-round victory. Four months later he met the tough but vastly undersized (170–75 pounds and five feet, eleven inches tall) Tommy Loughran, who should have been no match for Carnera but nonetheless outboxed the champion for fifteen rounds. Carnera somehow escaped with his title, but the Miami-based fight, which drew a mere 8,624 fans and grossed a disappointing $44,598, finally convinced almost everyone associated with the game or interested in it that Primo Carnera was not the answer to boxing's problems.[95]

The California Clown

The frantic search for a charismatic heavyweight champion had turned into a fool's errand. Promoters had looked abroad, to the South, to ne'er-do-wells, to has-beens. Then, perhaps remembering the call of Horace Greeley, they found what they hoped would be California gold: a handsome, bronzed, sometimes-Jewish boxer named Max (short for Maxmillian Adalbert) Baer. By 1933 boxing experts would generally concede that Baer, sometimes known as the "Livermore Larruper," was the most colorful figure to grace the ring since Jack Dempsey.[96]

Although Baer claimed German-Scottish ancestry, because of his Jewish background and the Star of David he wore on his trunks, the press, boxing promoters, and fans thought of him as a Jew. While there had been a distinguished, if not long, line of Jewish boxers before him, such as Daniel Mendoza, "Battling" Levinsky, Joe Choynski, and Benny Leonard, no Jew had ever won the heavyweight championship. In predominantly Christian, Anglo-Saxon America, that would have been almost as inconceivable as another black champion.

The Jewish experience in boxing was part of a larger process of acculturation. In eastern Europe parents had taught their children that moderation, goal orientation, intellect, and the cherishing of traditional values were legitimate "Jewish" characteristics, but preoccupation with the body, sensuality, rashness, and ruthless force were deemed "un-Jewish," or goyish. Avoidance of violence was an honorable trait among Jews but was often misconstrued as weakness and cowardice by an American society born in bloody revolution, expanded through violence, and defended by force, where the right to bear arms and protect one's property are guaranteed by law.[97] Discriminated against at all levels of society and ridiculed for their appearance, language, and manner, some Jews turned to boxing as a way to earn respect, a sense of belonging, and, for a few, money.

Although prizefighting was an unreliable socioeconomic elevator, successful Jewish boxers did bolster the morale of assimilation-oriented Jews. Men like Benny Leonard were highly visible role models for the boys of the slums. Despite traditional values that shunned physicality, by 1928 there were more prominent Jewish boxers than there were boxers from any other single ethnic or racial group. The succession had gone from Irish to Jewish and would pass on to Italians, to blacks, and to Latins,[98] a pattern that reflected the acculturation strategies of those ethnic groups located on the lowest rungs of the socioeconomic ladder. As each group moved up, it pulled its youth out of prizefighting and pushed them into more promising and meaningful pursuits.[99]

The stereotypes attached to Jewish boxers vividly underscored the prejudices they faced. Maxie Rosenbloom, as the light-heavyweight champion, received press coverage that was as demeaning as any given to blacks. So disrespectful was the media that it called him "Slapsie Maxie" and the "Harlem Harlequin"; indeed, readers who did not know his race wondered if he were black.[100] A *New York Times* article taunted: "He's a blooming bounder and the American equivalent of Fuzzy Wuzzy, Mr. Kipling's famous India rubber idiot on a spree."[101] In response to a NYSAC reprimand for hitting with open gloves, Rosenbloom was said to have asked if he could put zippers in them. When the man who was called boxing's "spasmodic opera bouffe" was dethroned as light heavyweight champion in November 1934, the Associated Press proclaimed that the loss ended the four-year reign of "the clowning champion of the light heavies."[102]

Rosenbloom did not stand alone in ridicule. Harris Krakow, known as "King" (or "Kingfish") Levinsky, was the universal whipping boy of boxing. Battered in the ring by almost every heavyweight of note, he got little respect or privacy out of the ring. When one of his marriages ended abruptly and unceremoniously, a wire release informed the public that "the whirlwind romance of King Levinsky and his fan-dancer bride, Roxanne Carmine, nil Golda Glickman, has found its way to divorce court."[103] Levinsky's forays into the fantasy land of professional wrestling and his well-publicized exchanges with the "Louisiana Kingfish," Huey Long, did little to encourage a reputation as a serious fighter.[104] Of course, one can argue that Rosenbloom and Levinsky *were* clowns and that the press merely covered what it saw—in which case Rosenbloom and Levinsky seemed to have performed societal roles prescribed for and expected of them, and their clowning was, in essence, a survival mechanism. Jewish boxers were faced with perpetuating stereotypes at the same time they were trying to chip away at them, and their mixed message was most powerfully delivered by Max Baer.

Jim Tully, a noted novelist, science writer, and boxing analyst, was not above imposing the clown image on Baer. After watching him prepare for his championship fight against Primo Carnera, Tully concluded that Baer had the "heart and nerve of a tiger" and would be known as "a killer clown."[105] The "killer" label was unfortunate, for Baer actually had killed another fighter, Frankie Campbell, brother of baseball great Dolph Camilli. Campbell's death must have affected Baer deeply, as he lost four of his next six fights. He had also beaten Ernie Schaaf a few months before his fatal encounter with Primo Carnera,[106] and Baer probably believed that he had contributed to that tragedy as well. Thus, "killer" served as a powerful reminder of better-forgotten tragedies, and "clown" perpetuated a stereotype largely reserved for Jews and blacks.

When Max Baer destroyed Primo Carnera on June 14, 1934, to take the heavyweight crown, he was stigmatized as "a wide open, wild and free-swinging novice, possessing hitting strength no doubt, but handicapped because of his wildness and uncontrollable desire to accomplish the downfall of a foe with one fell swoop of his arm."[107] More newsworthy, however, was Baer's life outside the ring as a wisecracking playboy. In reality he possessed a shrewd business sense and during his short reign as champion capitalized on lucrative radio, film, and advertising contracts. He left the ring as so few have, a financially secure man, but he was never a universally accepted boxing hero. His bout with Carnera grossed only $428,000, far below the gate receipts of the halcyon days "when Tex Rickard waved his magic wand."[108] Baer was not a replacement for Dempsey, only temporary "comic" relief from the depressing economic and social climate.

After Baer there was little degrading media treatment of Jewish athletes or the Jewish people, but boxing cannot really be credited with diminishing stereotypical images. While the sport allowed Jews to symbolically demonstrate American values, the rising political and economic power of the Jewish community did far more to reduce expressions of hate, ridicule, and degradation, as did the consciousness-raising impact of Nazi persecution and the Holocaust. Joseph Moncure March's *The Set-Up,* a narrative verse on prizefighting first published in 1928, was due for revision. The story involved a black fighter "who had already been defeated by race prejudice, but didn't know enough to stop fighting,"[109] a has-been whose only value came as a setup for promising young boxers. March had innocently (so he said) included a Jewish manager, a "thoroughly obnoxious and unscrupulous character," the modern version of Shakespeare's Shylock. By the late 1930s many Jews considered the treatment anti-Semitic. Although "no one," according to

March, "had thought *The Set-Up* anti-Semitic when it first appeared," even he had to admit that much had transpired since then.[110] Jews and others sympathetic to their cause embarked on a campaign to wipe out ancient stereotypes. According to March, one need only to have looked about "to see how successful this process of prophylaxis has been."[111]

Commenting on the need for heroes, Ralph McGill, a respected journalist for the *Atlanta Constitution,* looked back on the Golden Era of Sport in a clever and insightful piece called "The New Type Hero." He romanticized about the very serious young men—Babe Ruth, Jack Dempsey, and Bobby Jones—who had ruled America's games in the 1920s. Ruth's sins could be overlooked in view of his almost supernatural hitting feats, and Bobby Jones, who was "hermit like in his devotion to his home,"[112] need not be questioned as to how an amateur athlete could earn so much money. Dempsey "was good for a little publicity and mingling with the boys, [but] he never had any nightlife scandals," McGill contended—obviously ignoring the fact that Dempsey had barely escaped conviction on a morals charge brought by his first wife. To McGill these were aberrations, not true indications of character.[113]

The new hero was different, according to McGill, a lesser breed, "a strange mixture of crackpot and genius": men like baseball sensation Dizzy Dean and boxing champion Max Baer, "the daffier the better." But the supply was soon exhausted and McGill saw no others, not even the great Lou Gehrig, who reflected the growing tendency in baseball to stress a corporate appearance. Teamwork was more valued than individual eccentricities, publicity stunts, and even an occasional scandal. But a hero, by popular definition, has to stand alone, to assure people that human beings are still at the center of all things. With machines replacing people in the work force, with skyscrapers, supposed monuments to our genius, dwarfing us, the arenas for individual achievement were being diminished constantly. McGill willingly discounted Dizzy Dean's and Max Baer's antics because "they were never dull" in a time of economic depression,[114] but he hoped they would be passing phenomenon.

Indeed, Dean gave way in the 1940s to the noncontroversial efficiency of Stan Musial and Marty Marion. And Baer, following in the footsteps of so many of his predecessors, spent a year engaging in nontitle exhibition matches—none of which took place in New York, to the consternation of the boxing fraternity. He was neither a proper tonic for the prizefight industry nor an appropriate hero, and when he no longer drew large crowds to his fights or brought credit to the game, he quickly lost favor with boxing promoters and the press.

From Relief to Riches

Baer's replacement was James J. Braddock, appropriately named the "Cinderella Man," a clean-living journeyman boxer with a large family on public assistance. What better image to promote than someone who had escaped from the depths of the depression to rise to the top of his profession and, symbolically, to the top of the world? Yet Braddock presented a problem. While he identified with his supporters, he did not stand above them to point the way. His character and clean life-style may have made him worthy of the heavyweight title, but as a boxer he was nondescript.[115]

The possessor of questionable boxing skills, as evidenced by a mediocre record, Braddock nevertheless won a fifteen-round decision over Max Baer on June 13, 1935. Many people suspected a fix. The "Cinderella Man" did nothing to discredit the championship out of the ring; but he also did nothing in the ring to boost the sport's popularity. In the two years following his title bout he fought in only one three-round exhibition, and observers despaired of this champion who "knew better than to risk his title and who cannot beat more than three or four men in the game."[116] Braddock was merely a caretaker champion who would serve until his chosen successor had been properly groomed and the public effectively prepared.

5

Pugilistic Renaissance
Depression, War, and Joe Louis

During the pugilistic depression of the early 1930s, Madison Square Garden, the "Mecca of Boxing," lost money and prestige. Despite numerous management changes, attendance figures continued to lag far behind those of the arena's best years. The Garden's relationship with the Hearst press was a contributing factor to this decline. In 1933 the press reported that Mrs. William Randolph Hearst had sought a larger share of boxing proceeds for her Milk Fund for Babies, but the Garden refused. Contemporaries have alleged that Damon Runyon, Bill Farnsworth, and Ed Frayne, all Hearst reporters, were not happy with their earnings and "shook down" promoters in exchange for publicity.[1] Whatever their motivation, the three reporters enlisted Mike Jacobs, the former ticket scalper for promoter Tex Rickard, to aid the Milk Fund in return for their help in breaking the Garden's virtual stranglehold on boxing. To this end Jacobs promoted a fight at the Bronx Coliseum. The undertaking proved so successful that he subsequently leased the New York Hippodrome and, together with the Hearst reporters, incorporated the Twentieth Century Sporting Club in 1933.[2] Jacobs, on the verge of establishing control over boxing, only needed the right fighter. Being a religious man, he prayed; his prayers were soon answered.

In 1934 a powerful, good-looking, speech-impaired, light-skinned black boxer appeared on the scene. Everything about Joe Louis Barrow spelled success for some lucky boxing promoter, even his handicap, which ensured relative silence at a time when only a humble, quiet, unassuming black would do. Taught how to behave properly and how to fight, he was packaged as the perfect tonic for the ills of prizefighting and, in part, the larger society. As Joe Louis, a name he chose for himself, this son of an Alabama sharecropper would become the greatest living testament to William Hazlitt's adage, "Men do not become what by nature they are meant to be, but what society makes them."[3]

Louis's emergence on the prizefight scene coincided not only with the decline of the sport and a lack of heroes but, more important, with the social and economic deprivation wrought by the Great Depression. As domestic problems were compounded by external threats, Joe Louis stood as a fighting symbol, helping to knock out menaces from within and without while reviving a nearly moribund sport. If minimum qualifications for leadership are inversely dependent on the need for leadership, then Louis was a leader of the highest order.[4]

Color Him Hero

Eventually, to facilitate Louis's rise to the top of his profession and to hero status, promoters, handlers, and the press worked in harmony to develop the proper image for the young fighter. Even his "Brown Bomber" nickname reflected a concern for projecting his power, not his race; after all, no one called blacks "browns." Above all, Louis could not remind the public of another infamous black boxer, Jack Johnson. Appropriately, Louis accepted the prescribed role of a God-fearing, Bible-reading, mother-loving, clean-living, humble young man. His somewhat carefree and childlike habits, such as his voracious gum chewing and ice cream eating, revealed the wholesomeness of his "vices" and his naïveté.[5]

Despite some attempts to "whitewash" Joe Louis, to make him a "white man regardless of color," no one could forget that he was black.[6] The supportive white press and the idolizing black press made sure their readers remembered that fact during the fourteen years, between 1935 and 1949, that he stood at the center of boxing and racial issues. While boxing pundits valued him for his service to the sport, he received as much, if not more, attention for his influence on racial matters, and many people deemed him "a credit to his race."

Joe Louis Barrow's simple and obscure beginnings in no way suggested his future prominence. Born on May 13, 1914, to Lily Reese and Munrow Barrow, Louis grew up in a broken family, along with seven brothers and sisters.[7] His mother tried to escape the oppression of rural southern life by migrating to Detroit in 1926. Dropping out of school by the sixth grade, Louis ran the streets and in 1932 discovered boxing through a friend. He fell in love with the sport, worked hard at it, and before long reached the finals of the National Amateur Athletic Union boxing tournament. By age twenty he had turned professional.[8]

Under the tutelage of Jack "Chappie" Blackburn, Louis's trainer and father figure–confidant, and black managers John Roxborough and Julian Black, Louis escaped the ghetto, his job at Ford Motor Company, and obscurity. Long before Mike Jacobs or the press had reached him, the sagacious Roxborough had convinced Louis that black boxers needed friends as well as managers and that only other blacks could fill both roles. Because he understood the nature of racism in America, Roxborough also laid down a harsh set of strict guidelines to enable Louis to succeed:

1. He was never to have his picture taken alongside a white woman.
2. He was never to go into a nightclub alone.
3. There would be no soft fights.
4. There would be no fixed fights.
5. He was never to gloat over a fallen opponent.
6. He was to keep a "dead pan" in front of the cameras.
7. He was to live and fight clean.[9]

Armed with this moral guidance and the expert training provided by Blackburn, Louis set one of the most dazzling records in fight history. Between July 1934 and June 1935 he fought in twenty-two bouts, winning all of them, eighteen by knockout. In March 1935 Mike Jacobs approached Roxborough about promoting Louis's fights, an attractive offer since Louis had not met any big-name boxers and had battled before relatively small crowds in cities not known for boxing. Roxborough and Black had experienced much difficulty in promoting their fighter on a large scale; now Jacobs would change all that.[10]

The New York promoter quickly went to work. Promising to donate part of the proceeds from Louis's fight on March 28, 1935, against Natie Brown to Mrs. Hearst's beloved Milk Fund, Jacobs reaped enormous publicity for Louis from the Hearst press. He went so far as to hire a special train to bring sportswriters to the fight, which Louis won in a ten-round decision. Then he made plans for a heroic encounter with Primo Carnera.[11] Joe Louis was on his way. Unfortunately, he had already lost something, and so had black America. Although officially his managers, Roxborough and Black were now beholden to a white man, Mike Jacobs, who would determine who, when, and where Louis fought. With all his ability, with all the proper advice, it would still take expert promotion and acceptance by white society for Louis to succeed as a bona fide hero. The depressed national economy, the nearly bankrupt boxing industry, and the stirrings of fascism certainly signaled the need for a new American hero, but not necessarily a black one. The proper racial climate was critical to Joe Louis's bid for hero-status.

Timing Is Everything

Much has been said and written about Joe Louis as a race hero; biographers Anthony Edmonds, Alexander Young, Jr., and Gerald Astor give this aspect of Louis's career ample treatment.[12] Yet each writer analyzes the race issue from a predominantly northern perspective, an approach that has led to a significant gap in our understanding of Louis's influence. Only by knowing how the South also felt about him can we really assess his national impact. For all his achievements as a boxer, Louis's greatest contribution might have been the reactions he evoked and what they revealed about the society in which he lived. His rise to boxing prominence occurred during a period of relative racial calm in America. The xenophobia and paranoia following World War I had long subsided, and the twin specters of economic hardship and international turmoil diverted our attention.

With specific regard to the South, Louis's career began after the intense racial tension provoked by the Scottsboro tragedy and ended before the U.S. Supreme Court's landmark decision in *Brown* v. *Board of Education of Topeka* (*Kansas*) in 1954, which, according to C. Vann Woodward, helped to make the South "more deeply alienated than it has been at any time since 1877."[13] If there was one constant determinant of southern thought it was that "the South was and shall remain a white man's country."[14] In practice, this necessitated both white control of the institutions of society and the separation of the races.[15] Segregation was thus carried out at every level and in every sphere of society, including sport. Viewing confrontations between whites and blacks as disruptive and dangerous, southern officials strictly prohibited interracial boxing; they had no desire to see white assumptions about racial superiority tested in the ring. Under such circumstances Joe Louis's acceptance in the South appears remarkable, but in fact it was not all that it seemed. His reception below the Mason-Dixon Line indicated the interdependence of North and South and the influence of economics on racial issues.

Neither the northern nor the southern press was particularly enlightened or evenhanded in its treatment of blacks, including athletes. The northern press freely employed demeaning language, including the frequent use of "darky," and the black athlete's stereotypical image ran the gamut from "animal" to carefree "sambo."[16] The differences in treatment were, for the most part, a matter of degree and not kind. Although there were fewer blacks in the North, their power to influence what was said about them exceeded that of their more numerous but also more oppressed southern brethren. In the southern press "nigger" was freely used as both a noun and an adjective,[17] and the treatment of black athletes was equally derisive. Jesse Owens, a great athlete and American symbol, was laughingly referred to by a Birmingham sports editor as "Fast Black," a "dark horse" who would have been "a wonderful man to run errands if the telephone, telegraph, and radio had not been invented."[18] The Jim Crow tyranny of the South allowed such statements to be made with impunity.

One of the more remarkable and fundamental differences between the North and the South in the stereotyping of blacks was the northern media's willingness to create and play upon racial and ethnic confrontations in boxing as a way of attracting and exciting readers; the southern press purposefully avoided such coverage. After Jack Johnson's "reign of terror," Dixie did not waver in its belief that "the enthusiasm manifested over sports grows out of a love of contest for supremacy, hence, the whites and blacks of the South shall not engage in any contest which might upset the theory of social superiority or imply social equality."[19] This view was affirmed by the policy of the southern press to ignore "race contenders" for the heavyweight crown.

Joe Louis proved to be the exception. His character and origins, a less volatile racial climate, a desire for heroes and a love of sport, and the southern press's visions of increased readership all made him acceptable—at least from a distance. Louis's name appeared as early as August 1934 in a southern paper, although he was simply listed as a "negro" boxer.[20] Not until later that year, when he was scheduled to appear on the same fight card as Max Baer, did Louis receive recognition as a "race contender." The *Charlotte Observer* ran an Associated Press report that Baer would get a good look at the youngster he might be forced to fight for the heavyweight championship—"Joe Louis, sensational negro clouter from Detroit."[21]

While such reports appeared to indicate a change in attitude toward a black heavyweight challenger, remember that despite southern resentment of northern control of the media, professional sport, and the economy, there existed a symbiotic relationship between the two regions, as evidenced by their sharing of news service releases. Yet the promotion of Joe Louis posed a peculiar problem for the white southern press. It recognized his potential for reviving prizefighting, which could translate into newspaper sales; but the southern press also had to consider the sensibilities of its white readership and avoid arousing black readers. Thus, in part the use of national press releases offered a relatively safe and detached mode of delivery, without the risk of personal identification with the news being reported; moreover, these releases were more economical than sending a reporter to cover such events. At the time, almost all news coverage of an inflammatory nature had northern origins.

Louis and Carnera: Abyssinia and Italy

Although more than likely apolitical, Primo Carnera was closely associated in the press with a belligerent Italy and its dictatorial leader, Benito Mussolini. According to sport scholar John Hoberman, Mussolini was the "great political athlete of the fascist period." He was called a hero of sport and favored boxing because punching was "an exquisitely fascist means of self-expression." Observers of Mussolini noted that while ruling classes are normally associated with intellectuals, in Italy physical fitness and commanding presence were the primary requisites. In July 1930 American immigration officials nearly deported Carnera, and Il Duce became personally involved in the incident.[22] Mussolini had no qualms about politicizing boxing and appointed his brother to head the Italian Boxing Commission. One writer found the appointment disturbing; he concluded that Mussolini, a man known for his meddling, "has taken on added powers and is now running boxing in this country [America]."[23]

By 1934 Mussolini was on the verge of showing Italy's military might by attacking the small black nation of Abyssinia (now Ethiopia). Boxing promoter Mike Jacobs seized the opportunity afforded by world events to schedule a fight between Joe Louis and Carnera, Mussolini's "emissary" in America. The international situation made the bout far more attractive than was warranted by the relative merits of the men involved. Blacks wanted to see Louis destroy the representative of an aggressive Italy, whose conquering of Abyssinia would, in the words of John Hope Franklin, "symbolize the final victory of the white man over the Negro."[24]

Primo Carnera, who had gleefully entertained an imprisoned Al Capone, who had earned thousands of dollars for his handlers, now had no one to turn to for support. In April 1934 wild rumors suggested that he was for sale; his "gangland" backers wanted to unload him, but no takers could be found.[25] The large life insurance policy written for him before his fight with Max Baer seemed to indicate that his handlers either expected or wanted him to be killed, which he almost was. Stories circulated that Carnera was worth more dead than alive.[26] Louis, by contrast, was being launched as a prime heavyweight contender and "the symbol of America in the chaotic international situation."[27]

The northern press played freely upon the racial and political elements of the fight. For example, Jack Cuddy of United Press Inter-

national asserted that the contest commanded more attention and produced more betting than any interracial fight since Sharkey took on
Wills in 1926. Clearly, Cuddy hoped to stir race feelings with his descriptions of Louis as the "Black Menace," the "Dark Destroyer," the "Golden
Puma," and the "Brown Bomber."[28] Cartoonists in the North effectively
associated the smaller, darker Louis with Abyssinia and the hulking
Carnera with Italy.[29] Edward J. Neil of the Associated Press called it
"war in the prize ring instead of Africa."[30] Not surprisingly, the southern
press all but ignored the fight's racial and international implications. It
chose not to carry reports of loud and widespread complaints about the
Italian threat to Haile Selassie's throne and failed to link the small black
nation to the American black community or mention the status of
Abyssinia's emperor as a race hero.[31]

Under extremely tight security, in expectation of possible racial
unrest, the two fighters met at Yankee Stadium on June 25, 1935. Louis
punished his oversized but spent opponent for six rounds before ending
the carnage with a knockout.[32] As one writer put it, "What had started
out as an Alp looked about the altitude of a chicken croquet by the time
Joe got through with him."[33] After the bout, black youths reportedly ran
through the streets of Harlem shouting, "Let's get Mussolini next."
Anthony Edmonds concludes, "Joe Louis had done symbolically what
black Americans vehemently hoped Haile Selassie would do in fact."[34]
In a simple way Louis also represented black pride and a nascent
Pan-Africanism.

Lifeblood or Threat

The South continued to avoid inflammatory media coverage and
to downplay Louis's potential as anything but a good boxer—with one
notable exception, William McG. Keefe of the *New Orleans Times-
Picayune,* who condemned the Brown Bomber's victory over Carnera as
bad for boxing. Fearful of a return to the anxious moments of the Jack
Johnson era, he warned Louis about following in his black predecessor's
footsteps. For the most part, however, southern reporters assumed a
stance that could be characterized as moderate to liberal by regional
standards. They pointed to Louis's "shufflin'" or exposed what they
perceived to be his lack of intelligence,[35] but they also made prizefight
buffs aware that Louis, despite his Detroit domicile, was one of their
own—an Alabamian, an "ex-pickaninny," a "southern colored boy."[36]
They said he was a "good nigger," one who knew his place. To them Joe
Louis was a ferocious boxer in the ring and a quiet, humble man outside
it, someone "determined to live so that he will be a credit to his people

and undo what others have done before him in the ring." Northern observers agreed that blacks would benefit from Louis to the extent that he fulfilled white expectations.[37]

Once the southern press was convinced that Louis was no Jack Johnson and did not threaten the region's racial order, it joined the northern media in hailing him as the savior of a dying sport, a credit to his race, a true native son, and, reluctantly, the embodiment of the long-sought American hero. The South had difficulty ignoring the Hearst reporters and other writers whose "paeans of praise swept louder and louder until Louis' fights on the radio commanded a higher rating than the president, Franklin D. Roosevelt."[38] Boxing promoters and officials also could not ignore fans who clamored for a match between the new sensation and Max Baer, who had lost his heavyweight crown to James J. Braddock only twelve days before Louis defeated Carnera.

The two fighters met in September 1935. Advance ticket sales convinced the press and boxing pundits that glamor and excitement had returned to the ring and that attendance figures would reflect an improving economic climate.[39] The Buick Motor Company bought radio rights to the bout for the remarkably high sum of $27,500. The fight itself drew over 88,000 fans, as cash registers clanged to the tune of $1,000,832, the largest gate since the second Dempsey-Tunney extravaganza in 1927.[40] Unfortunately, the fight fell short of expectations, ending in the fourth round with Baer on one knee, able to get up but not wanting to, a sad finish that forever marked him as a quitter and a coward.[41] Louis appeared invincible; the northern boxing establishment and the press were overjoyed.

This Louis victory provoked exuberant and sometimes belligerent reactions among blacks. The fight had been broadcast over combined NBC, WEAF, and WIZ radio networks to some ninety stations, in addition to at least forty stations affiliated with the Canadian Broadcasting Corporation, which made the impact immediate and widespread. Blacks from Chicago to Detroit to New York heard the broadcast in taxicabs, saloons, restaurants, poolrooms, and private homes, then surged onto the streets in jubilant and sometimes destructive celebration.[42] These displays met with some criticism in the North and harsh condemnation from a white southern majority that considered such actions absolutely intolerable. Such outbreaks threatened Louis's status below the Mason-Dixon Line, which in turn worried the northern press, for without southern support boxing's complete revival was unlikely.

Northern promoters and the press concerned themselves with the health of the prizefight industry, but the South worried over perceived threats to the social order. To forestall outbreaks of violence, even public demonstrations, the southern press issued warnings about the "danger of overestimating the significance of a socker." According to the *Raleigh News and Observer,* "wise Negroes—as wise white men— will not put their pride in a prize fighter, but will watch the race's advance in the more important, less dramatic, things by which in the long view any race or any people must be judged."[43] Of course, the purpose of such warnings was to keep southern blacks in line, but they also revealed the progression in southern racial thought: more enlightened or sophisticated southerners now acknowledged that within the ranks of black people were those who could be of credit, if only to their own race. Highly educated blacks like Robert R. Moton, the president of Tuskegee Institute, and C. C. Spaulding, the president of the North Carolina Mutual Life Insurance Company, were singled out as appropriate role models.[44] "Progressive" thinkers had finally accepted and promoted education as a way to uplift the black race while controlling it, just as the North had "Americanized" and acculturated immigrant groups through education. The South proved very slow in accepting sports figures as appropriate models, however, and southerners did not fully realize the social and economic value of successful athletes until the 1970s.

A few opportunists in the North, fronted by Jack Dempsey, tried— but failed—to seize upon the South's fear by repeating the search for boxing's great "white hope." While hysteria and rage had marked the mad drive to dethrone Jack Johnson, the search for Joe Louis's conqueror had the look of a business venture. Indeed, Dempsey's role in and presence at a series of well-organized elimination tournaments probably stimulated more interest than did the fighters. For the most part, both the northern and southern media responded very cynically and unenthusiastically to these attempts to derail Louis before he had even won the heavyweight championship. The North opposed the movement because Louis was good for the sport, and it wanted him to reach the top and fend off challengers from that position. The desire to avoid unnecessarily disturbing racial issues largely shaped southern opinion on the matter. Moreover, regardless of location or ideology, many observers resented the movement because it implied that the likeable James J. Braddock was not a capable champion.[45]

Truly, an air of silliness surrounded the traveling spectacle. John Lardner recalled, some years after the "search," that Dempsey had once invited the press to meet his stable of challengers. When one of the writers noticed some young black men among the fighters, the following conversation transpired: " 'I thought this was a white-hope tournament, Jack,' . . . 'That's right,' said Mr. Dempsey proudly. 'Fine boys, too. Look at them wolf that beefsteak.' 'But I see a couple of colored kids in the crowd,' said the questioner. 'You certainly do,' said Mr. Dempsey, rubbing his hands. 'They're the best fighters I got.' "[46] Lardner jokingly called it "White Hopes on Whole Wheat," not realizing that Dempsey had actually come up with the black "white hope," a creation whose value was not recognized at the time because Louis was well-respected and popular and so near white.[47] Yet the black "white hope" would eventually become a serious and effective weapon in the war against undesirable black champions. For now, however, even the South found Dempsey's efforts laughable. The *Charlotte Observer* ran a photograph of an emaciated, sad-looking boxer with the caption, "the next 'white hope'."[48] If the press did endorse these tournaments, it usually did so for economic reasons.

As Dempsey searched, Louis conquered. He won his next two fights in impressive fashion, including a fourth-round knockout of the iron-chinned Paulino Uzcudun,[49] which removed any doubts about the Brown Bomber's punching power. This awesome display and lack of worthy challengers led many sportswriters to concede the heavyweight championship to Louis. Yet one more obstacle remained: former German titleholder Max Schmeling. Despite the expectation of another easy Louis victory, Schmeling's link to Hitler stimulated unusual interest in the fight. Northern press coverage and the popular reaction to it provide additional insight into the differences in thought and action on race, ethnicity, and international matters between the North and the South.

Return of the Germans

After his loss to Sharkey, a depressed and disillusioned Schmeling suffered two humiliating defeats at the hands of American fighters. The one administered by Max Baer in 1933 was particularly distasteful. Although Baer had vacillated about his religious affiliation, in the face of nazism he boasted of his Jewish background. The opportunity for a Jew to embarrass the Nazis again would not come easily. Although his fight with Schmeling in 1933 had seemingly little ethnic, religious, or international meaning, within a year Hitler openly campaigned against Jews: Dachau was set up in March 1934 and anti-Semitic boycotts began in April; by 1935 clear evidence indicated that Hitler discriminated against Jewish athletes by denying them places on the German Olympic team.[50] Schmeling remained Germany's only boxing hope, and Hitler, realizing the symbolic value of the heavyweight crown, thus stood behind his most active representative in America. Baer was very much aware of Hitler's anti-Semitism and used his own position as champion to goad the führer, proclaiming, "Every punch in the eye I give Schmeling is one for Adolf Hitler."[51] While some of his statements may have been designed to stir interest in a return fight, many people considered Baer sincerely anti-Nazi.

Although Baer offered to fight Schmeling in Hamburg, Hitler refused. He viewed the Jewish people as *the* extreme opposite of his own Aryan race and went to great lengths to characterize Jews as clever but not original, lacking in culture, physical strength, and morals; physical condition and form were directly related to intelligence, and those geniuses with ill-formed bodies were the exceptions that proved the rule. Should the Jewish Baer again defeat the classic symbol of German strength, Hitler's propaganda campaign for Aryan supremacy would have been dealt a serious blow. Indeed, Hitler had such high regard for boxing that he argued, "a German Revolution of fancy-men, deserters and similar riffraff would never have been possible" if the "intellectual upper class . . . had all learned to box."[52] Baer and Schmeling never met again.

Despite Baer's reputation for clowning, his attacks on the Nazis were more serious than the press or almost anyone cared to admit. Hitler's discrimination against Jews in sport betrayed his deep hatred for them and his desire to exclude them from all areas of German life. Unfortunately, many people in the sports world chose to ignore the signals from Germany when they were, in fact, in a position to witness and speak out against the rapidly escalating repression. Avery Brundage, president of the United States Olympic Committee, reflected this head-in-the-sand mentality in a 1935 address before a pro-Nazi group in America: "We can learn much from Germany. . . . Germany has progressed as a nation out of her discouragement of five years ago into a new spirit of confidence in herself. The question was whether a vociferous minority [the Jews], highly organized and highly financed, could impose its will on 120,000,000 [*sic*] people."[53]

This type of insensitive utterance and the decision of the committee to sponsor an American contingent to the 1936 Berlin Olympics sent a message to the Jewish people that their problems were imagined, or at least not important. Of more serious consequence was the signal such actions gave to the Germans: they could act against the Jews with impunity.[54] Such attitudes also took political form in the appeasement policies of some European leaders, which gave Hitler carte blanche to move across the continent.

In 1935 Schmeling avenged both his earlier loss to Steve Hamas and a draw with Paulino Uzcudun. He quickly returned to boxing prominence and was openly embraced by his führer. His remarkable comeback symbolized Germany's rise from the ashes to a position of world prominence. As one American writer put it: "With all the dogged determination characteristic of his race, Max Schmeling has picked himself off the floor and hammered his way back into the heavyweight picture after heart-breaking defeats by Max Baer and Steve Hamas."[55] Schmeling set out to win the heavyweight championship of the world as Hitler goose-stepped his way across Europe. Each would use the other to achieve his goals, and each would come perilously close to succeeding.

The stage was set for a Joe Louis–Max Schmeling encounter, but each man, in his own way, posed a serious dilemma for promoters, the press, and, to some extent, the public. On the one hand, there was uncertainty about the public's readiness for a black champion, despite the fact that Louis's fight with Baer had drawn the first million-dollar gate in eight years. On the other hand, the powers-that-be did not want Schmeling to win the crown and have it "held hostage by Adolf Hitler."[56] The matchup was a natural one, however, and simply could not be avoided: a representative of the "master race" against a son of Africa and a burgeoning American hero.[57]

The American press, speculating on Schmeling's delay in agreeing to meet Louis, in general concluded that the Nazis opposed a mixed bout and would not allow Schmeling to participate. Not long before, Julius Streicher, a Nazi official and an ardent anti-Semite, had expelled a black wrestler from a tournament in Nuremberg on the grounds that Aryans should not be allowed to suffer defeat at the hands of non-Aryans.[58] Yet despite such opposition, Schmeling and his manager convinced the Nazi leadership that the German fighter's only hope of gaining the heavyweight crown for the fatherland was to defeat Joe Louis.[59] The necessary parties agreed to a bout on June 22, 1936, at Yankee Stadium. Within moments of the signing, the German press launched a campaign to denigrate Louis. It called for a boycott by Schmeling on the grounds that no self-respecting Aryan should lower himself by entering the ring with a black man.[60] The attack provoked a verbal war on both sides of the Atlantic. The National Association for the Advancement of Colored People expressed disapproval of the fight because of German racial policies and joined with the Anti-Nazi League in denouncing Schmeling as an instrument of Hitler's oppression. Rumor had it that Schmeling, if crowned champion, would join Hitler's cabinet as minister of physical education.[61]

The North and South, to no one's surprise, differed in their reactions to the upcoming bout. Inspired by financial interests, anti-Hitlerism, and ethnic considerations, northerners supported Joe Louis. Despite the often bittersweet encounters between Jews and blacks, and Louis's emotion-laden victories over Baer and Levinsky, the influential Jewish population stood firmly behind the Brown Bomber.[62] The southern press, while it deplored Hitler's belligerence and his repression against Jews, chose not to associate Schmeling with Hitler or hold him responsible for his führer's actions. Although some writers justified their stance by separating politics from sport, the more detached response of the South seemed to be heavily influenced by the region's ethnic homogeneity, its attitudes on interracial confrontation, and a less direct financial stake in the affair.[63] Louis received support, but it was not framed in racial or nationalistic terms; rather, it had its foundation in his ability, his character, his birthplace, and the benefits that would accrue to boxing. Before the fight one southerner wrote, "Alabama looks forward to the day when the world's heavyweight champion hails from the cotton fields of Alabama."[64] Interestingly, outside the press race sentiment led many people in the South to support Schmeling. The *Charlotte Observer* reported scores of calls and letters objecting to predictions of a Louis victory, and other papers reported similar reactions to their positive coverage of Louis.[65]

Louis seemed to put too much stock in press reports and thus avoided serious training; Schmeling saw the fight as a do-or-die mission and prepared accordingly. The German rocked the champion early, and the courageous Louis took a tremendous beating before going down for the count in round twelve. The press turned on him like a lover scorned, questioning his will, his intelligence, and his ability; some suggested that he was no more than a media creation, having built his reputation on has-beens.[66] The northern press quickly jettisoned him as a symbol of America and let him sink alone. Its harshly critical treatment seemed to be a face-saving gesture to protect its own credibility as well as the national image. The southern press had only its reputation to protect and expressed a sense of betrayal and crushed pride. With few exceptions, racial or international concerns were absent.[67]

Louis's faithful and persistent southern critic, William McG. Keefe, gloated and hailed Schmeling's victory as a vindication of white supremacy. The "reign of terror in heavyweight boxing was ended by Schmeling. The big bad wolf had been chased from the door. It took the Black Uhlan to prove that the black terror is just another fragile human being."[68] In triumph Louis appeared as a threatening animal; in defeat he was just a harmless mortal. Keefe now felt free to exploit the supremacy issue, and he appealed to all those who delighted in a black man's reduction to puerility.

Schmeling had not only upset Louis and the best-laid plans of boxing's power brokers, he had also scored an enormous propaganda victory for Nazi Germany. As a result, German officials, the media, and the public immediately elevated the "Black Uhlan" to hero status, and the führer personally befriended him, holding a party in his honor and inviting him to state functions. Schmeling returned the favor by crediting the Nazi leader with his success. He told the press, "Hitler's inspiration, more than anything else, spurs us to achievement."[69] The German response to Schmeling's victory was, of course, carefully measured and directed. Rather than making the outcome of the fight a symbolic victory over the United States, the Germans tried to exploit the race issue; they hoped to convince white Americans in particular that they and the Nazis were on the same side. German propagandist George Spandau maintained that the fight symbolized white "honesty over black brutality and lack of discipline" and that "through the German Schmeling, the white race, Europe, and White America, defeated the black race."[70] American writers like Westbrook Pegler remained convinced that Schmeling represented the Hitler Youth, a group that "detests and is sworn to destroy American ideals," but many others fell for the racist appeal.[71]

They Out-Hitlered Hitler

America's hope, Joe Louis, tended his wounds and nursed his injured pride. Not only had he slipped out of the heavyweight championship picture, but his defeat had allowed Hitler's representative to position himself for a shot at the title. Few observers believed that Braddock, the reigning champion, stood much of a chance against Schmeling, yet promoters were determined not to let this foreign invader "take the title back to Germany and present it to Adolf Hitler for the German Museum."[72] At first backers insisted that $25,000 be withheld from the winner to guarantee a return match, but when they learned that politically active Jewish groups planned a boycott, which might seriously affect gate receipts, they decided that the showdown must be avoided altogether. America's boxing autocracy proceeded to give Hitler a bitter taste of his own medicine via an incredible series of shakedowns, intrigues, high jinks, and contract breaches. The time had long since passed when sport served solely recreational needs; it was now a highly useful ideological and political instrument.

The first prefight snafu came in August 1936 when Braddock suffered a "hand injury," forcing a rescheduling of the fight from September 20, 1936, to June 3, 1937. (In the interim, rumors reached the Madison Square Garden Corporation, promoters of the fight, that Braddock contemplated breaking his contract by fighting Joe Louis. The Garden filed a protest with the New York State Athletic Commission, which ordered Braddock not to meet Louis.[73]) When circumstances indicated that the Braddock-Schmeling bout would not take place in America, Frank Hague, mayoral boss of Jersey City and a friend of Braddock's undertook to "help" the champion by scheduling the fight in Europe. Although the ever-scheming, entrepreneurial Hague, a man of considerable wealth with little visible means of income, had ulterior motives—he planned to use the heavyweight championship as an entrée into the lucrative optical supplies market via a Dutch firm[74]—the episode demonstrates what was a clear link between sport, greed, and diplomacy.

In January 1937 Dennis Scanlan, a Hague protégé, met with representatives of the German government for the purpose of staging a fight between Braddock and Schmeling in Berlin. Douglas Jenkins, the American consul general in Berlin, considered the matter serious enough to warrant a full and detailed accounting to the Department of State. In his letter, Jenkins revealed that Scanlan had proposed that a Dutch firm handle payments to the fighters and rights to subsequent fights. In addition, remaining funds would be used to sell optical supplies to the United States, thus giving Hague and his associates a corner on this valuable market.[75] Even more astounding was Scanlan's ultimatum to the German representative, to the effect that if the offer was not accepted by the German government, Schmeling would have no chance to meet Braddock outside the Reich. Upon receiving the message, Hitler, who desperately wanted a German titleholder, lent his support and anxiously awaited Hermann Goering's approval of the financial arrangements.[76]

While this behind-the-scenes drama unfolded, Joe Louis was quietly but convincingly working his way back to the top. He amassed a string of five consecutive knockout victories, with Al Ettore of Philadelphia lasting the longest at five rounds. In comeback fight number six, the fast and clever "bicycle-riding" Bob Pastor lost to Louis by decision; about that fight Louis uttered one of his most memorable lines, "You can run but you can't hide," in reference to Pastor's boasts about staying away from his powerful punches.[77] Mike Jacobs sensed that his young charge had regained his form, confidence, and credibility, and he made his move. A ruthless promoter in his own right, belying his endearing nickname "Uncle Mike," Jacobs enticed Braddock to break his contract with the Garden—an offer the champion simply could not refuse: a 10-percent share of the promoter's (Jacobs's) profits from Louis's subsequent fights.[78] Given his financial condition and meager talents, Braddock willingly defied NYSAC and signed to meet Louis on June 22, 1937, in Chicago. Regardless, Schmeling, who believed in contracts and American jurisprudence, came to America set on winning the championship from Braddock on June 3.[79]

Shadows Before?

The international and racial implications of the Primo Carnera–Joe Louis fight are clearly shown, as a defensive, little Ethiopia seems no match for an aggressive, behemoth Italy. (From the *Washington Post,* June 25, 1935)

The Joe Louis brain trust: (left to right) comanager Julian Black; trainer and confidant Jack Blackburn; and comanager John Roxborough. (Mrs. Russell Black)

Julian Black, with a close friend, clowning for the cameras, in stark contrast to the serious, stylized portrait of Joe Louis. (Mrs. Russell Black)

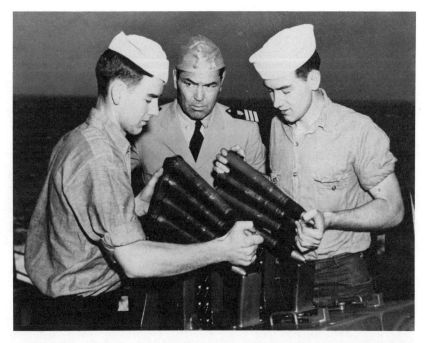

Lt. Comdr. Jack Dempsey oversees munitions handling while serving in the U.S. Coast Guard after the Army and Navy both rejected him because of his age. Dempsey, who avoided service in World War I, never captured the nation's imagination as a patriotic symbol, at least not to the extent that Joe Louis did. (Library of Congress)

Sgt. Joe Louis, after putting on a boxing exhibition in England, squeezes into the cockpit of a P-51. (Library of Congress)

Trading on the former champion's name, liquor distributors and vendors promote Joe Louis Kentucky Straight Bourbon Whiskey in New Orleans in 1952. Louis benefited little from this and other such ventures. (The Historic New Orleans Collection, Museum/Research Center, acc. nos. 1979.325.6033 and 1979.325.4295)

When Braddock failed to meet Schmeling on the appointed date, Madison Square Garden filed suit against the champion and sought an injunction to prevent the Louis-Braddock fight, a futile request in light of legal precedent. American courts rarely ordered injunctions in personal service suits, nor did they ever require specific performance—in this instance, the meeting of Braddock and Schmeling. In the court's opinion such a remedy would have caused Braddock unnecessary hardship; moreover, a loophole in the contract gave Braddock an easy out: the original negative covenant, which prevented Braddock from fighting anyone before Schmeling, had expired and had not been renewed in subsequent agreements. The Garden's argument that it carried over by implication was rejected by the court,[80] and Braddock was declared free to meet Louis, an encounter he must have awaited with mixed emotions.

As expected, the Germans reacted angrily, and both officials and the press denounced the legal outcome as a "farce" and "an organized fraud on Schmeling's rights."[81] They were not alone in their negative reaction. Garden promoter James Johnston criticized NYSAC for its lack of action and argued that stripping Braddock's title would have been appropriate. In Johnston's opinion the commission's failure to act resulted from an anti-Tammany state administration that resented Braddock's close ties to Jimmy Walker.[82]

Touching the Raw Nerve: A Black Champion

As Louis again moved closer to the throne, the South grew increasingly anxious about the impact of a black champion on the region. Lawrence Levine aptly interprets the attitude that prevailed in Dixie: "However quietly and with whatever degree of humility he succeeded, Joe Louis, like Jack Johnson before him, stood as a black man in the midst of a white society and beat representatives of the dominant group to their knees."[83] No amount of humility, Levine concludes, could preclude Louis's "becoming a breaker of stereotypes and a destroyer of norms."[84] Those very same southern sports pundits who had appeared so willing to see Louis succeed suddenly were overwhelmed by self-doubts and second thoughts on the acceptability of a black champion. With Schmeling and the foreign issue out of the way, race had no rival for determining loyalty.

The southern press, compelled to cushion the shock to itself and the white populace should Louis win the title, chose to play down the significance of the heavyweight championship bout. To this end it demeaned Braddock's ability, intimated that the outcome had already been determined, and even sided with Schmeling by reminding Louis that the German challenger really merited a title opportunity.[85] Louis was called a coward and was adversely compared to black boxers of the past, one writer predicting that he would never be the idol that Sam Langford was among the members of his race.[86] The media hoped to ensure a peaceful and quiet succession in heavyweight boxing by reducing the chances for blacks and whites to perceive Louis's victory—should he win—as a symbol of black superiority. Even non-sports editors joined the effort to ease tensions, arguing that championships could be quickly won and lost, that no one man would be around for a long time.[87] One editor suggested that the championship was valuable to children but almost meaningless in the progress of humankind.[88]

Joe Louis was prepared to face southern animosity and his boxing opponent. When the two men met on June 22, the Brown Bomber relentlessly stalked the game but outmanned Braddock, and by the eighth round almost everyone hoped the contest would end before the champion was killed. Braddock must have been relieved when it was over, for his description of Louis's punches revealed he had lived a nightmare: the left jab "was like someone jammed an electric bulb in your face and busted it"; the right was worse, "like someone nailed you with a crowbar. I thought half my head was blowed off. I figure he caved it in. I felt it after he hit me and I couldn't even feel it was there."[89]

For the first time in twenty-two years a black man fought for—and won—the heavyweight championship of the world, a remarkable, albeit logical, occurrence. The reaction to Louis's victory was even more remarkable. One southern editor, who perhaps viewed his role as a molder of public opinion rather than a reporter of it, stated that the general pattern of acceptance was evidence of "less race prejudice . . . less disposition to resent a Negro heavyweight champion."[90] Unfortunately, such assertions misrepresented the realities of southern race relations. Although changes had taken place in the South, especially regarding education for blacks, the lines of discrimination and segregation were still firmly drawn. Clearly, much of the reason for the southern response to Louis should be attributed to his behavior, his willingness to fulfill white expectations, and the fact that southern turf had not been invaded. A report in the *Columbus News Record* (Georgia) more accurately revealed some of the region's deep-rooted feelings about a black man fighting and beating a white man: "In the South we understand such matters better than they are understood in such Northern cities as Chicago and New York, and such a fight as occurred last night would not for a moment be thought of for a Southern city; indeed it would be criminal to attempt to stage such an affair in the South."[91]

A critical factor in the reserved white reaction to Louis was the humble and restrained behavior of southern blacks. While blacks in Harlem, Detroit, Chicago, and other major northern cities rejoiced publicly, their southern brothers and sisters hid their pride for fear of white retaliation.[92] Former President Jimmy Carter, who grew up in Plains, Georgia, recalled a time when his father, a staunchly anti-Louis man and a die-hard segregationist, allowed some black neighbors to listen to a fight on his radio. When Louis emerged victorious the guests showed no outward emotion. But upon reaching their own home, Carter reports, "pandemonium broke loose inside that house, as our black neighbors shouted and yelled in celebration of the Louis victory. But all the curious, accepted proprieties of a racially segregated society had been carefully observed."[93]

There was one notable exception to the subdued response of southern blacks: a racial disturbance in Durham, North Carolina, following Joe Louis's smashing victory to capture the heavyweight crown. According to Walter Weare, in *Black Business in the New South,* whites who drove through Hayti, Durham's black business and residential district, were confronted by blacks, who raced alongside the cars hurling rocks and shouting insults. The chief of police called C. C. Spaulding and demanded that he get "his" people off the streets. Spaulding, who had been extolled earlier by the Raleigh press as a more appropriate role model for blacks than Louis, "mounted a running board and commanded them to return home or invite the holocaust."[94] He and other members of the North Carolina Mutual Life Insurance Company had long been considered "shock absorbers," and city officials proudly bragged that they worked with black leaders because "the Negroes trust them and fall in line with what they say; that's the way for us to have peace."[95]

Durham, which became a center for cooperative interracial activities in the 1940s and 1950s was, in southern terms, progressive in its promotion of black economic development and, to a certain extent, black political self-determination. No doubt such an outbreak would have met with far harsher action in other areas of the South. In some ways this incident indicated that many blacks were chafing under the current conditions and would, with proper stimuli, express pent-up frustrations by a symbolic show of aggression. According to Lawrence Levine, "Louis' beating the white man at his own game served as powerful motivation for action among blacks."[96] What he had done, others dreamed of also doing, and sometimes they acted out that dream. Yet in most other areas of the South, where expectations ran so low and repression so high that blacks rarely challenged the system, fear and passivity remained the true secret to "good" race relations.

Hitler's Last Chance

The southern calm stood in marked contrast to the protests from abroad. Not willing to accept what they deemed was the unjust exclusion of their representative, the Nazis embarked on a campaign to discredit Joe Louis; at the same time they allied with the British to capture the heavyweight championship. Expressing either their ignorance or their tacit support of Nazi actions, the British Board of Boxing Control agreed in July 1937 to a fight between Tommy Farr and Max Schmeling for the heavyweight championship. The International Boxing Union had already declared Schmeling the champion, but that organization had little influence upon American prizefighting, making Schmeling's title almost meaningless. However, both the British and Germans felt that a Schmeling-Farr fight would legitimate the title.[97] Inexperience in the cutthroat boxing racket led the Nazis to once again underestimate the powers of Mike Jacobs, and it cost them dearly. Determined to stop at nothing to consolidate his hold on the sport, Jacobs undermined the Nazis' plans by luring Tommy Farr into a fight with Joe Louis. Farr's loss deprived both the Germans and the British of the crown.[98]

Joe Louis's greatness could never be certified until he fought and disposed of Max Schmeling. Their meeting was inevitable, and time now became Louis's ally. The longer the delay in setting a date, the more time Louis had to improve and Schmeling to grow older. At one point the Brown Bomber remarked: "I had two more years of experience and he had two more years of age."[99] The Germans understood this but were not willing to risk the embarrassment Jesse Owens and the "Black Auxiliary" had cast upon them at the Berlin Olympic Games. They were backed against the wall, however, and the only way out was through Joe Louis. Thus, after considerable debate, introspection, and persuasion by Schmeling, Hitler himself decided that the potential for glory outweighed the risks. The fight was scheduled for June 22, 1938, in New York City. Anti-Nazi groups objected and vowed to stop it by law suits and boycotts, but Jacobs brushed off their protests and threats.

The proposed bout took on the symbolism of democracy against fascism and became a vent for American ambivalence toward Nazi aggression.[100] The official American policy was strict neutrality, but by 1938 Hitler's intentions had become increasingly clear. His occupation of the Rhineland and the threatening of Czechoslovakia had disturbed the fragile international balance of power. The American public, although opposed to Nazi aggression and victimization of the Jews, feared U.S. intervention in Europe; in fact, as late as June 1940 less than 5 percent of the population favored declaring war on Germany.[101]

Consequently, the Louis-Schmeling bout typified for many the symbolic "single combat." Some writers denied that issues of race and international politics played any part in the contest, but these opinions clearly flew in the face of reality. Rumors had circulated in the German press that Herbert Lehman, governor of New York and a Jew, paid NYSAC to keep the title away from Schmeling.[102] No one could deny that Hitler and his associates blatantly exploited athletes for political purposes, forcing them to carry the banner of Aryan supremacy. Successful German athletes were highly rewarded, while failures paid a heavy price. For example, tennis star Baron Gottfried von Cramm, soon after his string of losses to Don Budge at Wimbledon and the U.S. Open and in the Davis Cup, was taken into custody on morals charges and was never heard from again.

Joe Jacobs, Schmeling's manager in America and himself a Jew, did his best to downplay the international significance of the fight. His actions did incalculable harm to the Jewish cause, however. In 1935 he created a storm of controversy when reports surfaced that he had saluted the führer with a "Heil Hitler." He openly scoffed at boycott threats as silly gestures, offering the opinion that "most of the trouble with the Jews over there [in Germany] is caused by the Jews in this country [America]." He described everyone in Germany as happy, "spending money like it was water." As for the talk of war, he said it "makes the Germans laugh." Joe Jacobs had no complaints, for the Germans treated him like a king.[103]

Mike Jacobs expressed his feelings about the boycott far more diplomatically and responsibly. While boxing was his business, he did not wish to denounce those who opposed the fight or dismiss the German treatment of Jews. He did offer to contribute 10 percent of the profits from the fight for Jewish refugee aid, but the Non-Sectarian Anti-Nazi League, a leader of the boycott, rejected what seemed to be a hollow gesture, demanding instead that Schmeling contribute funds as proof of his anti-Nazi sentiment. Regardless of the German boxer's feelings, to have acceded to such a demand would have been foolhardy.[104] Everywhere the fight was being billed as democracy versus fascism, pacifism versus militarism, and ultimately good versus evil. Even the southern press had come to regard it as a symbolic confrontation between Nazi Germany and the United States. Indeed, the normally taciturn Louis seemed emotionally charged, his deadpan expression giving way to a menacing glare. Ignited by his promotion as an American symbol and incensed by the racial slurs allegedly hurled by Schmeling, Louis promised, "I'm backing up America against Germany, so you know I am going to town."[105]

And "go to town" he did. Like a man on a mission, Louis struck with incredible quickness. The Brown Bomber unleashed a devastating, and vicious assault that made Max Schmeling "scream like a frightened girl or a stuck pig," before knocking him unconscious in just 124 seconds.[106] Louis had waged a "lightning war" of his own, and the American press hailed the outcome as a direct blow to nazism: "The Aryan idol, the unconquerable one had been beaten, the bright, shining symbol of race glory has been thumped in the dust. That noise you hear is Goebbels making for the storm cellar."[107] The northern press cast the victory as a unifying event that transcended racial boundaries, after which "white folks joined colored boys in national jubilation."[108] Although the South joined its northern counterpart in blasting the Germans as a race of "stupor men" and "not supermen," it tempered its tributes to Louis with reminders of his place in society; to southern journalists he was still a "colored boy."[109]

While America rejoiced the Nazis regrouped and moved quickly to minimize their losses. The Germans had interrupted radio transmission of the fight when a Louis victory became obvious, and they delayed releasing films of the one-sided battle until, according to Louis's manager, they could doctor them by interspersing action sequences from the first contest with those of the second. Roxborough angrily lodged an official complaint with Hugh Wilson, the American ambassador to Berlin, but the Germans assured him that they had done no such thing.[110] They, in turn, accused Louis of delivering illegal blows.[111]

The American press openly speculated that Max Schmeling would fall from grace, yet Hitler realized that he had been praised too highly to be easily discarded. Schmeling was still a hero to the German people and a highly visible international celebrity as well. With public opinion in mind, the führer sent a sympathy note to Schmeling's wife, accompanied by flowers from Goebbels, and reminded the public that the German boxer stood as a "model for the sports world."[112] Still, sensational stories circulated that Schmeling had been sent to a concentration camp and perhaps killed, which the Nazis viewed as the lies of a Jewish-dominated American press. To squelch these rumors the German government arranged for his return to the United States, announcing that "Schmeling's trip abroad will certainly achieve something but all agitators and Jewish criminals will invent another lie tomorrow."[113] However, the United States denied Schmeling entry, declaring that he had no acceptable reason for coming to this country (and they continued to withhold clearance until 1961). Evidently there was increasing concern on the part of American officials over Nazi actions and intentions. Unable to send their representative in person, the Germans resorted to a publicity campaign that highlighted Schmeling's contributions as a para-trooper and martial arts instructor.[114]

While Louis's stunning victory had little direct impact on world events, it had a positive influence on the home front. It was a morale booster and a confidence builder for the nation and especially for blacks. The Reverend Jesse Jackson, a modern civil rights leader, looks back on the fight as one that freed black people "from the midst of inferiority."[115] To others, memories of the fight border on the mythical. The popular and influential columnist Art Buchwald, in a 1981 reflection upon the Louis-Schmeling encounters, elevated the fights to legendary heights. Buchwald recounted that the kids in his town believed three things were certain: "Franklin Roosevelt was going to save the economy" and "Joe Dimaggio was going to beat Babe Ruth's record," but above all else, "Joe Louis was going to save us from the Germans."[116] Louis was their hero, and when he said, "America's going to win because we're on God's side," it meant as much to them as the president's reassurances during the depression that "we have nothing to fear but fear itself."[117] The Louis-Schmeling encounters were much more than prizefights; for many Americans, young and old, the battles became do-or-die situations for them and their country.[118]

Boxing's Return to Glory and Wealth

As Joe Louis's stock rose, so did boxing's. The second Louis-Schmeling fight drew 70,000 fans and grossed $1,015,012.[119] It also established Mike Jacobs as the most powerful promoter in the sport. With the heavyweight championship firmly in his clutches, Jacobs consolidated his hold on boxing by eliminating competition. He bought out the interests of Damon Runyon and Ed Frayne in the Twentieth Century Sporting Club, in which Bill Farnsworth became a working partner, having resigned from the Hearst press. A virtual monopoly was assured when Colonel John Reed Kilpatrick, president of the Madison Square Garden Corporation, announced on August 26, 1938, that Jacobs would copromote the Garden's boxing activities. "Uncle Mike" now owned the most prestigious boxer in the world and had direct access to the sport's most hallowed arena. Other fighters flocked to Jacobs, including Billy Conn, Rocky Graziano, and Sugar Ray Robinson.[120]

Louis was boxing's anchor and its genie. He was a human horn of plenty, supplying Jacobs with additional wealth and power, sustaining the prizefight business, and nourishing a hero-starved American public. Forsaking a long boxing tradition, Louis defended his title regularly, meeting almost anyone at anytime. The fans could not get enough of him, even against "the bum of the month." Of course, the press played upon ethnic and racial loyalties in promoting Bob Pastor, Jack Roper, Lou Nova, and "Two-Ton" Tony Galento as "white hopes," but these men were really little more than economic pawns. So clean was Louis's image, in fact, and so reassuring was his countenance that Congress eventually was convinced to lift the twenty-seven-year ban on the interstate transportation of prizefight films—one of the last vestiges of the Jack Johnson era and an obvious hindrance to economic gain.

The Return of Fight Films

The anti-fight film law had long outlived its usefulness and proved an endless source of irritation for promoters, the public, federal officials, and the courts. It was flouted with impunity, in part because of its ambiguity, but mostly because of changing attitudes and social conditions.[121] In a fit of hyperbole, one writer explained the irresistibility of a fight film: "You can listen to a fight on the radio, but you can actually see noise photographed by the camera. . . . Such method is only as old as Homer, who cut the light of Helen's beauty across the faces of the Trojan elders and let us surmise the power of the original from the radiance of the reflection."[122] Others attacked the law's lack of logic in an increasingly technological society. They saw no more harm in showing films than in permitting the fights themselves; moreover, round-by-round radio descriptions were allowed and still photographs appeared in the nation's newspapers. Critics pointed out that both state and federal governments already profited from legalized prizefights in the form of taxes, and if such film showings became legal, then additional revenue would be forthcoming.

In the fall of 1927 film exhibitors benefited from a favorable decision by United States District Judge Henry W. Goddard. In what appeared to be a violation of the 1912 law, New York theaters had openly exhibited moving pictures of the second Tunney-Dempsey fight. Goddard instructed a federal grand jury that the exhibition of such pictures, as distinguished from their transportation, was not a crime. On July 6, 1931, Samuel Busha of the Bureau of Investigation advised theater owners that he would not interfere with the showing of the heavyweight championship fight film featuring Max Schmeling and William Stribling. Busha arrived at his decision after a federal court had ruled that interstate transportation of original films did not constitute a violation of the 1912 law. This marked the first time that movies of a world's championship fight were seen in Philadelphia without government interference.[123]

As early as 1928 the legal community foresaw problems with the fight film law in terms of the radio transmission of pictures. Ralph Wilguss, in a *New York Law Review* article, predicted that the federal ruling in the *Pantomimic* case (see chap. 2) would serve as a precedent for declaring pictures of a prizefight transmitted via radio waves to be illegal.[124] This would clearly be within the purview of Congress since the sending of telegraph and telephone messages constituted interstate commerce.[125] Thus, although television was still in the experimental stage, in 1932 lawyers were predicting a confrontation between the new medium and the anti-fight film statute.[126] In 1939 the Lou Nova–Buddy Baer fight was telecast from New York and was almost certainly seen across the state line in New Jersey. Neville Miller of the National Alliance of Broadcasters anticipated more showings in violation of the law and urged its repeal.[127]

Senator Warren R. Barbour of New Jersey, a former boxer and an avid fight fan, had proposed corrective legislation in 1935, with the support of Congressman Emmanuel Celler, but that action proved unsuccessful.[128] Senator Barbour tried again in 1939, holding two days of hearings on a piece of legislation that would legalize the transportation of fight films. The hearings focused on four issues: the common flouting of an unpopular law; the acceptability and popularity of boxing as reflected in its legalization by all states; the allegedly changed racial conditions, personified by Joe Louis; and the burgeoning television industry.[129]

Ironically, two of the most important factors in the law's repeal were often unwelcome elements in the sport—women and blacks. Although others had to speak for them (only white males were called to testify), they virtually saved the day. Witness after witness cited countless examples of female fans as proof that boxing did not harm the public. A Connecticut official reported that 1,000,000 people had paid to see prizefights in 1938 and none had been arrested; he underscored the fact that women had comprised one-third of the total attendance. Others maintained that women enjoyed the fights as much as men and considered them good recreation.[130] Sol Strauss, the attorney for the Twentieth Century Sporting Club, testified that he followed his wife to prizefights and that more than 10,000 women had attended the second Louis-Schmeling fight in 1938. John J. Farrell, whose interests in boxing ranged from broadcaster to writer and promoter, testified that his mother had been a steady patron of boxing matches. Like other fans, he explained, "she enjoys a fight—not because she has a barbaric spirit . . . but she just likes it because it is a contest between two evenly matched men, and she has a little red blood still in her corpuscles."[131]

With regard to the race issue, Abe J. Greene, chairman of the New Jersey Boxing Commission, explained: "The measure came into being in the midst of a boxing contest which involved racial feuds; it was conceived at the time that the showing of such films might fan the flames of racial hatred. There is now, and for a long time there has been, no such condition, with the result that prize fight films have been shown in various states in violation of the law."[132] Senator Barbour willingly staked his own reputation on Louis, calling him the "first Negro heavyweight who was so respected across the country that boxing films could be sent interstate."[133] He was not alone in his assessment, as various boxing personalities and officials, including Gene Tunney, John Reed Kilpatrick, and even Jack Dempsey, testified before the Senate that Joe Louis provided no cause for alarm and that his fights did not upset racial "tranquility."[134]

On June 13, 1939, the Senate unanimously passed a bill to permit interstate shipment of prizefight films. Few people criticized the move, although the Women's Christian Temperance Union continued to loudly voice its opposition to boxing.[135] On June 29, 1940, Congress divested prizefight films of their status as objects of interstate or foreign commerce.[136] As expected, less than a year later state governments began to tax film revenues, an option that had been denied them earlier.[137]

Joe Louis's role in the repeal of the anachronistic, hate-inspired anti-fight film statute is difficult to overstate. But it would not be accurate to conclude that the repeal of the law was a measure of his influence on changing racial patterns. On the contrary, while there might have been relative calm and less tension at the time, this did not automatically translate into black gains. Blacks, for example, had only limited access to Louis's fight films because of exclusionary theater practices. Also, for most of Louis's boxing career professional and collegiate athletics remained largely segregated in the North and fully separate in Dixie.[138]

Lull before the Storm

By 1939 boxing had almost returned to the glory days of the past, and Joe Louis was largely responsible for its restoration. Even such fiascoes as his knockout of an aging Jack Roper did little to tarnish his or boxing's new lustre. The fight was so bad, in fact, that a legislative committee investigating boxing and wrestling in California in 1939 questioned athletic commissioners about the propriety of their having allowed it to take place. At the time Roper was thirty-nine and Louis was twenty-six; worse still, Roper had already been knocked out twenty times by virtual unknowns.[139] Clearly, Louis was having a hard time finding able opponents.

Soon ominous events abroad made heavyweight championship fights seem like child's play. On September 1, 1939, Germany invaded Poland and annexed Danzig, defying a British and French ultimatum. Within two days Europe was at war. Despite the "America First" movements, many people had to believe that it was only a matter of time before the United States became militarily involved. Yet, with a pall hanging over the world, on June 18, 1941, for one brief moment, everyone's attention was turned to what experts have called the best fight ever, "just before the world went to hell."[140]

In early 1939 a handsome young Irish light heavyweight named Billy Conn had come to the attention of Mike Jacobs. Unimpressed with Conn's record against unknowns in Pittsburgh and West Virginia, Jacobs decided to use him as cannon fodder for the popular Italian fighter Freddie Apostoli. But Conn won their first fight and then proved he was no fluke by beating the seasoned veteran in a rematch. By July of the same year he had fought himself into a title shot against Melio Bettina. "The Pittsburgh Kid," as Conn was called, decisioned Bettina and with his "movie-star looks" became the hottest fighter in boxing. Although he lacked the raw punching power fans had come to expect, his balletic grace and surgeonlike dexterity, his good looks, and especially his race qualified him for serious "white hope" status. All he needed was more weight. After three successful title defenses Conn gave up the light heavyweight crown to compete as a heavyweight. With increased weight came sudden power, and Conn knocked out five of the seven heavyweights he faced, including Bob Pastor, who had proven so elusive for Louis.[141]

Conn's mercurial rise to the top of the heavyweight division led to press reports of racially motivated friction between him and the reigning champion, which served to heighten expectations for an exciting showdown. On June 18 nearly 55,000 people packed into the Polo Grounds in New York to witness the fight. While the outcome may have disappointed many, the action satisfied everyone; in fact, the Louis-Conn fight soon took on legendary proportions.[142] Louis tipped the scales at 199½ pounds to Conn's meager 169, but Conn, noted for his footwork, soon began to outmove and, surprisingly, outhit the champion. By round twelve the challenger had convinced witnesses and announcers that he was clearly ahead and that only a knockout by Louis could save his title. Conn's handlers advised him to stay away, to stick and run, but a crunching left blow delivered to Louis's head at the end of the twelfth round convinced him that he could take the champion out. Conn stood toe-to-toe with Louis in the thirteenth round, ignoring the pleas from his corner, when Louis unleashed a crunching right to Conn's head. A rain of blows followed and Conn was counted out at 2:58 of the round. Although the official scorecards read 7-5, 7-4-1, and 6-6 for Conn, indicating a much closer fight than eyewitness accounts testified to, almost everyone concluded that stupidity or hot-headedness, not lack of skill, had cost Conn the fight.[143] A real "white hope" had been born and the stage was set for a rematch. But who would have expected that five years would elapse before the two would meet again, by which time Joe Louis would be a bona fide American hero and Conn an overweight, ring-rusty boxer.

World War II and a Black National Hero

From the very beginning of the European conflict President Roosevelt had clearly chosen sides, hoping to offer as much military aid to the Allies as he could without actually going to war. The fall of France in the spring of 1940 intensified the president's intention to rebuild America's military forces and to give England all aid short of troop intervention. By the summer of 1941 the United States was engaged in an undeclared naval war with Germany, as American forces protected shipping in the western half of the North Atlantic. Roosevelt's sympathy for the British belied neutrality, and his joint declaration with Winston Churchill, known as the Atlantic Charter, did everything except make the United States and Great Britain allies. The document not only spelled out the hopes of the two leaders for a better world but specifically referred to "the final destruction of the Nazi tyranny" as a war objective.[144] When F.D.R. said, "This nation will remain a neutral nation, but I cannot ask that every American remain neutral in thought as well," he was probably speaking for himself first.[145]

The situation in Asia was equally explosive. In 1937 Japan had renewed its attack on the nationalist regime of Chinese leader Chiang Kai-shek and shortly thereafter gained a foothold in northern Indo-China. The United States, committed to preserving the territorial integrity and independence of China, responded with various forms of economic pressure. In the meantime Japan signed the Tripartite Pact with Germany and Italy, in which each pledged to retaliate in response to an attack on any of the parties to the alliance. Thus emboldened, Japan continued its drive toward hegemony over eastern Asia, occupying southern Indo-China in July 1941. President Roosevelt imposed all-inclusive economic sanctions and issued an ultimatum to Japan: leave China alone or risk war with the United States.[146] The two countries continued on a collision course that finally culminated in the surprise attack on Pearl Harbor on December 7, 1941. Within hours America was at war. Its need for heroes would never be greater.

As symbols of American strength, the greatest boxers in the world were expected to join the greatest army in the world. The response was most encouraging: no less than five world champions stood tall among the more than 4,000 boxers in the military.[147] One of the most decorated soldiers in the war was welterweight champion Barney Ross, who, while wounded and suffering from shock and fever, helped to repel a Japanese attack at Guadalcanal.[148] Jack Dempsey, hoping to clear his name, practically begged to be inducted, but because of his age (forty-six) the Army and the Navy rejected him. The Coast Guard commissioned him a lieutenant commander, however, making him the highest-ranking professional boxer in the armed forces. Gene Tunney returned to the Marines as a captain.[149] Others made their contributions on the home front, such as James J. Braddock, who served as deputy director for the United States Civilian Defense in charge of boxing.[150] Even Jack Johnson displayed his patriotism by taking part in a Brooklyn War Bond boxing show that raised a record $3,000,000.[151]

Not to be outdone, boxing promoters staged numerous, huge war bond tournaments and sponsored special early morning boxing shows for the benefit of night-shift defense workers. The National Boxing Association pledged a 2-percent levy on boxing purses and managers for the war effort,[152] a patriotic yet self-serving gesture. NBA President Abe Greene candidly admitted that "we want to be able to do our part so that when the role of sports is recalled at the close of the struggle it will be found that boxing has played the part well in the true American style."[153] The war had removed boxing's biggest names, championships were frozen, and outdoor fights were virtually eliminated by blackout restrictions, making the NBA's pledge a clear case of opting for short-term losses in the hopes of long-term profits.

Few men in boxing sacrificed more and complained less than Joe Louis. Of all the athletic heroes, only the Brown Bomber occupied the summit as a national symbol. He set a stunning example through his acts of patriotism, and even the South responded appreciatively. Indeed, in the hearts of some, Louis's wartime heroism boosted him above the immortal Jack Dempsey.[154] Even before the United States had entered the war Louis promised to visit various U.S. military bases, a gesture that elicited unqualified praise from the southern press. The *Birmingham News* predicted that he "could become the most popular of them all if he would go on a tour of the army camps." Louis followed through on his promise, putting on exhibitions and delighting the troops with his very presence.[155] He also donated to the Navy Relief Fund his entire purse from the January 9, 1942, title bout with Buddy Baer.[156] While some viewed his generosity as a bid to delay his own induction and to reduce his tax burden, most people deemed it patriotic. Unfortunately, the donation was partly to blame for some of Louis's later, devastating financial difficulties. According to Truman K. Gibson, Jr., a top black War Department aide and close Louis associate, Mike Jacobs "screwed" his own fighter. Manager John Roxborough had allegedly reached an agreement with military officials that Jacobs and Louis would both donate their earnings to the Navy Relief Fund, but only Louis did so. Moreover, if Jacobs had arranged the fight as a charity event, Louis's share of the purse would not have been taxed; as it happened, he was taxed despite donating the money.[157]

Soon Louis was called up for duty. Attempts to have him commissioned were not taken seriously—nor did he approve of them—and Truman Gibson encouraged him to enlist in the army, which he did in February 1942. Louis took basic training at Camp Upton on Long Island and was then assigned to special services, although he wished to avoid charges of favoritism at all costs.[158] Shortly thereafter, on March 27, Louis defended his title against Abe Simon, in New York City. This time he donated his entire purse to the Army Emergency Relief Organization amid much fanfare, including a radio tribute by Under Secretary of War Robert Patterson, who praised him for his patriotism. The *Birmingham News* paid him the greatest honor by comparing him favorably to Jack Dempsey. Although Dempsey's avoidance of military duty in World War I was rarely mentioned, it clearly made him the object of criticism such as: "Joe Louis, Friday, became the first United States soldier to defend his heavyweight title. Despite wanting to be good soldiers Louis is the first to make the association a reality."[159] Another writer from the same paper concluded that "from almost every angle you can consider, there never has been a champion like Joe Louis in the ring."[160]

As a result of Louis's service above and beyond the call of duty, the Brown Bomber reached his greatest popularity and promoter Mike Jacobs wanted to take advantage of the situation. Whether he or Truman Gibson proposed a Louis-Conn rematch to benefit the Navy Relief Fund is not clear; what is clear is that Jacobs stood to be the main beneficiary.[161] After lengthy negotiations the War Department and the Louis camp arranged the bout. A committee in charge of the fight allegedly arranged for Mike Jacobs to collect $59,805 from Louis and $34,500 from Conn and John Roxborough to receive $41,145 from Louis, which represented money owed by the fighters to both men. When Jacobs demanded control of the first twenty rows of seats—prime scalping territory, the outcries were loud and immediate. Congressmen angrily called the arrangement "a mockery of the war" in which the "armed forces have taken upon themselves to pay the indebtedness of individuals."[162] Under congressional pressure, Secretary of War Henry Stimson called off the bout, despite rumors that Gibson had proposed such an arrangement to ensure Louis's cooperation. Gibson denied the allegation and maintained that Jacobs's insistence upon controlling the prime seats had destroyed the fight's chances.[163]

To many, Stimson's decision rendered meaningless the praise of presidential candidate Wendell Wilkie, who told Louis: "for your magnificent example in risking your championship [for free] that had bitterly been won through toil, tears, blood, and sweat, we thank you and the American people thank you."[164] Others felt that Louis should be allowed to earn money to pay his debts. The cancellation also added fuel to the fire of those critics, especially blacks, who had long been suspicious of the military's racial policies and who opposed Louis's donations to a fund that supported the armed services.[165] The decision confirmed Stimson's reputation among blacks as "a stubborn man . . . determined to continue color discrimination . . . war or not."[166] The secretary of war was fortunate that the man most affected, and the one who mattered most, showed no outward bitterness.

Joe Louis not only continued to visit military camps across the nation, he even purchased steak dinners for the soldiers. At Fort Riley, Kansas, where he trained in the cavalry, he bought uniforms for Jackie Robinson's entire graduating class. All the while Mike Jacobs was carefully noting each and every advance made to support Louis's philanthropy.[167] The man who has been described as a chemist with money (for his ability to break it down) would suffer tremendously for his charity, eventually owing his soul to Uncle Mike and his last dime to Uncle Sam.[168] But for now, because he was a tremendous morale builder, Louis was used by the government to gain black support for the war effort and to get black troops to accept a segregated army, even though he worked quietly behind the scenes to end segregation. His "Parade of Champions" exhibition not only entertained troops of all colors but helped to broaden the base of athletic competition on military installations by integrating blacks into the mainstream of recreational life. Before Louis came along, black athletic facilities were poor and black soldiers often could not find teams to play or had to compete against black high schools or colleges, sometimes penitentiaries.[169] Nonetheless, Joe Louis was on the horns of a dilemma.

Concern over treatment in World War I and unfulfilled hopes for equality in the postwar period caused many blacks to question blind support for American efforts in World War II. The *Pittsburgh Courier* launched a "Double V" campaign in which black support of the war effort was tied to black gains at home and in the military.[170] Many government officials considered the stand unpatriotic; their uneasiness arose from a guilt-ridden recognition that blacks were treated inequitably at home yet were expected to join an effort to destroy the racist, totalitarian Axis powers. This concern came through in a letter from Archibald MacLeish, director of the Office of Facts and Figures, to Secretary of the Interior Harold Ickes in March 1942. MacLeish warned, "There is no question but that enemy agitation will take advantage of this critical situation and that they will try to turn to [their] account the line taken by some zealous leaders who are seeking to advance their particular interests."[171] One response was a pamphlet, *The Negroes and the War,* by Chandler Owen, a black writer. Owen hammered so hard at the theme that a Nazi victory would cost blacks whatever they had gained that many people inferred from it that the War Department believed blacks wanted the Nazis to win and that blacks had to be persuaded to remain loyal to the United States.[172] A more subtle, positive, and glamorous approach was clearly necessary.

MacLeish suggested a multipronged attack on discrimination in the armed services, civilian defense, war industry, and even the deplorable Detroit housing situation.[173] Too little had been done too late in Detroit, where one of America's worst race riots took place on June 20, 1943.[174] Black government officials made similar recommendations, with W. J. Trent, Jr., of the Federal Works Agency suggesting that blacks needed visible evidence of their cultural and industrial development. The idea soon spread to the War Department, where William Hastie and his assistant, Truman Gibson, suggested to Under Secretary of War Robert Patterson that a film be made to show the accomplishments of blacks in and out of the military as part of an educational process.[175] Patterson took to the idea and contacted movie director Frank Capra; he also ordered the department's Special Services branch to give the highest priority to a film on the black soldier. Carlton Moss, a young black writer, was assigned by Patterson to collaborate on the script. The centerpiece of the film was none other than Sergeant Joe Louis, the heavyweight champion of the world.[176]

Louis had by this time become the most highly publicized noncommissioned officer in America. Regularly featured in wartime newsreels, he rivaled President Roosevelt and scenes from the battlefield in frequency and length of coverage. Now, in *The Negro Soldier,* released in 1943, he was teamed up with a black preacher who harkened back to the second Louis-Schmeling fight and made the war an extension of that battle, proclaiming that the "two men who were matched in the ring that night are matched again, this time in a far greater arena and for much greater stakes."[177] The film suggested to black people that if they loved and supported Joe Louis, then they must love and support America; that if their hero was committed to fight nazism, then so should they. To show further that blacks had no friend in Hitler, the preacher quoted a passage from *Mein Kampf,* where Hitler denounces the American belief in black progress: "it never dawns on degenerate America that it is criminal madness to train a half ape, till one believes he has made a lawyer of him."[178] He urged his flock to follow the heroic example of Joe Louis and support the nation, for the fight now "was for the real championship of the world to determine which way of life shall survive."[179] The film echoed a statement attributed to Louis that "there may be a whole lot wrong with America, but there's nothing that Hitler can fix."[180]

The Negro Soldier received rave reviews. Frank Capra reported that a skeptical group of 200 black publishers, editors, and writers who previewed the film expressed surprise and elation at the masterful creation. At other previews black and white soldiers were enthusiastic. Disregarding the objections of a small minority of blacks, who rightly felt the film glamorized the treatment of blacks in the army and their role in it, and a small group of whites, who felt the film exaggerated the role of blacks and described too close a contact between blacks and whites, the War Department approved wide distribution of the film. It was released to more than 3,500 white commercial theaters, and the army's chief of staff required all soldiers to see it. *The Negro Soldier,* a belated attempt to bolster morale and unity, not surprisingly overlooked numerous historical contradictions and completely ignored discrimination in the armed forces in the 1940s. One reviewer who complimented the film on its "distinct propaganda value" also asked, "When will truth and propaganda merge?"[181]

Despite the belief of some people that Capra's work sanctioned the historically segregated black army, blacks in general ignored the inequities of their situation and followed Joe Louis's example because they, like he, viewed soldiering as a way to prove their worth as Americans and break down the barriers of racism. They begged for the chance to fight, as typified in this emotional plea: "Train the Negro to fly those big bombers and fighter planes; give the Negro a good slap on the shoulder; treat him like an appreciated and loyal American soldier; give him a fair chance to operate submarines and warships and tanks and all of the modern devices used in modern warfare—then say to him 'go and do the job' and see how long Hitler's men can stand before them."[182]

While Hastie, Gibson, Trent, and Louis desperately hoped that *The Negro Soldier,* despite its inaccuracies, would have a positive effect with regard to racial issues, this was not achieved. In England, for example, entire towns would often be off-limits to black soldiers. Louis never used his celebrity status to gain special treatment, because he knew that for all his acclaim he was still a black man, a member of an oppressed group. The fact that he never lost sight of this endeared him to those people he stood above and with at the same time. Yet in spite of his quietness and his obvious use by the government, Louis fought injustice. While at Camp Sibert, Alabama, Joe Louis and Sugar Ray Robinson (a.k.a. Walker Smith) were ordered by military police at a bus station to sit in an area reserved for blacks; they refused and were taken into custody. Public outcry and Louis's reputation forced a change in policy.[183] Louis also helped to found an organization called Lend a Hand to Dixie, which attacked racial discrimination in the South.[184]

By war's end, Joe Louis had won boxing's most prestigious honor, the Edward Neil Memorial Award, for his sportsmanship and service. He was nominated for the Spingarn Medal for his civil rights work but narrowly lost to A. Phillip Randolph. In 1945 the army awarded him the prestigious Legion of Merit for his extraordinary service and sacrifice. Years later President Ronald Reagan, at the urging of Senator Paul Laxalt (who had been reminded by Truman Gibson of Louis's service to his country) bestowed an even greater honor on the Brown Bomber—burial in Arlington National Cemetery, the resting place of true military heroes.[185]

Although it is impossible to measure the extent to which Joe Louis helped to break down the color barrier or caused whites to look on blacks with favor, there can be no doubt as to his impact on his own people. Of course, not all blacks agreed with Louis's decision to cooperate with and represent the government and the armed forces. But he did command loyalty among his people, personifying their dilemma and offering a constructive, albeit far from perfect, solution. At the time, the choices of the black minority were not great. Noncooperation could engender resentment and repression, as Elijah Muhammad and his fellow Nation of Islam members discovered; unquestioning support could lead to the same experiences that followed the previous war. Louis, like a majority of black Americans, attempted to walk a tightrope between the two extremes, pursuing a course of extreme loyalty in public while quietly pressing for an end to discrimination. According to

Lawrence Levine, "No other contemporary member of the group was celebrated more fully and identified with more intensely by the black folk."[186] With such a role model, blacks could confidently enter the real fight for equality.

6

The Unholy Trinity
Television, Monopoly, and Crime

While World War II had taken much from boxing—New York State alone estimated a $75,000 loss in tax revenues with "Louis' shift from boxing trunks to an army uniform"—in the end the sport benefited from its patriotic sacrifices.[1] Soon the boxing industry was booming as impatient fans, who had suffered through wartime austerity, rushed to see boxing champions—many of them now war heroes—who had been held in suspended animation. In 1946 seven world championships protected during the war were contested. The biggest of them all was the long-awaited and much ballyhooed Joe Louis–Billy Conn rematch.[2]

Fans reacted as if the hands of time had stopped, as if June 18, 1941, were yesterday. Ringside seats for the rematch on June 19, 1946, sold for over $100 before the scalpers got them; in the end some 45,266 fans paid $1,925,564 to see an older, slower Brown Bomber manhandle his overweight, ring-rusty opponent. Conn himself called the fight a "stinkeroo,"[3] and it effectively ended his career, although after more than a year's absence he returned to the ring for two victories and a "swan song" exhibition in December 1948 with Louis.[4]

Due to the anticlimactic nature of the rematch, few people understood that the bout was a watershed in boxing, not because of the gate (it was surpassed only by the second Dempsey-Tunney fight) or the fact that millions listened to it on radios across America (that had been done before), but because it was the first heavyweight championship fight to be televised. The Louis-Conn rematch marked the beginning of a profound, profitable, but sometimes troublesome affair between boxing and the "picture box," a relationship that eventually turned symbiotic and then parasitic, nearly killing the host.

Birth of a Medium

By the 1920s radio had almost become commonplace in America, yet television, which was nearly as old, seemed to have little future. In the 1930s television was still a curious phenomenon of little social effect, the novelty stuff of international expositions.[5] One reporter at the 1939 New York World's Fair isolated television's problem: "People must sit and keep their eyes glued on a screen; the average American family hasn't time for it."[6] By 1946, however, Thomas H. Hutchinson, in *Here Is Television,* was enthusiastically proclaiming that "television means the world in your home and in the homes of all the people of the world. It is the greatest means of communication ever developed by the mind of man."[7] Time has apparently proven him correct. Television is a primary source of ideas and a most popular medium of entertainment, affecting the way in which we spend time with our families, transforming American politics, and influencing our outlook on the world.[8] When television merged with sport, America's games were forever changed.

In August 1931 the Columbia Broadcasting System's television station WZXAB broadcast a fight by "sight and sound," although satisfactory commercial undertakings did not begin until 1938.[9] Surprisingly, it was the government-owned and -operated British Broadcasting Corporation that spearheaded commercial development of the medium; even more surprising was the lead it took in profit-making sports broadcasts, such as the March 1939 transmission of the Eric Boon–Arthur Danahar fight for the championship of Great Britain. While the British did not intend to continue the commercial broadcasting of prizefights, their hesitancy did not deter American interests, which proceeded to catch up and quickly surpass the British pioneers. The National Broadcasting Company televised an exhibition bout between Lou Nova and Patsy Perroni in April 1939,[10] which was witnessed with great anticipation and optimism by promoters like Mike Jacobs, who saw a rosy future for televised boxing. Serious technical difficulties stood in the way of commercial success, however, since the extant telephoto lens could not bring the action in close enough for good viewing.[11]

By 1941 the television industry had made great strides toward commercialization, and prizefighting continued as its leading experimental subject. On May 9, 1941, the Radio Corporation of America, under the leadership of broadcast pioneer David Sarnoff, introduced large-screen theater television with the Billy Soos–Ken Oberlin championship fight, broadcast from Madison Square Garden to 1,400 "interested and privileged" guests seated in the New Yorker Theater. More than entertainment, this was a dress rehearsal designed to impress television's commercial potential upon sports executives, theater managers, and engineers. The equipment used included an optical system that was seven times more efficient than any previous system; it reproduced the action in the ring so clearly that virtually every blow was visible. Now the technology existed, but its cost prohibited widespread application.[12] Before the cost-profit threshold could be crossed, World War II intervened and research and development necessarily focused on defense production. Not until the war had ended did boxing and television resume their relationship.

Conceived in war, delayed by war, and hyped to limits reminiscent of the days of Tex Rickard, the rematch between Billy Conn and Joe Louis was a natural for television. The bout symbolized a return to normalcy, and the television and boxing industries were well aware that no other single event would so capture the nation's attention. Heavyweight championships were, according to Budd Schulberg, "a celebration, a ceremony, a profound rite, as truly a blood ritual as the sacrifice of the fighting bulls,"[13] and this would be the first televised championship.

Undistinguished and inferior coverage of such an event obviously would not do. New materials released from formerly inaccessible military stores enabled RCA to build "image orthocon" cameras with "turret" lenses that were 100 times as sensitive as prewar models. The resultant picture equaled the view from a seat approximately thirty feet from the ring. Despite the unevenness of the transmission, since prewar cameras were also used, the broadcast was a success. Yet television still lagged far behind radio in popularity and availability. The WJZ (New York) radio broadcast of the fight received a rating of 67.2 percent, far outdistancing the television rating.[14] Interestingly, most people who saw the fight watched it on someone else's television set. Reports from Washington told of the nation's legislators gathering at the Statler Hilton to witness the bout, while others watched it at special NBC locations. Few people were confident enough in the new medium to have purchased sets for viewing in the quiet and security of their homes.[15]

Perhaps the most common and revealing place for watching televised fights was the local bar. Tavern owners sensed that their customers were among the most rabid and knowledgeable boxing fans and invested early in television sets. "Fight Nights" were happenings, and the Louis-Conn rematch transcended all others. The scene at the Knife and Fork Tavern on Bleeker Street and West Broadway in New York City was typical of much of the East on June 19, 1946.[16]

Spectators inside and outside the bar watched the set, placed bets, and bragged about the virtues and economies of television viewing.

They expressed satisfaction with their vantage points, which they believed were "a hell of a lot better than a ringside seat" and certainly less expensive.[17] The excitement level rose as the owner turned the set on, the patrons seemingly as amazed by the medium as by the event. After the fight started viewers were attentive, but not always for the right reasons: often the principals would slip off the screen, to be brought back by the proprietor fiddling with the knobs; at other times the transmission came through so clearly that it swept the audience up in the illusion of being at the stadium. Some cried out, "Hit him, Billy!" only to be reminded that Conn could not hear them.[18] When panoramic shots reduced the size of the ring "to a tiny square of brightness with a couple of germs swimming in it," the customers hollered, "Fix it, Lou. We can't see nothing," or "Put us back on ringside, Lou." They did not realize that the "problem" emanated from the telecast, not from the set; nonetheless, the proprietor would finger a dial as if it might help matters. One spectator captured the essence of the event as she exclaimed, "First movies, now television! Next what?"[19]

The Louis-Conn rematch marked a new era and led boxing and television analyst Jack Gould to conclude that prizefighting's greatest moments on television came during the medium's infancy. The exchange was reciprocal, as word-of-mouth praise for the medium and the attendant publicity sold thousands of sets. By 1952 televised prizefights reached an average of 5 million homes; the figure rose to 8.5 million in 1955.[20] More significant than numbers, however, was the impact of televised boxing on diverse areas of society, not only changing people's habits but introducing new and unexpected social, economic, and legal forces that had to be accommodated. Specifically, the commercialization of television heightened the broadcasters' and users' concerns for ownership and gave rise to new and difficult legal questions. Boxing, a simple activity pitting man against man, found itself in the middle of complex legal battles that sometimes overshadowed and threatened those in the ring.

Commercialism and Legal Complications

By 1948 there were more than sixty television stations with an audience of 1,750,000; as estimates reached 65,000,000 by 1950, the networks maneuvered to limit and restrict use of their programs.[21] Fearing piracy and diminishing profits, televisors staked a claim to the air waves and tried to block transgressors. Prizefight telecasts were the catalysts for such concerns. The flurry of legal questions that arose included: (1) May a tavern pick up a television program for the entertainment of its customers without authorization from those who originate the telecast? (2) May a hotel furnish television to its guests in private rooms, perhaps rented at a premium, or in its public halls without the consent of the telecaster? (3) May a motion picture theater entertain its patrons by making television programs available, either on its regular motion picture screen or elsewhere in the theater, without authority?[22]

As a result of the Louis-Conn bout and subsequent improvements in broadcast technology, telecasts of boxing matches were in great demand.[23] For instance, on the eve of the second Joe Louis–Jersey Joe Walcott fight in 1948, the Hotel New Yorker reported that its television-equipped rooms were sold out. At the time the hotel had more sets under one roof than anywhere in the world—100 rooms with permanent sets and 50 wired for "roaming" sets.[24] One year later a televised fight was reportedly seen in 16,500 bars and restaurants in New York City alone.[25]

Success did not come easily, however. Just prior to the Louis-Walcott fight the promoters, the boxers, the broadcasters, and the sponsor of the match combined forces in a series of lawsuits to enjoin a motion picture theater operator in New York and a charitable organization in Boston from providing a telecast of the fight to paying patrons. In each instance the New York Supreme Court granted a temporary injunction, thus preventing unauthorized broadcasts of the contest. Although no opinion was offered, communications law scholar David Solinger reported that prevailing attitudes among jurists was that most national broadcasts by radio and television that did not fall under the category of news were protected by property rights legislation. Accordingly, promoters and broadcasters did have obvious quasi-property rights in a sporting event.[26]

Solinger's analysis was proven correct in 1971, when disputes arose over broadcast rights to the first Joe Frazier–Muhammad Ali fight. In this case promoters sought to halt an attempt by the Mutual Broadcasting Company to provide a summary after each round of the fight. Mutual had developed this ingenious plan to sidestep the ruling in *Twentieth Century Sporting Club, Inc.* v. *Transradio Press Service, Inc.* (1937),[27] in which the club successfully blocked Transradio's planned broadcast of a prizefight on the grounds that the use of the radio broadcast for its own news service was "an unlawful appropriation" of the quasi-property right that the club and the authorized broadcasting company had in the broadcast.[28] Mutual maintained, however, that by providing a summary after each round it was broadcasting news, not infringing on a property right. New York State Supreme Court Justice

Edward T. McCaffrey ruled in favor of Mutual, and a state appellate court upheld McCaffrey's decision.[29]

The problems of television and the law were complicated by the medium's commercial youth. Although in the 1940s laws regulating radio broadcasting also applied to the new medium of television, boxing-related tests of these laws soon forced a distinction. In 1949 the Maryland Court of Appeals rejected a promoter's claim that a contract to broadcast weekly fights via radio gave him the right to televise these matches. Judge Charles Markell concluded that "the privilege of broadcasting boxing bouts did not in 1941 and 1943, and does not now, include television."[30] His decision stood despite the fact that the Federal Communications Act (1934), in defining "radio communication," specifically included "the transmission by radio of pictures and sounds of all kinds."[31] Citing *Norman* v. *Century Athletic Club* as a precedent, subsequent decisions concluded that neither the promoter nor the radio station that held the broadcast rights could televise bouts except by agreement with the other.[32]

While the *Norman* decision established precedent in the area of broadcast law, one of the most revealing cases concerning the role of television and boxing in a changing society was *Ettore* v. *Philco* (1956),[33] for it showed how boxing had traveled light years since the days of side bets. The suit was brought in 1954 by Albert Ettore, a former professional boxer of no great fame, against the Philco Television Broadcasting Corporation for televising, without his permission, motion pictures of his fight with champion Joe Louis, staged some fifteen years earlier. Ettore, who still owned a percentage of the film rights, argued that the broadcast had violated his property rights.[34] Relying on *Norman,* the U.S. Court of Appeals for the Third Circuit concluded that "if a performer had contracted his services and the finished product is a motion picture in which the performer's services are embodied and the motion picture is employed in such a way as to deprive the performer of his right to compensation for the new use of the product, he is entitled to relief."[35] Simply put, the station had used the film for purposes that were unintended. Philco maintained that Ettore should have anticipated television broadcasts when he signed the contract, but the court, agreeing with scholarly observers, believed that in 1939 television was "little more than a gleam in inventors' eyes" and such a "different dimension" that Ettore could not have imagined the commercial potential when he signed the contract.[36]

Video broadcasts of boxing had, within a short time, created a vast audience for the sport. The new technology transformed prizefighting from a closed attraction to a mass spectator sport. While boxing itself remained the most basic of human activities, the business side of the sport was becoming incredibly modern, complex, and organized. That process would be accelerated by events in 1949, as the dominant individual entrepreneur, Mike Jacobs, gave way to the faceless corporation.

The Incorporation of Prizefighting

By December 1947 the declining health (due to heart trouble and old age) of Mike Jacobs gravely concerned both financial backers and managers of Madison Square Garden. His assistants had neither the personality nor the skill to maintain the operation. Boxing revenues, which peaked in 1947 at $1,246,000, fell to $646,000 by 1950.[37] Although many people blamed the ineptness of Sol Strauss, Jacobs's cousin and legal counsel, for the precipitous drop, television played a significant role.

The Tournament of Champions, Inc., a promotional subsidiary of the Columbia Broadcasting System, was formed in May 1947 by entrepreneurs who believed that boxing would help to develop television in the marketplace. Among the organizers were Lawrence Lowman, of CBS, and Charles Miller, of the Music Corporation of America. Shortly after its founding, the Tournament of Champions challenged the Twentieth Century Sporting Club by promoting the third bout between Rocky Graziano and Tony Zale, as well as Zale's loss to Marcel Cerdan; both were middleweight championship fights. The Tournament of Champions also promoted regular Wednesday night bouts, which were televised by CBS in competition with the Twentieth Century Club's Friday night contests on NBC. Before long the Tournament of Champions, which allowed boxers and their managers to negotiate for larger purses in an atmosphere of "free" competition, was engaged in a bitter promotional conflict with a weakened Twentieth Century Club.[38]

Then a shocking development occurred. On December 5, 1947, an aging Joe Louis defended his heavyweight title against "Jersey Joe" Walcott of Camden, New Jersey. Experts considered Walcott such a bad fighter that the bout was originally scheduled as an exhibition; it became a championship fight only at the insistence of the New York State Athletic Commission. The challenger knocked Louis from pillar to post, and only the judges' decision stood between him and the championship. Before the announcer read the cards Louis admitted defeat by leaving the ring. Then came the words, "Winner and still champion, Joe Louis." The champion was as stunned as his crestfallen opponent. The verdict met with widespread criticism, and prominent boxing writer Jimmy Cannon maintained that if any other fighter had fallen heir to such bad judgment, there would have been full-scale legislative and legal investigations.[39] Louis was not at all deluded by the outcome. His performance convinced him that the end of his boxing career was near, but financial considerations and pride prevented his immediate retirement. Although he knocked out Walcott in a rematch, he was determined to retire soon.

Louis had discussed his problem with Harry Mendel, a New Jersey press agent and promoter; the two men had become friends after Mike Jacobs hired Mendel to work as a publicist at one of Louis's training camps. While on a cross-country exhibition tour with Louis after the Walcott rematch, Mendel allegedly conceived a plan to control the heavyweight championship. (Although Gibson claimed it was his idea, boxing historian Barney Nagler refers to it as the "Mendel Plan" and credits Gibson with its execution, not its conception.) Under this simple, yet effective plan a new corporation, Joe Louis Enterprises, Inc., would be formed to contract the exclusive services of the four leading contenders for the heavyweight title—at the time they were Ezzard Charles, Joe Walcott, Lee Savold, and either Gus Lesnevich or Joey Maxim. Louis would then resign as champion and Joe Louis Enterprises would assign the four exclusive contracts to any individual or corporation ready and able to pay for the right to promote world heavyweight championship fights. The winner of the first match would be declared the champion and would then defend his title against the next challenger. Louis would retain radio, television, and movie rights.

Harry Voiler, a Florida hotel owner with connections to the Hearst press and tangential ties to boxing, was offered 49 percent of the corporation's stock in exchange for $100,000; Louis would hold the remaining 51 percent. When Voiler would not or could not provide the capital, Louis exerted pressure on Gibson to offer the plan to David Charnay, one of several partners in the Tournament of Champions. Charnay was not interested, at which point Mendel suggested that James Dougan Norris and Arthur Wirtz might buy the idea. Norris was a Madison Square Garden stockholder and heir to a huge financial empire built on grain speculation, real estate, liquor distribution, and large indoor stadium holdings; Wirtz was his partner.[40] Mendel called Norris for an appointment and Louis, Gibson, and Mendel met Norris in Florida. After relieving a hangover by hitting golf balls with Louis, Norris considered the idea, liked it, and asked the men to present the plan to Wirtz. After long and hard negotiations with considerable concessions by Louis, an agreement was reached, marking the establishment of the International Boxing Club (IBC) of New York. Norris and Wirtz paid Louis $150,000 in cash ($100,000 less than he had demanded) and gave him an employment contract and a 20-percent stock interest in the IBC.[41]

After receiving exclusive promotional rights to Charles, Walcott, Savold, and Lesnevich, Louis assigned them to the IBC and retired from boxing. Then Mendel, who was a friend of Abe Greene, president of the National Boxing Association, convinced Greene to recognize the winner of the first fight as the heavyweight champion. With the Mendel-Gibson plan in hand, Norris approached Madison Square Garden officials in March 1949 and warned them that it was in everyone's best interest to "work together now and keep the events for our buildings and not create a competitive situation that would be harmful to us all."[42] Without Joe Louis, who had walked out on him, Mike Jacobs could not fight back. In a move to reverse its sagging fortunes, the Garden bought out Jacobs's interests, including his exclusive leases with Yankee Stadium and the St. Nicholas Arena, as well as his contract with Sugar Ray Robinson, and assigned all of these to the IBC. This virtually ensured IBC control of nearly half of all championship boxing in the United States. For example, from 1937 to 1949, 45 percent of all championship bouts were held in Yankee Stadium, the Polo Grounds, or St. Nicholas Arena.[43] No wonder the IBC became known as the "Octopus."

With the acquisition of Jacobs's holdings, the one substantial competitor in New York boxing promotions was the Tournament of Champions, which had an exclusive lease with the Polo Grounds and an exclusive contract covering the next two fights of Marcel Cerdan, the middleweight champion of the world. In May 1949 Norris, through the Garden, bought out the Tournament of Champions. Although he paid dearly, the acquisition gave the IBC the potential for a virtual monopoly on a national basis.[44] Under the terms of the agreement, Norris paid $50,000 plus 25 percent of the net profits on the next two middleweight championship matches. CBS agreed, in perpetuity, not to invest in or promote any professional boxing matches in return for the right of first refusal to the broadcasting of certain matches staged at Madison Square Garden.[45]

In a period of four months the IBC had acquired exclusive control of the promotion of boxing matches in the heavyweight, middleweight, and welterweight divisions. It strengthened this hold by requiring each contender for the title to grant it exclusive promotional rights to his championship fights for a three- to five-year period.[46] Norris then increased his stockholdings in Madison Square Garden until he held a controlling interest and could thereby dictate the Garden's policies and boxing activities. This, combined with his ownership of Chicago Stadium, the Detroit Olympia, and the St. Louis Arena, gave Norris near total control over the participants, the sites, and the broadcast of boxing, or so he and many others believed. He was the president of Madison Square Garden, the IBC (New York), and the IBC (Illinois) and its parent company, the Chicago Stadium Corporation; he and Wirtz held directorships in all four organizations.[47]

A monopoly had quickly fallen into place. In the four-year period from March 1949, when the IBC staged its first championship fight, until May 1953, it held or controlled the promotional rights to thirty-six of forty-four championship prizefights staged in the United States, which included all of the championships in the heavyweight and middleweight divisions.[48] Clearly, the IBC controlled boxing, but who really controlled the IBC? It was not Joe Louis, who preferred golf to the rigors of business management; within a year after his appointment, Truman Gibson had taken over most of his duties. Norris and Wirtz had the titles, the money, the stock, and the legitimate contacts, but even that did not ensure control.[49]

Sharks and the Octopus

With all his wealth (estimated at $50,000,000–$400,000,000), James Norris anticipated few difficulties in running the boxing industry. However, problems arose with the Boxing Managers Guild of New York, which had been incorporated in November 1944 as a social club and benevolent protective union organization composed of managers and matchmakers, their purpose being to maximize both their own and the fighters' share of the live gate and broadcast revenues. The guild's leading figures were Jack Kearns, Bill Daly, "Tex" Pelte, Herman Wallman, and Charles Johnston—a rogue's gallery.[50]

In April 1949 the New York local of the Boxing Managers Guild struck the IBC and settled for a $1,000 share, above and beyond the purse, for each fighter who participated in a televised main event.[51] A year later, after making renewed demands for an increased share of television revenues, which the IBC considered excessive, the guild struck and picketed Madison Square Garden. Its action put a stop to boxing at the Garden and at St. Nicholas Arena for nearly two months, with the exception of the Jake LaMotta–Tiberio Mitri fight on July 7. On July 14 the guild and the IBC "settled," the agreement calling for a 2-percent allocation of the broadcast receipts for headline fights if that portion exceeded a guarantee of $4,500.[52] The strikers had Norris and the televised media tugging at their hair. Sponsors were clamoring about the instability of the boxing industry and had driven Norris to exasperation.

Problems with the guild continued until 1953, when Gibson and

Norris decided to make payments to Kearns and Pelte for peacekeeping purposes at the rate of $135,000 over the next three years.[53] Kearns, whom Randy Roberts describes as a man of "great courage and no ethics or morality," had not changed since his managerial tenure with Jack Dempsey, when he would "cheat, push, or connive his fighters to the top."[54] Although Gibson maintained that the payments were designed to ensure a steady flow of fighters without interruption from strikers, they represented, clearly and simply, protection money.[55] Shortly thereafter the IBC, through a subsidiary, the Neville Advertising Agency, secured the services of Miss Viola Masters—the future Mrs. Paul John "Frankie" Carbo. Gibson would later testify before a Senate investigating committee that she had been paid "to counterbalance or to negate any possible ill effect" from the Kearns arrangement, since Kearns and Carbo were "deadly enemies." This assessment was either deceptive or naïve, because Carbo controlled most of the managers in the Boxing Managers Guild of New York and at least one meeting between Carbo and Norris on boxing-related matters took place at Kearns's home; Bill Daly, a close associate of both Kearns and Carbo was also there.[56] Norris disagreed with Gibson, denying the counterbalance notion and frankly admitting that Viola Masters was simply a conduit for payoff money to Frankie Carbo. The IBC could not risk open and formal association with Carbo, but it needed him to keep the guild in line. The relationship between the IBC and the nefarious Carbo was paradoxically described by Norris as a "reluctant one" that he in some ways actively "sought out."[57] Who was Frankie Carbo and what did he have to offer to a legitimate business enterprise?

A Microcosm of Organized Crime

Despite predictions that it would signal the end of entrepreneurial crime, World War II ushered in a new and even more profitable era. According to Humbert Nelli in *The Business of Crime,* the war's diversion of public attention from the activities of crime syndicates, its shortages, its need for cooperation at any price between capital and labor, and its "frenzied emphasis on pleasure to compensate for the pains of sacrifice" produced the perfect climate for corruption.[58] Americans tended not to pay much attention to organized crime because it did not affect them—or so they thought. Crime commission reports from California, Michigan, and Illinois soon brought the matter to the public's and the federal government's attention, however. On September 14, 1949, Mayor DeLesseps Morrison of New Orleans, president of the American Municipal Association, asked the federal government to investigate the influence of organized crime on municipal government.[59] In December of that same year the association appealed to the U.S. Justice Department for aid against racketeering, insisting that the problem was too large to be handled by local officials because of the interstate nature of the crimes. Interstate gambling, in particular, had become a most serious problem.[60]

The criminal activities associated with the fight game were indicative of this larger problem. The cast of characters was the same, the tactics were the same, and so were the difficulties of detection and control. There were many villains, more victims, and few heroes. One of the latter brought the problem of racketeering in prizefighting to the surface. He knew both the extent and the depth of the cancer, yet only after more than twelve years of investigations, surveillances, arrests, and trials was he able to bring the central figure to justice and into the hands of the law.

In December 1946 Frank S. Hogan exploded on the scene, a virtual one-man crusade against sports gambling. What the television version of Elliot Ness was to the illegal alcohol trade, the real Frank Hogan was to criminal infiltration in sport. Formerly a vigilant assistant to Thomas Dewey, he made his mark with the arrest of the notorious gambler Alvin J. Paris.[61] A wiretap on Paris's phone revealed that he had attempted to bribe two members of the New York (football) Giants to throw the championship game with the Chicago Bears in 1946. Hogan also learned of betting information Paris had apparently passed along regarding an upcoming fight between Charley Fusari, a promising young welterweight, and Charles "Chuck" Taylor. New York detectives had reported earlier that insiders tipped them that the fight would be fixed, and these suspicions were substantiated by a switching of odds and the hedging of bets by local bookmakers.[62] The use of the telephone to place bets occurred regularly—just one year earlier, gambler Samuel Solomon, better known as Sam Boston, had been convicted of accepting boxing-related bets on his home telephone[63]—but detection and prosecution remained difficult.

These activities were overshadowed by the revelations of Rocky Graziano in 1947, following the mysterious cancellation of a scheduled bout against Ruben "Cowboy" Shank. Graziano had been a prohibitive favorite to beat Shank, but outside New York bettors put large sums on the underdog, indicating that insiders knew the outcome in advance.[64] Three days before the fight Graziano announced that he had suffered a lower back injury and would not be able to fight. Suspecting foul play, District Attorney Hogan and his aides questioned Graziano on January 26, 1947, and subpoenaed him to appear before the grand jury.[65] Graziano admitted under oath that he had been offered $100,000 to throw the fight and had feigned injury because he did not want to lose purposely; nor did he wish to face the consequences of double-crossing those who had tried to bribe him. This was not an isolated incident, for Graziano testified that bribes had been offered on three other occasions: one in May 1945, in a bout against Al Davis, and two in connection with Shank.[66] When Graziano refused to identify the three people who had made the offer, Hogan clearly understood the strength of his enemy and how fear had motivated this particular boxer's actions.

Politicians made the scandal a cause célèbre and seized the opportunity for public grandstanding and political point scoring. New York State Senator Isadore Dollinger, a Bronx Democrat, called for a legislative investigation. Sounding more like an attack on the Republican-led state government, his resolution declared that boxing fans had been "duped, fleeced, and otherwise damaged" and that the New York State Athletic Commission, under Edward Eagan, had failed to examine or correct the abuses.[67] As time would show, neither the legislature nor the commission seemed committed to a sustained attack on sports gambling or racketeering.

On February 7, 1947, NYSAC concluded that Graziano's decision to withhold information constituted a violation of the commission's rules governing collusion and sham exhibitions. Unable or unwilling to get at the criminals, it ruled Graziano's behavior detrimental to the best interests of boxing and revoked his license. Many people condemned the harsh penalty, especially when it appeared certain to destroy Graziano's chance to fight Tony Zale for the championship. However, subsequent events exposed both the hypocrisy and futility of the commission's actions.[68]

Shortly after the Graziano scandal, Sugar Ray Robinson, the welterweight champion, reported that he, too, had been approached by criminals who wanted him to weigh in over the limit for his bout with Marty Servo. Investigators caught Robinson in an apparent lie when reporter Lester Bromberg testified that in fact Robinson had been offered a bribe not to fight Servo. Robinson's penalty was a $500 fine and a thirty-day suspension.[69] Abe Greene argued authoritatively that the episode reeked of "unbalanced justice, if not of political witch hunting,"[70] and NYSAC's record in such matters certainly supported his charges. Greene pointed out that Freddie Fiducia had tried to report a bribe but the commission refused him an audience; he went ahead with the fight in question, then received a sixty-day suspension. Al Davis, who had been suspended for life in 1941, boxed six months later in the Polo Grounds; he was an easy target for bribers.[71] Even with Graziano the commission's rulings were ineffective, as he beat Tony Zale for the middleweight championship on July 16, 1947, in Chicago.[72] Independent state control of the sport clearly undermined each commission's punitive capability.

Hogan knew that boxing's problems ran far deeper than Paris, Graziano, Davis, Fiducia, or Robinson. Examples of worthy fighters being denied matches were commonplace because the boxers would not submit to the demands of racketeers. Most serious and prevalent was the criminal infiltration of the managerial profession. To correct the situation Hogan embarked on a sweeping campaign to expose and prosecute managers with criminal records. Although he mentioned no names, his sights were clearly set on the man he referred to as the "leading light" among the racketeers, a man who had the largest piece of many prominent fighters, despite the fact that he could not obtain a manager's license because of his long and serious list of crimes. The relentless district attorney noted that after the Graziano scandal this character had been missing from his usual haunts along "Jacobs' Beach," the nickname of the area near Mike Jacobs's Broadway ticket agency,[73] and that he had once testified before the New York State Athletic Commission that he did everything for Jacobs except sign commission form contracts.[74] The mystery man was none other than Frankie Carbo, a.k.a. "The Ambassador," "Mr. Gray," and "The Superintendent."

The Boss of Boxing

Born in New York City on August 10, 1904, Carbo wasted little time beginning his life of crime. At age twelve he was sent to a Catholic reform school. Carbo's police record shows seventeen arrests, escalating from vagrancy and suspicious character to felonious assault, grand larceny, robbery, and murder. In the language of his world, Frankie Carbo was "no two-bit petty criminal."[75] His first homicide charge came in 1924 when he was indicted for killing a cab driver. Carbo pleaded guilty to a lesser charge of manslaughter then fled from justice, spending four years at large before being apprehended and sent to Sing Sing Prison for a year. His most notorious murder-connected arrest came in 1939, following the Thanksgiving Day shooting of Harry Schacter (a.k.a. Harry Greenberg and "Big Greeney"), a member of the infamous Murder Inc. gang, outside his home in Hollywood, California. Among those indicted for the crime were Louis "Lepke" Buchalter, Benjamin "Bugsy" Siegel, and Frankie Carbo.[76] Al Tannenbaum, a member of Murder Inc., testified that Siegel had driven the getaway car and Carbo had fired five bullets into Schacter. The first trial ended in a hung jury; and during the second trial, the chief prosecution witness, Abe "Kid Twist" Reles, also of Murder Inc., fell or was pushed to his death from a hotel room window in Coney Island, ruining the prosecution's chances for a conviction.[77]

Carbo's record, and especially his connection to Murder Inc., boded ill for prizefighting, and his disproportionately low number of convictions pointed to the difficulties Frank Hogan and other scrupulous officials would have in attacking the criminal infiltration of sport. The Carbo–Murder Inc. connection also revealed a great deal about the sociology of organized crime; indeed, the multiethnic constituency of Murder Inc. spoke volumes about the expanding and coherent structure of criminal activity in the United States. As a result of prohibition, bootlegging became a new criminal occupation with less risk of punishment, greater potential for gain, and less social stigma. Organized crime began to take on many of the characteristics of legitimate business and served as a springboard into legal operations for criminals. Also, with the formation of heterogeneous gangs, many of the social and cultural distinctions that had separated the various ethnic groups of the underworld were dissolved. Subsequent criminal ventures had a mixed-ethnic flavor, as in labor racketeering under Albert Anastasia. When criminals infiltrated prizefighting, these ethnically mixed groups still figured prominently, as will become evident.[78]

After Carbo revealed to the New York State Athletic Commission that he controlled Mike Jacobs and the New York boxing market, NYSAC responded by fining the Twentieth Century Club $2,500.[79] The commission's action, a mere slap on the wrist, not only raised serious questions about NYSAC's sincerity but also revealed the extent of Carbo's power. Hogan's hands were tied because the New York State Assembly had not yet passed a law making it illegal to act as a manager, promoter, or second without a license; when it did, in June 1947, the penalty for violation was a laughable one-year prison sentence and a $5,000 fine.[80] For example, Jimmy Plumeri, alias Jimmy Doyle, appeared before Hogan's "boxing grand jury" and boasted that his record of one conviction out of nine arrests attested to his "political influence."[81]

There was little reason to think that Hogan could do any better against Carbo, especially when so many people were unwilling to help him or even take the matter seriously. A tongue-in-cheek column in the *New York Times* reflected the cavalier approach of the press, summoning sportswriters to investigate the situation because it would be "a lot of fun" but would reveal little.[82] The *Times* pointed to the "unblemished" record and image of Joe Louis to support its belief that crime was a matter of small significance in boxing. That Louis remained the bellwether of the sport is obvious from the newspaper's conclusion that "it may be stated with complete confidence that no professional gambler had approached him with a huge bribe, the election returns here speak for themselves."[83] Despite the sarcasm, even the most critical writers believed Joe Louis possessed an untouchable quality that at least kept his division clean. Jimmy Cannon, a boxing expert, called prizefighting "the swill barrel of sports," yet he admitted never having heard that Louis was party to a crooked fight. Despite Mike Jacobs's association with Carbo, most people believed that he never let his criminal friends tamper with the conduct of fights because he was convinced that fixed fights could only hurt the game; there was simply too much to lose should Louis's image be tarnished by gambling scandals.[84]

For all his efforts in the cause of justice, Frank Hogan found few allies, even from expected sources. John P. Powers, assistant attorney general of New York State, called Hogan's grand jury findings "interesting reading," but he did not believe they proved boxing to be as "heinous a sport as has been pointed out."[85] As for NYSAC, it reaffirmed its commitment to ensuring the integrity of the game but gave more attention to defending its own lax policies and enforcement efforts.[86] Sol Strauss, director of the Twentieth Century Sporting Club, boasted, "We've been investigated and what did they find? Nothing!"[87] Like so many others Strauss believed that boxing was a political football, "dead game for any legislator who wants his name in the papers."[88]

Ironically, Hogan's best ally was Hollywood, the "capital of make believe." The release of *Body and Soul,* a fictional yet representative account of prizefighting that starred John Garfield, stirred anger and fear among the game's functionaries.[89] Charles Johnston, president of the Boxing Managers Guild of New York, protested that the movie portrayed the protagonist as a fighting champion too eager "to take a dive" and painted the managers as "thieves, gangsters, fixers, connivers, double-crossers." He resented the "untrue and uncomplimentary" aspersions,[90] yet what really seemed to bother him was the truth. Indeed, if the film deserved criticism it was for understating rather than exaggerating boxing's ills.

The plight of Philadelphia-based fighter Ike Williams indicated both the geographic extent and the widespread impact of criminal infiltration in boxing.[91] Williams, the lightweight champion from 1947 to 1951, testified under oath in December 1960 that he had been boycotted in 1946 by the International Boxing Managers Guild and could not obtain fights until Frank "Blinky" Palermo became his manager.[92] Palermo, who had a manager's license, was the reputed numbers king of Philadelphia and maintained close ties to Mickey Cohen, a West Coast racketeer; John Vitale, the underworld leader in St. Louis; and Frankie Carbo.

Palermo, as Carbo's chief lieutenant, played a significant role in boxing for over twenty years.[93]

Like so many others in the profession, Williams had faced a classic dilemma: damned if he did and damned if he didn't. His options limited, he submitted to the mob but paid a heavy price. Williams claimed that Palermo stole two of his championship purses, amounting to $65,000, although the money may have been taken as payment for cash advanced to him by his manager. Unfortunately, fighters kept very bad financial records and rarely knew how much they owed; their benefactors often fudged records and charged exhorbitant interest. Williams also reported that he had received uncounted bribe offers to lose major contests and that Palermo had always relayed the messages.[94]

One such offer, which Williams refused, came in a scheduled fight against Freddy Dawson in 1948. About ten minutes before the bout, Williams allegedly received information that officials would take the fight from him, and he informed writers Red Smith, John Webster, and Jack Sarnes, "After I fight tonight, come back, I'll have a story for you."[95] When word reached the officials that Williams planned to talk to reporters, they decided to play it straight. Williams won the fight and was later fined $500 for casting doubt on the integrity of the officials. Interestingly, the chairman of the Pennsylvania State Athletic Commission, which assessed the fine, was Leo Raines, a friend of Blinky Palermo; they had earlier traveled together to California to watch Williams fight.

LaMotta and the Mob

Perhaps no series of events indicated the degree of influence and control organized crime wielded over boxing than that which surrounded Jacob "Jake" LaMotta, the "Raging Bull." Long considered the uncrowned middleweight champion, LaMotta attributed his predicament to an unwillingness to cooperate with underworld figures. Then, after years of frustration, he tried to make a deal in June 1947 that would propel him to the championship. His brother and quasi-manager, Joseph "Joey" LaMotta, supposedly relayed an offer of $100,000 to throw a fight against the handsome Tony Janiro. LaMotta said he would lose only for a guaranteed title opportunity, which the bribers refused. Consequently, LaMotta beat Janiro to a pulp for ten rounds.[96] Connected with that offer was Joseph Di Carlo, known in the underworld as "The Boss" and "The Wolf," who police had characterized in 1934 as "Buffalo's Public Enemy Number One."[97] Di Carlo's long criminal record included numerous arrests for assault, vagrancy, and violation of election laws. He also wielded considerable power in Buffalo politics and controlled the city's labor racket. Among his close associates were Mike Lascari, brother-in-law of Charles "Lucky" Luciano; the Fishetti brothers, members of the Al Capone gang; and Frankie Carbo.[98]

Harry Stromberg (a.k.a. Hyman Chaim, Joe Bloom, and, more commonly, Nig Rosen) also was implicated in the attempted fix of the LaMotta-Janiro fight. He had an arrest record commensurate with his aliases, including robbery, illegal possession of firearms, attempted burglary, unlawful flight to avoid prosecution, suspicion of possessing narcotics for sale, and conspiracy to run an illegal lottery. Among Stromberg's associates were Meyer Lansky, the notorious international criminal, "Big Al" Polizzi of Cleveland, and Frankie Carbo, with whom he had been partners in a New Jersey bookmaking enterprise. Stromberg's influence in boxing extended over Herman Taylor, Philadelphia's leading promoter, Felix Bocchicchio, the manager of Jersey Joe Walcott, and Blinky Palermo.[99] Clearly, the already expansive criminal network in boxing was growing rapidly. Less than a year after the Janiro incident the underworld was able to guarantee LaMotta a shot at the middleweight championship in exchange for a loss.

On November 14, 1947, Billy Fox, an undefeated black light heavyweight with an incredible forty-three straight knockouts, fought Jake LaMotta. A convincing win by Fox would not only position him for a title fight against champion Gus Lesnevich but improve the betting odds for his next bout. When Fox knocked out a passive and powerless LaMotta in four rounds, the New York State Athletic Commission withheld the purses of both boxers and began a so-called investigation on November 17.[100] LaMotta claimed that an internal injury had debilitated him. When questioned about the dramatic change in betting odds just before the fight, he said that gamblers had apparently learned of his injury, although he had concealed it from the commission, the examining physician, and even his own manager.[101] NYSAC accepted LaMotta's story but concluded that such action for personal gain militated against the best interests of boxing and fined him $1,000, ordered his indefinite suspension, and kept both purses. Seven months later, under threat of a lawsuit, the commission lifted the suspension.

Democrats in the state assembly labeled the investigation a cover-up.[102] Certainly no one could convincingly explain why the examining physician had been unable to detect the alleged injury before the fight. Critics considered the Fox-LaMotta debacle the culmination of a whole series of questionable bouts resulting from the inaction or incompetence of much-criticized commission chairman Edward Eagan, who Democrats accused of failing to probe deeply into alleged underworld links to New York boxing. If the fight had been fixed, however, the criminals had covered their tracks so well that Assistant District Attorney Alfred J. Scotti, head of the Rackets Bureau of the New York County District Attorney's Office, turned up nothing in an independent criminal investigation.[103]

Out of this furor came a legislative ruling to fingerprint applicants for boxing-related licenses and to deny licenses to anyone who had been convicted of a felony or certain misdemeanors. Unfortunately, the law had little effect on undercover managers and the manipulation of fighters by the underworld.[104] The depth of the problem went unnoticed until Jake LaMotta revealed the "true" story in 1960 at the Kefauver hearings on professional boxing, which focused on criminal and monopolistic activity in the sport.[105] According to LaMotta, his brother Joey had relayed an offer from Blinky Palermo, Fox's manager of record, and Bill Daly, another Carbo associate, to throw the fight with Fox. LaMotta refused to lose for money but agreed to accept the offer when Thomas Milo, the moneyman in the New York underworld, assured him that a championship fight would come his way. According to LaMotta, no one expected that he would lose so badly, but it was his way of telling the world that he was losing on purpose.

On February 28, 1947, Billy Fox met Gus Lesnevich for the light heavyweight title, losing in ten rounds; he also lost a rematch one year later, suffering a first-round knockout that effectively burst the overrated fighter's bubble.[106] After the underworld allowed the air to clear, it arranged a middleweight championship fight between the Raging Bull and Frenchman Marcel Cerdan.[107] According to LaMotta, he had to pay $20,000 to Lew Burston and Sam Richman, American representatives of Cerdan and close associates of Frankie Carbo. Since his share of the purse amounted to only $19,000, LaMotta claimed that he covered the difference by betting $10,000 on himself to win. Both Burston and Richman denied knowledge of the $20,000 ransom for the crown, and when he was questioned, Joey LaMotta pleaded the Fifth Amendment.[108] Many others did the same.

This refusal to testify at the Kefauver hearings underscored the problem of dealing with organized crime. A code of silence, both voluntary and forced, proved a major obstacle to law enforcement. Although neither Jake LaMotta nor anyone else would admit that Frankie Carbo was behind the fixes and bribes, investigators were sure that he was.[109] Frank Hogan continued his quest but did not succeed until Carbo's fingerprints had covered much of boxing via his association with the IBC.

An example of the International Boxing Club's leadership and power in the fight game. From a drawing by George Lee. (Truman Gibson)

Racketeer and boxing czar Frankie Carbo was taken from his prison cell to testify before the Senate Anti-trust and Monopoly Subcommittee on December 14, 1960. Carbo refused to cooperate, pleading the Fifth Amendment thirty times. (UPI/Bettmann Newsphotos)

District Attorney Frank S. Hogan of New York, Frankie Carbo's chief adversary, testifies before a congressional committee on May 11, 1961. (UPI/Bettmann Newsphotos)

Television and the Feeding of a Monster

In the relationship between television and the International Boxing Club, the villain cannot be easily identified. To many observers the
IBC, which clearly monopolized the sport, was the devil to which
television had sold its soul. The industry supported this feeling, claiming
that its partnership with the boxing organization stemmed from necessity.
Television executives explained that in their early efforts to provide
weekly broadcasts they were frustrated by haphazard and unreliable
arrangements with jackleg promoters; the IBC, however, was a reliable
operative. In the course of events, each used the other to its own
advantage. While television helped the monopolistic and criminally
infiltrated IBC to expand, it also captured high ratings and exerted
influence over the IBC and boxing in general. In 1952 televised fights
reached an average 5 million homes, representing a whopping 31 percent of the available audience; by 1955, that figure climbed to 8.5
million, with the IBC pulling in $90,000 per week. In less scientific
terms, boxing in the 1950s reportedly sold as many television sets as
Milton Berle, and it rivaled "I Love Lucy" in the ratings. Fans could
watch prizefights nearly every night of the week.[110]
The almost exclusive association between the IBC and television
eventually threatened the viability of the sport, for it drastically reduced
attendance at small boxing clubs. These local clubs were to boxing what
the minor leagues were to baseball; as they declined so did the number
and quality of available boxers.[111] By 1952 experts reported that the
ranks of professional boxers had been depleted by 50 percent and "town
fight nights" had been wiped out. Newspaperman Arthur Daley aptly
described the situation: "Then came television, on Wednesday for suds
[Pabst Blue Ribbon beer] and on Friday for blades [Gillette razor blades].
There aren't that many good prize fighters any more. They are brought
up before they are ready for that quick buck. They go down as fast as
they rise."[112] Indeed, television's role in boxing raised the issue of who
was in control of the sport.
A 1953 fight between lightweight champion Jimmy Carter and
Tommy Collins of Boston underscored this concern. Before a large
television audience the veteran Carter floored the inexperienced Collins
more than ten times. Critics blamed the sponsors and the network for
the poor showing,[113] but no one involved with the fight really wanted to
take responsibility for it. The IBC blamed the Boston sportswriters who
had plugged it; Sam Silverman, the Boston promoter who had arranged
it; and the Massachusetts State Boxing Commission, which had approved
it. A. Craig Smith, a Gillette company spokesman, told the critics, "You

can't make a tea party out of a boxing match," and then scoffed at the suggestion that sponsors controlled or should control the matches. To such charges he snidely retorted, "We don't know anything about fighting, our business is razor blades."[114] As broadcaster, NBC had no official comment on the affair; unofficially, it disclaimed responsibility for the event, the control of which rested "within the hands of the lawful body set up to supervise such matters." When queried as to why it had not stopped transmission, NBC responded that its switchboard would have been deluged by angry fans wanting to know what had transpired.[115]

Despite the denials of the network and the sponsor, both may have had a great deal of influence as to who fought and the nature of the fight. An early ending to the main attraction might result in a substitute fight and the possible quick switching of the dial by home viewers, which did not appeal to the network or the sponsor. There was even the possibility that they exerted pressure on ring officials, who ultimately decide whether to stop a fight based on the condition of one or both of the fighters. Moreover, many observers alleged that sponsors helped to change the style of boxers. Charles Einstein of *Harper's* described the typical boxer of the time: "Today's fighter is primarily a slugger. The boxer, the hitter, the combination man is gone. The sponsor does not want him. The sponsor wants a man who'll sell his product, somebody popular, and colorful."[116] What Einstein spoke of was a "media creation," whose first and most important characteristic was that he be white. According to Truman Gibson, television sponsors were particularly sensitive to the overexposure of blacks, and the record bears him out. Even a popular entertainer like Nat King Cole could not attract one national sponsor for his show, which departed the airwaves after fifty-nine consecutive weeks. Cole blamed the advertising industry for not trying to sell his program to a national account, claiming that "the advertising industry and their big clients didn't want their products associated with Negroes."[117] He astutely observed that "racial prejudice is more finance than romance,"[118] a position the advertising industry and its clients held with regard to boxing. All-black boxing matches, like all-black shows, were not desirable.

One of the most famous media creations was Charles P. Davey, a National Collegiate Athletic Association boxing champion from Michigan State University. White, attractive, and flashy, Davey became a great success on the video screen after a considerable number of professional fights. Television fans thought that he was unbeatable, not recognizing that his success rested in part on a shrewd, well-handled buildup. Matched against opponents who fitted his style, Davey appeared to be a far better boxer than he was. Not until he received a devastating beating at the hands of welterweight titleholder Kid Gavilan in 1953 did fans realize that he was not championship material.[119]

Carbo and Control

Although Frankie Carbo was added to the IBC payroll in 1954, in the form of payments to his fiance, Viola Masters, he had exerted considerable influence within the organization before that date. In 1951, for example, Jake LaMotta would not agree to an IBC-promoted bout with Sugar Ray Robinson until he had consulted with Carbo. In fact, Carbo even had a hand in setting the terms for an IBC heavyweight championship bout between Rocky Marciano and Jersey Joe Walcott.[120]

After four heartbreaking attempts at the heavyweight title, Walcott finally took the crown from Ezzard Charles, a black boxer, on July 18, 1951, and successfully defended his title in a rematch with Charles one year later. Then, on September 23, 1952, Walcott lost the championship to Rocky Marciano, the "Brockton Blockbuster." An aging Walcott had outboxed the rugged, aggressive, and unstylistic young Marciano for twelve rounds, until his tired old legs and punch-weary arms gave way to relentless youth. A bloody, battered Marciano, drawing upon seemingly endless inner reserves, won the title in round thirteen,[121] the first white heavyweight champion in fifteen years. But unlike the days of old, there was no running and hiding from black opponents. The public demanded a rematch, and Marciano agreed to a May 15, 1953, meeting in Chicago. However, the challenger's demands threatened to delay or cancel the fight. The issue was financial, not racial. Felix Bocchicchio, Walcott's manager, was holding out for more money, and James Norris evidently asked Frankie Carbo for assistance. Carbo and Bocchicchio discussed the fight with Gibson and Norris, and according to Gibson, "The result of the conversation was disastrous for us because we paid $250,000 for the challenger which antagonized Marciano and forever alienated him from us."[122] Chances are good that Carbo was responsible for Bocchicchio holding out in the first place.

After 1954 Carbo's role in the IBC escalated dramatically. He first acted as a "convincer" in lining up four former champions for IBC bouts: LaMotta, Carmen Basilio, Willie Pep, and Tony Demarco.[123] Shortly thereafter, through Billy Brown, an IBC undercard matchmaker, Carbo allegedly began to arrange fights in New York. More than one manager admitted to the impossibility of getting matches in New York without Carbo's approval.[124] By 1955 he had taken over the IBC, according to Aaron Kohn, managing director of the New Orleans Crime Commission. Kohn stated that Carbo and a New Orleans businessman,

Blaize D'Antoni, had visited James Norris in his New York office. Carbo, approaching a wall map of the United States, told them, "Jim, from now on you got the upstairs, Dan's [D'Antoni] got the downstairs"; as he spoke his finger moved across the width of the map, slicing the country in half.[125]

Just what did Carbo have that could make an otherwise powerful Norris agree to such an arrangement? Clearly, the IBC needed Carbo more than he needed it. Although Norris had the media, the sites, and the license to operate, he could do nothing without fighters—and they were controlled by Carbo through his hold over managers and match-makers. According to Truman Gibson, Carbo's control meant that a manager representing a fighter could do exactly nothing for that fighter unless he consulted Carbo.[126] Whether Carbo had the power and backing to exercise such control was moot. In the words of Senator Estes Kefauver, "Sometimes it is not whether you really have the stick or not, but whether a fellow thinks you might have it."[127] Those men who evidently believed Carbo had it included Willie Ketchum, manager of featherweight champion Davey Moore (1959–63); Bernard Glickman, manager of welterweight champion Virgil Akins (1958); John DeJohn and Joseph Metro, managers of welterweight and middleweight champion Carmen Basilio (1955–58); Ernie Braca, briefly comanager of Sugar Ray Robinson; Emile Shade and Angel Lopez, managers of welterweight champion Kid Gavilan (1951–54); Sam Silverman, Massachusetts boxing promoter; Rip Valenti, manager of welterweight champion Tony De Marco (1955); Johnny Buckley, manager of middleweight champion Paul Pender (1962); and Babe McCoy, the notorious California matchmaker.[128]

For an illicit manager-promoter Carbo was quite bold in his activities, frequently holding court in public places. In March 1958 undercover agents sent by District Attorney Hogan observed Carbo with the following people at Goldie Ahearn's Washington, D.C., restaurant: Benny Magliano (a.k.a. Benny Trotter), a Baltimore promoter; Billy Brown, an IBC employee in New York; Sam Margolis, Blinky Palermo's partner in a Philadelphia restaurant; Tony Ferrante, the manager of middleweight champion Joey Giardello (1963–65); Goldie and Helen Ahearn, the owners of the restaurant and boxing promoters; Mike Snyder, the manager of Jimmy Archer and errand boy for Palermo; and Angelo Dundee, the trainer and manager of many ranking fighters.[129]

The relationship between Angelo Dundee and Carbo was not clear, but it was a well-known fact that Dundee's brother Chris maintained close ties to Carbo. Evidence of that relationship came in testimony from Truman Gibson and was corroborated by witnesses before a New York grand jury on April 4, 1958. Gibson testified that Chris Dundee had called him about closed-circuit television rights for a Sugar Ray Robinson–Carmen Basilio fight in March 1958. Dundee wanted to obtain a franchise for the Georgia and Florida closed-circuit telecasts, but Gibson told him that a deal could not be worked out. At that point Dundee put Carbo on the phone in an attempt at "friendly persuasion." The fact that Dundee did not get the rights shows that even Carbo's power had its limits.[130]

Still, Carbo's influence could not be questioned. He controlled many high-ranking fighters from coast to coast, made possible by televised boxing. Although racketeering had invaded the sport some time ago, it had not been able to exert well-organized, highly centralized control before the advent of television. In the pretelevision era, nonchampionship matches usually interested only a local audience, especially among bettors. Television, however, made local bouts interesting on at least a regional, if not national, level. More bettors were attracted and live gates mattered less. Criminals had more incentive to invade and conquer promotional ranks throughout the land.[131]

Frankie Carbo's relationship with Herman "Hymie the Mink" Wallman shows just how complicated criminal dealings could get. Wallman, a furrier by vocation and a shady character by reputation, "managed" former welterweight champion Johnny Bratton (1951), lightweight contender Orlando Zulueta, and a host of lesser known fighters. As part of his duties Wallman allegedly paid boxing officials to score bouts in favor of his fighters; then he would pass the information along to Carbo, who placed his bets accordingly. In return for his services Wallman was allowed to handle his fighters with little interference from Carbo. But Carbo had control over so many managers and their fighters that his interests in a particular contest often led to a conflict. In 1957, when Wallman's fighter, Orlando Zulueta, was scheduled to meet lightweight champion Joe Brown, Carbo told Wallman that if his man won the title he had to give a piece of the fighter to Lou Viscusi, Brown's manager (and the former manager of the great Willie Pep), who had been close to Carbo for many years.[132] Perhaps fortunately for Wallman, Zulueta lost.

Carbo could not have been so effective without the acquiescence, and even indirect collusion, of the various state athletic commissions. The behind-the-scenes machinations for a crucial match in 1958 shed much light on underworld influence over the IBC and, in this instance, over the New York State Athletic Commission. In 1957 welterweight champion Carmen Basilio abandoned his title after winning the middleweight championship. To fill the vacancy NYSAC ordered an elimination tournament, but the IBC had trouble lining up contenders. Two of the contestants, Virgil Akins and Isaac Logart, were managed by Carbo associates Bernie Glickman and Jimmy White, respectively. Glickman, confident that his fighter could defeat Logart, threatened to pull Akins out unless the two fought against each other. James Norris paid Carbo between $10,000 and $15,000 and the match was scheduled.[133] Then Julius Helfand, the NYSAC "reform" chairman, got word that the tournament was likely to be held outside New York. The Colorado Athletic Commission was willing to declare the Logart-Akins winner the new middleweight champion, and Carbo supported a Denver-based fight. Norris alleged that Helfand emphatically ordered him to book the fight into Madison Square Garden, no matter what; his exact words were, "Now I expect you to bring that match to New York. The match belongs in New York and dammit, you had better bring that match to New York."[134] Although Glickman did not reveal his association with Carbo until later, Helfand should have suspected who was behind the delay and how Norris would meet his demands.

Norris took Helfand's demand literally and called a meeting with Carbo, Billy Brown, Herman Wallman, and Jimmy White to discuss the upcoming tournament. He told them of Helfand's orders, and they quickly reached an agreement.[135] In his zeal to reap the prestige and material benefits for his state that were associated with a championship fight, Helfand had indirectly consorted with criminals, an action that, although surprising on the surface, was in effect a natural by-product of an unhealthy, indiscreet friendship between the commission chairman and the promoter.

What was the basis of this relationship? When Averill Harriman took office as governor of New York in 1955 he listed among his goals a determination to clean up boxing. To that end he appointed former King's County assistant district attorney and "racket-buster" Julius Helfand to chair NYSAC. Ironically, as Harriman cited, "the bowing under of the commission to threats" by promoters to remove fights from the state, unless proper conditions were met, was a prime reason for the continuance of criminal infiltration. Yet that is what Helfand seems to have ordered in the Logart-Akins mess.[136]

Helfand had started out like the gang-buster he was reputed to be. First, he launched an investigation into the practices of the New York Boxing Guild, the most powerful arm of the newly formed (1952) International Boxing Guild (the result of an internal dispute and the need for a new image). He called the NYBG "a continuing menace to the integrity of boxing in the state,"[137] and in December 1955, after seven months of investigation, concluded that it had "arrogated to itself the conduct and regulation of boxing in New York."[138] Helfand specifically charged that: (1) It violated commission rules forbidding matchmakers from acting directly or indirectly as managers. (2) It conspired to "ground," or boycott, fighters who were not in its good graces. (3) Out-of-state managers were compelled to "cut in" a guild manager before obtaining a fight in New York. (4) Guild managers admitted association with "the sinister and shadowy" Frankie Carbo.[139]

As a result of these and other findings, NYSAC denied recognition to the International Guild. Charles Johnston, president of the International and a member of the New York City local considered the ruling unconstitutional and vowed to fight it.[140] This time the guild was part of a lost cause. Its activities were blatantly disruptive and over the years its reckless use of power had brought it many enemies. In September 1955 a matter implicating the International Guild reached a Cleveland, Ohio, grand jury; the charges included: boycotting of televised fights not approved by the guild; boycotting any shows involving a fighter who appeared in a televised studio bout; and refusing to match its fighters against those with nonguild managers.[141] Although the defendants were eventually acquitted, the indictment landed a significant blow against the organization's effectiveness.[142]

In New York, Helfand tested the courts and found them willing to support his suspension of all guild-related licenses. In *London Sporting Club* v. *Helfand* (1956),[143] Stephen Sullivan, head of the London Sporting Club of New York, a small promotional organization, appealed a NYSAC ruling that had revoked his license and levied a $5,000 fine. He had been accused of circumventing the commission's rulings concerning the New York Guild by removing televised matches from St. Nicholas Arena in New York to Baltimore so that guild managers could receive the benefits of the televised fights and still continue as members of the outlawed organization. Sullivan's appeal was turned down by two New York courts.[144]

A key to the success of Helfand's all-out attack on the guild hinged on the stand taken by James Norris, who had frequently conducted business with guild members and was expected to side with them to protect his television contracts. To the guild's surprise, on January 7, 1956, Norris unexpectedly aligned with the boxing commission,[145] a move that gave backbone to the New York ruling. The guild quickly began to topple as pessimistic members conceded, "We can't have fights without a television contract and only Norris can give us that."[146] Although members voted sixty-six to zero to ignore the Helfand order, the defection of Al Weill, manager of heavyweight champion Rocky Marciano, signaled the end of the group's cohesiveness.[147] For all practical purposes the guild died with Norris's decision and was buried by the courts.

At last, in Julius Helfand, Frank Hogan seemingly had the help he needed to crush the criminal element in boxing. The two men emerged from the defeat of the guild as saviors of the sport. Yet the nature of the breakup raised serious problems that few people seemed to consider. While spectacular and sensational, the actions of the Helfand-led commission in reality did little to halt Carbo's influence; he controlled the managers whether they belonged to the guild or not. For that reason alone some people accused Helfand of little more than political posturing. One such accuser was former NYSAC Chairman Robert K. Christenberry, who announced his candidacy for New York City mayor in 1957 and was blasted by Helfand for having given comfort to racketeers by not eliminating the guild. Christenberry called the charges a "low, despicable, and unwarranted political smear" made on behalf of Tammany Hall,[148] and he demanded that Helfand produce a list of underworld characters he had eliminated from boxing.[149] Helfand refused, which prompted Christenberry to intimate that there was no such list; if there was, Frankie Carbo certainly was not on it, for he still lurked in the shadows and controlled many important managers.

Unknown to the press or the public, Norris's decision to back Helfand had emerged under very questionable circumstances. According to Norris, his alignment with the commission had been forced by Helfand in a conversation during which the chairman asked if Norris were on the side of law and order, to which Norris responded in the affirmative. At that point Helfand told him, "Well, what I expect you to do and want you to do and order you to do is to go right back from here and make an announcement that you will not recognize the managers' guild anymore, that you will not use any of their fighters, and just tell them you are through."[150] The two became extremely close after the incident, and authorities later discovered that Norris had paid Helfand's expenses to attend an IBC-sponsored fight in Havana, Cuba.[151]

On the basis of this relationship and the past performance of NYSAC and other boxing commissions, not much real reform could be expected. Meaningful change and good-faith efforts to eliminate organized crime would emanate from sources other than the commissions. Ironically, the fight that Helfand ordered be held in New York led to the downfall of Frankie Carbo, as the Justice Department and the courts closed in on the IBC.

Dismemberment of the Octopus

James Dougan Norris had alienated scores of people in high places. The vastness of his empire, his close association with criminals, and the monopolistic practices of the International Boxing Club ran him headlong into a sort of new populist mood among some very important public officials. The most prominent of these officials was Estes Kefauver, a Tennessee senator with presidential aspirations, who, from his chairmanship of the Senate Judiciary Committee's Subcommittee on Antitrust and Monopoly, would hit at the monopolistic practices as well as the criminal infiltration of the International Boxing Club. In 1949 the Congress, urged on by Kefauver, had demonstrated an enthusiastic interest in punishing businesses that acted to restrain trade. The House of Representatives proved its seriousness in the summer of 1951 by investigating the possible violations of trade by the baseball industry.[152] The Senate, not to be outdone, established the Subcommittee on Antitrust and Monopoly, giving itself the needed mechanism for investigating possible monopolistic enterprises, among them the IBC.

Not content with the staging of fights but also determined to control how the fights would be viewed, Norris had figured out an ingenious way to make maximum profits from a bout. The public wanted as many bouts televised as possible, and most of the time so did the boxers, yet large stadium contests often brought greater financial reward to the fighters than television revenues did. Despite the protests of sponsors and television officials, who argued that an attraction of significant appeal would be unaffected by broadcasting, Norris went ahead with plans to offer television viewers a number of second-class club fighters, saving the best fighters for more profitable stadium bouts. As a result, the television industry suffered from reduced advertising revenues as disgruntled advertisers pulled out.[153]

Norris further antagonized the industry by arranging for closed-circuit broadcasts of the most popular fights; paying customers at selected theaters would help him eliminate home television entirely and gain considerable profits for himself and the IBC. The first such showing came on June 15, 1951, when Joe Louis met Lee Savold in a comeback fight.[154] Arthur Daley's tongue-in-cheek comments on the arrangements reflected the attitude of many toward the "public-be-damned" posture of the IBC:

> Everyone knows about Louis, of course. The Bomber has been on television display all during his pitiful "comeback" campaign. However, the stay-at-homes won't get this sterling struggle between these eager young kids for free. There will be no television. There will be no radio. There might not even be any gate receipts. New Yorkers will have to pay at the Polo Ground's turnstyle and a few selected out-of-towners will be afforded the privilege of seeing it on television at special theaters where they also will have to pay.

But if the entire fight were to be televised for free, there would be no spectators at the ringside except in the working press rooms.[155]

Yet the cynical Daley missed the mark, misjudging both the public's loyalty and respect for Joe Louis and, perhaps, its gullibility. The interest in the fight was amazingly high, and when rain forced the contest indoors, after two postponements, Madison Square Garden received over 200 letters, telegrams, and postcards condemning the move to a smaller site. Even so, the fight drew 18,179 fans to the arena and filled eight movie theaters in six cities.[156]

Heeding only the profits and not the protests, Norris quickly sold the television rights to the Jake LaMotta–Bob Murphy light heavyweight battle, scheduled for June 27, 1951, in Yankee Stadium, to theater owners for at least $10,000. As in the Louis-Savold bout, the closed-circuit telecast went to Albany, Pittsburgh, Cleveland, Washington, D.C., Baltimore, Chicago, Richmond, and Philadelphia; ten of the eleven theaters were filled to capacity, which meant more money for Norris's organization, as the deal included a percentage of the gross receipts.[157] This led to other telecasts, including the Rocky Marciano–Rex Layne mismatch in Salt Lake City on July 12, 1951, and the Sugar Ray Robinson–Randy Turpin middleweight championship fight in September 1951, which signaled a new turn in broadcasting.[158] The Robinson-Turpin match marked the first time motion picture exhibitors had outbid both television and radio for the exclusive rights to a prizefight. The terms proved most pleasing to Norris and the IBC, which, as promoters of the bout, shared in the profits of the film rentals in addition to theater receipts.[159]

Norris and his associates had sorely tested the public's level of tolerance. The fans reacted indignantly, and even state and national legislators joined in the battle against television blackouts of closed-circuit bouts. Representatives called for a congressional investigation, insisting that the failure to provide for home radio and television violated "a right that should not be denied the tax-paying public of America."[160] Some even suggested, contrary to legal precedent, that a bout of the magnitude of Robinson-Turpin was in the public domain. Norris was playing the role of a robber baron, out of place and out of time. Worst of all, he was tampering with people's emotions. No matter how much the audience's size proved that boxing was a big business, with all its attendant implications, fans only saw the sporting element and delighted in its entertainment value. Boxing seemed to fill a variety of psycho-sociological needs, ranging from vicarious participation to ethnic identification to compensatory hero worship. Norris saw profits before people and believed that boxing fans, despite their protests, would do anything to see a match. Despite a threatened boycott of the closed-circuit showing of the Robinson-Turpin contest by the TV Owners and Viewers League of Cleveland and a similar group in Washington, D.C., the bout went on as scheduled, with more than desirable financial results. The IBC imposed similar restrictions on the Joey Maxim–Sugar Ray Robinson light heavyweight championship contest in June 1952. Ironically, however, the greed of the IBC enabled many fans to beat the blackout by eavesdropping on the Dominion Network of the Canadian Broadcasting Corporation, which had bought the radio rights and whose signal could be picked up by many Americans.[161]

In August 1951, amid all of the antimonopoly activity in the Congress, Senators Warren Magnuson and Harry P. Cain of Washington and Herman Welker of Idaho introduced resolutions calling for an investigation of the IBC. Their concern with the organization's activities focused on Harry Matthews, a light heavyweight boxer from Seattle by way of Idaho. A complaint from Jack Hurley, Matthews's manager, and a review of his record led the senators to believe that the IBC was depriving Matthews of a chance at "big-time" fights. Despite subsequent information that indicated Matthews was not a worthy contender, the publicity surrounding the fighter quickly led to a Department of Justice investigation into the potential violation by the IBC of federal antitrust laws. In March 1952 a federal grand jury recommended that the government file an antitrust suit to end the restraint of trade in the promotion and broadcasting of championship matches.[162]

On March 17, 1952, the Justice Department filed suit against the International Boxing Club, authorizing Melvin C. Williams, head of the antitrust division in New York, and Harold Lasser, special assistant to the attorney general, to argue the government's case. Charged as defendants were the International Boxing Clubs of New York and Illinois, the Madison Square Garden Corporation, James Norris, and his partner Arthur Wirtz;[163] conspicuously absent from the list was the name of Joe Louis. Although Louis's consent had made the original deal possible, and despite the fact that he supposedly owned stock in the IBC, the government chose not to name him as a defendant. The ostensible reason for the decision was that Truman Gibson and Theodore B. Jones of Chicago, who served as trustees for Louis, actually controlled the stock; apparently, prosecutors believed that Louis was more victim than accomplice and was incapable of nefarious and complex business dealings—a testament to his character but possibly an insult to his intelligence.[164]

The Justice Department's complaint charged that, beginning in

1949, Norris and his associates had combined and conspired to restrain and to monopolize interstate trade and foreign commerce through the promotion, exhibition, broadcasting, telecasting, and motion picture production and distribution of professional championship boxing contests in the United States. Allegedly, these men controlled championship boxing on a worldwide basis. The distinction between championship and nonchampionship fights loomed critically in the government's case, as did the Justice Department's ability to prove that boxing should be considered interstate commerce and subject to antitrust laws.[165]

Not to be outdone, the New York State Athletic Commission, under its new chairman, Robert Christenberry, opened its own investigation of exclusive service contracts between promoters and boxers. As could be expected, NYSAC found no serious problems; after all, it had more than peacefully coexisted with Mike Jacobs during his twelve-year stranglehold on boxing in New York. There were other serious irregularities about which NYSAC also did little or nothing; namely, the question of whether the IBC had such a cohesive alliance with people who operated beyond the legal control of the commission that it's functioning in New York was detrimental to boxing. Again, the same question had been asked of Mike Jacobs; like him, the IBC continued to operate with little interference from NYSAC.

Federal efforts seemed more earnest and determined, although they were temporarily derailed by judicial precedent and congressional softness on another, related antitrust case. On February 5, 1954, in U.S. District Court, Judge Gregory T. Noonan dismissed the government's suit against Norris and the IBC in a forty-five-minute hearing with no written opinion. Noonan based his decision on the Supreme Court ruling in *Federal Baseball Club* v. *National League* (1922), confirmed in *Toolson* v. *New York Yankees* (1951), which exempted baseball from antitrust legislation. The Supreme Court had put the burden on Congress to change the law, but Congress remained unwilling to do so. In his ruling the judge agreed with Whitney North Seymour, counsel for the IBC of New York, who maintained that no valid basis existed for distinguishing between boxing and baseball.[166] By contrast, Harold Sasser argued for the Justice Department that the Supreme Court's sport-related antitrust decisions applied solely to baseball and that the issue of broadcasting and televising fights added a new dimension that had not been a part of the baseball rulings. Judge Noonan responded to Sasser's assertion by informing him of baseball's frequent use of both radio and television. Apparently no one wanted to accept the burden of equating sport and business.[167]

The baseball rulings and the controversy that surrounded them were and would remain a source of embarrassment for the Supreme Court. According to Steven Rivkin, in his article on "Sports Leagues and the Federal Antitrust Law," the conundrum signified more than the illogic of the baseball rulings; it also reflected the court's entire reshaping of the Sherman Antitrust Act. That act, in broad and unequivocal terms, was intended to protect trade and commerce, yet judicial interpretation of the practical meaning of the act has determined that prohibitions be limited to contracts or combinations that "unreasonably" restrain competition.[168]

Judge Noonan's ruling for the IBC placed an unwanted spotlight on the Supreme Court, which would be forced to explain again and again its ruling in *Federal Baseball* and other cases involving the Sherman Act. In his closing statement Noonan asked the burdensome question the high court could not ignore: "Do you think the Government should take the position that the Supreme Court meant only baseball as against football, college or professional, and basketball? Where would the snowball end?"[169]

The Justice Department wasted little time in asking the Supreme Court for a determination on whether the International Boxing Club was subject to antitrust laws. Collaborating in the appeal was the New York State Athletic Commission, as amicus curiae; it was represented by Manuel Lee Robbins, special assistant attorney general of New York. (Subsequent actions by NYSAC cast serious doubt as to its suitability as a "friend of the court.")[170] The prosecution was superbly prepared, dedicated to proving that the IBC's promotion of professional boxing fell under the provisions of the Sherman Act. Central to their case was the laundry list of complaints that the IBC used interstate trade and commerce to:

> (a) negotiate contracts with boxers, advertising agencies, seconds, referees, judges, announcers, and other personnel living in states other than those in which the promoters reside;
> (b) arrange and maintain training quarters in states other than those in which the promoters reside;
> (c) lease suitable arenas, and arrange other details for boxing contests, particularly when the contests are held in states other than those in which the promoters reside;
> (d) sell tickets to contests across state lines;
> (e) negotiate for the sale of and sell rights to make and distribute motion pictures of boxing contests to the 18,000 theatres in the United States;
> (f) negotiate for the sale of and sell rights to broadcast and

telecast boxing contests to homes through more than 3,000 radio stations and 100 television stations in the United States; and

(g) negotiate for the sale of and sell rights to telecast boxing contests to some 200 motion picture theatres in various states of the United States for display by large-screen television.[171]

In arguing the government's case the Justice Department focused on the distinctions between baseball and boxing with regard to trade, pointing out that although an already significant portion (25 percent) of the IBC's earnings came from the sale of television, radio, and motion picture rights to championship matches, improvements in and expansion of television capabilities would greatly increase revenues from interstate communications vehicles. Justice Department predictions were correct, for in good years the IBC earned upwards of $8,500,000, most of it on telecasts of one kind or another. Even the IBC could not deny this.[172]

Recognizing the futility of arguing against the prosecution's facts and figures, the IBC merely contended that, stare decisis, the club was exempted from legislation under the Sherman Act; in other words, its exemption should stand without reexamination of the underlying issues because of the baseball rulings. The Supreme Court rejected this logic, maintaining that the ruling in *Federal Baseball* did not apply to all businesses based on professional sport. The justices submitted that the question before them was not whether a previously granted exemption should continue but whether a new exemption should be granted. In a display of clever and precise ballhandling, they converted a judicial problem into a political football by putting the onus on Congress to change the law. Of course, the court suspected that Congress would do nothing, as in 1951, when it had taken no action on four bills that extended to all sports the exemption afforded baseball in 1922 and 1951. True to form, Congress threw the antitrust ball back to the Supreme Court, postponing legislation until the status of *Federal Baseball* had been clarified. The stalemate continues to this day. The Supreme Court has not declared baseball subject to antitrust laws, and Congress has not extended the exemption, despite the blatant illogic of the subsequent decision against the IBC.[173]

On January 31, 1955, the Supreme Court ruled by a seven-to-two vote that boxing fell under the scope of the Sherman Act, thus reversing the decision of the lower court. Justices Felix Frankfurter and Sherman Minton dissented, thereby exposing the inconsistencies, subjectivity, and human frailties within the nation's highest court. An exasperated and embarrassed Frankfurter lamented, "It would baffle the subtlest ingenuity to find a single differentiating factor between other sporting exhibitions, whether boxing or football or tennis, and baseball insofar as the conduct of the sport is relevant to the criteria or considerations by which the Sherman Law becomes applicable to a 'trade or commerce.' "[174] Moreover, he argued, the broadcast issues were totally inapplicable to this case because baseball had more interstate aspects than prizefighting.[175]

Justice Minton rejected the decision for entirely different but equally revealing reasons. To him the IBC's activities presented no violation of trade or commerce regulations. He saw only a perfectly legitimate contract for personal service—Joe Louis's—and argued that because the commodity that helped produce the monopoly was Louis, the monopoly was gained through competition, not interference. Minton contended that if others wanted to start an elimination contest, they were free to do so; he did "not suppose that Joe Louis had to go back into the ring and be wallopped to a knockout or a decision before he could surrender his championship."[176] Borrowing from the considerable legacy of Justice Oliver Wendell Holmes, whose comments in the 1922 *Federal Baseball* decision had led to the present controversy, Minton opined that boxers have nothing to sell but their personal services, which do not constitute commerce. He reduced the majority decision to the absurd, chiding his colleagues that "when boxers travel from state to state, carrying their shorts and fancy dressing robes in a ditty bag in order to participate in a boxing bout, which is wholly intrastate, it is now held by this Court that the boxing bout becomes interstate Commerce."[177] What the court had declared incidental in *Federal Baseball* now became more important than the exhibition, "as fine an example of the tail wagging the dog as can be conjured up," Milton quipped.[178]

Why did the majority rule as it did? Justice Frankfurter admitted sarcastically but rightly that "the Court gave a preferred position to baseball, because it is the great American sport."[179] Baseball represented civilized entrepreneurial America and the middle class; it was supposedly everything boxing was not—clean, wholesome, pastoral, and strategic. To change baseball might threaten its existence, and few members of the Supreme Court were prepared to expose the sport to a loss of public confidence. Prizefighting, by contrast, already suffered in the public eye and often in the halls of justice. Kenesaw Mountain Landis, appointed the commissioner of baseball following the Black Sox scandal, knew this and had jealously cultivated a favorable image for baseball by maintaining considerable distance from the corrupting influences associated with the world of boxing. For example, in 1930, when Chicago White Sox player Art Shires engaged in a prizefight, Landis issued a stern decree: "Hereafter, any person connected with any club in this organization who engages in professional boxing will be regarded by this office as having permanently retired from baseball."[180] He emphatically added that the "two activities do not mix."[181]

Justice Frankfurter sensed that the other members of the court not only disliked James Norris, whose control of a single, monopolistic enterprise left him more vulnerable than the baseball owners' cartel-like arrangement, but they also disliked boxing. He saw the dangers and warned, "Whatever unsavory elements there be in boxing contests is quite beyond the mark."[182] Nor did he approve of the Supreme Court's intrusive attempt to remedy a state problem. If the states found boxing distasteful, Frankfurter believed, they had the means available to eliminate the sport. He charged the states to abolish boxing exhibitions or sanction them only under conditions that safeguarded the states' notions of the public good.[183] Whether he was right or wrong, Frankfurter nonetheless had little impact on his fellow justices. The government had won a major battle—making the IBC subject to antitrust law. Now the Justice Department had only to prove that the "Octopus" had violated the law.

Following the Supreme Court decision the IBC made desperate attempts to shed the obvious trappings of a monopoly. The original contract with Joe Louis was allowed to elapse, and all exclusive contract practices were abandoned. Leases on Yankee Stadium, the Polo Grounds, and St. Nicholas Arena were also dropped. Moreover, the IBC could prove that it had no control over the new heavyweight champion, Floyd Patterson. Still, on July 2, 1957, the U.S. District Court for the Southern District of New York found the International Boxing Clubs of New York and Illinois, the Madison Square Garden Corporation, James D. Norris, and Arthur Wirtz guilty of violating the Sherman Antitrust Act, based on the evidence provided earlier to the Supreme Court.[184] The presiding judge, Sylvester J. Ryan, struck what appeared to be an uncompromising and devastating blow against the defendants by ordering a complete reorganization and virtual dissolution of the IBC.[185] He was neither fooled nor impressed by their change in appearance but instead considered the overwhelming evidence that Norris and Wirtz still possessed all the power of monopoly and restraint, especially over championship fights. Truman Gibson later confirmed the judge's sagacity by admitting that between 1949 and 1959 the IBC had staged 99 percent of all championship fights;[186] in actual numbers, the IBC was directly involved in thirty-seven championship contests from May 15, 1953, until March 1957.

The IBC's nearly complete stranglehold on championship contests convinced Judge Ryan that only drastic steps would ensure meeting the

criteria set forth in *Schine Theaters* v. *United States* (1948) with regard
to punishing monopolies. According to *Schine,* a dissolution decree
should put "an end to the combination or conspiracy when that is itself
violative," deprive "the antitrust defenders of the benefits of their
conspiracy," and "back up or render impotent the monopoly power
which violates the Act."[187] Ryan therefore proceeded to break up the
monopoly, ordering Norris and Wirtz to divest themselves within five
years of all stock owned directly or indirectly in Madison Square Garden.
This was more a blow to their pride than their bank accounts, for
according to Truman Gibson, stock purchased at $7.00 per share was
sold for $25.00 per share (actually, $18.23 per share, which was still a
sizable increase from the $7.85 per share paid at the time of purchase; in
fact, Norris and Wirtz more than doubled the value of their investment,
from $1,723,580 to $3,948,300).[188] Ryan also ordered the two men to
dissolve the International Boxing Clubs of Illinois and New York, and
he enjoined the Chicago Stadium and Madison Square Garden from
staging more than two championship bouts annually. Finally, he banned
all exclusive agreements for the promotion of boxing events and required
Madison Square Garden, for a period of five years, to lease its premises,
when available, at a fair and reasonable rate to any qualified promoter
who applied in writing for such.[189] Judge Ryan maintained, in essence,
that to destroy the monopoly the clock had to be turned back to 1949,
when the Norris-Wirtz group promoted boxing contests in the Midwest
and Madison Square Garden promoted them in New York.[190] This was
easier said than done.

Strangely enough, the IBC's harshest critics came to its rescue,
often agreeing with supporters that destruction of the monopoly would
kill the sport. Arthur Daley declared that dissolution of the IBC
"would create a vacuum with nothing but chaos on its outer fringes."[191]
Although a persistent critic, he viewed the IBC as a necessary evil,
"the cement that holds together the diverse fragments" of the business.[192] Boxing insiders had grown accustomed to monopolies and
considered the IBC little more than a technologically newer version
of Tex Rickard's and Mike Jacobs's operations, working on the same
principle of signing up the champion and letting the others fall in
place.[193] To most boxing fans, supporters, and officials the concern
was not so much who controlled boxing or how they controlled it but the
results, and no one could question the IBC's results: the boxing industry
was stable; there was a steady flow of outstanding fights; and the
television industry and advertisers had been given a tremendous boost
in fortunes. Of course, in most instances the fighters had to sign with

the IBC or not fight, and, needless to say, the terms were best for the IBC. For this reason the Supreme Court had ruled that such activity gave the IBC "an odorous monopoly background" that was "feared in the boxing world."[194]

The IBC had no intention of submitting to Judge Ryan's orders. It appealed directly to the U.S. Supreme Court, which heard the case on November 13, 1958. The decision was handed down on January 12, 1959,[195] ending some seven years of investigation and litigation during which Norris, Wirtz, and Gibson had strengthened their hold on the prizefight industry and showed little regard for antitrust laws or lawsuits. In affirming the district court's decision, the Supreme Court justices, incensed by the IBC's activities, angrily commented: "it appears that appellants had continued exercising their unlawful control long after they well knew that this activity was within the coverage of the Sherman Act. In view of the fact that no denial was made on that appeal of the sufficiency of the Government's complaint it is reasonable to assume that appellants, subsequent to our opinion knew that their conduct violated the Sherman Act, obedience to which is so important to our free enterprise system. Still they continued their illegal activity. In fact from all appearances, it is continuing today."[196]

Still, those who controlled the IBC refused to submit easily or gracefully, deciding that if direct confrontation with the courts did not work to their advantage, then circumvention would. In Judge Ryan's decree and the Supreme Court's affirmation of it, one major loophole had been ignored: the Chicago Stadium Corporation, parent company of the IBC of Illinois, could organize new entities to handle its boxing promotions, as could the Madison Square Garden Corporation vis-à-vis the IBC of New York.[197] To this end Truman Gibson organized the National Boxing Enterprises. The NBE would promote the two allowable championship fights and all nonchampionship contests, and Title Promotions, Inc., another new company, would, under Gibson's alleged direction and ownership, promote other championship fights. Both companies represented little more than a paper reorganization of the IBC; in fact, James Dougan Norris still exercised fiscal control.[198]

Gibson and Norris both realized that their promotional future hinged on gaining control of the heavyweight championship. Since Constantine "Cus" D'Amato, manager of Floyd Patterson, had broken relations with the IBC in 1957, Norris had been unable to promote any of the champion's fights, and now, in 1959, the most prized crown in boxing rested in enemy hands. Norris seemed determined to get it back—in any way he could.

The Octopus's Last Gasps

Through Gibson secret payments were made by Norris to Blinky Palermo, undercover manager of Charles "Sonny" Liston, to control Liston's television appearances.[199] The mean and powerful Liston had great difficulty attracting opponents, and Norris wanted to expose Liston to the public under the most favorable circumstances so that he would, by popular demand, become an undeniable contender for the heavyweight crown. Norris also moved in on the young promoter William P. Rosensohn, who had gained apparent control of the unbeaten and unknown Swedish fighter Ingemar Johansson before Johansson defeated Floyd Patterson for the heavyweight championship in June 1959. Once again Truman Gibson worked out the details for a new company, Worldwide Boxing Promotions, Inc., with Rosensohn as president. (Norris also bought a one-third interest in Rosensohn Enterprises but pulled out when advised that he might be in direct violation of the IBC dissolution decree.)

In July 1959, when Gibson met with Johansson and Edwin Ahlquist, his adviser, he learned that Rosensohn had no real standing with Johansson; moreover, it was revealed that Charley Black, a former second-rate bookmaker, and crime figure Tony "Fats" Salerno controlled two-thirds of Rosensohn Enterprises. Norris broke off negotiations with Rosensohn and decided to go after Johansson directly. However, before he made any headway, the smart and frugal Swedish boxer, who had a mind of his own and little fear, proceeded to expose the strongarm tactics used against him in a series of magazine interviews. Apparently, Johansson had been forced to take on Rosensohn as his American manager after Rosensohn had allowed Salerno, a known criminal, to secretly buy into his promotional enterprise in return for Salerno's help in getting Cus D'Amato to agree to a Patterson-Johansson fight.[200] Since Charley Black, D'Amato's friend, had gained Salerno's support for Rosensohn, he also received a one-third share in Rosensohn Enterprises.

After NYSAC suspended Rosensohn's matchmaking and promoter's licenses, the brilliant, opportunistic lawyer Roy Cohn, notorious for his role as counsel to Joseph McCarthy during the anti-Communist hearings of the 1950s, and his partner, Bill Fugazy, took over Rosensohn Enterprises, buying Rosensohn's shares for $78,000 and the remaining shares for an undisclosed figure from Vincent Velella, who represented Tony Salerno. Cohn and Fugazy then formed Feature Sports, Inc., and promoted the first two fights between Patterson and Johansson. This left Norris and company without a heavyweight champion and with no immediate way to get one.[201]

Federal Intervention

Already damaged by civil law actions, IBC members now faced more serious criminal charges. The siege began shortly after the Virgil Akins-Isaac Logart match that Julius Helfand, NYSAC's reform chairman, had demanded be held in New York in March 1958.[202] Although Helfand had placed Frankie Carbo under varying degrees of surveillance and investigation for eleven years, District Attorney Frank Hogan had not acquired any indictable evidence against him. The big break came in 1958, as Hogan's persistent efforts to obtain court orders for wiretaps finally paid dividends. The official eavesdropping revealed that Carbo had issued orders to Hymie Wallman and Bernie Glickman with regard to the elimination tournament for the vacated middleweight championship. Hogan and his men also learned what had long been suspected: that James Norris obediently took orders from Carbo as well.[203]

In July 1958 Frankie Carbo was indicted in New York County for his undercover managing and matchmaking activities, and on October 10, 1959, he pleaded guilty, placing himself at the mercy of the court.[204] In December 1959 boxing's shadow power was sentenced to two years on Rikers Island, New York, after Assistant District Attorney John G. Bonomi assessed the limits of his power: "The evil influence of this man for many years, permeated virtually the entire professional sport of boxing."[205] Unlike so many others, Bonomi saw nothing but evil in Carbo's association with prizefighting, going so far as to say that "the name of Frankie Carbo symbolizes the degeneration of professional boxing into a racket."[206] After twelve years of pursuit, District Attorney Frank Hogan could only secure a misdemeanor conviction against Carbo. In fact, had it not been for Hogan's pressure on the state in 1947, the charge of unlicensed managing and matchmaking would not have carried any penalty at all. Even with the conviction, Carbo fled once again and continued his mischief, but this time he would go too far.

As the Supreme Court suspected in 1959, the IBC had indeed moved to extend its control over boxing, this time geographically. Although James Norris had given up his role as president of the IBC of both New York and Illinois, to be succeeded by Truman Gibson, no significant change had taken place in the real operation of the business. The IBC had ostensibly discontinued exclusive contracts practices, but in actuality it had turned that operation over to Frankie Carbo and Blinky Palermo;[207] boxers still signed with the IBC or they did not fight. Legal pressure to reduce monopolistic practices seemed to have the unintended effect of increasing underworld influence in the boxing organization.

Driven by Norris and his seemingly unquenchable thirst for power,

Gibson had set out in 1958 to entrench the IBC on the West Coast by securing control of two suitable arenas for boxing promotion—the Hollywood Legion Stadium and the Olympic Auditorium; he succeeded in obtaining the services of both but controlling only the former. The Olympic Auditorium was owned by George Parnassus and run by the unflappable Aileen Eaton, known to many people as the "Queen of the Jungle." Even with its criminal connections the powerful IBC could not influence Parnassus or Eaton, a novelty in this male-dominated arena who began her boxing-related career in 1942 as a "trouble shooter" at the Olympic Club. The club's owners had assigned her to find the source of and correct the Olympic's financial difficulties; when she fingered her boss she was rewarded with his job. Mrs. Eaton performed so skillfully that she soon emerged as the country's most powerful local promoter,[208] whose hard-nosed negotiating with managers earned her the title "Dragon Lady."[209] More important, she stood out for her integrity in a sport that many people believed was "built on lies."[210] Aileen Eaton paid more than lip service to her conviction that boxing did not have to be a "smelly dirty business,"[211] and she and Parnassus could not be bought or muscled out by the IBC and Frankie Carbo.

Jackie Leonard (born Leonard Blakely) was both less principled and less competent. The possibility of sharing in television revenues totaling $180,000 weekly from the Wednesday (ABC) and Friday (NBC) night fights was too tempting to pass up, and he agreed to be the IBC's chief West Coast promoter. Gibson proceeded to form the Hollywood Boxing and Wrestling Club, for the purpose of leasing the Hollywood Legion Stadium.[212] Leonard was named president of the club and acted as its promoter and matchmaker. The International Boxing Club lent $28,000 to the new organization, making Leonard financially indebted and personally vulnerable; moreover, he was now dependent on Gibson for televised fights.[213] And like so many other managers, matchmakers, and promoters, he also owed money to Frankie Carbo. In October 1957 Leonard had guaranteed a payment of $12,000 to Kid Gavilan, a used-up, Carbo-controlled fighter, for a bout with Gaspar Ortega. The fight did not draw well and Leonard could not meet his obligation. Facing pressure from Gavilan's handler, Angel Lopez, Leonard called on Carbo to intercede. Gavilan subsequently received $7,000; the remaining $5,000 was never paid.[214] Carbo never forgot his debtors or their debts.

Leonard soon understood how much his plea for help would cost him. His unwanted involvement with Carbo escalated when Donald Nesseth, a friend of Leonard's and manager of promising young welterweight Don Jordan, repeatedly begged Leonard to obtain a nationally televised fight for his boxer. Leonard approached Gibson on the matter and Gibson agreed to arrange a match. Jordan fought the number one welterweight contender, Isaac Logart, and won a ten-round decision. After winning three more fights, two of them against the cagey but declining Gaspar Ortega, he became the leading contender for the welterweight crown.[215] Gibson guaranteed Jordan a fight against Carbo-controlled Virgil Akins, and shortly thereafter Leonard allegedly received a phone call from Blinky Palermo, who was obviously acting on behalf of Carbo. Palermo warned Leonard, "We are in for half the fighter [50 percent of the manager's share] or there won't be any fight."[216] Leonard claimed to have balked at the ultimatum, but on the insistence of Gibson, who was with Leonard during the conversation, he accepted because of Gibson's assurances that he would "take care of everything." When Gibson and Leonard relayed the conversation to Nesseth, the feisty manager rejected the arrangement. He neither trusted Gibson nor wanted to risk double-crossing the underworld.[217]

Gibson and Leonard nevertheless led Palermo to believe that he and Carbo would receive their share should Jordan beat Akins. On December 5, 1958, Jordan won a fifteen-round decision over Akins and took the crown. Palermo and Carbo's payoff was to come after the prearranged rematch on April 24, 1959, in St. Louis, which Jordan also won. When Palermo demanded the money from Nesseth, to his surprise Nesseth stood his ground and refused. Palermo and Carbo realized that not only had Jordan beaten their fighter but he and his manager had stolen the crown from them, and they responded with threats that betrayed Carbo's violent history. On April 28, Leonard received a telephone call from Carbo, who threatened to hire someone to take care of the promoter by gouging his eyes out. According to Leonard's best recollection, Carbo warned, "We are going to meet at the crossroads. . . . You will never get away with it. I have had that title 25 years and no punks like you are going to take it away from me. . . . When I mean get you, you are going to be dead. . . . We will have somebody out there to take care of you."[218]

Palermo and Gibson tried to find a way out for Leonard and Nesseth. They proposed that Jordan fight Sugar Hart, another Carbo-controlled fighter, but Nesseth feared that Hart had a good chance of beating Jordan and refused. Gibson allegedly promised Leonard money for convincing Nesseth to sign for a Jordan-Hart match, but his effort failed. Palermo and Carbo then sent underworld "strong-arm man" Joe Sica to convince Leonard that the only way to get his head out of the "noose" was "to grab hold of Nesseth and make him take the fight with Sugar Hart."[219] Nesseth told Gibson of the threats, and although Gibson suggested that the easiest way out was to take the Hart fight, he agreed to call James Norris about disarming Carbo. He did call Norris but met with no success, and on May 4, Louis Dragna, another "enforcer" paid Leonard and Nesseth a visit.[220] The next day the Los Angeles Police Department put a tap on Leonard's home phone and hid a microphone in his office. As a result of the surveillance they obtained evidence that Gibson had applied financial pressure to get Leonard to arrange the Hart-Jordan fight.[221]

On May 11, Gibson allegedly invited William Daly, of the defunct International Boxing Guild and a close Carbo associate, to Los Angeles. The purpose of his visit was persuasion, but it seemed more like intimidation, which Leonard earlier sensed it would be. Gibson asked Leonard to meet with Daly, which he did; he was wearing a hidden microphone that enabled the police to tape the conversation. Daly related Gibson's and Carbo's anger over Leonard's and Nesseth's actions. According to Daly, Gibson felt betrayed because Leonard had let the welterweight title get away from the IBC and Frankie Carbo and he allegedly vowed to destroy both men.[222] An accurate and vivid description of the consequences for noncooperation were deemed instructive, so Daly inarticulately but effectively related the near fatal assault on boxing promoter and manager Ray Arcel, whom Carbo had once controlled: "They use a water pipe . . . lead pipe . . . and they just get an ordinary piece of newspaper, see, newspaper don't show fingerprints . . . and you sitting in a crowd. . . . and they try to give you two bats, and they kill you with two if they can. But they whack you twice and split you—fracture your skull. And knock you unconscious, and they just drop it. . . . and after they drop it—the law—they're protected by the law. They have to have witnesses."[223]

Leonard, desperately seeking to protect his boxing interests as well as his life, reported the incident to the California State Athletic Commission and allegedly received a severe beating for his admission, although a police investigation turned up no evidence to corroborate the assault. On May 14, 1959, however, the CSAC met and, as a result of the evidence from Leonard and Nesseth, turned the entire matter over to the U.S. Attorney's Office in Los Angeles for federal grand jury action.[224] On September 21, 1959, the grand jury returned indictments against Carbo, Palermo, Sica, Dragna, and Gibson for "extortion affecting commerce and conspiracy to extort in violation of the Hobbs Act, for interstate transmission of threats and conspiracy to transmit an offense against the United States."[225] In addition, Carbo and Palermo were charged with obtaining $1,725 from Leonard through threats of physical injury and violence. Palermo and Sica were charged with attempts to coerce Nesseth, through fear and threats of violence, into giving up part of his contracted control of Jordan by agreeing to a fight with Sugar Hart. Carbo and Palermo were charged on five other counts with the interstate transmission of threats to injure Leonard and Nesseth.[226]

A groundswell of concern and interest erupted after public disclosure of the indictments. Governor Edmund G. Brown's hue and cry that "boxing smells to high heaven" was the loudest and most prominent of a chorus of calls for federal control of prizefighting to combat criminal penetration. One day after the governor's emotional statement the Senate Subcommittee on Antitrust and Monopoly opened its investigation, ostensibly concerning monopolitistic practices in professional boxing. In reality Estes Kefauver, who chaired the subcommittee seemed to be more interested in resuming his public crusade against organized crime, which dated back to 1950. The investigation gave Kefauver new political life and an effective vehicle for stealing some of the Government Operations Committee's thunder. The famous Appalachin, New York, meeting of gangster chiefs in 1957 had provided insight into the scope of control and the sophisticated coordination of organized crime in American society. Shortly after that meeting the Senate, through its Government Operations Committee, headed by William McClellan, began an investigation into labor racketeering.[227] With the election of John F. Kennedy in 1960 and the appointment of his brother Robert to head the Department of Justice, the legislative attack on organized crime gained aggressive support from the U.S. Attorney General's Office. Robert F. Kennedy, who had made the conviction of Jimmy Hoffa a personal crusade, seemed dedicated to stopping organized crime wherever it existed, including boxing. Although he inherited the Carbo case from the Eisenhower administration, Kennedy supported vigorous prosecution of the defendants, including Gibson, who complained after his arrest that he had been "picked up and handled like a murderer."[228]

In February 1961 Paul John Carbo was found guilty on two counts and was sentenced to twenty-five years in prison and fined $10,000; bail was denied pending an appeal (which failed, in 1963). Frankie Carbo finally felt the fury of the justice system, spending the rest of his life in prison. Blinky Palermo received a fifteen-year sentence and a $10,000 fine; when his appeal failed in 1963 he followed his long-time friend and partner to prison. (Palermo was paroled in 1971, an old but still very active man.) Joseph Sica was sentenced to twenty years in prison and fined $10,000; upon appeal in 1963 he had two judgments against him reversed, but his sentence was not changed. Louis Dragna received two concurrent five-year sentences but was acquitted upon appeal in 1963.[229] Truman Gibson, who insisted that he had been framed by Daly and Leonard and prejudicially tried by the court, was sentenced to two concurrent five-year terms and fined $10,000. The judge, taking into account Gibson's most distinguished government and legal career, suspended his sentence and placed him on five years' probation.

Gibson appealed in 1963, hoping to clear his name and record, but he failed to convince the court that he had not unduly used his influence, power, and authority to force Leonard and Nesseth to unwillingly give up the championship without justification or remuneration. According to the court Gibson kept Jordan, Leonard, and Nesseth from capitalizing on the welterweight championship by denying them profitable promotions and television dates. The one thing that Gibson could not deny, which probably doomed him, was his association with Carbo and Palermo. He admitted that the IBC had dealings with the underworld in order "to maintain a free flow of fighters without interference, without strikes, without sudden illnesses, without sudden postponements." When asked whether he knew what certain nefarious figures might do on his behalf Gibson answered, "Not completely, no," leaving the court to conclude that actions benefiting Gibson might come through any channel, including illegal ones.[230]

Whether Truman Gibson was a bad guy or a fall guy remains one of the mysteries of this entire episode. Even his attempt to clear his name was colored by controversy. He maintained, to his possible detriment, that prior to the trial the Department of Justice had promised to dismiss the indictment against him. However, the government responded that the documents upon which Gibson pinned his hopes were forgeries and that Gibson knew this at the time of his appeal. Nonetheless, Gibson still maintains that he is innocent.[231] A letter to Arthur Wirtz on March 6, 1962, shows how little Gibson gained financially from his involvement with Carbo and who he believed was responsible for his downfall:

Dear Art:

Your letter dated February 26, but mailed without postage on March 2, greeted me on my return to Chicago from Sarasota and Bradenton, Florida, on Sunday.

Since you sent the letter to my home, I had all of Sunday to consider it. You refer to the $6,000. What about the balance which was due me but unresolved at the time of payment of the $6,000. In this connection, note the enclosed copy of the stipulation you had drawn. Note the reference to the amount. Your memory may also be jogged by referring back to the meeting in your office at the Chicago Stadium on the night of the Kennedy rally and in the presence of your partner.

So, at our meeting add all of this and not just the $6,000 to the agenda. You measure everything in terms of money. You are probably correct since you have been so successful.

What measure do you put on a man's life? Was your shrewd bargain, when we last met, your determination?

I could not help but think then and now that I never knew Carbo before the organization of the IBC. I never cleared championships with him. I talked with him most infrequently. I certainly did not clear the Akins-Jordan fight with him. Some one did, and the fact that I didn't indicates who put me in the soup. While you are remembering things in the past, please also recollect that I didn't collect any of the profits (nor did Joe Louis, despite his agreement) from the split up IBC operations from behind a nice insulated shield.

I thought of all these things in your office. I would not have said or written them except for your last letter. So, at our meeting, let us include everything on the agenda.[232]

The Betrayal

With Truman Gibson gone the IBC was virtually dead. The civil suits, dissolution, reorganization, and criminal proceedings against Gibson had all taken a heavy toll, yet the unkindest blow came from a most unexpected source—television. This betrayal was not so much a question of morals as of economics.

As early as 1958 low ratings had dictated that the networks cut back on boxing telecasts. As one writer explained, "Boxing shows had gone the way of television comics; the novelty had worn off and viewers lost interest."[233] The figures bore him out. In 1952, 31 percent of the available audience watched boxing telecasts; by 1959 only 10.6 percent watched televised fights. Boxing's failure to keep pace with the expanding television audience made sponsorship of a prizefight a poor proposition for return on investment.[234]

By 1959 television had grown enormously as a commercial venture, and the industry had made great technological, programming, and artistic advances as well. Consequently, boxing was no longer the ideal subject, the major attraction, or even a necessary evil. While all the networks cut back, NBC was the first to drop the sport, in September 1960.[235] Many people reacted bitterly to the decision, blaming television for turning its back on the game when it had put boxing in its present predicament. James Farley, Jr., of the New York State Athletic Commission summed up the mood in claiming that "television not only destroyed clubs, but took the personality out of boxing. . . . Most of the ills of recent years have stemmed from the control of television through the auspices of Jim Norris, the IBC, and their associates. They reduced boxing to the shell we have today."[236] This emotional and not altogether accurate criticism was as much a defense of the sport as an attack on television. The game he so loved stood defenseless against what must have appeared to be a total onslaught, including an attack by the federal government.

Federal Control: Politics or Public Interest

The problems of controlling boxing were not new to the 1960s. As early as 1920 members of various state athletic commissions had realized that the individual rules and regulations of the states made effective control and coordination difficult. Consequently, a few state athletic commissioners organized the National Boxing Association "for the purpose of assuring greater efficiency and uniformity in the supervision of professional boxing and for more effective control and regulation of professional boxing."[237] In this regard the organization failed miserably. Sports editor John Kieran of the *New York Times* defined the problem in 1930: "A fighter banned in New York can fight in National Boxing Association territory and that includes twenty-six states. A fighter banned in NBA territory can fight in New York or Pennsylvania. A fighter banned in Pennsylvania can fight in New York. Seldom do these different organizations get together on a verdict. They have different customs, opinions, and rules."[238] Of course, two of the biggest boxing states, New York and Pennsylvania, refused to join the NBA, but even those that did zealously protected their own authority and argued that no state could delegate its authority to any other group or entity; each state thus reserved unto itself the power to make its own decisions. As a result, anytime a state or states did not agree with the NBA, it/they could and often did deviate from the umbrella body's directives.[239] In 1930, for example, Primo Carnera, although banned in twenty-six states, was allowed to fight in California.[240]

Congress recognized as early as 1940 the failure of state control and the NBA, as well as the infiltration of organized crime into the fight game. On April 9, 1940, Representative Ambrose J. Kennedy of Maryland offered a joint resolution in Congress to establish a national boxing commission. Kennedy cited an alarming array of specific concerns that: "(1) The evil practices that have grown up in connection with commercial boxing have attained the proportions of a national scandal. (2) The alleged . . . control of commercial boxing by gangsters and racketeers has reached such a stage that the states are powerless to cope with the problem. (3) It is necessary for the Federal Government to assist the States in eradicating such control and evil practices for the general welfare of the whole United States."[241] Among other things, the resolution called for a five-man commission appointed by the president; federal licensing of fighters, managers, and promoters for world championship contests; and strict penalties for violating the rules.[242] The resolution died in committee and twenty years passed before Congress resumed serious efforts to handle the situation.[243]

In 1960 the Kefauver-led investigation and hearings into professional boxing did much to inform the public and its officials about the problems in the sport. After hearing some thirty-six witnesses, who produced 1,847 pages of testimony in ten volumes of transcript, Kefauver and many other public officials were convinced that direct action had to be taken to combat boxing's problems, especially incursions by organized crime.[244] On March 29, 1961, Kefauver and Senator Claire Engle of California introduced Senate Bill 1474, which, like the Kennedy resolution of 1940, proposed to "aid the states in their effort to drive racketeers and gangsters out of boxing and to end the monopoly of one of our major sports."[245] The two crusaders set out to accomplish their goal by establishing in the Department of Justice a national boxing commission, which would be responsible for setting up a federal licensing system. A commissioner would be authorized to require all professional boxers, managers, and matchmakers engaged in interstate bouts to obtain a federal boxing license, and violators would incur severe penalties. The bill's sponsors took great care to explain that the measure was in no way intended to preempt the states' authority and responsibility to regulate professional boxing; to that end sponsors limited jurisdiction to bouts of an interstate nature.[246] In reality, by 1961 very few professional bouts had been anything other than interstate in nature, so despite its denials the federal government would be assuming duties that had been the province of the states. Surprisingly, most state boxing commissions endorsed the need for a federal regulatory body. Resistance to the legislation came from another source—the Justice Department and the Congress itself.

Robert Kennedy, as counsel to McClellan's Government Operations Committee, commonly known as the Labor Rackets Committee, proposed a national crime commission to coordinate information about and efforts against gangsters. Estes Kefauver supported that plan as well, and both men linked the scheme to a federal boxing commission.[247]

When Kennedy became attorney general, however, he no longer saw the necessity of a national crime commission, believing that the Justice Department could achieve the same objectives; he cautioned against establishing a federal boxing commission for the same reasons. Although he recognized the need for additional legislation to combat crime, he suggested that it be directed toward expanding the jurisdiction of the Federal Bureau of Investigation. Kennedy promised he would not oppose the bill, but his lack of enthusiasm for it proved costly.[248]

The Kefauver-Engle bill failed, as did similar bills introduced in 1962. In 1963 an undaunted Kefauver tried again and received encouraging support from a New York State legislative committee that recommended passage of a bill sponsored by him in the Senate and William T. Ryan in the House. Before debate on the issue ended, Kefauver died, on August 10, 1963. With his death many people believed that any hope for federal control of boxing died too.[249] However, in June 1964 the Congress did pass and President Johnson signed into law an amendment to Title XVIII of the United States Code "to prohibit schemes in interstate or foreign commerce to influence by bribing the outcome of sporting contests. . . . "[250] Penalties included a maximum fine of $4,000 and a maximum ten-year prison sentence. The amendment proved the closest that Congress would come to the regulation of professional boxing.[251]

While Congress Fiddled

The IBC was defunct and Frankie Carbo was in prison, but boxing's problems remained. When Carbo and his associates were convicted, Special Prosecutor Goldstein stressed that it was everyone's duty to do something about organized crime. "If we stop with this conviction," pleaded Goldstein, "the practice will continue."[252] He could not have been more correct.

Frank Marrone, a detective in the office of District Attorney Frank Hogan, described Carbo's influence in boxing as "unique" in that "he controlled a racket solely and to himself."[253] Once imprisoned in 1960 Carbo did not lose control but, according to Marrone, delegated the "hands-on" responsibility to Blinky Palermo.[254] When Palermo joined Carbo behind bars there were others on the outside who could take over. Although no longer able to effect pervasive control over the sport, as in the past, organized crime still played an important role in boxing. In fact, through Charles "Sonny" Liston, Carbo and associates would regain boxing's most prized possession, the heavyweight championship of the world.

The Sharks and the Bear: Criminal Control of Sonny Liston

Sonny Liston was a tragic figure whose early fall into a life of crime made him a prime candidate for control by the underworld. The New York State Athletic Commission aptly described Liston in one sentence: "A child of circumstances, without schooling and without direction or leadership, he has been the victim of those with whom he has surrounded himself."[255] At age fourteen he was sent to a detention center after being arrested for breaking and entering; not long after his release he earned a stay at the state penitentiary in Jefferson City, Missouri, for a string of restaurant robberies. As the story goes, in prison Liston met a cleric named Father Stevenson who challenged the wayward youth to harness his fighting spirit in a constructive manner. Liston took up boxing and quickly and easily went through all of his early opponents. An impressed Father Stevenson asked Frank Mitchell, the black publisher of the *St. Louis Argus* and a small-time boxing manager, to arrange a bigger match. Liston demolished Mitchell's fighter, a professional, and at age twenty-two or twenty-three (no one was ever sure of his birth date) turned professional, in 1953. Frank Mitchell became his manager of record.[256]

Mitchell had a long arrest record but no convictions, and he associated freely with criminals in St. Louis. Soon after Liston's release from prison Mitchell got his young charge a job, working for John Vitale. On record as president of the Anthony Novelty Company, Vitale was in reality a labor racketeer who exerted an extraordinary influence in the St. Louis underworld and on union activities. When two leading St. Louis union officials were killed in 1952, the trail led to John Vitale but nothing could be proved; arrested fifty-eight times, he was convicted on only three occasions. Vitale hired Liston as a laborer in his cement company; in reality the young fighter mainly kept black laborers in line.[257]

With his criminal record, fierce reputation, and St. Louis base, Liston had trouble getting professional opponents. The Missouri Athletic Commission suspended him in 1957, but by lying to Illinois officials he obtained a fight there within weeks. Despite his liabilities Liston possessed enormous potential, and with the championship in "enemy" hands, Norris, Carbo, and Palermo saw in Liston a splendid chance to wrest the crown from manager Cus D'Amato and his fighter, Floyd Patterson.[258]

Informants reported to St. Louis police that Vitale and Mitchell had made numerous trips to Chicago, and on one of them Liston's contract was divided up between Vitale and the "combination."[259] (A check of long-distance telephone calls made on March 8, 1958, from Mitchell's St. Louis office showed a call to the residence of Blinky Palermo.[260]) As a result of the negotiations John Vitale got 12 percent through Mitchell (who was totally out); Palermo also got 12 percent; Joseph "Pep" Barone got 24 percent and became Liston's manager of record; and Frankie Carbo got a controlling 52 percent. Shortly thereafter Liston moved to Philadelphia and lived for two years in the Hamilton Court Hotel (Palermo had an interest in a restaurant located there). With Carbo's imprisonment in 1960 Palermo assumed his interest, thus allowing Carbo to share in the fighter's control and earnings while behind bars.[261] In early 1961 Liston applied for a Pennsylvania boxer's license and the chairman of that state's athletic commission, Al Klein, informed him that "he would have to be clean before he could fight in Pennsylvania."[262] On April 24, 1961, Liston "acquired" a new manager, George Katz of Philadelphia, who was approved for a license after convincing the Pennsylvania State Athletic Commission that he had no connections to Palermo or Carbo. The commission also forced Liston to buy up Barone's interest in his contract (although as late as 1964 Liston still owed Barone some $42,000).[263]

By late 1960 Liston had fought his way to the top of the heavyweight division with the support of Norris. A match with champion Floyd Patterson was scheduled for the spring of 1962, and promoters wanted it in the "Big Apple." On April 17, 1962, Liston applied for a New York boxing license, but unlike the Pennsylvania body NYSAC found the Katz-Liston relationship highly suspect. Under the terms of their arrangement Katz received only 10 percent of Liston's earnings, "a most unusual distribution" (the normal manager's share was 33 1/3 percent).[264] As boxing managers were not known for their philanthropy or naïveté, the commission concluded that Katz managed Liston on paper only and that the 10-percent distribution was payment for his services as a front man. Liston confirmed NYSAC's suspicions when he revealed, "In connection with the bout with Floyd Patterson, Mr. Katz has not and will not act in my behalf."[265]

Under the chairmanship of Melvin Krulewitch, who had been appointed by Governor Nelson Rockefeller, NYSAC rejected Liston's application and, in the process, the bout for the heavyweight championship of the world. The action represented one of the few courageous and bold decisions that any state commission would make in the face of the fiscal and prestige potential that a heavyweight championship fight carried. Why did NYSAC take such action? Simply put, it believed the risks outweighed the benefits. The official NYSAC statement read in part: "The history of Liston's past associations provides a pattern of suspicion. His association with Vitale, Palermo, Mitchell, and others is a factor which can be detrimental to the best interests of professional boxing and to the public interest as well. We cannot ignore the possibility that these longtime associations continue to this day. The wrong people do not disengage easily."[266]

The Illinois State Athletic Commission, a true boxing scavenger, once again showed little concern for Liston's criminal association and allowed the fight. On September 25, 1962, Sonny Liston knocked out a petrified Floyd Patterson in one round,[267] and the underworld again owned the heavyweight championship and a powerful symbol to the world. What remains surprising is the lack of attention and concern paid to this state of affairs. The rise and fall of Sonny Liston indicated the extent of criminal infiltration in sport, the problems of illegal gambling, and the difficulties of coping with the problem.

Behind the Liston-Clay Fiasco

When Blinky Palermo went to the federal penitentiary in Lewisburg (Pa.), Sam Margolis, a Palermo business associate, tended the store and took over as Liston's advisor and keeper.[268] In the spring of 1962 Margolis arranged for Liston to meet Robert, James, and John Nilon, concessionaires and security service contractors for sporting and entertainment events who had known Margolis since their youth in Leeperville, Pennsylvania. As a result of the meeting Robert and James Nilon entered into an agreement with Liston to form Inter-Continental Promotions, Inc. In exchange for 50 percent of the stock Liston agreed to fight exclusively for the new corporation; the Nilons distributed the rest of the stock to their best advantage. On December 16, 1962, Liston transferred 275 of his 500 shares to Sam Margolis, who turned over 50 shares to his lawyer, Salvatore Avena; one can safely assume the rest of Margolis's shares belonged at least in part to his incarcerated bosses. Margolis justified the transfer as repayment of Liston's debts to him.[269] Then, in early 1963 Liston completely severed ties with George Katz, his manager on paper only, and Margolis hired Jack Nilon to serve as manager, ostensibly at Liston's request. On February 28, 1963, Liston agreed to give Jack Nilon the standard one-third of his earnings.[270] He had little feel for money management and, in fact, testified that if given a check he would not be able to determine its amount. Illiteracy and certain mental deficiencies left Liston at the mercy of others with regard to his fiscal affairs and career directions.[271]

Inter-Continental Promotions was soon ready to handle a Sonny Liston–Cassius Clay championship "grudge match." Liston was the heavyweight champion, but the young, handsome, brash, witty, and loud-mouthed Clay was stealing his thunder. Clay's mercurial rise to the top of the boxing profession after his gold medal performance as a light heavyweight at the Rome Olympics in 1960 was more a product of his style in and out of the ring than his boxing skill. A predicted knockout against an over-the-hill Archie Moore, a controversial decision over the tough Doug Jones, and a close call against Henry Cooper did not indicate championship material, but his perfection of the art of self-promotion did. Even during the buildup for the second Liston-Patterson showdown in Las Vegas, it was Cassius Clay who provided the excitement, upstaging both champion and challenger by threatening to destroy the "big ugly bear" Liston.[272] Although his publicity-seeking banter was harmless, Clay's antics polarized the boxing community and the public: the man inspired either adoration or contempt. Still, no one could deny that he had given a much-needed spark to a static sport. What mattered most was that both friend and foe would gladly pay to see him fight.

In the spring of 1963 the Pennsylvania State Athletic Commission secretly requested the Liston-Clay fight for the Keystone State. Upon formal application in the fall, a new administration's deputy attorney general ruled that the PSAC should not license Inter-Continental to promote the fight because Liston owned stock in the company and would therefore have a financial interest in his opponent—a violation of the boxing code in Pennsylvania.[273] A PSAC member unofficially suggested a way around the statute to Garland Cherry, the Nilons' lawyer: "You can still promote in Pennsylvania by using another local promoter. Sell the rights to him or make some kind of a contractual relationship with him. In other words, deliver the bundle of rights to some local promoter who is acceptable to us, make your money as you will, and whatever provisions or commitments you want, as long as the man who applies to the boxing commission is one who is acceptable to us, and there are not commitments between himself and one or the other fighters."[274]

Inter-Continental refused to stoop any lower and decided not to reapply in Pennsylvania. They turned to New York and California, where they met with rejection because of Liston's unacceptability. However, New Jersey, Nevada, and Florida were all willing to license the fight and reap the prestige and profits it promised. Florida won out when William B. MacDonald, Jr., and his partner Chris Dundee agreed to buy the promotional rights to the live gate for the staggering sum of $625,000, which removed the issue of a fighter having a financial stake in his opponent.[275] While many other irregularities remained intact, on October 29, 1963, arrangements were finalized for the much-ballyhooed fight, scheduled for February 25, 1964, in Miami Beach. Clay would receive 22½ percent of the profits, plus $50,000 if he won the heavyweight championship, in return for which Inter-Continental gained the right to promote his next fight, to name his opponent, and to determine the site; half of Clay's purse was placed in escrow to guarantee a return fight. Gordon Davidson, an officer in Clay's Louisville sponsoring group, maintained that the $50,000 payment was intended to increase the challenger's earnings to approximately 25 percent, which Liston had opposed. Robert Nilon disagreed and admitted that by locking Clay into a return match the money represented insurance for Liston against loss. Florida state's attorney Richard E. Gerstein speculated that such an arrangement might have induced Liston's defeat by making it profitable.[276] Liston was an overwhelming favorite to defeat his younger, smaller, and less experienced opponent, and if "smart money" bettors backed Clay because they knew Liston was going to lose, they would reap a financial bonanza. His handlers would be the first to know of such a deal and would gain in the short-run as well as the long-run via the return match clause. Although this scenario was based on circumstantial evidence, a drastic change in betting odds just before the contest indicated the possibility that inside information had been responsible for the shift to Cassius Clay.[277]

The Miami Beach Boxing Commission never received the contract in question and Liston himself never signed it. Another contract drawn up on the same date and signed by Liston—one that did not include a rematch provision—was filed with and accepted by the Miami Beach Boxing Commission.[278] The many irregularities might have gone unnoticed were it not for the bizarre circumstances that occurred during and after the fight. In the fifth round the challenger had to be pushed into the ring by his trainer, Angelo Dundee. Clay later said that liniment on Liston's gloves had gotten into his eyes and blinded him. Then, at the beginning of the seventh round Liston refused to leave his corner, complaining of a shoulder injury, and the title changed hands with the champion seated in his corner, apparently suffering only from a mouse under his left eye. Cries of "fix" came from far and wide.[279] Investigations followed in rapid order and from a variety of sources, including the U.S. Senate, but none found any illegalities, only irregularities and unethical behavior[280]—a result that can be attributed more to a lack of commitment than to the circumstances. Based on his office's investigation of the fight, the report of Florida state's attorney Gerstein proved particularly revealing, mostly for the questions it raised.

Known gambler Ash Resnick, director of sporting events at the Thunderbird Hotel in Las Vegas, had had the full run of Liston's camp.

He was present in Liston's dressing room prior to the fight, accompanied Liston to the ring, and watched the contest from Liston's corner. Despite the fact that Resnick had been barred and/or ejected from every race-track in South Florida as a recognized bookmaker, the Miami Beach Boxing Commission made no attempt to remove him from the Liston camp.[281] In addition, Pep Barone and Sam Margolis accompanied Liston through much of his training in Miami Beach.[282] Notwithstanding the presence of these and other suspect individuals, the investigation uncovered no evidence of a fixed fight. A panel of eight competent physicians agreed that the injury to Liston's arm could have prevented him from continuing the fight, although they speculated that the injury had occurred prior to the fight, a fact confirmed by Gerstein's independent investigation. Apparently the injury had not been detected, or at least not reported, by the commission-appointed physician who examined Liston, even though Liston had received cortisone shots until five days before the fight (according to his personal physician and handler).[283] While the outcome of the bout might not have been predetermined, those who knew of Liston's condition had valuable information for betting purposes. The state's attorney's report concluded there was no real move to fix the fight because betting odds had not fluctuated on a national scale, in localized gambling centers, or at ringside.[284] However, CBS–TV revealed on February 26, 1964, one night after the fight, that the odds went wild, fluctuating from seven-to-one to ten-to-one, with four-to-one odds at ringside and ample Clay money available.[285]

What seemed to bother Americans more than these irregularities was the news of Cassius Clay's religious conversion. While the newly named Cassius X ("X" symbolized the stolen African name of black Americans) seemed convinced of the righteousness of his cause, few accepted the religious message of the Nation of Islam. Its racial rhetoric, proposing radical if not violent solutions to domination by "white devils," betrayed a hatred that in turn provoked widespread hostility against its leaders, Elijah Muhammad and Malcolm X, and their followers.[286] Even enemies of organized crime openly stated their preference for mob control of the heavyweight crown rather than have it in Black Muslim hands.[287] The championship was too important to relinquish to "enemies" of American values, and extreme measures would be employed to recapture it.

7

Civil Rights to Rebellion to Reaction
The Era of Muhammad Ali

For all of its "flabbiness and self-satisfaction and gross materialism," its sprawling suburban complexes with rows and rows of ticky-tacky houses, the fifties managed to unleash a series of developments, both positive and negative, that spawned the social activism of the sixties. A decade characterized as "the dullest and dreariest in all our history"[1] and about which historian Eric Goldman wrote, "We're grown unbelievably prosperous and we maunder along in a stupor of fat,"[2] nurtured the events that were to follow. Two stand out: when President Dwight D. Eisenhower made the "biggest damnfool mistake" in his life by appointing Earl Warren as Chief Justice of the Supreme Court,[3] and when he ordered his representative not to sign the Geneva Accords of 1954 no matter what the results, thereby committing the United States to a policy of "nation building" in South Vietnam.[4] Civil rights and Vietnam would dominate the sixties; and the man once known as Cassius Clay would, as Cassius X and then Muhammad Ali, transcend his profession to become an iconoclastic symbol of that turbulent decade—proof of Budd Schulberg's claim that "America gets the champion it deserves."[5]

The Fight for Integration

By the late 1940s the National Association for the Advancement of Colored People had embarked on an all-out legal attack against racial inequality and discrimination in such diverse areas as public accommodations, jobs, and voting rights. The NAACP's actions sounded a clarion call, alerting blacks to their rights and urging white America to honor its commitments to grant "due process of law" and "equal protection" to all within its borders.[6] Of course, its most notable breakthrough came in the fight against discrimination and segregation in public schools, which culminated in the landmark case *Brown* v. *Board of Education of Topeka, Kansas* (1954). The Warren-led Supreme Court attacked the long-standing segregationist principles of *Plessy* v. *Ferguson* (1896) in deciding the *Brown* case. Although its ruling was technically limited to a constitutional declaration outlawing racial segregation in the public schools, it served as a basis for later Supreme Court rulings that declared all state-imposed racial discrimination unconstitutional per se.[7] The *Brown* decision and a subsequent order for its implementation marked the beginning of a new era in the legal struggle for black equality.[8]

The integration efforts of the NAACP had a widespread impact and were not lost on even the obscure and ordinary citizen, such as I. H. "Sporty" Harvey, a quite mediocre black boxer from San Antonio, Texas. Having languished in the sport for little money and less renown, fighting only members of his own race under difficult conditions, Harvey sought relief via state legislator and liberal lawyer Maury Maverick, the son of a famous congressman. Maverick had earlier introduced a bill to repeal the discriminatory Texas prizefight statute; that met with no success. Thus, when Harvey came to him in June 1953 he was more than happy to take the issue before the courts. Maverick enlisted the support of a Chicano lawyer and future superior court judge, Carlos Cardena, and set out to challenge the constitutionality of the 1933 Texas law banning prizefights between whites and blacks. Initially, the elitist NAACP offered no help, as it was committed to the school desegregation issue and chose not to expend valuable energy on a seemingly frivolous boxing case—one that it believed was doomed in the state courts. Maverick defied convention, however, and confronted the local courts, not the federal courts. It was a bold step.[9]

Despite his poor record of only seven wins against nine losses, the brief filed by Harvey's attorneys stated that since boxing titles in Texas were for whites only, the state had unfairly denied him access to a championship. District Court Judge Jack Roberts, motivated by career considerations, entered a judgment upholding the 1933 law on the ground of compelling state interest; in other words, he supported the contention that mixed prizefights threatened stable race relations.[10] An anonymous source maintained that Roberts privately admitted, "I'd a ruled for the nigger, were it not for the heat I'd feel."[11]

The *Brown* decision in February 1954 gave Harvey and his attorneys new hope. Still spurning the federal courts, they petitioned the

Texas Court of Civil Appeals, using *Brown* as precedent to argue that Harvey's civil rights had been violated according to the provisions of the Fourteenth Amendment and the Civil Rights Act. Harvey's opponent in the suit, the Texas Commission of Labor Statistics, which controlled boxing in the state, contended once again that "professional boxing matches have a tendency to and do provoke disorders, quarrels, and breaches of the peace."[12] But witnesses provided convincing evidence that blacks and whites had lawfully engaged in mixed sporting events without racial incident. Moreover, Deputy Boxing Commissioner Louis Quintanilla testified that interracial boxing matches had occurred and there had been no unfavorable or disruptive fan reaction. Nonetheless, M. B. Morgan, the commissioner of labor statistics and a defendant in the original suit, repeated the rationalization that trouble would result from mixed bouts; he said he knew this from his conversations with the "man on the street."[13] The court was not convinced, however, and concluded that although the 1933 legislation may have anticipated evil results from mixed boxing, the record indicated beyond doubt that such fears lacked foundation. Moreover, based on *Brown,* the court ruled that "even if riotous conditions did result from mixed boxing exhibitions, we doubt if this statute would be sustained by the Federal Supreme Court in some of its opinions."[14] The Commission of Labor Statistics appealed to the Texas Supreme Court but was denied a rehearing on November 17, 1954.[15]

The Texas courts had moved some distance since *Sweatt* v. *Painter* (1950), in which the U.S. Supreme Court overturned a state court ruling of separate but equal facilities and ordered that the University of Texas Law School admit a black student. Now, in *Harvey* v. *Morgan,* the Texas courts demonstrated that they would uphold the laws of the land. But would the public follow suit? The answer was yes and no. While not nearly as defiant as many other southern states, Texas did maintain many elements of segregation; for example, in several areas of the state public schools remained segregated well into the sixties and seventies. Politics also proved to be an area in which old practices died hard; and, true to its geographical location, Texas seemed to be somewhere between the South and the West on civil rights issues. In prizefighting and other sports racial mixing was permitted, although there were limits: the municipal golf course in Corpus Christi was integrated in 1953, yet blacks were not allowed to use the locker room and clubhouse facilities.[16]

On February 24, 1955, Sporty Harvey became the first black man to legally fight a white man, Buddy Turman, in Texas. Unfortunately, Harvey found himself on the losing side of a unanimous decision. The fight was a promoter's dream, drawing the largest boxing crowd in Dallas in more than ten years. More important, the almost evenly divided interracial crowd of 2,400 witnessed the event without incident.[17] Other mixed bouts took place with no racial flare-ups, yet at least one boxer saw no reason to credit racial egalitarianism or even fair play for the calm with which these fights were received. He was convinced that black defeat ensured peaceful reactions. Although his allegations were difficult to prove or refute, his story is worth telling, if only for its humor.

Bob Baker was known in the trade as a "ham and egger," a second-rate fighter, but also a first-class raconteur who could more easily talk himself into a place in history than fight into one. The following account of one of his Texas prizefight experiences, carried by *Time* magazine in 1957, although distorted, reveals his flare for embellishing stories, even at the expense of history and poor Sporty Harvey. According to Baker:

> I went down to Texas to fight that kid. Roy Harris, that's his name. It was the first mixed bout in Texas. I knew I was going to lose. I was fighting a white boy and no colored man is going to beat a white boy in Texas. I hit him and he went down and I thought "Why this boy can't fight at all."
>
> But I can hear that crowd and they're counting on this boy. So I said, "Kid please get up." I know that if he didn't get up they weren't going to let me out of that town alive. I love my wife and I love my kids, and most of all I love me. And I told the kid to get up, and I'm thankful that he did. And after that I was careful not to hit him. So he won.[18]

Baker was certainly correct about one thing—Roy Harris from Cut'n Shoot, Texas, could not fight. He became one of Floyd Patterson's "bums of the month" and a sacrificial lamb for Sonny Liston. The fact that Liston demolished Harris in the first round of a fight in Texas in 1960, with no demonstrably adverse fan reaction, casts even more doubt on Baker's talent and veracity.[19]

Texas stood in stark contrast to Louisiana, where a pitched battle was being waged to prevent interracial boxing matches. Interestingly, by 1953 Louisiana had eased separatist practices at sporting events by allowing whites and blacks to fight on the same program; a sixty-year-old rule had prohibited this. Of course, white and black seating arrangements were still subject to rigid segregation at these events. In a series of steps leading toward "integration," the state athletic commission also revealed that no laws existed to prohibit white and black athletes from playing against one another in football, basketball, baseball, and other sports.[20] But the state government, perceiving federal civil rights activity as a threat to the established social order, which brought back painful memories of Reconstruction, retrenched and tried to turn back the clock on black social and civil rights.

In June 1956 a bill reached the legislature that would prohibit "dancing, social functions, entertainment, athletic training, games, sports, or contests and other such activities involving personal and social contact in which the participants or contestants are members of the white and negro race." Blacks protested in letters to Governor Earl Long and threatened boycotts of professional fights, but the bill passed anyway, in violation of the spirit of recent Supreme Court decisions regarding state-imposed segregation.[21] The New Orleans Branch of the NAACP led the fight, and in its "Action Program for 1955" demonstrated the seriousness with which it approached the issue: "Equal opportunity to recreational facilities is almost as necessary as equal opportunity in education and work in our fast moving society."[22] Condemnation of the new Louisiana law came from boxing interests all over the nation. The National Boxing Association's executive committee called it "completely repugnant to the spirit of America and to the principles of freedom so clearly enunciated by the United States Supreme Court in its recent decisions."[23] Until Louisiana rescinded the act, the NBA urged boxers and their managers to avoid that state.[24] With the legislature and the governor refusing to yield, the controversy festered and then erupted in a bizarre series of events surrounding a top lightweight contender.

Ralph Dupas, a tan-complexioned young man, found himself caught up by the new law and the racial hatred that infected much of Louisiana society. Mrs. Lucretia Gravolet, a seventy-four-year-old resident of Davant in Plaquemines Parish, wrote to Senator W. M. Rainch, chairman of the joint legislative committee on segregation, and asserted that she knew and could prove that Dupas was in fact a black man from Plaquemines Parish who was formerly known as Ralph Duplessis. The accusations alone brought Dupas and his family considerable embarrassment and hurt.[25] If proven correct, he would be barred from fighting against whites in Louisiana, thereby causing inestimable damage to his career. Of immediate concern, however, was an upcoming fight against Vince Martinez. (Hispanics were judged on color, not blood content.) The Louisiana State Athletic Commission heard testimony behind closed doors from a variety of individuals who attested that Dupas was born in Orleans Parish and that his family was white. Dupas's lawyer, Sam Yelden, offered documentary evidence, including a statement from a doctor and a Roman Catholic nun, to support Dupas's claim that he was white.

The athletic commission found no truth to the charges and granted

Dupas permission to meet Martinez. After the ruling, a much-relieved boxer said, "I knew it would end this way. But its' been an embarrassing experience." His mother, echoing her son's optimism, added, "Maybe all Ralph's troubles are over now."[26] They were both wrong. Shortly after the beleaguered fighter's victory over Martinez, the Louisiana State Boxing Commission, reacting to pressure from the state attorney general's office, demanded that he produce a certified record of birth before it would approve any future bouts. The agency responsible for providing the necessary documentation, the Bureau of Vital Statistics, held that Dupas was legally black and, indeed, his birth certificate appeared to support that claim (under Louisiana law "black blood" traced back within five generations makes the bearer black[27]). The probe revealed that Dupas's mother had been reared by a black family named DuPlessis, but she maintained that they took her in after she had been orphaned and that she did not know her real mother or father. Unable to read or write, she had eleven children before she officially declared Peter Dupas the father of all of them. The city of New Orleans never issued a birth certificate for Ralph Dupas and its records had allegedly been altered to classify him as a member of the "Negro race." Death certificates for Dupas's paternal grandmother and grandfather listed them as white.

The Louisiana attorney general's office, which officially considered Dupas black, ruled that his highly important upcoming fight with Ramon Fuentes was illegal. Although the athletic commission continued to support him, it was no match for the state's highest legal authority.[28] In the meantime Dupas sued for a delayed birth certificate, and in October 1957 he won a short-lived victory. Civil District Judge Rene Viosca ordered the city of New Orleans to issue a delayed white birth certificate to lightweight boxer Ralph Dupas. Judge Viosca believed the city had failed to establish that Dupas was of "colored" ancestry; he also took into consideration the fact that Dupas was "a man who has been commonly accepted as caucasian."[29] In late February 1958, however, the Orleans Parish Court of Appeals reversed Viosca's decision, maintaining that city officials could not be ordered to issue a birth certificate to the fighter because Dupas had not proved he was born in Orleans Parish.[30]

The court battle continued. On June 27, 1958, Dupas was granted a hearing before the Louisiana Supreme Court, which ruled that his right to his own birth records had been denied on specious grounds—clearly, there was a lack of evidence that Dupas was black, and the city also did not want to be exposed for altering birth records. Unable to prove its point, the attorney general's office reversed itself[31] and Dupas, whose life history had been aired before the public like clothes on a line, won the right to be white. Yet his victory was a mixed one, because as a white man he could not fight blacks in Louisiana; hence, a proposed bout with Joe Brown for the lightweight championship would await a change in the law.

A little-known fighter named Joseph Dorsey soon found himself at center stage in the fight against discrimination in Louisiana. Although the Dupas controversy had attracted more public attention, Dorsey's case, along with five other NAACP-sponsored lawsuits against the New Orleans public school system, the city parks, the city buses, and the trade schools,[32] showed the depth of Louisiana's racial problems. His lawyers argued along the same lines that Harvey's had in the Texas case—that state law prevented their client from fighting for a championship. Having no luck in the state courts, Dorsey's NAACP attorneys, among them James Nabrit III and A. P. Tureaud, Sr., turned to the federal courts and found a sympathetic ear. A three-judge panel ruled that Louisiana's athletic segregation law was unconstitutional, as was the state athletic commission's ruling that prevented interracial bouts.[33] Louisiana officials, determined to challenge this "pernicious" decision imposed by misguided federal judges, appealed on the grounds that the state had been sued without its consent, in violation of the Eleventh Amendment. As expected the U.S. Supreme Court upheld the federal court ruling and reaffirmed the unconstitutionality of the Louisiana law.

Immediately boxing promoters and officials hailed the decision, rejoicing in the prospects of increased interest generated by inter-racial bouts. More altruistic supporters believed the ruling would open Louisiana's eyes "to the things that are steadily taking place in our society."[34] However, Joseph E. Viguerie, president of the South Louisiana Citizens Council, spoke for a great many people in protesting the federal action. He assured like-minded citizens that "segregation in athletic games, dancing and similar activities will continue to be the custom" and condemned the profit seekers, adding that "common sense and good judgment will prevail."[35] Indeed, schools, buses, athletic events, and prizefights in Louisiana remained segregated, which frustrated blacks and moved them from legal action to civil disobedience.

From the Courts to the Streets

By the mid- to late 1950s, blacks had assumed a more militant position, combining legal tactics with boycotts and Ghandi-inspired civil disobedience. The catalyst, of course, was Rosa Parks's courageous refusal on December 1, 1955, to yield her bus seat to a white person. According to historian Lerone Bennett, Mrs. Parks's arrest in Montgomery, Alabama, "did what no other event, however horrible, had been able to do: it unified and focused the discontent of an entire Negro community."[36] The Montgomery bus boycott that followed introduced the country to Dr. Martin Luther King, Jr., who would lead a national resistance movement cloaked "in the disarmingly appealing garb of love, forgiveness, and *passive* resistance." Blacks had long been ready for change; now they had Rosa Parks to symbolize their quest for equality and Martin Luther King to show them the way.[37] Afro-Americans would no longer wait for the courts to solve their problems; instead, they would take to the streets, armed with the belief that truth and righteousness would prevail.[38] Blacks proudly marched down the road of activism, joined by a number of athletes, especially boxers.

Sugar Ray Robinson, not one to pull punches in or out of the ring, had a penchant for approaching discrimination head on. The same man who had refused to enter an Illinois boxing auditorium through a back entrance designated for blacks, who had confronted segregationists in the South, now took aim at the governor of Arkansas and the president of the United States. Commenting on Governor Orval Faubus's recalcitrance during the Little Rock school desegregation crisis in 1957, Robinson declared, "I never interfere in politics, no kind of way, but I'd give that Faubus my whole purse and take him on after Basilio." Of President Eisenhower, who had been indecisive during the crisis, he said, "There he is playin' golf and his country is darn near a revolution."[39] A remarkably free-spirited and determinedly independent man, Robinson's civil rights efforts were never focused or sustained, yet they reflected the potential pressure that could be applied by America's most visible and acclaimed blacks. The embodiment of that potential was still developing his boxing skills in a Louisville Police Athletic League gym.

By the early sixties the country was certainly in turmoil, if not on the verge of revolution. The new black militancy gained strength in the larger society and filtered through the semipermeable membrane that separated sport from the real world. Gradually, many black Americans awoke to the reality that black athletes were being used to cover up the transgressions of a repressive system. They no longer accepted the theory that the athletic accomplishments of blacks were confirmation that the present system worked for all its citizens; that if the masses of blacks were competitive, disciplined, hardworking, patriotic, and God-fearing, they too could realize the American Dream.[40]

For Floyd Patterson, who seemed content to take his cues from past legends, the change would make him a man out of place and out of time. After taking Rocky Marciano's vacant title in 1956, Patterson assumed that he should follow in the tradition of Joe Louis, Ezzard Charles, and Jersey Joe Walcott, which he did, becoming a relatively popular champion despite the dreadful quality of his opponents. However, his accommodationist stance found less and less support in the black community. His idea of radicalism was to drink from a whites-only water fountain in the South and remark that the water tasted the same.[41] Where Louis and his successors' passive and patriotic roles were appropriate and heroic to most blacks, the same posture from Patterson stigmatized him as an "Uncle Tom," an enemy of the people. Howard Cosell was among those who sensed that Patterson was playing to the crowd but that the crowd had grown tired of his act.

While Joe Louis's victories in the ring were often symbolic achievements for all blacks and stimulated immeasurable pride, Patterson's later battles carried little or no significance.[42] Militant and astute blacks had finally come to the realization that too much had been made of the accomplishments of black athletes; that black champions and the integration of sport did not generate, or even contribute to, meaningful changes in political, economic, or social conditions. Moreover, the athletes themselves often did not benefit from their own accomplishments. Jesse Owens, who had expected riches and fame after his "stupendous feats" against the Nazis in the 1936 Olympics, instead found himself stripped of his amateur status and forced to run against horses and work as a janitor to earn a living.[43] Joe Louis became a professional wrestler in a desperate attempt to pay off his staggering tax indebtedness; because those people he had counted on during his boxing career had taken advantage of him, the same government he had served so nobly during World War II now hounded him for money.[44]

When Sonny Liston and Floyd Patterson met in 1963 the new breed of blacks struggling for social equality and economic progress believed that the real fight was being waged in the streets, not in the ring. *New York Times* sportswriter Robert Lipsyte captured these sentiments in interviews with militant blacks protesting housing discrimination in New York. Attempting to explore the historic link between sport and civil rights, Lipsyte asked the protestors about the significance of the upcoming heavyweight bout. To his surprise he got answers like, "They'll always give us an opportunity to act like animals," or "We're beyond the point where we can get excited over a Negro hitting a homerun or winning a championship." To them the battle in the ring meant nothing compared to the big one "raging in a way of life."[45]

Among those interviewed was Malcolm X, later described by Budd Schulberg as "a black intelligence who had a burning scorn for 'the collective white man' and 'the so-called American Negro'."[46] As chief spokesman for the Black Muslims, his fiery oratory and uncompromising challenges to authority made him one of the most feared men in

America. Malcolm X considered boxing to be exploitative of blacks; to him prizefights were laughable affairs in which promoters "let a Negro excel if they [sic] are going to make money for them."[47] Such opinions notwithstanding, he was considerably interested in the outcome of Floyd Patterson's fights, because Patterson had crossed him by offering disparaging comments to the media on the Nation of Islam, insults that he believed had come at the urging of whites. Consequently, Malcolm X hoped that Sonny Liston would "shake Patterson up."[48] Liston obliged, uncrowning Patterson in short order. What Liston could not do was seal Patterson's lips or negate his influence among Christians and integrationists. Patterson still symbolized the moderation that most liberal Americans wanted, in stark contrast to Liston, the former convict with long-standing connections to organized crime and the man Maurice Berube characterized as the "stereotypical nightmare of the bad nigger, the juvenile delinquent grown up."[49]

Although Malcolm X downplayed the importance of prizefighting, he had no qualms about stage-managing the next heavyweight champion to ensure that his points of view and deeply felt religious convictions would find a mouthpiece in one of America's most visible symbols. The heavyweight champion's throne would be the public power base of the Nation of Islam; the standard bearer would be Cassius Marcellus Clay. According to Maurice Berube, Clay was destined to become "a folk hero, one of the first truly black men to challenge America in black terms." He was neither "the humble Negro champion like Joe Louis" nor "the 'non-white' champion, Jack Johnson, who terrified whites by seeking white prerogatives."[50]

When Cassius Clay first appeared on the boxing scene he was a breath of fresh air, someone who might restore boxing's tainted image and sagging fortunes. The scene was so familiar to prizefight fans that few of them paid serious attention to the open, outspoken youngster. When he won a gold medal as a light heavyweight at the 1960 Rome Olympics, however, Clay established himself as an American hero. At first his professional career was carefully managed by a group of white Louisville businessmen, led by William Faversham, Jr., who admitted, "We were presumptuous enough to think we could help boxing by bringing along this clean and colorful kid from Louisville."[51] When Clay showed signs of black consciousness in his selection of a young, black, female lawyer named Alberta Jones to negotiate his contracts, no one thought anything of it. He was the "Johnny Appleseed of boxing," and his loud mouth and impudence were assets. Over 16,000 fans paid up to thirty dollars each "in hopes of seeing Archie Moore button the brash kid's lip."[52] They still did not realize that the fresh breeze would turn into a dragon's breath or that Johnny Appleseed would sow the seeds of discord.

Angry observers would later accuse Malcolm X of poisoning the young fighter's mind, but Budd Schulberg believed that Clay fooled the American public by hiding his true feelings from the people who watched him "roll his marvelous brown body and bark with laughter like a frolicking young sea lion."[53] No one sensed the lurking racial anxiety within, "producing anger as causatively as boiling water releases steam." Malcolm X merely harnessed that steam, gave it purpose, and directed it against his enemies.[54]

Cassius Clay and his brother, Rudolph, met Malcolm X in 1963 at a Detroit mosque. The charismatic leader convinced Clay that he could serve as a warrior for the Muslim cause, combatting the power of white Christianity that had conditioned blacks to accept inferior status. His battles against Christian opponents would be "a modern crusade," with satellites beaming the action to the world. The fighter invited his Black Muslim mentor to his training camp before the first encounter with Sonny Liston in February 1964 and their relationship was made public. The boxing world and society at large were shaken by the link, even before the challenger's public announcement of his new spiritual and political directions.[55]

The elements of Clay's departure from what society expected of him had roots in the more traditional civil rights movement. Black revolutionary and radical protest movements have usually had a deep religious component; in fact, the spiritual base of the black community is so significant that any movement planning to make a substantial social impact must tap it. Throughout the history of the Nation of Islam its leaders have recognized that any move away from Christianity required a more familiar and trustworthy anchor than a purely secular movement could offer. Indeed, Malcolm X established a religious organization, the Muslim Mosque, Inc., before he left the Nation of Islam to found the Organization of Afro-American Unity.[56]

The Nation of Islam's religious underpinning mattered little to most Americans. Promoters sensed this and nearly cancelled the Liston-Clay fight when they learned of Clay's conversion. They feared the revelation would threaten the salability of a bout that had been billed as a clash between good and evil, or as Clay put it, "Little Red Riding Hood" against the "big bad wolf." Backers were convinced that when fans learned of Clay's espousal of an alien religion and a radical political doctrine, "they'd pray for the wolf to win."[57] Their concerns were financial, whereas the general populace really feared these "black avengers" against white injustice. The media and law enforcement agencies, on a variety of levels, conducted "a veritable witch hunt" against the Black Muslims, who seemingly dictated the terms for their own freedom and development.[58]

Crowning the "Black Prince"

Cassius Clay, in reality Cassius X, took the heavyweight championship from Sonny Liston on February 25, 1964, and immediately became a supposedly dangerous alien in his own land. Budd Schulberg maintained that the brash warrior "would fight with weapons never before carried into an American ring," including his faith in a non-Western religion and his belief that "he was part of a global family of nonwhites among whom Caucasians were in turn a minority doomed to eventual defeat."[59]

Shortly after his disciple's religious conversion and boxing victory, Malcolm X fell completely out of favor with his leader and second father, Elijah Muhammad, ostensibly for his comments about the assassination of President Kennedy but more likely because he was becoming too powerful. A drastic change in the movement followed his ouster.[60] Deemphasizing politics, the Nation of Islam now focused on economic self-sufficiency and social improvements for blacks. Elijah Muhammad changed Cassius X's name to Muhammad Ali, in recognition of his faith and to reflect the shift toward a less threatening stance. Ali was commissioned by his new mentor to serve as the most visible spokesman for the new, moderate, economically oriented, more religious Nation of Islam.[61] And he supported the party line, even on Malcolm X, his dear friend. Most Americans, however, still associated the Nation of Islam and Black Muslims with Malcolm X and hatred—an image that was solidified in late 1959 by Mike Wallace's "kaleidoscope of 'shocker' images" captured in the documentary "The Hate That Hate Produced."[62]

This reaction was not unexpected. According to C. Eric Lincoln, the first scholar to study the movement, the fact that the Black Muslims grew out of the same social conflict that spawned other black protest groups was not enough to make them "acceptable to the spirit of protest which has won universal respect and frequent admiration."[63] The major difference between the Nation of Islam and other groups lay in the former's reluctance to appeal to the "white man's conscience." Instead, its leaders sought a "more dependable protection" for their "interests than came from sharing the white man's power."[64] This novel approach alienated many blacks and threatened most whites; once Malcolm X left the group Ali became the prime target of their concern.

When the World Boxing Association threatened to strip Ali of his title for what it considered "conduct detrimental to the spirit of boxing,"[65]

most observers concluded that his religious and racial views were the
real reasons for the proceedings against him. The NAACP suspected as
much and so did Senator Richard Russell of Georgia. The diehard
segregationist urged his colleagues to stay clear of the dispute, for "those
who direct this WBA are so intolerant, narrow-minded, and bigoted to
threaten to strip a champion of his title for his religious belief."[66] This
coming together of three disparate interests—the Nation of Islam
(separatist), the NAACP (integrationist), and Russell (segregationist)
—indicated the importance of the issue and the dynamics of race
relations at the time.

Southern politicians had historically cited examples of northern
racial intolerance to expose the hypocrisy of a region that tried to apply
different standards to southern racial problems than it did to its own. An
arch segregationist, Richard Russell often supported causes for seemingly egalitarian reasons when in reality he simply wanted to preserve
southern order.[67] Such thinking dictated Senator Russell's surprising
support of Muhammad Ali, who he predicted from the moment of his
conversion would be surrounded by a storm of controversy.[68] After the
WBA temporarily removed Ali's title in March 1964, Russell called the
decision and the public's acceptance of it evidence of "the grip of
intolerance on this country." He argued that such demands for conformity posed a serious threat to every American citizen and that the federal
government was failing to guarantee the people's Constitutional rights.
Russell conjectured: "What if the situation had been reversed and
Patterson had been the champion and had joined a sect of any kind
which believed in utilizing the Federal power to mix races? If any boxing
association, or even any individual, had undertaken to take his title away
from him for believing in integration and race mixing, the editorial
pages in every newspaper in the land would have sizzled with ringing
denunciations."[69]

Senator Jacob Javits, a liberal Republican from New York, agreed
with Russell, albeit reluctantly. Careful to maintain his distance for fear
of falling into the same "political bed," Javits took the floor and offered
this advice to his colleagues and, ultimately, to the nation: "Perhaps it is
a good thing to demonstrate to the country that whatever may be the
differences between the Senator from Georgia and me—and probably
they are as profound as any in the Chamber on the issue of Civil
rights—we can also see eye to eye on a question such as this without
inhibition."[70]

The fact that Ali was being discussed in the Senate was clear proof
that the heavyweight title was an instrument of symbolic power beyond
the sport. Senator Russell astutely understood that Ali commanded the

attention, if not the allegiance, of a large segment of the black population and thus found in him a brave and popular black proponent of segregation. Russell wanted to prove to all Americans that even blacks believed in separation of the races. Implicit in his statements and his stance was the message that the South could not be all bad if a southern representative was speaking out for the beliefs of a black man as the rest of the nation remained quiet.

Three major athletic commissions (New York, California, and Pennsylvania) refused to support the WBA action, reflecting an age-old tradition that even "villainous" champions should be fairly treated. Consequently, most of America and the world still recognized Ali as the heavyweight titleholder. For the time being, at least, even his detractors were willing to wait for someone to take his crown in the ring. The questions remained, Who would redeem America? Would there be another search for the great "white hope?"

The Black "White Hope"

Boxing promoters, politicians, and the media all sensed that the time was not right for a blatantly racist campaign to neutralize Ali. With the enactment of new civil rights legislation, the American government seemed on the verge of fulfilling the promises of its Constitution and motto. Fortunately for Ali's opponents, his association with the Nation of Islam not only put him outside white values but also distanced him from many blacks. The climate was perfect for a black "white hope," and Floyd Patterson, who had carried integration to its furthest extreme by marrying a white woman, was it. Ironically, in Jack Johnson's era Ali would have been the hero and Patterson the villain. Now, Patterson saw in Ali the opportunity to regain the championship and become a hero, even a legend—something his fighting ability, personality, and prior circumstances had not permitted; it was his last chance for boxing immortality.[71]

Although the Patterson-Ali rivalry conjured up images of a "holy war," a battle between the forces of Islam and Christianity, religion was not the real issue; racial ideology, patriotism, and society's standards for proper athletic behavior were at the heart of the dispute. Ali had alienated much of the sporting public and boxing officialdom. Howard Cosell claimed to be the only person in the media to call him "by the name he adopted"; an angry and ugly public responded by labeling Cosell a "White Muslim."[72] Irrespective of the artistry and grace Ali brought to a sport that had previously thrived on naked power, his cockiness and his political and religious dissent flew in the face of society's rule that athletic heroes must hang their heads in humble appreciation and stay out of politics. Mainstream liberals, as lineal descendants of those who had supported Jackie Robinson's integration of baseball, did not want this iconoclast to threaten its vision of American order and the role athletes must play in it.[73]

Ali was the perfect foil and Patterson relished his role, playing it with an enthusiasm that must have either delighted or embarrassed his supporters. His once close friend Howard Cosell was offended by Patterson's "good guy" routine and his invidious comparisons between the Black Muslims and the Ku Klux Klan.[74] His characterizations of the Nation of Islam as a hate group perpetuated the very image it was working so hard to shed. The Black Muslims' non-Christian religion, their conscientious objection to war, and their separatist racial philosophy were convincing evidence to Patterson and many citizens that the followers of Elijah Muhammad could not be true Americans. The country's rising level of intolerance was reflected in Patterson's declaration to Ali: "I challenge you not only for myself, but for all people who think and feel as I do." He was, of course, speaking to the self-righteousness of the cause.[75]

Patterson got his big chance on November 22, 1965, but his fists proved far weaker than his mouth. His refusal to call Ali by his new name—he insisted on calling the man "Clay"—showed disrespect not only for Ali's religious beliefs but for the man himself. Yet the proud and egotistical Ali could not bring himself to hate Patterson. Although most observers believed Ali tortured Patterson for twelve rounds, refusing to end the fight with a "merciful" knockout, Howard Cosell believed otherwise after Ali made the potentially dangerous admission that he had "carried" Patterson. (In boxing parlance, "to carry" is to refrain from hurting an opponent or making him look bad.) Ali saw himself as a victim, trapped in an impossible situation; he once complained to Cosell, "When I knock a man out I'm cruel. When I don't I can't punch."[76] Whatever his reason, Ali seemed to have a soft spot for Patterson. Maybe the former champion's accomplishments, despite his small size, influenced Ali; or maybe he believed that Patterson was simply a product of another age, playing a prescribed role. He showed his true feelings when he agreed to fight Patterson in September 1972. The thirty-year-old Ali took on the thirty-seven-year-old Patterson not because he delighted in torturing an older man but because Patterson had fallen on hard times. Bad financial management and accounting had caused serious tax problems for the former champion, and most of what he owned was taken by the Internal Revenue Service.[77]

All this is not to say that Muhammad Ali was not capable of hatred

I. H. "Sporty" Harvey, the first black man to legally box a white man in Texas. (I. H. "Sporty" Harvey)

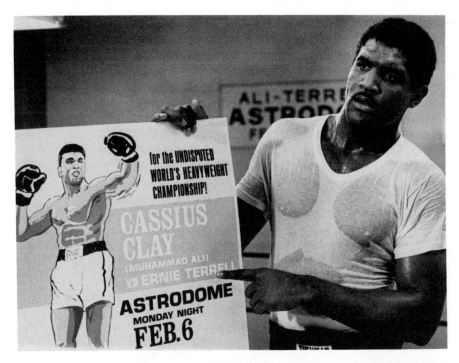

A relatively unmarked but very angry Ernie Terrell threatened not to fight Muhammad Ali until something was done about the advertisement for the fight, which displayed a large likeness of Ali and none of Terrell, the WBA champion; Terrell's name is also printed in smaller letters. (UPI Photo by Walt Frerck)

This postfight photo indicates the beating Ernie Terrell suffered at the hands of Muhammad Ali, whom Terrell repeatedly referred to as Clay. (UPI Photo by Walt Frerck)

A young, handsome, and trim Muhammad Ali posed for this publicity shot. (Reverend Ray Martin, Progressive Amateur Boxing Association, Inc., Houston, Tex.)

A defiant heavyweight champion Muhammad Ali, still referred to as Cassius Clay by UPI, talks to Howard Cosell and other newsmen shortly before his scheduled induction into the U.S. armed forces on April 28, 1967. (UPI/Bettmann Newsphotos)

or cruelty. When he fought Ernie Terrell in February 1967 he was not able to hide his disdain or his meanness. Terrell was six feet, six inches tall and weighed 200 pounds, which gave Ali no reason to pity him; moreover, Ali viewed Terrell as a usurper who had gained the World Boxing Association belt by beating Eddie Machen after that association had "permanently" stripped Ali of the title in the fall of 1964 for his unauthorized rematch, scheduled for May 22, 1965, against Sonny Liston in Lewiston, Maine. Terrell criticized Ali's stand on the draft and, like Patterson, insisted upon demeaning Ali's religion and calling him "Clay"—a "slave name" Ali had come to despise. Above all, Terrell's attacks on Ali simply came at the wrong time. He mirrored a society that sought to destroy Ali by making him a social outcast and denying him the right to earn a living. Ali, in a wicked display of rage, taunted Terrell, punctuating each punch with the demand, "What's my name?" In torturing and humiliating Terrell, Ali was striking back at his enemies.[78]

After his fight with Patterson, Ali hosted his own "bum of the month" club, which included the tough but punchless Canadian George Chuvalo; Henry "The Bleeder" Cooper of England, who had floored a young Ali in 1963 before losing the fight on cuts; Brian London of England and Karl Mildenberger of Germany, two nondescript fighters; and Cleveland "Big Cat" Williams, who had distinguished himself by surviving a bullet shot at close range into his stomach by a policeman.[79] As challengers dropped one after another the anti-Ali forces struggled to find answers. Unlike the outrageous and controversial Jack Johnson, Ali's moral character was not vulnerable to attack. He was a notorious womanizer, but so were many other famous Americans: presidents, generals, even Joe Louis had been known to make the rounds, and with the sports media dominated by men and nurtured by a sexual double standard, chasing women was hardly grounds for character assassination. Although some people did try to exploit Ali's marital infidelity as proof of religious insincerity, they were not very successful. Ali was careful to avoid alcohol, drugs, cigarettes, and, most of all, white women.[80]

Muhammad Ali symbolized America under siege. Its urban black population was growing increasingly frustrated and embittered. In the minds of these angry city dwellers an act of police brutality was no longer an isolated occurrence but was representative of institutional racism and injustice, which could and did set off riots across the nation. The new black consciousness of the sixties, with its activism and militancy, touched the sensibilities of whites, moving many of them to rethink their attitudes about and behavior toward America. Racism, the atomic bomb, poverty, and American involvement in Vietnam became focal points of unprecedented skepticism and protest. The nation's leaders were threatened, and in their insecurity they sought to silence the opposition. Ali had become a personification of the discontent and unrest; he was a "crossover" artist before the term found its application in youth culture and the music world; he was the "Fifth Beatle," a deracinated, classless, alien, antiestablishment figure of broad appeal.[81] The government concluded that one way of shutting Ali up was to "co-opt" him (a catchword of the sixties, meaning the authorities tried to subvert the opposition by absorbing or buying members to their side).[82]

Love It or Leave It: War Psychosis

In 1963, at a time when Ali was considered charmingly obnoxious, he had been classified 1-Y for draft purposes—mentally incompetent to serve in the armed forces. A few disgruntled congressmen called the classification an "insult to every mother's son serving in Vietnam,"[83] and before too many years passed a chorus of voices called out for his reclassification. Shortly before his fight with Ernie Terrell in February 1967, the Selective Service reclassified Ali, making him draft eligible with 1-A status. The government sought to have him replay the role that Joe Louis had performed in World War II and guaranteed him that he would not see duty in Vietnam. Ali not only refused, he poetically challenged the government:

> Keep asking me, no matter how long.
> On the war in Viet Nam,
> I sing this song
> I ain't got no quarrel with the Viet Cong.[84]

His response brought angry denunciations from the highest levels. Representative Frank Clark of Pennsylvania came close to branding Ali a traitor. On the floor of Congress he rebuked the champion, "To welch or back off from that commitment is as unthinkable as surrendering to Adolf Hitler or Mussolini would have been in my days of military service."[85] The comparison was misleading at the very least, for the undeclared war in Vietnam bore little resemblance to World War II.

Foisted upon the public as a necessary and inescapable duty to preserve a democratic government against the forces of communism, the war was, in reality, created in part by America's insistence upon protecting resources of economic and strategic interest, blocking indigenous revolutions, and subscribing to the domino theory as an article of faith. American efforts were marred by a lack of understanding or appreciation for the complexities of Vietnamese politics, culture, and nationalism. Moreover, as the nation's own intelligence sources showed, at the time of the Geneva Accords, Ho Chi Minh had the overwhelming support of the Vietnamese people. Yet the United States wedded itself to Ngo Dinh Diem, president of South Vietnam, a man who had little popular support and few democratic principles. By 1957 an insurgence had begun in South Vietnam, which the U.S. government maintained was the product of North Vietnam's desire to impose communism on its southern neighbor; critics called it an indigenous revolt. According to William Duiker, the insurgence was a legitimate revolt based in South Vietnam with organization and direction from Ho Chi Minh in North Vietnam.[86]

No matter the source of the rebellion, the American government viewed Vietnam as a cornerstone to the stability of Indochina. Post-World War II policy of containment dictated that wherever possible the United States would do whatever it could to prevent the spread of Soviet, and later Chinese, influence.[87] Although many people in the Kennedy and Johnson administrations questioned the likelihood of success, the apparent belief in the righteousness of the cause and the assurance that God was on our side pushed America deeper and deeper into a war that eventually proved both unwinnable and unpopular. In retrospect, protecting the reputations of policymakers and discouraging "unfriendly" national liberation movements seemed more responsible for the failed initiative.

When President Lyndon B. Johnson ordered direct attacks on North Vietnam and later sent over thousands of land troops, many people began to voice the question, What are we fighting for? The Students for a Democratic Society organized protests against the government's actions, as the nation's growing uncertainty and insecurity bred extreme intolerance, even threatening long-standing constitutional rights. (For example, during the October 1967 antiwar demonstrations, 3,000 U.S. troops and marshals were dispatched to protect the nation's capital, marking the first time since the 1932 Bonus March that such force was used against American citizens.[88]) *Newsweek* columnist Emmet John Hughes sensed "a feeling—a tension in society and a stress among men—not known since the 1930s."[89] The Central Intelligence Agency and the Federal Bureau of Investigation infiltrated the antiwar movements and frequently engaged in smear campaigns, the most common tactic being to label key leaders as communists or communist-linked.[90]

History has shown that the government alone could not have created this atmosphere of intolerance. When President Woodrow Wilson had explained to the American public that World War I would be the war to end all wars and that those who disagreed were opposed to righteousness in a fight against evil, his "idealistic rhetoric was intended to appeal to people's nobler instincts." Unfortunately, some Americans, even those in the government, "used the passions of war to unleash campaigns of hatred against the enemy and against 'slackers' at home."[91] Such a response by a large segment of the American population to a similar justification for intervention in the 1950s and 1960s was possible because of the government's ability to shape popular dissent, not only through ideological domination, but by the development or support of an entire set of practices and expectations that established the norm for most members of the society. In this context hegemonic ideology became a part of everyday life and action; it derived from the dominant group but was sustained by collaboration of the dominated.[92]

Under such a system the government did not need to dictate the actions of its people. Television networks were, for a long time, able to discredit the antiwar movement through trivialization, polarization, and distortion. War critics suffered at the hands of ordinary citizens, as killings, physical assault, and bombings (three in the spring of 1966 alone) spoke to the hostility. Public opinion polls for the war years documented the "consistently high levels of intolerance for the anti-war critics," according to historian Charles De Benedetti. Other forms of harrassment, such as job dismissals, petty vandalism, or questionable arrests, cannot be quantified easily but were numerous, as were harrassment of war critics' families and relatives and the receipt of death threats.[93] Representative Frank Clark evinced this mood in suggesting that the war necessitated limitations on freedom of expression because "there is some stage at which our use of free speech and open discussion becomes a transgression on good common sense."[94]

Feelings about American involvement in Vietnam notwithstanding, Muhammad Ali had broken no laws, and for the time being Congress and his other opponents had no grounds for legal recourse; Clark did, however, call for a boycott of his fights. When Ali sought a military deferment as a conscientious objector, Mendel Rivers, a South Carolina congressman and the powerful chairman of the House Armed Services Committee, warned, "If the theologian of Black Muslim power, Cassius Clay, is deferred by the board in Louisville, you watch what happens in Washington."[95] Since the Kentucky Senate demanded that he be drafted, Ali's lawyers expected that the Louisville Federal Induction Center would reject his appeal and decided that he should establish residency in Houston, where one of his lawyers suggested he might get a better deal. Optimism quickly turned to despair when Selective Service Director General Lewis B. Hershey predicted that Ali would not be deferred (Hershey's wife was the sister of Hayden Covington, a member of Ali's legal team). Considering the fact that Joe Namath (the football player with bad knees) and George Hamilton (the actor who was dating the president's daughter) had been spared military service, Hershey's forecast prompted Covington to tell Ali, "They want to make an example of you."[96] Pressure from Washington and the court of public opinion proved strong and the review board denied Ali's request.[97]

Although Muhammad Ali had many faults, religious insincerity was not among them. He did not "tone down his Muslim affiliation, although it cost him millions in endorsements, appearances, and television and recording contracts."[98] Ordered to report for induction on April 1, 1967, Ali was met at the courthouse by black students who carried signs that read, "Stay Home, Muhammad Ali," and who chanted, along with black power activist H. Rap Brown, "Hep! Hep! Don't take that step." A triumphant Ali emerged from the building after refusing to take the traditional step forward that signified entry into the armed services.[99] His opponents finally had the grounds to crush him. The New York State Athletic Commission stripped him of his title, declaring his conduct "detrimental to the best interests of boxing."[100] Only three years earlier that same commission had backed his right to free expression, announcing that "within the limits of the Constitution, the right to freedom of speech and to religious belief are inviolate."[101] Now other athletic commissions followed New York's lead and refused to recognize him as the heavyweight champion, rescinding his boxing license and consequently denying him the right to earn a living.

On June 20, 1967, a federal court found Ali guilty of draft evasion; sentencing him to five years in prison and levying a $10,000 fine. "Establishment" America had demanded a conviction and had gotten it. The prosecuting attorney warned, "We cannot let this man get loose, because if he gets by, all black people who want to be Muslims will get out for the same reasons."[102] Given the large percentage of blacks in combat, the concern was real. Another Ali critic commented, "If any one individual contributed to the contagious disrespect for law and love of country, then it would have to be our disposed [sic] fighting king."[103] (Ali rivaled Martin Luther King, Jr., in this category, a connection that was more than coincidental.) The sentiment was institutionalized by its inclusion in the *Congressional Record.*

Ali faced imminent incarceration, revocation of his passport, unfavorable press coverage, and hostility from much of the American public. Although financially able to retain good legal counsel and to exhaust the appeals process, his resources could not match those marshaled against him. Solace came from his religion, the encouragement of friends, and support from fellow pacifist and philosopher Bertrand Russell, who assured the man he would never meet, "The air will change. I can sense it."[104] Ali was buoyed by this prophecy but nonetheless teetered on the brink of disaster.

Revolt of the Black Athlete

The public backing that Ali received came at first from a small but influential minority. Howard Cosell did not waver in his support of the embattled fighter. Along with Robert Lipsyte and writers for *Esquire, Newsweek, Sports Illustrated,* and *Christian Century,* Cosell praised Ali for his sincerity and nobility while mocking "his opponents as self-righteous hypocrites who arbitrarily prosecuted him and took his title away."[105] Perhaps many more people agreed with Ali but feared the consequences of speaking out. The avalanche of criticism, oppression, and legal action that followed Ali's refusal to serve in the military unveiled a level of paranoia not felt in this country since the McCarthy era.[106]

Just when he seemed most alone, aid came from an unexpected source: a group of black athletes, led by Bill Russell, the Boston Celtic basketball great.[107] Unable to convince Ali to compromise his beliefs, the athletes chose to publicly back him. They were certain that he was sincere and upset with the infringement of his civil rights; they also recognized their own importance as role models. Instead of using their position to bolster the status quo, these athletes would become agents for change and freedom. They realized the risks but felt they could no longer close their eyes to the artificiality and fragility of their lofty status. Playing the part of the "good Negro" was no longer acceptable.

This open support for Ali heralded a revolt among black athletes which threatened the existing social order. Until now they had been, for the most part, perfect models of passivity, subservience, and blind patriotism despite blatant injustice. In the 1940s and 1950s Paul Robeson, the great Rutgers athlete and a modern "Renaissance man," had dared to call for peaceful coexistence with the Soviet Union. He became a "nonperson" and was unmercifully persecuted. When he was investigated by the House Un-American Activities Committee, even the proud and assertive Jackie Robinson found himself in the difficult position of making statements about black Americans and communism that appeared to directly attack Robeson.[108] Unfortunately, no black athletes came to his assistance.

Although stripped of his title, boxing licenses, the right to travel abroad, and his livelihood, Ali still had something very important: he was an inspiration to black youths, especially proud, dissatisfied young athletes. The adoption of Islamic names by American heroes such as basketball great Lew Alcindor (Kareem Abdul-Jabbar) and football star Bobby Moore (Ahmad Rashaad) symbolized the new mood.[109] When symbolic names turned to symbolic acts in the form of an Olympic boycott, which Jabar endorsed and obeyed, the crisis extended from the realm of sport into the halls of Congress. To counter the rising tide against a black boycott of the Mexico City Olympic Games in 1968, George Hansen, an Idaho congressman, submitted what he believed was a representative article for entry into the *Congressional Record*. The following excerpt reflects the prevailing myths of the time and their questionable assumptions:

> Until the 1950s schools in the South were not yet integrated, Negroes in many cities rode in the rear of buses and housing and restaurant accommodations were segregated.
>
> In athletics, progress toward equality for the Negroes has come by leaps and bounds as compared to two centuries or more of struggling for freedom from oppression across the land. Certainly, though, it is hard to see why so many Negro collegians should be screaming racial prejudice. All one has to do is check the lineups when attending any major college basketball game, or to attend one of the bigger track meets around the country or to watch a pro football game.[110]

Black athletes had, in the past, accepted this outlook, reinforcing the dominant ideology; now they defied it. Ali and others pointed out the cracks in this facade and, amid widespread dismay, spread their message to the white athletic community. Although certainly in the minority, once clean-cut All-American boys who could have taken their places next to Parris Island marine recruits now sported shoulder-length hair and drooping moustaches; even more alarming, they questioned the authority of their drill-instructor-like coaches. A few white professional sports stars soon began to challenge the cult of athletics for its glorification of a cutthroat world of competition, money, and militarism. Dave Meggyesy of the St. Louis (football) Cardinals retired from the game because he felt it was reflective of a sick society, declaring that it was "no accident that the most repressive political regime in our history is ruled by a football freak, President Nixon."[111] Linebacker Chip Oliver of the Oakland Raiders "dropped out" of football to "find himself" in a California commune, calling professional football a "silly game" that "dehumanizes people." He quit because he felt he "wasn't doing anything positive toward making the world a better place to live in." Having been turned into charging "slabs of beef," he and his teammates had lost "their esthetic soul" and with it the feeling that they could "accomplish higher things."[112] Meggyesy, Oliver, and all the gurus of the athletic consciousness movement clearly owed much to Ali.

A Rolling Snowball

Sensing the broader implications of the sanctions against Ali, militant black groups vocally protested the punitive measures and staged boycotts. The list of people opposing a Joe Frazier–Buster Mathis fight in March 1968 to decide the new heavyweight champion of New York, Massachusetts, and Illinois could have been a directory of the new black militancy: Floyd McKissick, national chairman of the Congress of Racial Equality; Jarvis Tyner, national chairman of the W. E. B. Du Bois clubs; Carlos Russell, chairman of the Black Caucus of the National Conference for New Politics; John Wilson, of the National Black Anti-War, Anti-Draft Union; the Student Nonviolent Coordinating Committee; and Amiri Imamu Baraka (Le Roi Jones), cultural leader of the new black nationalism. The group unanimously resolved that "white America cannot tell black people who deserves to be the world Champion and decide for black people who the world's Champion is."[113]

On May 3, 1968, Ali learned that his first appeal had failed. Despite the setback, a muffled chorus of support could be detected in the outcries of incensed American youths who were determined to be heard. As a sign of the changing mood, "Ali became a 'radical-chic' cause when entertainers, writers, and intellectuals" defended the former champion's right to fight. Even Robert Kennedy believed that Ali should be allowed to box and to express his opinions.[114]

The antiwar movement found new strength in the Tet Offensive, a full-scale synchronized attack against the major urban areas of South Vietnam. On January 30, 1968, a team of Vietcong soldiers blasted through a wall surrounding the U.S. Embassy in Saigon and for six hours fought American marines inside the compound.[115] All of the embassy invaders were killed and the Vietcong were routed in most of the other battles, but not before they inflicted heavy casualties among soldiers and civilians and caused considerable destruction in the cities. Further damage was done in the United States as "wire service reports exaggerated the success of the raid on the Embassy" and "televised accounts of the bloody fighting in Saigon and Hue made a mockery of Johnson and of Westmoreland's optimistic year-end reports, widening the credibility gap."[116]

Campaigning on an antiwar platform, Senator Eugene McCarthy of Wisconsin was boosted into national prominence by a group of disenchanted young people and some established politicians. He even came within a few hundred votes of defeating the incumbent president in the New Hampshire Democratic party primary on March 12, 1968. A few days later Bobby Kennedy formally announced his candidacy for the Democratic presidential nomination. Lyndon Johnson could not fight or ignore the rising public opposition to his presidency or the internal rebellion of sorts being led by Defense Secretary Clark Clifford. (Along with corporate lawyers and former Cabinet officers, ambassadors, and generals, Clark told the president that the war was too costly in lives and money and that further escalation would threaten the American social fabric.[117]) Sensing certain defeat, a highly unpopular Johnson revealed on March 31, "I shall not seek and I will not accept the nomination of my party for another term." At the same time he announced a deescalation of the war effort, calling a halt to the bombing raids on population centers in North Vietnam and inviting the North Vietnamese to join him in a "series of mutual moves toward peace."[118]

After the Tet Offensive the American media elites moved more toward a liberal position on the war. Although not casting the radical Left in a flattering light, this slight shift did help to produce powerful images that rocked the Democratic party and the supporters of the war. Perhaps the clearest sign of the media's changing attitude and its effect surfaced at the tumultuous Democratic National Convention in Chicago in June 1968, a convention wracked, if not wrecked, by the Vietnam debate. Bitter floor fighting between forces for and against the war was exacerbated by the rough tactics of city police, who shoved and harrassed anti-Vietnam delegates and spectators; and the nation watched on live television as more of Mayor Daley's "finest" brutalized demonstrators outside the convention center.[119] The media now seemed ready to back the antiwar movement, as evidenced by its support and fostering of the "Clean for Gene" (McCarthy) campaign, in which students shaved off their beards and wore suits to distinguish themselves from "Irresponsible Radicals."[120]

Muhammad Ali benefited from the more liberal media, but the courts, which would ultimately determine his fate, were unimpressed and unmoved by the sentiments of outraged youths and disgruntled legislators. In early 1969 Ali appealed his conviction to the U.S. Supreme Court, which, without hearing the merits of the case, remanded it to the original district court to determine whether evidence gathered by illegal wiretaps had been used to convict him. The district court decided in July 1969 that it had not,[121] so Ali's fate again rested with the Supreme Court. Considering the pro-Nixon, pro-Vietnam, and pro–law and order posture of Chief Justice Warren Burger and his conservative allies, Ali's cause appeared to be lost.

While his lawyers continued to fight for Ali's freedom they also pressed for his right to earn a living as a boxer. In August 1969 Ali applied for a license in Macon, Georgia, but was turned down. The mayor, under pressure from Governor Lester Maddox and the public, explained that Ali was "against the system both blacks and whites are fighting for."[122] In December 1969 he was denied a license by the city of Tampa, which cited similar reasons.[123]

Despite these disappointing and frustrating setbacks, Ali had regained some recognition and acceptance from the media and the field of entertainment. By spring 1970 he had performed in a short-lived Broadway musical, frequented television talk shows, appeared in a documentary film, and served as a commentator for an ABC–TV broadcast of a boxing match involving U.S. and Soviet fighters. The network's decision met with criticism from a variety of sources, including Jimmy Elder, a black boxer scheduled to fight in the event who protested Ali's involvement and called it un-American. Legislators quickly seized the opportunity to exploit the young man's viewpoint, especially Representative Fletcher Thompson of Georgia, who maintained that "Cassius Clay should not be the commentator for an event of this sort because of the overt disrespect he has shown to this Nation and its people and I, like Mr. Elder, consider this an affront to loyal Americans everywhere, although it will obviously receive much applause in some of the hippie circles." Thompson wrote letters of condemnation and protest to all of the networks and to the Federal Communications Commission in an attempt to prevent such occurrences in the future.[124] His comments and actions not only threatened Ali but undermined all Americans' right to express themselves freely.

While Thompson's message implied that Ali's appeal was to marginal elements in American society, in reality he was waging an increasingly difficult battle to halt the wholesale erosion of prowar values. As the popularity of the war decreased, Ali's acceptability among the public and even the boxing world improved. Even the denial of a license to fight in Tampa gave Ali hope, for the governor of Florida had at first given his approval and was then forced to retreat in the face of hostile congressional and local reactions. The boxing industry, concerned with profits, saw that with Ali out of the ring both fan interest and gate receipts had declined. As he became less a political untouchable, however, promoters decided that he was useful to the sport. The prospects of enormous financial returns from a fight between Ali and the new heavyweight champion, "Smokin' Joe" Frazier, put profits ahead of prowar patriotism. Risk taking had always been a part of boxing—Tex Rickard had taken a calculated risk with Jack Johnson and lost; Mike Jacobs had taken one with Joe Louis and won—and the time seemed right to try again. Few ring observers, officials, or financial backers believed that the exiled, ring-rusty Ali could possibly cope with Frazier, but they were willing to bet that the fans would pay to find out.

As Ali moved a step closer to the ring he was forced to suffer technological humiliation—a computerized fight with Rocky Marciano. Although neither man was supposed to know the outcome of the fight, Ali could not possibly have expected to win. A reporter for the *Philadelphia Inquirer* allegedly informed him:

> The Computer knows who's who in the equation. Take you, a loud-mouth black racist who brags "I'm the greatest! I'm the King!" You won't submit to White America's old image of black fighters, you won't even submit to White America's Army. . . . Every self-respecting made-in-America computer knows how to add that up. They killed you off but can't get rid of the ghost you left behind. And there's not a white fighter around to chase it away. . . . They want your ass whipped in public, knocked down, ripped, stomped, clubbed, pulverized and not just by anybody, but by a real Great White Hope, and none's around. That's where the computer comes in.[125]

Complete with carefully choreographed boxing action between a heavy Ali and a trimmed down but noticeably aged Rocky Marciano, the mock battle was released to the public in January 1970, a true indication of the level to which boxing had sunk in Ali's absence. Marciano himself must have been ashamed. Throughout his career he had avoided playing on racial and political issues, but money and the need for attention may have made him act against principles. In any event he managed to do on film what no fighter had done in the ring—he miraculously knocked out Ali in the thirteenth round despite sustaining a terrible beating himself.[126]

The staged morality play was a soothing tonic to many Americans who longed to see Ali dethroned in the ring. However, British fans, whose sense of fair play and distance from American politics allowed far more objectivity, rejected the outcome flatly.[127] Ali's flair, his wit, and his consummate boxing skills had made him a hero to the British, even though he had twice beaten Britain's Henry Cooper. When shown the original films of the pseudo-fight, British fans complained so vehemently that promoters provided a revised version that had Marciano with arms upraised in protest after the referee stopped the bout on cuts.[128]

Ali persevered, but the politically controlled state boxing commissions and the courts, working in tandem, proved formidable. When subsequent applications in 1970 failed to secure a license from any of the major boxing commissions, Ali sought to have the ban on his travel lifted for a bout in Canada, where so many draft evaders had sought refuge. The courts refused him permission to leave the country.[129] A disheartened Ali turned to, of all places, Mississippi for relief, his advisers reasoning that because that state was not affiliated with the WBA, officials could be convinced to issue a boxing license. According to Ali the governor approved the license, as did the mayor of Jackson, in exchange for a large donation to the Salvation Army.[130] But both officials retracted the offer and denied ever having issued a license when the public reacted angrily to news of the agreement. Ali and his supporters tried Georgia again, this time concentrating on Atlanta, whose emerging black political power base seemed promising. State Senator Leroy Johnson and a host of prominent businessmen had helped elect a white liberal mayor, Sam Massell, and Johnson, a longtime friend of Ali, asked the mayor to approve an Ali-Frazier fight. When Frazier refused to meet Ali, Massell agreed to let Ali fight in Atlanta against a respectable opponent.[131]

With public discontent over the Vietnam situation on the rise—due in part to the outspoken criticism of disillusioned GI's and the repercussions of the Kent State tragedy—Ali found himself a brother-in-cause with a distinguished southern statesman, Senator J. William Fulbright, whose long-term objections to the war were becoming angrier and more persistent.[132] Even the Nation of Islam had shed its radical image and found acceptance as a peace-loving self-help group. Indeed, the changing racial climate, symbolized by the burgeoning black political movement in the South, played an important role in Ali's bid to resume his boxing career. At the bargaining table when an agreement was reached with Mayor Massell sat Maynard Jackson, who in 1974 became the first black mayor of a major southern city (Atlanta). His breakthrough was followed in New Orleans, Birmingham, and a few smaller southern cities—places where blacks had not been allowed to vote less than a decade before.[133]

Now that Ali had a license, who would be the "respectable" opponent? Jerry Quarry, who had been robbed in a title elimination bout against Jimmy Ellis, was anxious for another chance and seemed to be eminently qualified. Ali mused: "Who could be more respectable in Georgia than a white hope ranked as top contender in the World Heavyweight Division, Jerry Quarry? And Irish at that."[134] The matchup was a "natural," a fight pitting white against black; it would "bring in the loot" and "appeal to all that is primitive and basic, in this most primitive and basic of all sports." According to some estimates, over half a million people saw the fight in more than 200 theaters and arenas across the country.[135] Unfortunately, the fight itself, on October 26, 1970, was anticlimactic. Ali shattered Quarry's title aspirations with a third-round technical knockout and proved to the world that he could still "throw the leather."

From the Squared Circle to the Halls of Justice

In 1969 Ali's lawyers had filed suit against the New York State Athletic Commission, which continued to deny him a license. Although the courts had not prohibited Ali from engaging in any lawful activity while appealing his conviction, NYSAC had decided that he was detrimental to boxing. Many people felt that NYSAC's position had been dictated by Governor Nelson Rockefeller, a staunch supporter of the war, who Ali believed took his cue from the Nixon White House[136]; moreover, the commission had a long history of members who had served in the armed forces, General John J. Phelan and Colonel John Reed Kilpatrick being just two of many.[137] Taking these factors into consideration, Ali's lawyers sued on the basis of prejudice against their client. A Manhattan District Court judge, Marvin E. Frankel, ruled that the evidence did not support Ali's claim that his First and Fourteenth Amendment rights had been violated, but he agreed to hear the arguments again if new evidence were submitted. Unfortunately, Ali's legal advisors had not done their homework and failed to present sufficient evidence to convince the judge on the second try. Objective legal minds, in reflecting on Frankel's decision, agreed with his judgment based on the facts.[138]

A new strategy was then launched by some concerned individuals from the Columbia University Law School, along with representatives of the NAACP Legal Defense Fund. Bolstered by the Freedom of Information Act, this ad hoc legal task force gained access to NYSAC records and figuratively hanged the commission with its own rope.[139] Facing the same court but a different judge, Ali's lawyers this time presented what the presiding judge called "astounding" new evidence. They found in the commission's records "at least 244 instances in recent years where it (NYSAC) had granted, renewed, or reinstated boxing licenses to applicants who had been convicted of one or more felonies, misdemeanors, or military offenses involving moral turpitude,"[140] including murder, sodomy, and rape. The court concluded that for the commission to license individuals convicted of such heinous crimes yet refuse Ali a license did in fact constitute arbitrary denial of equal protection. The commission countered that since Ali's conviction was recent and since he had not served a prison sentence, it was withholding his license to help rehabilitate him, but the court found this shaky defense totally devoid of merit and ruled in Ali's favor.[141]

Fighting in the Interim

While awaiting the U.S. Supreme Court ruling on his draft evasion conviction, Ali remained optimistically active. His New York boxing license restored, the "people's champion" prepared to regain his title from Smokin' Joe Frazier. The buildup to the fight took on some of the racial and patriotic overtones of the second Joe Louis–Max Schmeling bout, despite the fact both men were black and both were American. Although Frazier was less inclined and less prepared than Floyd Patterson had been to voice his opposition to Ali and his life-style, he too insisted on calling Ali "Clay." Not surprisingly, the media spoke for Frazier long after he thought enough had been said. Print and broadcast journalist alike did not let the public forget the differences between the two men, even if those differences had to be created or exaggerated.[142]

Robert Lipsyte described Ali as an enigma, "never what anybody wanted him to be . . . a black symbol who rejected Malcolm X, a champion who boasted, a selective pacifist, a separatist libertarian, a lovable religious zealot, and a campus speaker who denounced marijuana, unmarried sex, and integration."[143] Ali had alienated some of "liberal America" with what it perceived to be cruel and humiliating beatings of Patterson and Terrell; and his refusal to be drafted had totally alienated "patriotic America."[144] He was too black and too un-American. Frazier, by contrast, was a surrogate "white hope." Lipsyte claimed that "everyone who knew Joe Frazier liked him. An honorable, decent, hard-working slugger, Frazier had always been willing to sacrifice his flesh, in bits and pieces for our viewing pleasure."[145] In reality Smokin' Joe was a rather average, uncharismatic, and inarticulate man—but that did not stop the Madison Square Garden publicists from proclaiming: "Not since the days of Joe Louis and Ray Robinson and Floyd Patterson has a black man brought so much dignity to boxing."[146] Through all of this Frazier remained remarkably unaffected, never losing sight of his mission (beating Ali) or his own importance. In his simple and sincere way he put the fight and himself in the proper context, saying, "The thing I want most . . . is to fight Clay and to settle this thing."[147]

Politics and race certainly played a role in stimulating interest in the fight, but money was the major concern of the promoters. Randy Roberts's assessment of a bout between Jack Dempsey and Georges Carpentier pertained here: "Give the masses of people . . . Lancelot to cheer and some . . . Simon Legree to boo and jeer, and the money would roll in in waves and people of both sexes and all classes would perk up and take notice."[148] And take notice they did: profits totaled at least $20,000,000, although the actual sum will never be known because the "bout had created the most feverish demand and most outlandish ticket-scalping in sports history."[149]

On March 8, 1971, the attention of the world was focused on Madison Square Garden. Unlike most highly promoted affairs, this event lived up to the hype. Even the boxers looked upon it as more than just a fight or a grandiose spectacle, truly believing that personal honor and perhaps a way of life hung in the balance. Ali seemed more intent on proving his manhood than on winning the championship. He had long maintained that boxing was more dangerous than war and was bent on showing everyone that cowardice in no way motivated his refusal to serve. He told the *Chicago Daily News,* "I am laying out my life on the line for the Government. Nine out of ten soldiers would not want to be in my place in the ring, it's too dangerous."[150] Ali's foolish show of courage and machismo guaranteed a brutal affair, the challenger standing toe-to-toe with his opponent, hands down, taking Frazier's best punches with headshakes and laughs. Frazier, who had soaked his face in brine to harden it in expectation of Ali's slashing, rapierlike punches, absorbed tremendous punishment of his own; but getting hit was his style, not Ali's.

The punishment and the long layoff eventually drained Ali's energy and led to a knockdown in the fifteenth round, when Frazier caught the tired challenger with a long, looping left hook. Ali regained his feet to beat the count—even his detractors had to admire his courage—and gathered enough strength from a seemingly inexhaustible reserve to hang on until the final bell. Despite the knockdown the outcome remained in doubt. The decision was a very close one, but it went to Frazier and "Patriotic America." As Frazier's supporters reveled, Ali's fans cried "foul," not without some justification. Robert Lipsyte intimates that ring officials were at least subconsciously biased by the conviction that a Frazier victory would be good for boxing and for America.[151] Joe Frazier's grotesquely swollen face and his three-week hospital stay after the fight raised even more doubts. Ali attempted to discredit the undisputed champ, questioning the reasons for his victory, something Frazier resented so much that he decided to deny Ali a return fight before risking the heavyweight title in a bout with George Foreman. That decision cost Frazier untold profits and the loss of his reputation.[152]

If the nature of the fight itself was not proof that the stakes were far higher than money and a belt, the reactions to it were. Ali supporters took the loss personally and refused to accept it. According to militant

Cornell student leader Donald Reeves, "When Ali tasted defeat for the first time, I was crushed. Few things have so destroyed my spirits as to see Muhammad Ali lose. Despite the fact that he proved to be more of a man in defeat than many of us are in victory, psychologically, people everywhere who loved Ali, for whatever reason, also felt his defeat as a personal loss."[153] Among those welcoming his loss were some of the troops in Vietnam. Ali was called "the most debated athlete in the prisoner of war camps,"[154] and his exploits in and out of the ring had long been the subject of propaganda radio broadcasts by the enemy. One prisoner of war vividly recalled that while most sporting news came from new prisoners, "the V (Vietcong) told us about Cassius Clay on the loudspeaker."[155] Not surprisingly, his loss pleased many soldiers on the battlefield,[156] as well as countless supporters of the war. Representative James R. Mann of South Carolina, speaking out for Lieutenant William Calley, Jr., who had been found guilty of sanctioning atrocities against civilians in Vietnam in the My Lai massacre, argued that he could not understand the justice in Calley's standing "convicted of murder" while "Muhammad Ali still walks the streets of America, a couple of million dollars richer by virtue of his failure to serve."[157]

Now that Ali was down, calls came from far and wide to bury him. The man who often bragged about having the most recognizable face in the world faced the specter of invisibility. Black novelist Ralph Ellison painfully described a fate suffered by so many of his race: "You ache with the need to convince yourself that you do exist in the real world, that you are part of all sound and anguish, and you strike out with your fists, you curse, and swear to make them recognize you. And, alas, it is seldom successful."[158]

Justice Prevails

On April 19, 1971, Ali's lawyer, Chauncey Eskridge of Chicago, argued his draft evasion case before the U.S. Supreme Court. The prospects appeared bleak. Chief Justice Warren Burger, a staunch Nixon supporter, sensed that "the silent majority" wanted Ali to pay for his evasion of military duty. A host of concerned citizens wrote to the court, asking that justice be done, and quickly at that. Harry R. Gaines of Grand Rapids, Michigan, was convinced that he represented the majority view:

> How long has this [Ali's case] been in the U.S. Supreme Court? How much research and reference does [a case] such as this require? What about the thousands of other men who have

responded to the call to the armed forces; many of whom have been killed in action? How many others have been allowed (after conviction) to go on about their business receiving hundreds of thousands of dollars? What effect does such delay (of decision) have on the general public in respect to and regard of courts—of all kinds? (We hesitate to quote some of the comments heard on this delay.) How many other future draftees will seek delay and stall?[159]

William S. Watrous of Glen Ellyn, Illinois, when informed that Chief Justice Burger could not "give advisory opinions on the basis of correspondence," threatened to expose the high court's delay in handling the case to the *Chicago Tribune.* Watrous refused to accept the fact that the court was bound to consider cases brought before it in the regular course of events. The operations manager of a Charlotte, North Carolina, radio and television station inquired about the case and suggested that the court act quickly because "most people convicted of draft evasion go to the penitentiary immediately, but Clay remains free to get rich off the American system which he has defied."[160]

Chief Justice Burger knew that something had to be done. Ali's case had come up two terms before, at which time the court had voted against hearing it, thus allowing the conviction to stand. Fortunately for Ali, a late disclosure by the government that he had been monitored on a national-security wiretap on Martin Luther King, Jr.'s phone had precluded an official decision on the matter; instead, the justices remanded the case to a lower court for rehearing.[161] The 1970 Supreme Court decision in *Welsh* v. *United States* opened another door for Ali, forcing the high court to grant a writ of certiorari on the basis of a petition that cited *Welsh* and argued that "denial of conscientious objector status to Ali" may have been based upon the Department of Justice's erroneous characterization of his objections to participation in any war on "political and racial" rather than "religious grounds." In the *Welsh* decision the Court had ruled that moral and ethical objection to war was as valid as religious objection, thus broadening the qualifications.[162]

By the spring of 1971 President Nixon's obsession with repressing any opposition to the war had infected Chief Justice Burger.[163] On April 20, the day after Ali's case had been heard, the court accepted an emergency petition from the Department of Justice that sought to reinstate a lower court order to evict antiwar veterans from camping on the mall in Washington. In reinstating that order Burger was convinced that the veterans threatened national security, which signified how close the Nixon administration had come to governing by court injunctions.[164]

Such actions seriously jeopardized the separation of powers, and it was in this ominous atmosphere that Ali's case was decided.

Newspaper reporters Bob Woodward and Scott Armstrong, in a controversial and unprecedented look inside the Supreme Court, revealed that only Justice William Brennan wanted to hear the case. Aside from the draft question, the racial overtones made any decision extremely difficult, and the early rounds went against Ali. Solicitor General Erwin N. Griswold, the nation's chief prosecutor, had convinced five members of the high court that Ali was not a conscientious objector but instead a selective objector who would fight in a holy war or a Muslim war if asked to do so by his leader, Elijah Muhammad. Six inches of FBI evidence gained from wiretaps on Elijah Muhammad's phone since 1964 seemed to prove his point. It appeared that Ali's conviction would be upheld and he would go to prison. Chief Justice Burger assigned Justice John M. Harlan to write the majority view, but according to Woodward and Armstrong, Harlan's clerks were convinced that Ali's willingness to fight in a holy war lacked relevance. The holy war was really Armageddon, the war of good against evil, the same war that Jehovah's Witnesses would fight—and they were accepted as conscientious objectors.[165]

Harlan's clerks suggested that the justice read the *Autobiography of Malcolm X* and *Message to the Black Man,* by Elijah Muhammad, two books that had convinced them of Ali's sincerity. A seemingly unmoved Harlan returned to work a changed man, "persuaded that the government had mistakenly painted Ali as a racist and had unduly ignored the Justice Department's own hearing examiner's findings that Ali was sincerely opposed to all wars."[166] Now the high court was deadlocked at 4–4; a tie would go against the petitioner, but because the justices were equally divided, there would be no written decision and Ali would go to jail never knowing why he had lost his case. Justice Potter Stewart was upset by this prospect and offered a compromise solution— that Ali be set free, citing a technical error by the Justice Department. This proposal had two advantages: the ruling would not set a precedent; nor would it broaden the categories for conscientious objector status. Seven justices accepted Stewart's plan, and Burger, fearing that his dissent might be construed as racist, joined in, now convinced that "an 8-0 decision would be a good lift for black people."[167] The only black member of the court, Justice Thurgood Marshall, had disqualified himself because he had been the solicitor general at the time Ali was originally prosecuted.[168]

A seldom humble Ali responded to the decision gratefully and somewhat naïvely. He thanked Allah and "the Supreme Court for recognizing the sincerity of the religious teachings that I've accepted." Armstrong and Woodward commented that "he did not know how close he had come to going to jail."[169] Ali's spiritual leader, Elijah Muhammad, had served three and a half years in the federal penitentiary for refusing to be drafted during World War II, but times had changed. The Supreme Court was becoming very sensitive to antiwar pressures and was even more concerned with racial unrest. The last thing it wanted was to render a decision that might make all Black Muslims eligible for conscientious objector status[170]—which might have spawned a much larger Nation of Islam and a much smaller U.S. military force.

Even though Dr. Daniel Ellsberg had surrendered that same day, June 29, 1971, to the U.S. attorney in Boston for arraignment on charges of unauthorized possession of secret documents, the Ali decision dominated editorial comment in the nation's news media. The outcome was viewed more as a vindication of the American judicial process than a victory for Ali. The *Kansas City Times* reflected white press sentiment in its opinion that "the Court must decide matters on the basis of the law as defined by the Constitution, equally applied to all, and immune to transient fevers. That is what has been done in the case of Cassius (Muhammad Ali) Clay, and while many may disagree with the decision emotionally, the rationale of the 8-0 decision is difficult to refute."[171] Ali's hometown paper, *The Louisville Times,* set the tone of his future: "He has at long last won the measure of justice which the Courts can provide. It is now up to the rest of us to provide the fuller benefits."[172]

The Comeback Trail

Although Ali's legal battles were behind him, he still stimulated controversy wherever he went, whatever he did. He remained the "black menace" of his time, and in the absence of bona fide "white hopes," other black boxers were still expected to humble him. The boxing world hoped for a long and profitable rivalry between Ali and Frazier. But Smokin' Joe spurned Ali, and less than two years after their brutal contest he chose to defend his title against the huge, powerfully built, but raw George Foreman in Kingston, Jamaica, on January 20, 1973. To the surprise of boxing experts and observers, Foreman jack-hammered Frazier into a humiliating second-round knockout.[173] The crown was on a different head, but it was a perfect fit as far as white America was concerned. The fit depended not on head size but on mindset.

Foreman, even more than Frazier, strove to be a symbol of patriotism, conformity, and acquiescence. Five years earlier, at the Olympics Games in Mexico City, Foreman had walked around the ring waving a tiny American flag to celebrate his gold medal victory—quite a contrast to

Tommie Smith and John Carlos, the track stars who stood on the winners' stand with clenched fists in protest of racial injustice. Foreman capitalized on the incident in "Don't Knock the American System to Me,"[174] a patriotic message that found currency with the boxing crowd and with politicians of various persuasions who jumped at the chance to justify their own ideologies and further their own programs. With the assistance of a ghost author, Foreman wrote: "There were more than 2,000 black athletes in those Olympic Games in all sports. I was afraid—even with the USA on my jersey—they might not know I was an American. And I wanted everybody to know, and to know that at that moment, I was one of the happiest Americans who ever lived. So, I took the little American flag from the pocket of my robe and waved it as I took a bow to each of the ring's four corners."[175] The old theme of black against black would be subtly replayed by the media, but an ingenuous Foreman continued, "What never occurred to me then was this little thing I did would be translated into an opposing view to the 'black power' fever which was so much a part of that Olympics. . . . I was so proud, I was just doing what came naturally to me. It was my 'thing' and thank God, it is still my 'thing'."[176]

Conservative Congressman Frank Clark of Pennsylvania cited the champion for his patriotism and the example he set for the black race. Foreman had impressed Clark as a man "who has won the admiration and respect of Americans everywhere, not only for his ring accomplishments, but for his public statements outside of the ring."[177] Black liberal Yvonne Braithwaite Burke of California capitalized on Foreman's crediting the Job Corps with taking him from a life of "pool halls and wine" to the heavyweight championship of boxing simply by introducing him to the sport.[178] She held him high as a shining example of what could be accomplished by a worthwhile program that was being threatened with cutbacks and possible extinction by the Nixon administration, which was set on dismantling the remains of Lyndon Johnson's Great Society. Even the racially and fiscally conservative governor of California, Ronald Reagan, found himself agreeing with Burke that the Job Corps had done great things for George Foreman.[179]

Shortly after Foreman beat Frazier, a former college football player, Marine, and angular but awkward fighter named Ken Norton shocked the boxing world by winning a twelve-round decision over Muhammad Ali. He broke Ali's jaw in the process, leading many fans to wonder if this might be the end for the former champion. For the first time in many years his name was no longer in the forefront of the boxing world, and Ali went home to recover from his physical wounds and salve his injured pride. Meanwhile, George Foreman was surrounding himself with an aura of invincibility, crushing Joe "King" Roman in one round and then flooring Ken Norton with an awesome second-round barrage.[180] (Interestingly, Norton seemed to have lost as much from paralytic fear as from the punches.) He was content to wait for Ali to reestablish himself, which Ali did, winning close decisions over Ken Norton and Joe Frazier. With Ali's detractors gleefully awaiting his total destruction at the hands of Foreman, another flamboyant figure lit up the boxing scene and deflected much of the negative publicity.

A New Scapegoat

Don King, black businessman extraordinaire, raised a storm of controversy by entering the closed world of boxing promotions. Despite the fact that blacks had long been an important force in prizefighting, their roles were limited to the ring or its corners. Ali said it best in his admission that boxing always gave him the feeling of "two slaves in the ring."[181] Despite its plethora of black boxers, New York State had only two licensed black referees in 1970.[182] Black referees in general received less pay and fewer assignments, especially at the major arenas; for example, as late as 1970 no black referee had ever officiated a main-event bout at Madison Square Garden. The reality of the situation troubled black boxers, many of whom viewed the referee as a policeman in the ring. They did not feel comfortable with white referees when fighting white opponents, expecting no more fairness and understanding than ghetto residents received from white police officers.[183]

Despite all the publicity about Joe Louis's two black managers, John Roxborough and Julian Black, they had been dwarfed by Mike Jacobs after he took an interest in the Brown Bomber.[184] Even the powerful and brilliant Truman Gibson, the chief promotional operative in James Norris's International Boxing Club, profited little from his efforts. In fact, when the axe fell on the IBC, Gibson took much of the blame, although the evidence indicated that Norris both knew of and approved Gibson's actions. Black boxing commissioners were even more rare, until the late 1970s when Floyd Patterson, Althea Gibson, and Jersey Joe Walcott served on state athletic commissions in New York and New Jersey.[185]

Perhaps the most striking example of blacks' disproportionate sharing of boxing profits was the first Ali-Frazier fight. While promoters and exhibitors reaped approximately $20,000,000 from the event, made possible by the immense talent and appeal of Ali and Frazier, the only blacks to benefit directly, other than the combatants and their associates, did so through the Congress of Racial Equality. CORE earned $75,000 for its sponsorship of the only Harlem showing of the fight, and only threats to boycott the live fight and theater showings made even that small breakthrough possible. Since blacks owned so few restaurants, hotels, movie theaters, and newspapers, they were in no position to capitalize effectively on the residual profits either. Then along came Don King, the self-proclaimed "first strong black promoter of national repute."[186]

King, not unlike Roxborough, Black, and a host of other successful black businessmen, had learned his trade on the streets. His capital came from the illegal betting operation known as the numbers, or policy. With so few opportunities for legitimate businesses, blacks of considerable education and social standing often made money illegally, investing it in real estate, bars, and even baseball teams. Gus Greenlee, owner of the Pittsburgh Crawfords of the Negro Baseball Leagues, and his rival Abe Manley of the Newark Eagles both made their money from gambling. Like so many others they remained or became the pillars of their communities.[187]

As inmate #6178 at the Marion (Ohio) Correctional Institution, where he was serving a four-year term for killing a numbers racketeer who had double-crossed him, Don King polished his business skills. Within four years of his release in September 1971 he had become the most powerful promoter in boxing and one of the most successful black businessmen in America. His success depended largely on his ability to relate to black fighters and to reward them more substantially than others did; of no little importance were his determination to be his own man and his belief that he was a symbol for all of black America. King's outrageous hairstyle—described by television sports commentator and former Miss America Phyllis George as "electric hair"—and his outspokenness, often punctuated by malapropisms, made him an unforgettable figure.[188] Black Ohio Congressman Louis Stokes recognized King's importance and introduced him to his colleagues via a series of articles in the *Congressional Record.* These journalistic snippets, especially the one headlined "Cleveland's King Shocks Boxing's White Establishment," clearly reinforced King's image of independence and race consciousness, characteristics that made him the Ali of promoters.[189]

King knew the barriers to black success, but he refused to drown in his "own tears over past injustices." He exercised practicality—referring to it as "a pragmatic approach"—and refused to exclude whites from his business. On responding to criticism from a separatist group, King explained, "I am a black man, my strength comes from blacks, but this is not a strength or a commitment that means polarization, isolation, or alienation."[190] This philosophy and its application did not go unrecognized, for King received a Heritage Award in April 1976 for his work in promoting better understanding and harmony among all people.[191]

Like Ali, King made an impression beyond the ring. His promotional undertakings in underdeveloped countries had far-reaching economic, political, and racial implications. Aware of the uses of sport by major powers, the so-called third-world countries quickly grasped that athletics could be used to raise their standing in the pecking order of nations. Because of its universal appeal and symbolism, prizefighting provided an excellent vehicle for increased visibility. Although the fight game had belonged traditionally, in a fiscal sense, to a very small group centered in New York City, developing nations considered it an American asset, and to them control of prizefighting represented American power, money, and prestige. Any inroad into this perceived American monopoly opened the possibility of a redistribution of the assets of international influence toward the Third World. Foreign control of the World Boxing Association and World Boxing Council symbolized a shift in boxing politics.[192]

In March 1974 King promoted the championship bout between George Foreman and Ken Norton in Caracas, Venezuela. Although Foreman ended the bout in short order, considerable drama surrounded the affair.[193] The fight had been contracted with the understanding that the boxers would not be subject to Venezuelan taxes, but King and the fighters did not know that the government had never approved the arrangement in writing. As a result, the Venezuelan authorities detained both fighters after the contest and did not release them until they had paid an 18-percent tax and forfeited bonds of between $60,000 and $100,000.[194] The American press characterized the affair as an international disgrace, and it proved acutely embarrassing to King who, as a novice, an outsider, and a flamboyant black man in a white man's business, had been expected to fail.

In spite of the "Caracas Caper," King won the favor of Herbert Muhammad, Ali's manager. Having quickly established a reputation for delivering huge purses, the flamboyant promoter soon shocked the boxing world by arranging a $10,000,000 heavyweight championship fight between Ali and Foreman in the tropical nation of Zaire, the first such event in Africa.[195] The decision made sense fiscally and also meshed with the "buy black and support black" philosophy of the Nation of Islam. The fight in Zaire would be an attempt "to prove to the world that blacks can do the job with efficiency . . . and sophistication," a word King believed "the world is reluctant to associate with black people."[196]

In the process of assembling what would be the most expensive single sporting promotion venture in history, King joined Video Techniques, a closed-circuit television firm. His relationship with the white owner, Hank Schwartz, was stormy, a result of King's independence and his feelings of self-importance. A promotional flyer for the Ali-Foreman fight, to which Video Techniques had the television rights, barely mentioned King, and his reaction led Schwartz to comment, "He is mainly responsible for the fight. With the diverse personalities of Foreman and Ali, he was the only one in the world capable of bringing them together."[197] King accepted that as an apology and explained that his intent was not to make waves but "to be treated as an equal." In a somewhat patronizing way Schwartz added, "He's a welcome addition to our company and he'll probably have me riding in the back of the bus in a couple of months."[198]

Press reaction to the Ali-Foreman fight was as expected—replete with attempts to discredit the host nation and the bout itself. Prefight publicity emphasized the negative, despite the fact that the matchup had all the ingredients of a classic contest. The media reported a hopelessly chaotic situation and seemed to discourage attendance, stating that visitors would be forced to stay in dormitories and on ships, or else in extravagantly priced hotel rooms.[199] Joseph Desire Mobutu (Sese Seko), the president of Zaire, was the frequent target of press attacks, and while the ruthless autocrat no doubt deserved condemnation, sportswriters had not usually directed their ire at leaders of other nations staging championship contests.

Despite negative press coverage, a month-long delay caused by a cut over Foreman's eye, and logistical complications, the Zairians hosted a successful live event. They took pride in the fact, as one native store clerk put it, that "we showed to our people and the Africans and the world that black Africa can produce an international event that brings the world to us."[200] Financial losses for the promoters approached $4,000,000, but Zaire was not to blame. Video Techniques, the American promotional organization that had hired King to ensure television rights to the fight, had overpriced closed-circuit tickets, which seriously affected volume and profits.[201]

Zaire's reputation may not have grown as much as it expected from the "Rumble in the Jungle," as Ali dubbed it, but Don King's did. He was enough of a force to warrant courting in 1976 by Democratic presidential candidate Jimmy Carter, who King described as a farmer "who could go from the fields to the Oval Office, the most powerful office in the world." Because King saw himself as "a product of the hard-core ghetto, an ex-number operator and ex-convict who could rise to the pinnacle of the boxing world," he concluded that "Carter and I have had a somewhat synonymous life."[202]

George Foreman, after his gold medal performance at the 1968 Olympic Games in Mexico City. Many viewed this patriotic display as an intentional counterprotest to the black power salutes of trackmen John Carlos and Tommie Smith, but Foreman said he was just "doing my thing." (Photo by *Houston Chronicle*)

Truman Gibson, a low-profile black boxing promoter of the 1950s and 1960s, working behind the scenes for the International Boxing Club in Chicago. (Truman Gibson)

Don King, a high-profile, flamboyant black boxing promoter of the 1970s and 1980s, with champion Larry Holmes (left) and challenger Gerry Cooney (right) before their 1982 fight. (UPI/Bettmann Newsphotos)

Above: Rocky Marciano lands a forearm to the face of his aging idol, Joe Louis, in a 1951 fight. *Below:* Although never relishing his role as the great "white hope," Marciano agreed to repeat it against Muhammad Ali in a mock computerized contest in 1968. (UPI/Bettmann Newsphotos)

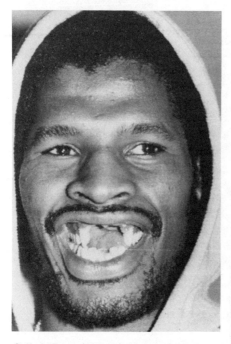

Called "Dracula" by Muhammad Ali, Leon Spinks is captured in unflattering, stereo-typical poses by a UPI photographer. Such images did little to enhance his reputation in or out of the ring. (UPI/Bettmann Newsphotos)

His association with a presidential candidate did not persuade the sporting press to resent King less. Not able to criticize his business acumen, detractors mercilessly ridiculed his appearance and language. *Washington Star* writer Tom Dowling, for example, gave a sardonic appraisal of King's most salient attributes: "There are some who give the vote to his Afro, which stands straight up on his skull, like a cartoon figure who has just put a penny in the fuse box"[203] (raising the image of Buckwheat, in the "Our-Gang" comedy series, whose hair stood on end when he was frightened). Dowling continued: "Others are more smitten with King's memorized rhetoric, a combination of gibberish, Mrs. Malaprop, and Palgrave's Golden Treasury of English Verse"[204]—reminiscent of a long-standing racist stereotype of blacks as imitative creatures blessed with good memories but meager reasoning capacities. Dowling seemed to be taking a page from Harvard Professor Nathaniel Southgate Shaler, who had argued in 1884, as part of his retrogression theory, that white people were great organizers and builders; black people were imitative.[205]

Even Norman Mailer, in his account of the championship bout in Zaire, *The Fight* (1975), could not resist exploiting King's pseudo-intellectualism.[206] Yet at least one writer viewed such characterizations as typical of the racist attitudes that had always pervaded boxing and the larger society. King certainly did not stand alone as a target, for the press consistently reinforced stereotypes by reproducing interviews with black athletes, especially boxers, in which their speech took on the character of an Amos 'n Andy dialogue.[207] By comparison, no one seemed to address Angelo Dundee's questionable command of the English language; instead, they concentrated on his talents as a boxing trainer and a manager.

In the spring of 1977 the press and the boxing establishment finally had something more tangible to attack King for—the scandal-ridden U.S. boxing championships. His opponents never doubted that this controversy would rid the sport of its new black menace. As Michael Katz attested, there were "many people in boxing waiting with glee for King to be knocked out."[208] But the black press, which appreciated King's contributions to blacks as a model of race consciousness and business skill, came to his rescue. Dr. Carlton B. Goodlet, president of the National Newspaper Publishers Association of the black press, charged, "We as newspapermen who uphold the tradition of the free press and a responsible press have examined the evidence before us and are forced to conclude that King has not been given fair play in the white press."[209]

If King was guilty of wrongdoing, so were many others, including a major network, *Ring* magazine (the "Bible of Boxing"), and scores of individuals. In July 1976, ABC Sports, Inc., for the sum of $2,035,000, had contracted with Don King Productions, Inc., for exclusive broadcasting rights to the boxing championships. The event would feature a series of elimination bouts among American boxers designed to produce U.S. champions in eight weight classes; to compensate for a lack of name boxers, titles were offered to attract fan interest. The contract in part specified that Don King Productions would organize and promote the tournament; that the quality of fighters participating would be the best possible, as determined by rankings established by *Ring* magazine at the time the tournament started; and that ABC Sports would have certain exclusive "first negotiation/first refusal positions" with respect to the broadcast of subsequent defense and title fights by the winners or subsequent tournaments of the same or a similar type promoted by Don King Productions. Unfortunately the ratings, the selection process, and the first-refusal provision led to the tournament's undoing.[210]

Despite prior knowledge pointing to inaccurate ratings and obviously uneven matches, the network televised six events from January 1977 through mid-April 1977. Not until the semifinal round, when heavyweight Scott LeDoux charged that the tournament was rigged in favor of Don King's associates and that kickback payments had been made, did ABC halt further broadcasts of the tournament.[211] The charges provoked an immediate rash of inquiries ranging from a federal grand jury investigation in Maryland, a field investigation by the Federal Communications Commission, congressional hearings, and several internal investigations conducted by the American Broadcasting Corporation, the parent body of ABC Sports. The grand jury inquiry produced no indictments and was supported by the ABC-commissioned Armstrong Report, which found that the irregularities in the running of the tournament did not warrant criminal prosecution "but did indicate a good deal of unethical behavior by individuals involved with the administration and organization of the tournament."[212] Some of the irregularities included fabricated rankings, prize money kickbacks disguised as agents' fees, and unqualified boxers.

Both the FCC and a congressional communications subcommittee held ABC Sports responsible for negligence and careless conduct. Although no laws had been violated, the FCC issued a harsh reprimand and asked for assurances that the network would not again fall "below the standards expected of a broadcaster."[213] ABC Sports temporarily disassociated itself from Don King, despite the fact that he had not been charged with a crime (King often insisted that his only crime was "to beat my fighters over the head with hundred dollar bills"[214]), and was soon replaced by NBC. King's unparalleled entree with good black boxers made him one of few promoters who could put together an entire card for television, and in the cutthroat ratings game, ethical considerations weighed less than market shares.[215]

In 1978 Madison Square Garden, long a place where blacks could not even fight, contracted for King's services. The innovative David A. "Sonny" Werblin, president of the Garden, explained: "My philosophy is to get the best management people I can in the front office, the best coaches and the best players. Don is tops in his field."[216] While a racial barrier had been breached, economics, not egalitarian concerns, had motivated Werblin. King's worldwide promotions had upstaged the Garden, and Werblin astutely concluded that he would rather have King as an ally than a foe. Red Smith put the matter a little differently: "In another business it would seem a curious union, but in the fight racket unlikely alliances are formed and dissolved from week to week."[217]

Don King is certainly not a saint. Like all promoters his overriding aim has been to profit from boxing, and to that end he could employ charm, devious persuasion, and outright coercion.[218] A New Jersey crime commission once suggested that King, like so many other businessmen, had no compunctions about taking lightly laundered money from organized criminals for closed-circuit television rights.[219] More recently, on December 13, 1984, a federal grand jury handed down a twenty-three count indictment charging King and an aide with income tax evasion, filing false income tax returns, and conspiracy in connection with the concealment of over $1,000,000 in unreported income.[220]

The Acceptance of Ali

While King was becoming boxing's most controversial figure, Ali profited from the redirection of the firestorm, encountering the "changing air" Bertrand Russell had predicted. Observers attributed the acceptance of Ali by the American public to a change in the man, but it was really the country that had changed. Ali was still brash, outspoken, and a Black Muslim; the country, which had ended its direct involvement in Vietnam and eased the troubles in the streets, had by 1974 entered the throes of a leadership crisis that made Ali's words and actions seem like child's play. The public's preoccupation with Nixon and Watergate allowed Ali to take full advantage of his revenge victories over Joe Frazier and Ken Norton. Many people now saw him as a great and courageous fighter, a man who stood up for his principles. When the time came to match him against George Foreman, race and politics played a far more minor role than they had when Frazier and Ali first fought. Ali was winning the hearts of a more tolerant, less hostile American public, and

Foreman had in some ways become a reminder of a time many Americans wanted to forget.[221]

Ali, as the grand old man of the ring, was David against Foreman's Goliath. Armed with a defensive strategy appropriately dubbed the "rope-a-dope," Ali let Foreman hit away at his closely guarded head and body. He believed that Foreman would grow tired and frustrated from hitting the arms and gloves of an opponent leaning on the ropes, and by the sixth round his tactics appeared to be working. Ali then took the offensive and floored a weary Foreman in the eighth round. Rising too late to beat what many observers thought was a quick count, a stunned Foreman lost his crown and his confidence. The victory returned to Ali the much-coveted heavyweight title and, even more precious, respect. He received the prestigious Edward J. Neil memorial plaque as "Fighter of the Year," bestowed by the Boxing Writers Association (which not long before had consistently vilified him). His home city of Louisville gave its endorsement to the new champion by naming a street after him. The country had finally caught up to Muhammad Ali.[222]

In 1976, America's bicentennial year, Ali shared "Fighter of the Year" honors with Joe Frazier as a result of their death-match "Thrilla in Manilla." A poll sponsored by Cutty Sark, the scotch whiskey maker, named him the best boxer of all time; his frequently heard claim, "I am the greatest," was at last endorsed by some 500 sportswriters, editors, and broadcasters who chose him over Joe Louis, Jack Dempsey, Sugar Ray Robinson, and Jack Johnson.[223] And his influence outside the ring was attested to by his surprising appearance on "Face the Nation" in May 1976, a show traditionally reserved for world leaders, politicians, business executives, and civil rights leaders. Although the panelists asked Ali many questions regarding his profession, they also addressed subjects of far-reaching importance, including philanthropy, black politics, and the Nation of Islam. When some of the questions betrayed lingering doubts about his religious convictions and sincerity, Ali's answers clearly revealed a mind that worked as fast as his hands and feet, one that had long kept the press off-guard. Fred Graham, legal correspondent for CBS, and Ali engaged in a classic exchange:

> GRAHAM: Well, you have a reputation as—you're separated from your wife, and you have a reputation as a man who has a sharp eye for the ladies. Now, how is that going to be consistent with your role as a religious leader in the years ahead?
> ALI: Well, as far as my personal beliefs are concerned I don't talk about them in public; as far as my personal problems with family, these are things I don't discuss in public, especially on high-class

shows like I was told yours would be, so I don't even expect to talk about that here.[224]

Ali's performance so impressed Senator Mike Mansfield of Montana that he entered the complete transcript into the *Congressional Record*.[225]

White Hopes, Black Stereotypes, and Ali

Notwithstanding the fact that Ali had become an acceptable champion, even a decorated one, the nature of the sport demanded rivalries and adversarial relationships. With patriotism relegated to the past, race still lent itself to exploitation. Yet the search for the great "white hope" turned up more "dopes than hopes." Shaky promises of fame and wealth had little appeal to whites, who had more tangible opportunities outside the ring. The two most prominent white fighters, Jerry Quarry and Duane Bobick, stumbled short of their goals and promoters' expectations, Quarry losing two fights to Ali and Bobick failing against lesser opponents.[226] By 1978 Joe Frazier had retired and the Norton-Ali rivalry was growing stale.

Promoters turned to Leon Spinks, a ghetto child turned Marine who had won a gold medal at the 1976 Montreal Olympics in the light heavyweight division with a rip-roaring street-fighter assault on his opponents. Spinks rode the crest of the Olympic wave into the professional ranks and, with an exclusive network contract in hand that guaranteed frequent television appearances, soon became a household name. He had only a handful of professional fights under his belt when backers pushed him into contention for Ali's title.[227]

Ali accepted and prepared for an easy payday, but Spinks had other ideas. Taking advantage of the out-of-shape and mentally unprepared champion, the raw but game challenger won a unanimous decision on February 15, 1978, in Las Vegas, and took over the heavyweight crown. He had gone from Pruitt Igoe in St. Louis, one of the nation's most horrible high-rise, low-income housing projects, to the pinnacle of sports success, a quantum leap. But his lack of education and social skills put him at the mercy of the press, which saw him as the "Emperor Jones" of the pugilistic world, a throwback to D. W. Griffith's black legislators in *Birth of a Nation*. He was the epitome of the ignorant, childlike black who had freedom and power but did not know what to do with them, a little of Jack Johnson, Battling Siki, and Sonny Liston rolled into one; but he resembled most closely Tommy "Hurricane" Jackson, the media's whipping boy and Sambo of the 1950s.[228]

Hurricane Jackson had been a sportswriter's dream. Here was a grown man who allegedly only wanted to eat hot dogs, ice cream, and pie; who supposedly liked to canoe but could not swim; who thought he was Eddie Arcaro but could not ride horses. The press characterized him as an illiterate who blamed his losses on everything from a meddling mother to taking in too much air. His trainers dubbed him "nanimal," which they defined "as a throwback to the man of the gutter"[229] but may have been the combined form of "nigger" and "animal." Unlike Spinks, poor Hurricane Jackson never had the glory that came with a gold medal or a heavyweight championship. He also never had the shame that came with a fall from the top.

The euphoria of victory led Leon Spinks on a widely publicized odyssey of arrests and lawsuits. The press pursued him relentlessly. When he finally signed for a return bout with Ali, rather than with the World Boxing Council's number one contender, Ken Norton, the Latin American–controlled boxing oversight body withdrew its recognition of him as champion, which made a shambles of the boxing world. Norton became the WBC heavyweight champion by default.[230] On June 9, 1978, less than six months after winning the crown, Leon Spinks lost to Muhammad Ali and went from the penthouse to the outhouse of the boxing world. *Philadelphia Inquirer* reporter Martin Ralbovsky, kinder than most, called Spinks "an interesting sociological story" who "never did understand why he couldn't take the ghetto with him." Having "failed to conform to championship form the protectors of the image came calling."[231]

Despite his disastrous and short reign, Leon Spinks deserves recognition for one outstanding accomplishment: he made America aware of Ali's value as a champion in and out of the ring. Cal Fentress of the *New York Times* remarked that while Spinks would be remembered "only by trivia buffs, the memory of Ali—sleek and strong and sassy—will be young and easy under the apple boughs."[232] Senator Charles Percy of Illinois was quick to understand that and gave Ali the long overdue and unqualified praise from national leaders that had been accorded Dempsey, Louis, Frazier, and a host of lesser boxers. In a speech that only the bravest of souls could have made in the very recent past, Percy told his congressional colleagues: "He became the symbol of racial pride to millions of blacks in the heat of the civil rights movement. He became a hero to the thousands of young people during the tumultuous sixties because of his stand against the Vietnam War."[233] According to Percy, Ali's victory over Spinks was not just another comeback, it "was a victory for all that he stands for nationally and internationally."[234]

Ali: A Lost Cause?

Muhammad Ali retired in 1979 and boxing was the worse for it. But like so many past greats, money and the need for a stage and an audience soon brought him out of retirement. He suffered some terrible beatings at the hands of WBC champion Larry Holmes in October 1980 and Trevor Berbick on December 12 of that same year, which convinced him to retire permanently. Today, the once quick-witted and sharped-tongued Ali is a shadow of his former self—his speech slurred and muffled, his gait slow and unsteady, his mind less than nimble. After a series of tests and a hospital stay, doctors diagnosed Parkinson's syndrome, concluding that the cumulative effect of hundreds, if not thousands, of blows to the head had caused a deterioration of brain cells. In boxing parlance, Ali was punch-drunk; he was unable to perform before an audience (and even had to give up his roach spray commercials). The public was emotionally torn between ridicule and pity.[235]

Then Ali did what would have been unthinkable in his prime—he supported Ronald Reagan's bid for the presidency. To a majority of blacks, the way in which he endorsed Reagan was more disturbing than the endorsement itself: Ali was photographed taking a friendly tap from Reagan, with Joe Frazier and Floyd Patterson beside him; the caption read, "We're voting for the man."[236] Of course, Patterson and Frazier had long been cast as two of Ali's arch enemies, representing everything he was not, so that association was paradoxical. But for Ali to accept the caption with the highly emotive phrase "the man" was intolerable to anyone who had joined him in fighting the police and the general authority of the state, both of which had been dubbed "the man." The implications of his act were that all was well in America, and even his most loyal supporters now considered him a "sell out."[237]

In probing the depths of the man to fathom his more recent actions, we are likely to find clues to the real Muhammad Ali, both past and present. Why did he endorse a presidential candidate who had attacked affirmative action, voting rights, and civil rights? Why did he support a man whose policy of "constructive engagement" with South Africa (with which Ali agreed) has been condemned by black leaders here and abroad? Ali's answer was that "Reagan is the best man out of all of them because he's trying to keep prayer in the schools."[238] Did Ali think that Reagan and his Christian fundamentalist supporters would promote Islamic prayers in the schools? Or was Ali's seemingly inexplicable action the end result of diminished mental capacity?[239] Ali had made some equally paradoxical decisions in the past, but they had been attributed to naïveté, egotism, opportunism, and conservatism. For answers we must look to Ali and South Africa.

Ali and South Africa

Faced with exclusion from international sports, in 1971 South Africa unveiled a "multinational" sports policy that allowed whites and blacks to compete with each other on the national level. Mostly a sop to external pressure, the new policy also represented a critical step toward legitimizing the ultimate dispersal of blacks into "independent national states" commonly known as homelands, Bantustans, or dumping grounds. The probability of resistance at home and alienation abroad led the South African government and sporting officials to seek the assistance of American promoter Bob Arum, who in turn secured the services of Muhammad Ali. If Senator Russell could have so effectively used Ali to defend the southern way of life in 1964, the South African government saw value in doing the same in 1972,[240] reasoning that a person of Ali's background and stature guaranteed favorable publicity for the increasingly shunned nation.

The South African press enthusiastically supported a proposed November confrontation between Ali and another black American, Al Jones, at the prestigious and spacious Ellis Park Rugby Stadium in Johannesburg.[241] But anti-apartheid forces countered quickly, having realized that an Ali visit could hurt their cause. Only timely and forceful persuasion by Ambassador Abdulrahim Farah of Somalia, chairman of the United Nations Special Committee on Apartheid, and South African exile Dennis Brutus prompted Herbert Muhammad, Ali's manager, to refuse the offer. The two men had convinced him that the long-range consequences might be disastrous for Ali and even the Nation of Islam.[242] Instead, light heavyweight champion Bob Foster fought Pierre Fourie in Johannesburg in December 1973. According to the South African press, Fourie's performance, even though he lost, showed that despite boycotts and sanctions South African boxing could "compete—though not yet on level terms—with the sport in other countries";[243] in other words, the boycott was ineffective.

The Foster-Fourie bout was held up as false proof of hope and movement in South Africa. Conventional wisdom maintained that contact and communication would produce more change, but the Soweto riots of 1976, in which more than 700 people died, exposed in flames and death the emptiness of this illusion. Antigovernment sports groups within South Africa warned against further contact. The Black Peoples' Sport Council, in October 1977, explained, "We believe that sport or any other activity cannot be divorced from the realities of the present political system."[244] Thus, equality in society became a requisite for cooperation with the government's so-called normalization of sport. The position was expressed by the call to action, "No normal sport in an abnormal society."[245]

Facing even more opposition from international sporting associations, South Africa continued to use boxing both as a wedge to break the boycott and as a propaganda tool. Having established a strong presence in the World Boxing Association through officials and top-ranking contenders since its entry in 1974, South Africa launched a multipronged attack on its enemies in sport and politics. Ali again figured prominently in the government's plans, as promoter Bob Arum reached a tentative agreement in 1978 with a South African hotel chain (Sun Hotels) to stage the Muhammad Ali–Leon Spinks return match in Bophuthatswana— although proclaimed an independent state by the South African government, no other nation recognized it as such. South African officials clearly intended to make the fight a showcase event for the homeland policy, in which blacks allegedly exercised self-rule and controlled their own destinies in perfect contentment and harmony. Sun City, the Las Vegas–style resort with legalized gambling, "blue" movies, and lawful race mixing was to provide a cover for the virtually nonarable, mineral-free, industryless land; of course, there would be no mention that South Africa controlled Bophuthatswana's defense, police, civil service, currency, and postal service.[246]

With a guarantee of $14,000,000, Arum pressed on with attempts to justify the bout. Ali remained uncharacteristically silent and deaf, perhaps the visions of dollar signs and misinformation from the apologist promoter dulling his senses to the reality of the situation. His silence amounted to consent, especially when measured against the comments and actions of many black leaders in sport and the larger society. Arthur Ashe, who had gone to the land of apartheid in 1973 and who had criticized India in 1974 for refusing to play the South African Davis Cup (tennis) team, reversed his position. He now believed that the opening up of South Africa to foreign nonwhite athletes simply covered up the continuing racial discrimination there.[247] The Reverend Jesse Jackson, who spearheaded the black American movement against apartheid, warned that "no black fighter could fight there and gain respect."[248] Another black leader called the fight "a betrayal of the African people" in which Ali would be "endorsing apartheid."[249]

Although the protests forced Arum and Ali to consider another site, the island of Mauritius, they did not put an end to the plans for a South African–sponsored fight. Actually, economic considerations determined where the fight would be held, as a refusal by the United States government to permit foreign tax credits on the purses and the threat to picket closed-circuit showings made the fight too risky financially.[250] (It eventually took place in New Orleans on September 15, 1978; Ali won a fifteen-round decision.) By refusing to take a moral stand, Ali guaranteed that he would never be able to shake free of South Africa and its damaging associations, something that would haunt him during the 1980 Olympic boycott crisis.

When the Soviet Union invaded and occupied Afghanistan in 1979, a shocked world reacted with angry denunciations, which changed nothing. President Jimmy Carter, who had promised American support for human rights around the world, felt compelled to act. Armed intervention was out of the question, for nuclear weapons had tied his hands. Instead, Carter took the unprecedented step of threatening to boycott the 1980 Moscow Olympics, along with the more traditional threat of a grain embargo, unless the Soviet Union withdrew its troops—a strategy designed to hit the Soviet stomach as well as its sporting heart. Although the move was doomed to fail, based as it was on the faulty assumption that the Soviet Union cared more about sport and grain than it did spheres of influence, Carter believed that with the participation of other countries he could succeed. Convinced that he needed the African nations for support, the president turned to Ali for help. The man who dubbed himself the "Black Kissinger" gladly accepted the rare opportunity to serve as an official emissary on an important political mission.[251] His dream of statesmanship had come true, but it would end as a nightmare.

In sending Ali to Africa, Carter demonstrated a serious ignorance of history and United States–African relations; moreover, he failed to sense the uneasiness of black African leaders with Ali, who in turn understood neither the realities of the Afghanistan situation nor the limits of his own importance in influencing policy decisions. America was associated with colonialism and racism in the minds of many Africans, while the Soviet Union was associated with anti-imperialism. Also, Africans had not forgotten the negative American reaction to their boycott of the Montreal Olympics in 1976, when the International Olympic Committee had refused to expel New Zealand for violating sanctions against sporting contact with South Africa. Clearly, black Africa hoped, through nonsupport, to show that South African racism and aggression were as repugnant to them as the Russian invasion of Afghanistan was to the United States.[252]

Africans resented Carter's selection of an uneducated athlete to consult with national leaders, many of whom had already been alienated by Ali's loose tongue. (He was once denied entry to Zambia for allegedly denouncing Africans in comments made at the United Nations; he claimed they had failed to protest the plight of blacks in the United States.) Ali's relationship to South Africa also was a point of contention. Thus, black Africa put so much pressure on Ali during the trip that he reversed his position and, to the dismay of the American delegation and the president, admitted at a press conference that had he known the history of America and South Africa he would have turned down Carter's request. Africa refused to support the boycott, prompting one observer to remark, "as a presidential envoy, 'The Greatest' looked like a rank stumblebum."[253]

Knowing all of this, one is prompted to ask how an athlete who threw aside tradition at a nervous juncture in American history had since become so basically conservative and so easily manipulated. The truth is that the radical who had abandoned Christianity to become a Black Muslim, who had refused military induction and in general defied the Establishment, was never really a radical—society merely perceived him as one because he did not follow the guidelines that had been set. In its post–Malcolm X era the Nation of Islam was no more threatening to the American order than Booker T. Washington's Tuskegee group. Both stressed cleanliness of body, moral character, racial solidarity, and self-help; they differed in that Booker T. Washington hoped for the ultimate assimilation of blacks into mainstream America while Elijah Muhammad wanted permanent separation.[254] Similarly, thousands applied for conscientious objector status during the Vietnam era, and a great many more Americans protested our involvement in Southeast Asia, but it was Ali who became a symbol of the radical draft dodger because, as an athlete, he could influence America's youth.[255]

With his departure from boxing, Ali as a symbol of rebellion had been exposed as a relative conservative, someone with a self-help mentality. Those who adored him in his fighting days felt betrayed by his words and actions. Sadly, he is now lost without boxing but also lost because of it. The sport took him to greatness and earned him millions of dollars and millions of fans but taught him little about sustaining greatness or preserving his fortune. This fate has been shared by almost every great boxer, yet it does not deter young men hoping to follow in their footsteps, most of whom will never experience even a small part of Ali's glory but will surely endure a large part of his pain. If nothing else, Ali's tragic demise forces us to look beyond the ring and its glitter and into the depths of boxing's despair.

Conclusion
The Myth and Reality of Boxing

Prizefighting surely must be one of the supreme anomalies of our time. As boxing developed from an illegal activity to sanctioned sport it remained primitive, with only the trappings of modernity. But like a weed shooting up through a crack in the sidewalk, it is firmly planted in the foundation of our highly advanced society. Why would a nation with a history of discounting tradition accept, support, and even protect a throwback to an uncivilized past? Is there a method to society's apparent madness? The answers to these questions not only shed light on boxing but on the larger society.

Some of the qualities that have opened boxing to attack have, at the same time, been its salvation. While brutality and death have often stirred calls for reform and/or abolition, they have also served as alleged proof of manhood and even national resolve. Boxing's brutal physicality has provided an escape from the dwarfing structures, choking pollution, crowded urban centers, and uncontrolled technology that threaten our primacy as the architects of modernity. The stench of a dimly lit gymnasium, the sight of two sweaty gladiators standing tall in the ring, and the sound of glove against flesh all open a window to a simpler, more human-oriented past when muscle, might, and perhaps intelligence allowed us to control our own destiny.

In the end boxing reveals America's ambivalent attitude toward tradition. We choose not to let tradition stand in the way of progress, but that progress is often antithetical to individual primacy. The fact that the odds weigh heavily against success for the great majority of boxing hopefuls does not seem to matter. When an underprivileged boxer succeeds against overwhelming odds and insurmountable obstacles, at enormous personal costs, the hopes of all Americans are buoyed. In this role boxers become integral elements in a belief system that thrives on the willingness of an overwhelming majority of its faithful to dream the impossible—that success is there for the striving. The fact that former heavyweight boxing champion George Foreman (now on the comeback trail, apparently for economic reasons) was among the winners of the Horatio Alger Award offers credence to the notion that the myths of prizefighting success are caricatures of the American Dream.

It is because of, rather than despite, its contradictions that boxing has survived. The sport has been effectively packaged, marketed, and sold as a natural activity possessing redeeming social values ranging from socioeconomic escalation to character building. Thus, a significant portion of the public has been convinced that boxing's benefits far outweigh its harmful effects and that protest against the sport is almost un-American. Indeed, boxing has been directly associated with American strength and spirit, some observers claiming that the sport is as old as the Anglo-Saxon race and a maintainer of its "courage and pluck."[1]

Once the people had been assured that undesirable elements and practices had been minimized in boxing, convincing them that the sport had something positive to contribute was fairly easy. Over the years, far fewer critics have objected to the inherent dangers of two men striking each other than they have to gambling and fraud; in fact, boxing injuries and deaths often have been attributed to corrupting external agents, not to the blows delivered and received in the ring. Although watching a fight may be painful to many, it in no way compares to the often grisly experience of hitting and being hit repeatedly. Yet young men continue to stock and sustain the sport. Why?

Boxing as the Magic Carpet: A Perilous Ride

There can be little doubt that the desire for monetary gain, fame, and enhanced social status have motivated many a young man to enter the prizefight ring. Lawrence Perry described boxers in the 1800s and the early 1900s as men of "a lower order of intelligence, their haunts, mainly roadhouses and saloons,"[2] and that has not changed in modern times. Studies in 1952 by S. Kirson Weinberg and Henry Arond and in 1971 by Nathan Hare demonstrated that nearly all prizefighters had low socioeconomic backgrounds and little education, qualities that ensured their victimization and virtual peonage. Boxers without money, useful work skills, or education simply fought to live, and any display of success made the profession attractive to others, offering hope of reward without deviant behavior. Of course, success was often defined broadly within the narrow context of the boxing world, and a lack of monetary gain was compensated by displays of courage, moments in the limelight, and the sense of belonging to a special brotherhood.[3]

Well-educated and financially secure young men have not generally succumbed to the lure of the prize ring. For them, fighting carried too many risks with only meager rewards. According to the legendary sportswriter Grantland Rice, these fellows have always had available far too wide a range of viable options to allow them "to jump into the roughest, toughest, richest, lowest scale of professional sport." They also declined the stigmatization that accompanies even the most respected champions; as Rice concluded, middle- and upper-class lads "don't mind professional baseball and football, but to be labeled a 'prize fighter' is something they can't quite swallow."[4]

Without this perspective and a history of advancement through traditional means, underprivileged youth believe what they see and hear. Newspaper stories and word-of-mouth tales about the lucrative sums allegedly earned by boxing champions have often obscured reality. For example, in 1932 New York boxing clubs dispensed nearly $1,500,000 to prizefighters, but considering there were some 945 licensed boxers, the average income was only $1,500—a sum not far from the poverty line.[5] Worse yet, the average income in no way reflected the fiscal shortfall for the average boxer: 100 main-event boxers shared $1,000,000 while the rest were left with $500,000 to divide among themselves; their average yearly earnings totaled less than $600.[6]

Looking at success in terms of advancement to the top also sheds critical light on the likelihood of that success. In a localized vertical mobility study of 127 boxers from 1938 to 1951, sociologists Weinberg and Arond found that very few boxers reached the top of their profession: 107 (84.2 percent) progressed no farther than the local preliminary or semiwindup category; 11 boxers (8.7 percent) became local main-event fighters; 8 (7.1 percent) achieved national recognition as top contenders; and just 1 fighter became a champion.[7] A financial study conducted on a national scale during the same period found that only 600 professional fighters earned enough money to sustain themselves and only 60 became headline fighters.[8]

Time has had little impact upon these statistics. The experience of undercard boxer Malik Dozier of Washington, D.C., is representative of the false hopes, the misperceptions, and the shattered dreams. According to Dozier, "If you got a name like Sugar Ray Leonard, boxing's great, but not if you're at rock bottom like me." He was looking from the bottom up, having fought preliminary bouts on the same card as the former Olympic champion's early professional fights. To Dozier, Leonard's

$30,000 purses appeared astronomical in comparison to the $150 he received (before expenses); indeed, on one occasion his pay was not sufficient to cover medical costs for a broken jaw and teeth.[9] Like many other boxers, Dozier had to supplement his income with money from a nine-to-five job. Fighters would often drive 100 to 400 miles for a $75 or $150 fight, sleeping in their cars to cut expenses. One boxer aptly remarked, "Ain't no dues like boxing dues."[10]

Yet a well-publicized event like the 1976 Olympic Games in Montreal, with the hero status and lucrative television contracts it brought to Ray Leonard and the other four American gold medalists, stirred tremendous interest among poorer youths. Such success stories, along with the rags-to-riches boxing film *Rocky,* brought glamour back to boxing. Long-time boxing expert Mike Capriano revealed the power of these symbols in his simple observation that "these kids hear about this Davis kid and those Spinks boys getting all that money to box, and they come down to the gym . . . figurin' maybe they can make a good score, too."[11] But even those who "score big" earn far less than the public has been led to believe. For example, Jose Stable's $10,000 purse from a 1965 fight with Emile Griffith was divided among his trainer ($840), his manager ($2,500), and his training and fight expenses ($1,600); Stable's net earnings before taxes thus totaled only $5,040, of which his manager gave him $540 and doled the rest out in $70 weekly payments, a common practice.[12]

If expenses and taxes have not totally eroded a boxer's ring profits, unscrupulous managers and promoters often have accelerated the process. The most frequently cited example of managerial exploitation has been the loan or advance system. Through this system managers encourage fighters to borrow money from them, which they tend to squander while the managers look the other way. The boxer's indebtedness means that each fight becomes collateral for another advance, and the one-third limit on a manager's share of a fighter's purse is rendered meaningless. For example, Ike Williams, lightweight champion and victim of the loan system, had entire purses withheld from him by his managers on at least three separate occasions. And Johnny Saxton, a welterweight champion in the 1950s with links to organized crime, reported that he never received more than "a couple of hundred dollars" after each fight.[13] Even before organized crime's involvement in boxing, the great Robert Fitzsimmons received not one cent for three of his world championship fights.[14]

Often compounding a boxer's fiscal problems were hangers-on, or "parasites," people who read about huge boxing purses, associated with the fighters, and drained them. Because of their high visibility and reputations, boxers often felt obligated to protect their image even when they could not really afford to. They suffered the "big man, big spender syndrome" in which failure to pick up the tab was perceived as a betrayal of their status and profession. Danny Cox, a promising young heavyweight in the 1940s, admitted that the stereotype of boxers as spendthrifts was all too true. According to Cox, fighters liked "to spend their dough fast; part of their training seems to be reaching for the tab." He cited Mickey Walker, Jack Dempsey, Joe Louis, and Beau Jack as prime examples of boxers who spent most of their money being "good sports." "Camp followers" try to embarrass a thrifty boxer into spending money by telling the story of a boxer who was so sparing that "when saying his prayers he refused to say amen because he did not want God to get all of his money."[15] Unfortunately, most of the money spent on friends was not tax deductible.

For many years the lion's share of a boxer's earnings went to the Internal Revenue Service. Joe Louis and Sugar Ray Robinson stand out for the depth and extent of their tax miseries. Both grossed over $4,000,000 in their long and heralded careers, but taxes and poor financial advice and management left both men bankrupt. Robinson was relatively fortunate in that he ended his career with virtually nothing but also owed nothing; Louis was another story. Robinson's tax troubles reached a climax after he had agreed to defer the income from a certain fight to avoid excessive taxes. The IRS refused to accept the deferment and withheld his purse from a subsequent fight. Robinson sued, and on April 6, 1965, the U.S. Tax Court ruled in his favor, ordering the IRS to release the $313,449.82 withheld. However, out of that amount Robinson realized only $123,000, using the remainder as a credit on his income taxes.[16] Had the decision gone against him, he might have suffered as badly as his friend Joe Louis, who in 1956 owed the IRS $1,250,000 in back taxes.[17]

Joe Louis's tax problems reveal the untold pitfalls of the unincorporated professional boxer with bunched income potential. By 1946 he owed the government $98,000 in back taxes, due in part to the fact that even though he donated two of his purses to war-time relief funds, the fights themselves were not considered charity events and he was liable for taxes on both purses. When he fought Billy Conn after leaving the military in 1946, his best fighting years having been spent in service to his country, his tax burden increased even further because the $591,116 income from that fight and an additional $93,250 in earnings raised his gross annual income to $700,000, placing him near the 90-percent tax bracket. Moreover, bad financial advice clearly exacerbated his already serious problems.[18]

Louis's trouble with the IRS worsened following his second match with Billy Conn in 1946. After deducting various business expenses from the Conn fight earnings, Louis reported an income of $163,419, on which he paid $115,992 in taxes. However, the government disagreed with some of his deductions, rejecting the arrangement he had with his first wife, Marva, to pay her 25 percent of his purse from the Conn fight for services as one of his managers, in lieu of a cash alimony settlement. The IRS also refused to accept a deferred payment agreement that Louis's manager had worked out for the Mauriello fight, and it disallowed certain other expenses and business losses. The government calculated Louis's adjusted gross income at $448,465, increasing his tax bill from $115,992 to $362,048 and leaving Louis with only $86,417, which was reduced to $57,722 after New York State taxes were paid. Unfortunately, Louis was not aware of his tax situation until 1950, after his initial retirement from the ring, at which time he learned that the government had also found discrepancies in his income tax returns for 1947, 1948, and 1949.[19] Part of the problem stemmed from Louis's borrowing at will from his own company and then failing to report the loan either on his individual or corporate returns.[20]

Louis came out of retirement in an attempt to ease his indebtedness, but he only added to his woes. To have settled his tax debt within twenty years, while at the same time paying current income taxes and interest on the debt, he would have had to earn $310,000 per year. Unfortunately, he had surrendered control of the heavyweight crown to promoters Norris and Wirtz, and though he got 20 percent of the IBC stock in return, according to Barney Nagler "he could put his income from his stock holdings . . . into his right ear." The shrewd Wirtz, who had outsmarted financial minds far greater than Gibson's or Louis's, arranged for most of the earnings of the IBC in Chicago and in New York to go into arena rents (from which he and Norris profited), not the boxing clubs themselves. Since the financial records reflected consistent losses for the IBC's first year and small profits thereafter, Louis did not collect any dividends during the years he held stock in both corporations. By 1956 his annual income was estimated at $40,000, and despite good-faith efforts to pay his back taxes, he could not even reduce the interest on his debt. In early 1957 the government seized a $64,000 trust fund that had been set up for his two young children.[21]

The public did not sit idly by and allow an American hero to be totally destroyed. Louis's tax problems became a cause célèbre and supporters urged Congress to act on his behalf; others appealed to the IRS to reach a compromise. Finally, in the late 1960s the Brown Bomber's third wife, Martha Jefferson, a very able lawyer, convinced the IRS that further pursuit of her husband would only make gainful employment a futile exercise. Belatedly, the IRS consented to tax Louis only on his current earnings and at the standard rates.[22]

Even without the fiscal mistakes, Joe Louis's net earnings still would have been dismally out of proportion to his gross earnings. From 1947 through 1949, when as champion he received his biggest purses, the tax rate for individuals who earned $200,000 was 88 percent;[23] it was not until 1982 that legislation was passed to reduce the tax rate to a 50 percent maximum. Like other individuals whose incomes fluctuated, boxers who made far less than Louis also paid large percentages of their earnings to the IRS.[24] In 1964 Congress enacted legislation allowing for five-year income averaging, but until then people with highly unpredictable earnings levels suffered both in good times and in bad.[25] Additional relief came from the aforementioned case involving Sugar Ray Robinson, commonly referred to as *Ray S. Robinson* (1965), which permitted boxers to receive deferred payments for fights if they filed the appropriate papers before the event.[26] However, even now there are few fighters who take advantage of that option, and even fewer opt for incorporation, which can facilitate deferred payments as well as provide other tax savings, including deductions for retirement plans. The complexity of the process has deterred many, but the more compelling reason seems to be the desire for immediate and large earnings.[27]

Whether manifested in alcoholism, drug addiction, or ostentatious spending, this immediate gratification syndrome has been disastrous for boxers and other athletes, especially in light of the short length of a professional athletic career and the bunched income potential that accompanies it. On the average boxers have seven or eight years in which to earn a living, and few have the necessary fiscal management skills to build a nest egg prior to their retirement from the fight game. A dearth of marketable skills outside the ring has also been a major cause of economic collapse for boxers both during and after their careers. Sugar Ray Robinson and Joe Louis stand out in this regard, although they were far from alone.[28]

Early in his career Robinson was considered a shrewd businessman. In 1951 he held investments worth some $450,000, including a café, a six-chair barber shop, a dry cleaning business, a lingerie store, and several apartment buildings. But a combination of poor management and Robinson's extravagant life-style (which included a personal traveling barber, a traveling golf instructor, and a traveling jester) led to the collapse of his small empire.[29] Although boxing did nothing to prepare Robinson for life, he still believes in the sport. As of early 1987 he was encouraging young men to better themselves through boxing and had institutionalized the message in Sugar Ray's Youth Foundation for

Imparting Values Through Sports, located in Los Angeles.[30] (Robinson is reportedly suffering from Alzheimer's disease, which doctors have linked to head trauma.)

Joe Louis experienced business failures for remarkably similar reasons. He too lived extravagantly and made miserable investments, losing $10,000 in a restaurant and bar, $30,000 in a black newspaper, and $35,000 in a Chicago nightclub. The few sound investments he did make were, unfortunately, short-term. For example, he and his partners constructed and sold 200 homes in the $12,000–$14,000 price range but built no more; and they opened a trade school in Chicago to train returning veterans to be automobile mechanics, but somehow they ran out of veterans.[31]

Such problems did not respect race, as white champions before Robinson and Louis met comparable fates. Tommy Loughran, who held the light heavyweight title from 1927 to 1929, reportedly earned over $250,000 in the ring but lost everything in part through unwise investments. His predecessor, Paul Berhlenbach, who supposedly garnered $500,000, "advertised in the papers for a job to keep from starving" and appealed "to the court to get back a trust fund of depreciated securities."[32]

Robinson, Louis, Loughran, and Berhlenbach had something else in common: each fought long after his prime, and each came out of retirement to fight indebtedness. Time has not changed the trend. In August 1985, Jose Torres of the New York State Athletic Commission announced that three former three-time world champions, Roberto Duran, Alexis Arguello, and Wilfred Benitez, who together reportedly earned more than $6,000,000 in the ring, were making comebacks out of financial need. Benitez had filed for bankruptcy in Puerto Rico; Arguello, who was reportedly insolvent as a result of bad investments and tax debts, had to forfeit his property in Florida for taxes and turn over all revenues from his Lite Beer commercials; Duran, too proud to admit his financial troubles, allegedly spent $8,000 per week to support his life-style. All three men fought in 1985–86, Duran as a middleweight. The latter insisted that he was pursuing a goal no boxer had ever achieved—titles in four weight classes—but his hopes were dashed by Robbie Sims, who won a split decision on June 23, 1986, in a title elimination bout in Las Vegas.[33]

These men were all exceptions in that they were champions and had earned substantial amounts of money. But in their handling of finances and their postboxing careers they were just like most other fighters. Sociologist Nathan Hare, himself a former boxer, observed that "the tragedy of the fighter's life is... when his career comes to an end—he feels that the best years of his life are already behind him."[34]

The postscript for too many boxers reads like the classic line by Marlon Brando's tough-guy character in *On the Waterfront:* "I could have been a contender. I could have had class. I could have been somebody."[35]

While boxing frequently served as an instrument of status attainment for rising fighters, many of them experienced a sharp decline in status in their postboxing lives, which often resulted in temporary or prolonged emotional difficulties in terms of readjusting to life outside the ring[36]—a common occurrence for many professional athletes. An extreme, but not atypical, example was Johnny Saxton. Three years after winning the welterweight championship, Saxton was destitute and desperate. He committed two burglaries in the Philadelphia area, for which he was tried, convicted, and incarcerated. While in jail he attempted suicide and was admitted to an institution for the insane. Less extreme, but no less depressing, were the postboxing careers of Beau Jack, a shoeshine man; Kingfish Levinsky, an ambulatory tie salesman; and Joe Louis, a professional wrestler, wrestling referee, and "official greeter" at Caesar's Palace Hotel and Casino in Las Vegas.[37]

The 1980–81 comebacks attempted by two once-magnificent champions, Joe Frazier and Muhammad Ali, graphically illustrate the problem of maladjustment. Frazier likened his return to being "alive again." He admitted that boxing was his life, that he knew nothing else, and that creating boxers in his own image was simply not satisfying enough. Moreover, ridiculous as the notion might seem, Smokin' Joe honestly believed that he owed the public something—another look at his great skill and courage. But he was living in the past, and his lackluster performance against an inferior opponent persuaded him to accept the inevitable. He has not lost his love or enthusiasm for the game, however, and continues to fight vicariously through his son and a nephew, whom he manages and trains—which is not surprising given that he once said, "The most important thing is, I love to fight."[38]

Ali's postboxing life is more depressing because many observers believe that his talents transcended the narrow confines of the "squared circle." Despite his self-proclaimed status as "the Greatest" and "the Black Kissinger," it is clear that boxing made him what he was and is. He has no skills outside the ring which compare favorably to his once-extraordinary boxing dexterity and in recent years has exhibited a form of social disorientation. While the physical punishment associated with the sport has taken its toll, the return to "ordinary" life has been a demoralizing experience for a man of such former lofty status. Sportswriter Dave Anderson remarked, "People who need people don't retire."[39] Ali still needs people—an audience—but he is an actor in search of a stage.

Surprisingly, the most revealing messages about the plight of former boxers have often come in the pleas of the sport's most ardent defenders. Mrs. Tony Zale, the wife of a former middleweight champion and an unequivocal supporter of boxing, admitted during congressional hearings in 1974 that she watched too many fighters go around groping because of too few opportunities in the boxing world or the "outside one." She believed that both boxers and their sport were discriminated against, a criticism that addressed the system in which other sports found a training ground in colleges and universities and therefore were able to provide young men with the opportunity to get an education while they competed. She complained that while boxing was "in the gutter, now it's going to the sewer."[40]

Although Mrs. Zale had a valid argument, that unless boxers had incentives to pursue an education they would not, she ignored the discouragement boxers face from others in the sport. Professional boxing has not only failed, historically, to equip its own graduates for other work, but according to Nathan Hare, those in management positions often try to prejudice fighters against other endeavors. The boxer who has to work outside the ring to support himself and his family is considered a failure; he has betrayed the "order" by admitting that boxing does not always provide an adequate paycheck. Moreover, unlike other sports that have sophisticated and lucrative pension and disability plans, boxing remains in the Dark Ages in caring for its own.[41]

Those people who are closest to the sport agree that a majority of boxers are in bad shape financially, mentally, and physically, and that those who make good are exceptions. Yet few effective measures have been taken to improve their plight, although the Veterans Boxers Association is one benevolent group, composed of former boxers, that provides handouts to some of the many boxers in need.[42] However, the states, which reap significant benefits from professional boxing, have contributed little. Massachusetts recognized that it had a significant number of indigent boxers and responded in 1957 with the formation of the Boxer's Fund Board for the use or benefit of former boxers in need of financial assistance. The board, like the private benevolent groups, provided piecemeal relief at best. Selfish interests have prevented more from being done.[43]

In 1979 California commissioned an actuarial study to lay the basis for a comprehensive disability and pension plan for boxers. The plan was opposed by those with a vested interests in boxing and fell prey to the "reduction to the lowest common denominator" phenomenon: if one state required additional taxes or levies for a pension plan and others did not, a promoter who sought to maximize profits would arrange matches in those other states.[44] Only a federal commission could ensure that pension funds would be established for boxers nationwide, but there is little likelihood of such a commission and, to paraphase Congressman Pat Williams of Montana, less promise that boxers will ever have a "16th round."[45] Talent, luck, hard work, and personality are essential to success in boxing, and only a disproportionate few make it to the top, notwithstanding the myth of unlimited opportunity.[46]

The Physical Aspects of Boxing

Fiscal dependency and readjustment trauma, although very serious problems in and of themselves, pale in comparison to the prospects of serious injury and death faced every time two boxers enter the ring. The reality of the inherent danger in boxing has been denied by the promoters, managers, and officials, and even by the somewhat naïve positions of the boxers themselves. Why would anyone encourage another person to pursue a dangerous occupation, and why do so many accept the challenge? Although not everyone associated with boxing is evil, no one involved with the sport seems capable of escaping its addictive qualities. Somehow, supporters and fighters have deluded themselves into thinking that boxing, when properly conducted, is safe. The classic justification goes something like this: "Boxers are not two brawling brutes seeking to maim or kill each other. They are two closely matched athletes seeking, through the use of such skills and footwork, timing, accuracy, punching, and feinting, to determine who is the better man in the ring."[47] Dead boxers tell a different story.

On August 29, 1951, George Flores, a journeyman fighter, collapsed after taking two hard blows to the head in the eighth round of a fight. He died four days later from a cerebral hemorrhage and cerebral edema. Although referees had stopped Flores's two previous fights when he was obviously too badly hurt to continue, physicians approved by NYSAC's Medical Advisory Board cleared him to fight again, only one month after the first technical knockout and two weeks after the second.[48] Flores's family sued the state for negligence and won, but on appeal the Appellate Division of the Superior Court of New York overturned the lower court's decision and dismissed the case. The ruling not only showed the risks boxers and their families faced, with little chance of recovery in the case of injury or death, but also revealed the nature and objectives of boxing. The court had decided that no relief should be forthcoming because:

> Decedent (Flores) was engaged in a concededly dangerous activity. From his experience he knew that he would likely be struck by

blows to the head. In fact, the very objective of the contestants, well-known in advance, is to "knock out" the opponent and cause him to fall to the floor in such condition that he is unable to rise to his feet for a specified time. Decedent assumed the risks known to be inherent in the fight. . . . Because the State undertook to make a dangerous sport less dangerous by some regulation does not make the State an insurer of the participants.[49]

Although many boxers have denied the ring's dangers or even their own injuries, there have been some who have begged the world to sit up and take notice. Gene Tunney, known as a fast and clever defensive fighter, chronicled an incident that took place while training for his second fight with Jack Dempsey:

I went into a clinch with my head down and my partner's head came up and butted me over the left eye, cutting and dazing me badly. Then he stepped back and swung his right against my jaw with every bit of his power. It landed flush and stiffened me where I stood. Without going down or staggering, I lost all consciousness, but instinctively proceeded to knock him out. Another sparring partner entered the ring. We boxed three rounds, I have no recollection of this, nor have I any recollection of anything that occurred the next morning when I awakened, wondering who I was and what I was doing there.[50]

Tunney maintained that this incident convinced him to retire at the first possible opportunity. He feared becoming a victim of the fate that had befallen so many others before him—*pugilistica dementia,* or punch-drunkenness. Tunney had heard all the horror stories, like the tale of former lightweight champion Ad Wolgast who spent his last days in a mental hospital getting ready for his fight with Bat Nelson, a fight that "was always scheduled for 'tomorrow'."[51]

More recently, the "classic" third and final encounter between Muhammad Ali and Smokin' Joe Frazier in October 1975 serves to illustrate the extent of pain and suffering exchanged in an "evenly matched contest of skill and courage." Jay Stuller describes the two "gladiators" who took it "to the mountain" one last time in their bitter five-year rivalry:

His body heavier with age, Ali still fired those flashing and vicious left jabs, now backed with real power and they snapped Frazier's bobbing but unguarded head in the first three rounds. Then Frazier crouched low, began waging his own personal inquisition in the sixth. Like a starving and desperate wolf, he ripped at the champion's chest and kidneys, unleashing that legendary and evil left hook to Ali's jaw. The fight festered into a noble, but wicked war until the 14th, which Ali later described as being "like death. The closest thing to dying that I know of." Ali barely stumbled off his stool for the last round, but Frazier's manager, Eddie Futch, saw his fighter as a spent shell lying cold, with not a wisp of smoke remaining, "Joe, I'm going to stop it," said Futch.[52]

Just how much this particular fight took out of both men will never be known. Although it was Frazier who did not come out for the fifteenth round, Ali had also suffered mightily. The champ still showed speed and skill, but Frazier often found the mark with punches he claimed "would bring down the walls of a city."[53]

A pioneering 1973 study found that championship fighters often suffered the most brain damage because they met the toughest opponents, had longer careers, and consequently took more blows to the head.[54] Less scientific studies have reported similar findings. A 1980 *Playboy* survey judged boxing "the toughest job in sports."[55] On the basis of some twenty categories that touched on courage, physical skill, preparation, athletic intelligence, and danger, the magazine concluded that prizefighting had no equal; in terms of serious injury and frequency of injury, only auto racing surpassed it.[56] Boxing stood out clearly as the ultimate in interpersonal conflict, a conclusion that found support in a 1980 study by Patrick Malone of the Knight-Ridder News Service. Malone argued that boxing was the most deadly contact sport, and the statistics seem to bear that out: from 1970 through 1978 an average of 21 deaths per year among 5,500 boxers, or 3.8 deaths per 1,000 participants, compared to college football's 0.3 deaths per 1,000 and high school football's 0.1 deaths per 1,000.[57]

Deaths and serious injury suffered in boxing contests reveal only a small percentage of the potential for danger. Unfortunately, the damaging effects of the sport are cumulative and often difficult to diagnose, sometimes resulting in death, serious illness, or blindness long after a fighter's career has ended. However, convincing evidence has mounted over the years to the effect that brain damage and other forms of physical injury are frequent companions of the sport. Dr. Harrison Martland, a New Jersey pathologist who began his pioneering studies of the punch-drunk boxer in the 1920s, found that the opinion of laypeople, most of them men who made a living handling boxers, was more substantive than that of medical experts. These handlers led Martland to former boxers who exhibited the symptoms—a flopping leg, foot dragging, staggering, and slurred speech—of brain-damaging illnesses such as epidemic encephalitis (inflammation of the brain) or advanced syphilis. However, the doctor's findings, published in the *Journal of the American Medical Association* in 1928, were not substantiated through actual examination of boxers' brains after death.[58]

In 1936 Dr. Edward Carroll repeated Martland's assertions, concluding that brain-jarring punches caused tiny hemorrhages and scarlike injuries that were irreversible.[59] In 1950 researchers at the United States Naval Hospital in Bethesda, Maryland, found that punches to the head caused the brain to bounce inside the skull, hitting against the bony sphenoidal ridge, which then bit into the frontal lobes and destroyed tissue.[60] Yet neurosurgeons continued to disagree about the damaging effects of blows to the head, even knockout punches. Some concluded that the knockout punch, landing between the chin and the point of the jaw, "is the cleanest sort of a blow," temporarily shutting off consciousness and motor impulse, and that "ninety-eight times out of a hundred the man knocked out is upon his feet, his head cleared within fifteen or twenty seconds."[61]

Such opinions were the result of, among other things, imperfect technology and insufficient research and analysis. In 1962 Dr. Harry Kaplan, a New York neurosurgeon, found that only 1 out of some 3,800 boxers who had been knocked out and later underwent electroencephalography (EEG) showed significant brain-wave changes. He concluded that a knockout punch produced temporary unconsciousness with no lasting effect on the brain and that anyone who disagreed with him was relying on impressions, not facts. According to Dr. David Loiselle, a neuropsychologist and neurophysiologist, the EEG is a gross measure that often fails to pick up subtle changes in the brain, such as swelling, tears, and bruises, and is of no validity in measuring injuries to the brain stem produced by the twisting effects of hard blows to the chin. His conclusion was supported by the research of Dr. Harvey Levin and Dr. Stanley Handel, who have used 1980s technology, including magnetic resonance imaging to look for actual changes in the brain structure. MRI blends radio waves, magnets, and sophisticated computer software to produce definitive pictures of the brain. It allows physicians to detect abnormalities that might not be seen any other way and can pinpoint where minute changes may occur over time.[62]

A major breakthrough validating the long-term effects of boxing did not occur until 1973, when a team of British researchers led by Dr. J. A. N. Corsellis published a study that detailed the posthumous examination of the brains of fifteen boxers who had fought between 1900 and 1940 and had died in the past sixteen years, between the ages of fifty-seven and ninety-one. The pathology reports were complemented

Photographer Herb Scharfman captures the knockout punch delivered by Rocky Marciano (right) in the thirteenth round of his title bout with champion Jersey Joe Walcott at Philadelphia's Municipal Stadium on September 24, 1952. (UPI/Bettmann Newsphotos)

Referee Ruby Goldstein keeps a tight hold on a still eager and angry Emile Griffith as Benny "Kid" Paret sags on the ropes, felled by what UPI described as "a murderous barrage of blows." (UPI/Bettmann Newsphotos)

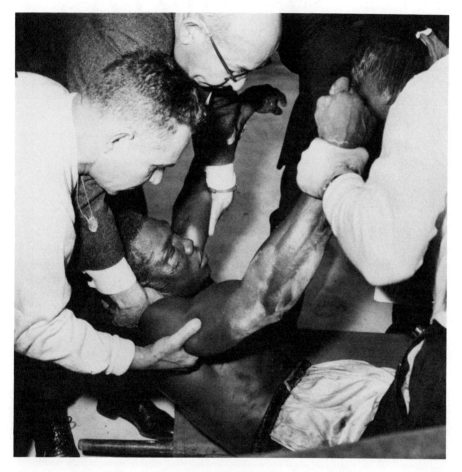

An unconscious, defeated welterweight champion, Benny Paret is placed on a stretcher as officials prepare to remove him from the ring. Paret's condition was described as serious, but he never regained consciousness and died on April 3, 1962. (UPI/Bettmann Newsphotos)

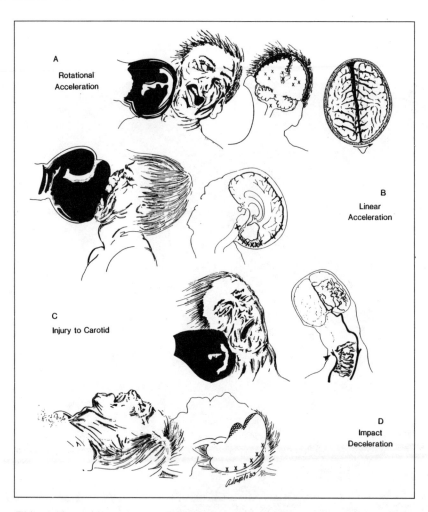

This vivid graphic shows the effects of four types of blows to the head. (A) The hook or cross to the jaw area produces rapid twisting of the brain, which results in bleeding and widespread trauma to fibrous tissue, from white matter to the base of the brain. (B) The straight punch or heavy jab snaps the head backward, which produces tears in the cerebellum and damage to the brain stem. (C) The downward blow to the side of the face and neck compresses the main artery to the brain and stops the flow of blood. (D) The hard landing against mat or ropes thrusts the brain against the skull, which causes tears to the front and sides of the brain. From "Morphological Changes in the Brains of Boxer," Peter W. Lampert, M.D., and John M. Hardman, M.D. *Journal of the American Medical Association* 251 (May 25, 1984): 2676–79. (Copyright 1984, American Medical Association)

by interviews with relatives and friends as well as written accounts, from which the researchers discovered that most of the deceased boxers had developed speech difficulties and the drooling and tremors characteristic of Parkinson's syndrome, in these cases the symptoms of a punch-drunk boxer. Upon microscopic inspection of cerebral tissue, clearly all of the men had suffered serious brain damage.[63] Additionally, researchers compared the nerve cells in the brains of former boxers with those of nonfighters who had died at similar ages and found that the former evidenced greater degeneration and loss. Moreover, three-fourths of the former boxers had openings in the membranous partition (septum) between the two halves of the brain, a condition that could easily lead to hemorrhaging; within the control group, only 0.3 percent showed such a condition.[64] Corsellis and his associates concluded that detection and prevention of brain damage in living subjects remained difficult because the condition did not simply result from an accumulation of blows; further, there was a danger that, at any moment and for some unknown reason, one or more blows could be fatal. Thus, no head injury was ever too trivial to be safely ignored.[65]

The boxing fraternity, the medical profession, and society at large virtually ignored the invisible damage done to boxers until November 13, 1982, when South Korean Duk Koo Kim, the son of a rice farmer, "was lifted out of obscurity on a stretcher."[66] Kim suffered irreversible and fatal brain damage in a brutal Las Vegas slugfest with Ray "Boom Boom" Mancini for the World Boxing Association lightweight championship. The ending to this nationally televised fight, in which both men gave and took enormous punishment, stunned the American people and millions more around the world.[67]

Kim's death four days after the fight prompted examination of boxing by regulatory and legislative bodies throughout the country. While most proposed tightened regulations, the American Medical Association took tentative and confusing steps toward the only real solution to boxing injuries and death—abolition of the sport. In January 1983 Dr. George Lundberg, editor of the *Journal of the American Medical Association,* published an impassioned plea to that effect, arguing that the "principle purpose of a boxing match is for one opponent to render the other injured, defenseless, incapacitated, and unconscious."[68] He cited recent medical studies that conclusively revealed atrophy in the brains of boxers and criticized those who defended boxing as an avenue of opportunity as well as those who argued that an illegal and more dangerous form would replace sanctioned boxing. Lundberg thought that boxers paid too heavy a price for occasional success, and he sarcastically suggested that if boxing was legal, gunfighting should be legal too. Boxing, in his opinion, had no redeeming value; it was "a throwback to uncivilized man [and] should not be sanctioned by any civilized society."[69] Lundberg clearly lit a fire under the status-quo-oriented medical organization, which had never taken a stand on the dangers of boxing.

The AMA's Council on Scientific Affairs, which commissioned a panel to study the dangers of boxing, recommended better regulation rather than abolition. It did not believe boxing was any more dangerous than some other sports accepted by society and considered abolition of the sport totally unfeasible. The council's report was clearly unsatisfactory to Lundberg and apparently to other physicians as well.[70] Their unhappiness surfaced in June 1983 at the annual meeting of the AMA's 351-member House of Delegates, when the Ohio delegation proposed a resolution that called for a ban on amateur scholastic, intercollegiate, and government-sponsored boxing programs. The object was to shut off the supply of boxers to the professional ranks by attacking the apparently more vulnerable, less popular, and less profitable amateur forms. The resolution passed with little fanfare.[71]

In 1984, after clear indications that adequate regulation was impossible, the AMA called for the total and complete ban of boxing because the intent of the sport was to do harm.[72] Boxers had been saying this for years, but few people had paid attention. When Sugar Ray Robinson appeared before a board investigating the death of Jimmy Doyle in 1947, he was asked if he knew that Doyle had been in serious trouble. "They pay me to get them in trouble," Robinson cooly answered.[73] In May 1986 the AMA renewed its call for a ban on professional boxing amid evidence that serious eye injuries occurred far more frequently than boxers, officials, promoters, or even doctors admitted. Dr. J. I. Maguire and Dr. W. E. Benson reported on nine cases of detached or torn retinas caused by boxing blows which were treated at one Philadelphia hospital between 1983 and 1985.[74] Although the damage had been caused by direct blows to the eyes, Maguire and Benson suggested that blunt trauma to the head could predispose boxers to a high risk of retinal detachment.[75]

The medical profession remained divided on the boxing issue. Dr. Russell Patterson, a New York neurosurgeon who has relied on John Stuart Mill, Isaiah Berlin, and Immanuel Kant to provide a libertarian justification for boxing, insisted that "the ban on boxing could be looked on as telling boxers that their desires and their values do not count." Such action would smack of paternalism and would represent the worst kind of slavery—absence of free will. Patterson's theory assumed that boxers truly understand the risks, although the evidence indicates otherwise—indeed, how could they be expected to understand when even doctors disagree. (For example, the fifteen-year-old Association of Ringside Physicians, founded by Dr. Max Novich, has consistently maintained that thorough physical examinations, better physician control, and uniform regulations can make boxing a safe sport.[76]) Patterson also assumed that boxers are aware of the real chances for success; once again the evidence indicates that they have been deluded. Finally, Patterson suggested that there should not be laws that inhibit risks in a free society; yet American legal codes are full of such restrictions: seat belt laws, antismoking ordinances, and many other acts against self-endangerment.[77]

Why Does Boxing Exist?

Although the desire for fame, money, escape, and status in part accounts for why young men box, the desperation and delusion that often drive the disadvantaged on a narrow and obstacle-ridden avenue toward the distant American Dream cannot be overlooked. However, neither status climbing nor materialism nor greed nor even corruption can fully explain the hold this primitive activity called boxing has on modern people. The real answer lies in human nature. Supported by a culture that values physicality and manliness, boxers pursue a sport at once scorned and glorified for its violence by a confused people who have prided themselves on civility and modernity but who cling to atavistic instincts. Boxing reflects society's fear of and need for violence, which is why reform movements that have attempted to sterilize and conventionalize "unnecessary" brutality have often been counterproductive. The kicking, biting, and scratching of the bare-fisted days has given way to padded, bright-colored gloves that protect the hands, give leverage to punches, and do untold damage to the brain as boxers now concentrate on blows to the head, when in bare-knuckle times the prospects of broken hands forced pugilists to aim for softer targets. Moreover, the regulation of boxing by fancy-titled state agencies, with little substance behind the facade of modernity, only masks the primitive nature of two men locked in serious and sometimes deadly combat.[78]

Society's need to conventionalize violence does not, in and of itself, fully explain the power of boxing; that violence must also be justified, must have some socially redeeming value. For the individual fighter, boxing has been promoted as a builder of character and a prover

of manhood; for the American people, boxing and other violent activities supposedly have purgative values. Governor Gifford Pinchot of
Pennsylvania, an ardent supporter of boxing, said in 1926 in justification
of his decision to allow the Jack Dempsey–Gene Tunney contest: "I call
your attention particularly to the fact that the nations in which boys and
men are in the habit of doing their fighting with their fists are precisely
those in which they are not in the habit of using the knife or the bullet
for that purpose."[79] Despite contradictory opinions that linked boxing to
warfare, Pinchot found considerable support, then and later, for his
position.

Laypeople, social scientists, and psychiatrists have all updated
Pinchot's assertion that boxing is a safety valve or outlet. According to
one theory, expressing hostility reduces the level of aggressive tendencies or relieves the actor; watching violent activities can have the same
effect. A leading proponent of this thesis was Dr. Seymour Feshbach,
who in 1961 published the results of an experiment to test the cathartic
effects of boxing on spectators. Feshbach showed that angered subjects
displayed less aggressive attitudes and tendencies in response to a word
test after viewing a violent prizefight film.[80] However, Dr. Leonard
Berkowitz's classic 1963 study on aggression demonstrated that quantita-
tive research had not been consistently kind to the catharsis theory. He
revealed that investigations of the theory have not always differentiated
between the instigation to aggression arising from frustration and an
individual's customary level of aggressiveness in social situations. Furthermore, although a person might feel relief after exhibiting hostility,
tension reduction might not invariably signify a lessened likelihood of
future aggression.[81]

Berkowitz believed that Feshbach's results indicated inhibition
rather than catharsis, and he set out to prove he was right using a
sequence from the brutal prizefight scene in the 1949 movie *The
Champion,* starring Kirk Douglas.[82] Critical of the lack of sophistication
in Feshbach's experiments, Berkowitz modified the film for his experiment,
prefacing one version with a characterization of the brutalized boxer as
a scoundrel receiving his just reward; in the other version the boxer was
portrayed as a man beginning to show remorse for a seamy past. The
catharsis theory should have predicted reduced viewer hostility in both
circumstances as a result of the viewer's vicarious experience of violence.
On the contrary, the first version heightened the hostility level of the
viewers and led them to perceive punishment of the boxer as justified
aggression. The combination of a deserving target and the revenge
factor overpowered inhibitions about aggressive impulses, indicating

that the viewers accepted what they observed to be appropriate behavior and applied the learning experience to their own circumstances.[83]

Even tests on boxers have failed to sustain the notion that release of aggression diminishes the desire for more hostility or else induces pleasure. In a 1955 study, B. F. Husman found that boxers seemed to experience an aggressive anxiety reaction rather than pleasant feelings following the discharge of hostile impulses.[84] Boxers showed presumptive signs of tension rather than ease, and tests indicated that fighters' aggressive behavior during the match made them feel anxiety or guilt even though the violence had social sanction.[85]

Lay critics of the purgative claims of boxing have equally valid counterarguments. The same Bertrand Russell who offered Ali solace insisted that boxing came dangerously close to real fighting and war and appealed to our sadism and lust for cruelty. Russell's evidence came from fans who complained "when there is no knock out or heavy hitting" or who roared savagely with excitement "when a hitter connects and his unfortunate opponent staggers groggy from the blow."[86] Even boxing's most ardent supporters have contended that fans are bloodthirsty to the point of exacerbating the brutality in the ring. Promoter Mike Jacobs admitted in 1935 that he searched for killers, sluggers, and maulers because the people wanted them. When asked if he should be taken literally, he responded, "They don't come out to see a tea party. They come to see a man hurt."[87]

Norman Cousins, as editor of the *Saturday Review,* openly stated his belief that fans contributed to the death of Benny Paret at the hands of Emile Griffith in April 1962. The tragedy evoked a worldwide outpouring of criticism and denunciation of boxing, along with a host of meaningless investigations that centered on whether the referee, Ruby Goldstein, had acted properly; whether doctors had failed to detect prior injuries; or whether ruthless managers had pushed their warrior into a fight before he had fully recovered from recent beatings. Cousins called the focus of these inquiries misdirected; blame rested, in his opinion, "on the prevailing mores that regard prize fighting as a perfectly proper enterprise and vehicle of entertainment."[88] *Commonweal,* a Catholic weekly, appealed to a higher law for help in righting a mortal sin: "The gospel law of love does not permit brethren to exchange wanton violence for mere renown or profit. There is no charity in a licensed assault that unleashes the beast in the boxer and the sadist in the spectator. As for natural justice, we who have no right to mutilate ourselves for external gain certainly cannot endow others with the right to attempt mayhem upon us by virtue of a contract."[89]

Boxing in the Eighties

Calls to a higher law notwithstanding, boxing's future seems secure. Not only will the sport continue to thrive, but there is little reason to believe that it will ever be affected by significant reform. Support of this view appeared in March 1984 when the State of New Jersey Commission of Investigation (SCI) made public its findings and recommendations on the inadequate regulation of boxing. The investigation produced damning information on the sport and its officials.[90]

The investigative commission reported that despite the appearance of a modern, bureaucratic system in control of the sport, prizefighting was conducted under barbaric conditions and control was lax or nonexistent. Robert Lee, deputy commissioner of the New Jersey Athletic Commission (Jersey Joe Walcott was its titular head), described his operation in terms of "horse sense," "gut feelings," and "rat systems." Instead of computers to check on the status of boxers, the athletic commission relied on Lee's instincts to determine if a boxer might be telling the truth about his health, age, or identity. As for verifying the suitability of referees, Lee relied heavily upon "whistle blowers" or "rats" for information that might disqualify an official.[91] In the words of the SCI: "Its [NJSAC] organizational structure is passe, its operation lacks administrative expertise and policy supervision, and its inadequate staff is devoid of essential skills, most noticeably in medical monitoring and fiscal controls." Countless examples of improper physicals, underage boxers, and unenforced suspensions were uncovered.[92]

The problems were not New Jersey's alone. Rump organizations such as the World Boxing Council (Mexico), the World Boxing Association (Panama; formerly dominated by South Africa), and the International Boxing Federation (United States) made effective control even more difficult for the various state commissions. The SCI noted allegations that ratings of fighters by these organizations often had little or nothing to do with ability and records but much or everything to do with money. Rumors were rampant that fighters could "buy into" the WBA and WBC.[93]

The distressing fact about these findings was that problems occurred, for the most part, in a state-authorized agency that was "well-intended." However, those good intentions were misplaced, in that the agency did not "put the public interest ahead of the industry's."[94] The situation deteriorated with casino development in Atlantic City and the use of prizefighting to promote gambling casino business. The demand for boxers with less than minimal physical and professional ability intensified, which prompted the SCI to conclude that an increasing number of boxing contests would be conducted with laws being bent and some-times broken. To prevent further tarnishing of the integrity of this sport, the SCI felt compelled to call for "an immediate legislative effort ... to modernize the regulatory process and repair the corroded administrative machinery by which the industry is governed."[95] On December 16, 1985, the SCI's final report concluded that boxing could not be salvaged through reform; thus, "no human endeavor so brutal, so susceptible to fraud, and so generally degrading should be afforded any social standing." What had pushed the SCI to take such a radical stand was the "incursion by organized crime into professional boxing."[96]

Hampered by the customary "code of silence," which the SCI argued has shielded organized crime's "depredations from even the most aggressive law enforcement scrutiny," investigators were not able to prove that any particular boxer was a mob pawn or that organized crime had fixed prizefights. But it did find ample evidence of harmful practices exacerbated by underworld intrusion, including weight falsification, name switching, and last-minute substitutions by overmatched and unqualified boxers. These often dangerous, unethical, and illegal actions demand description.[97]

In July 1982 Anthony Adams and Tony Coster met in a North Jersey boxing event. Adams weighed 176 pounds and had suffered losses in all five of his professional fights; his opponent weighed 217½ pounds and had won all three of his contests. How could such a fight be allowed? Adams testified that Deputy Commissioner Robert Lee had adjusted his weight to 190 and Coster's to 210½ (which Lee denied) to reduce the appearance of a total mismatch. Adams lost on a technical knockout in the first round, a result he had expected, for in his opinion the matchup was "a massacre."[98] He received $250 for his performance, a typical fee for boxers of his caliber, and was suspended for not putting up a good fight.

Using the name Clifford Smith, Adams lost a "setup" fight three weeks later at the Tropicana Hotel and Casino in Atlantic City. "Setups" to enhance a fighter's record were a specialty of John "Fix Man" Barr, who managed Adams. Barr's best clients were believed to be organized crime members or their associates, who valued his reliable service in providing "sure losers."[99] Fighters often used false names to evade suspension orders, and the SCI even found one instance in which a boxer used an alias to hide the fact that he was an escaped convict.[100] Kenny "Boom Boom" Bogner, Tony Ayala, and Reggie Boyer were just three of the many boxers named in the SCI report who had committed serious crimes or had criminal associations.[101] Thus, not only did the SCI reveal character problems among people behind the fighters, but the boxers themselves, contrary to the imagery of discipline and integrity, are often poor, uneducated, and desperate; at worst they are criminals.

Men like the late Frankie "Frank Flowers" D'Alfonso (Scarfo-Bruno family of the Delaware Valley), Frank Scaraggi (Genovese family of New York and North Jersey), and Michael "Mad Dog" Taccetta (Luchese family of New York) were just a few of the crime figures named by the SCI who had ties to boxing and whose influence extended far beyond illicit gambling, loan-sharking, and drugs. Many of these men were involved in legitimate enterprises, among them closed-circuit television, and some of their closest associates were present and former law enforcement and prosecuting officers.[102] So pervasive and threatening was their influence, in fact, that when the President's Commission on Organized Crime opened its hearings in June 1985, the SCI felt compelled to give instant exposure to "the insidious presence of organized crime" and also to seek federal help in resolving a problem that state action alone would be powerless to combat.[103]

Personifying the persistence of organized crime was Frank "Blinky" Palermo, who served seven years of a fifteen-year prison term before returning to Philadelphia to continue his long-standing involvement in boxing. The SCI made clear Palermo's connections with the Scarfo gang and his association with licensed promoters and managers in the Delaware Valley such as Frank Gelb, Steve Traitz, Sr., and Joe Hand. It concluded that Palermo and D'Alfonso had invested regularly in closed-circuit television boxing shows, including the Ali-Holmes contest in 1980 and the Cooney-Holmes match in 1982, from which they earned sizable profits (although cash transactions made proof of involvement difficult).[104]

The SCI also uncovered a plan by certain crime figures to gain control of the New Jersey Athletic Commission by arranging for Larry Doby, the first black baseball player in the American League, to head the commission. A resident of Montclair, Doby had frequent contact with Frank Scaraggi, from whom he purchased cars, and a mob-linked tailer named Al Certo, who also served as a booking agent for Mustafa Hamsho, a top-ranked middleweight contender. Without actually stating as much, the SCI implied that Doby obtained good deals or favors from both Scaraggi and Certo. Logic would dictate that, if made commissioner, Doby would be expected to return those favors.[105] Interestingly, his candidacy was openly supported by Buddy Fortunato, then a New Jersey assemblyman who had played a leading legislative role in enacting the 1984–85 program of boxing reforms. Fortunato, who had known Scaraggi for almost twenty years, refused to appear before the SCI, but in an off-the-record statement he admitted involvement in the "Doby for commissioner" affair although contradicting testimony by Scaraggi that he (Fortunato) had initiated the plan.[106]

How can such machinations be allowed and accepted? The SCI posed that question to the President's Commission on Organized Crime, proclaiming, "If the same mob presence we have found in boxing existed, for example, in professional baseball or football, it would constitute a massive public scandal."[107] Some observers have suggested that the answer is that no one cares about boxers or boxing. Since most of the participants are society's "throwaways" or "castoffs," their welfare is of little importance. Money has also been offered as the answer, but while there is money to be made from boxing—especially by those who never throw or receive punches yet encourage others to do so—those who share in the profits have not constituted a mass-based self-interest group.

I believe the answers can be found in human nature, mythology, and social control. Organized criminal involvement seems to enhance the rough-and-tumble, rags-to-riches, survive-against-all-odds aura of the sport; and if people can somehow blame the evils of boxing on an external agent, not on the activity itself, their guilt is more easily assuaged. While the public might be genuinely ambivalent about violence, there are manipulators who know this and who willfully hide behind and profit from organized crime. If the criminal element is removed, then boxing stands alone in public judgment.

On the level of myth, to have men rise above all the muck and emerge as knights in shining armor serves to reaffirm our faith in the traditional values that glorify the strong, solitary, noble individual. Joe Louis, Rocky Marciano, and Muhammad Ali, for example, were often surrounded by people with ties to organized crime, but none of these fighters has been viewed as an associate or a pawn of mobsters.

Critical observers have long argued that Americans are dangerously absorbed in compensatory distractions that tend to "dissipate the intellectual and moral energy which they need to foresee and confront their social and political abuses."[108] Since boxing plays a key role in a system that employs diversionary or deflective strategies to good advantage, to significantly modify or reform the sport would be to threaten its very existence. The abolition of boxing might then lead to an erosion of support for other activities of relatively marginal value to society's progress and welfare, which in turn might alert people to problems that have been obscured by the successes and failures they have shared vicariously. The ideas and attitudes of the privileged, those who have the time and money for leisure, recreation, and spectator sports, have filtered down to the masses. The message that sport is necessary is clear, but no one has revealed how and for whom.

Notes

Chapter 1: Crime or Sport?

1. Benjamin Rader, *American Sports: From the Age of Folk Games to the Age of Spectators* (Englewood Cliffs, N.J.: Prentice-Hall, 1983), pp. 24-29.
2. Quoted in Dale Somers, "The Leisure Revolution: Recreation in the American City, 1820-1920," *Journal of Popular Culture,* 4 (Winter 1971), p. 127.
3. Guy Lewis, "The Beginning of Organized Collegiate Sport," *American Quarterly,* Summer 1970, pp. 225-26; Arthur C. Cole, "Our Sporting Grandfathers: The Cult of Athletics at Its Source," *Atlantic Monthly,* 150 (July 1932), pp. 88-90.
4. James C. Whorton, *Crusaders for Fitness: The History of American Health Reformers* (Princeton: Princeton University Press, 1982), pp. 271-72.
5. Rader, p. 43; Whorton, pp. 271-72; Cole, p. 92; John C. Miller, *The Federalist Era* (New York: Harper and Row, 1960), p. 6.
6. Cole, p. 89.
7. Ibid.
8. Ibid., p. 92.
9. Ibid., p. 90.
10. Quoted in "Is Prize Fighting Legal?" *Law Times,* 35 (Apr. 28, 1860), p. 74.
11. Elmer M. Million, "The Enforceability of Prize Fight Statutes," *Kentucky Law Journal,* 27 (1938-39), pp. 153-54.
12. Albert Payson Terhune, "The Gilded Sport," *World's Work,* Mar. 1929, pp. 84-88.
13. Million, pp. 153-54.
14. *Commonwealth* v. *Colberg,* 119 Mass. 350, 20 Am. Rep. 328 (1876).
15. "Tiny West Virginia Town Site of First Heavyweight Championship," *West Virginia Review,* 1943, reprinted in *Congressional Record,* 88th Cong., 1st

Sess., July 15, 1963, p. A-4408. During the transition period between bare-knuckle and glove competition and English and American control of prizefighting, the heavyweight championship was in dispute. When English and world champion Jem Mace retired in 1873, American Tom Allen claimed the title on the basis of a loss to Mace in 1870. The English, however, refused to recognize Allen and supported Jem Smith. Mace subsequently came back to reclaim his title in 1873, but American boxing officials and promoters refused to recognize him. Thus, when Joe Goss met Paddy Ryan in 1880, the heavyweight situation was in such turmoil that some promoters decided this fight would settle the dispute. It did not, as England and America continued to recognize different champions until James J. Corbett defeated Charlie Mitchell in 1894.

On July 15, 1963, Senator Robert Byrd entered into the *Congressional Record* an article from the *Weirton* (West Virginia) *Daily Times* that recalled the history-making Goss-Ryan fight. The article read, in part: "Back in 1880 Ryan and Goss brought fame to the town of Colliers, and that city will always be remembered as the site of the world's first heavyweight championship bout.... And, even more important, modern ring history and the championship succession dates from that Goss-Ryan bout." This completely overlooks the fact that the dramatic match between James Camel Heenan of the United States and Tom Sayers of England in 1860 is generally considered the first international heavyweight championship fight. According to Melvin Adelman, in *A Sporting Time: New York City and the Rise of Modern Athletics, 1820–70* (Urbana: University of Illinois Press, 1986), p. 233, that fight drew more public comment than any other single sporting event between 1820 and 1870. At work here seems to be the phenomenon of relevancy and modernity.

16. "Tiny West Virginia Town," p. A-4408.
17. Dale Somers, *The Rise of Sports in New Orleans, 1850–1900* (Baton Rouge: Louisiana State University Press, 1972), p. 160.
18. Ibid.
19. James Cox, "The Great Fight: 'Mr. Jake' vs. John L. Sullivan," *Smithsonian*, 15 (Dec. 1984), pp. 157–58.
20. Ibid., p. 158.
21. Ibid., p. 156.
22. The most important development in the modernization of boxing came with the drafting of the Queensberry Rules in 1865, their publication in 1867, and their wide adoption in 1892. Before 1892 most important matches were fought under the London Prize Ring Rules, which were adopted in 1838 from Broughton's Rules of 1743 and revised in 1853 and 1866. The twenty-nine London Prize Ring Rules generally spelled out Broughton's Rules at greater length and in greater detail; they also specified fouls more explicitly. The "square of a yard" in Broughton's Rule 1 was replaced by the old "scratch" line: after the thirty seconds between rounds elapsed and the umpire called "time," each man had eight seconds to walk to the

scratch unaided; this prevented seconds from carrying boxers to the scratch who were unfit to continue. Also, spikes were limited on the boots, and fouls, such as butting, gouging, biting, scratching, kicking, and the use of stones in the hands, were clarified. The Queensberry Rules, which were probably drawn up by a classmate of Broughton's at Cambridge, John Graham Chambers, removed the wrestling aspect, introduced gloves, extended the time between rounds to a minute, banned spiked shoes, and limited rounds to three minutes. See Peter Arnold, *History of Boxing* (Secaucus, N.J.: Chartwell Books, 1985), pp. 34–35; John Grombach, *The Saga of the Fist* (New York: A. S. Barnes and Co., 1977), pp. 236–37.

23. Somers, *New Orleans,* pp. 163–64, 185; Cox, p. 160.
24. Somers, *New Orleans,* pp. 162–66.
25. Cox, p. 168.
26. Grombach, p. 44.
27. Somers, *New Orleans,* p. 170; Cox, p. 160.
28. Cox, p. 166.
29. Somers, *New Orleans,* p. 170.
30. Ibid., p. 172.
31. William Adams, "New Orleans as the National Center of Boxing," *Louisiana Historical Quarterly,* 39 (1956), p. 94.
32. Cox, pp. 162, 168.
33. Somers, *New Orleans,* p. 173.
34. Ibid.
35. *Sullivan v. State,* 7 Southern 275 (1890), p. 276.
36. Ibid., pp. 276–77.
37. Ibid.
38. Million, p. 155.
39. Elmer M. Million, "History of the Texas Prize Fight Statute," *Texas Law Review,* 17 (Fall 1939), p. 153; Peter Arnold, *History of Boxing* (Secaucus, N.J.: Chartwell Books, 1985), p. 124.
40. Somers, *New Orleans,* p. 174.
41. Adams, p. 96.
42. Ibid., p. 98.
43. Ibid., p. 99; Somers, *New Orleans,* p. 175.
44. Alan Trachtenberg, *The Incorporation of America: Culture and Society in the Gilded Age* (New York: Hill and Wang), pp. 3–5.
45. Ibid. The corporate-like atmosphere in which the Olympic Club operated and conducted its prizefights was not only evident in its hierarchical structure, shareholding membership system, and professional conduct of boxing contests but also was attested to by the advertisements in the souvenir program. These ads were for local business establishments and far-ranging firms like the Emerson Drug Company of Baltimore, which made Bromo-Seltzer to treat the headache caused by Paducah Club Whiskey of Paducah, Kentucky. See "Souvenir Program for the Carnival of

Champions" (Olympic Club, New Orleans, Sept. 6, 7, 8, 1892), pp. 1–6, in Louisiana Collection, Tulane University Library, New Orleans.

46. Somers, *New Orleans,* p. 177.
47. Ibid.
48. Adams, p. 100. According to photographs, etchings, other renderings, and souvenir programs, the Olympic Club was a remarkable structure. Having won a prize of $250 and the right to design the edifice, a local architect by the name of Einsiedel prepared a plan in an ornate French Renaissance style. The first floor included spacious parlors and reading, smoking, and retiring rooms; billiard, pool, and card rooms and a bar were located on the second floor; offices and four large apartments filled the third floor. The gymnasium, which occupied the rear of the building and measured 74 by 180 feet, was particularly well equipped, with locker rooms, Turkish and Russian bathrooms, a 35-by-75-foot natatorium, a bowling alley, and a rifle range. The showpiece of the club was a separate building known as the arena amphitheater, which covered an area of over 163 by 183 feet and could seat 9,000 spectators. Everyone who entered the arena was guaranteed a place to sit so that the boxing contests could be viewed in "absolute serenity." Ringside seats were reserved for the press; behind them were 49 boxes for various dignitaries; some 1,000 seats were offered on a reserved basis; and the remaining space, including the four galleries, was for general admission. Class divisions were maintained by the Olympic Club in the form of separate entrances for the elite, those with reserved seats, and general admittances; and membership in the club itself was limited to those who owned at least one share of stock, which cost twenty-five dollars in 1891 but by 1892 had risen dramatically. See "Souvenir Program," pp. 1–6.
49. Somers, *New Orleans,* p. 178.
50. Adams, p. 101.
51. Somers, *New Orleans,* p. 180.
52. Adams, pp. 102–3. Of the six boxers on the Carnival of Champions program, the description of George Dixon differed markedly from the others in three important respects: color was mentioned only in connection with Dixon; only Dixon was referred to as "boy"; only Dixon was characterized as modest, unassuming, and bashful. This characterization seemed to be designed to remind Dixon and others of his color as well as his place in society. To the credit of the tournament publicist, Dixon was also said to possess characteristics often reserved for whites, such as "super generalship" and devotion to profession. See "Souvenir Program," p. 10.
53. Adams, p. 104.
54. Ibid.
55. Elliot Gorn, "Gouge and Bite, Pull Hair and Scratch: The Social Significance of Fighting in the Southern Backcountry," *American Historical Review,* 90 (Feb. 1985), pp. 18–43.

56. Somers, *New Orleans,* p. 186.
57. Glenn C. Altschuler and Martin W. La Forse, "From Brawn to Brains: Football and Evolutionary Thought," *Journal of Popular Culture,* 16 (Spring 1983), p. 80.
58. Adams, pp. 106–7.
59. Ibid., pp. 107–8.
60. *State v. Olympic Club,* 46 La. Ann. 935, 15 So. 190 (1894), pp. 191–92.
61. Adams, p. 108.
62. *State v. Olympic Club,* p. 191.
63. Ibid.
64. Ibid., p. 196.
65. *New Orleans Weekly Times Democrat,* Sept. 7, 1892, quoted in Adams, pp. 102–3.
66. *State v. Olympic Club,* p. 198.
67. Ibid.
68. Ibid. The contract, used as evidence, read as follows: "We the undersigned, Stanton Abbott of London, England and Andrew Bowen of New Orleans, Louisiana, do hereby agree to engage in a glove contest to a finish before the Olympic Club . . . for a purse of two thousand five hundred dollars, the winner to receive two thousand dollars and the loser five hundred dollars of said purse. . . . The contest to be with five-ounce gloves and according to Marquess of Queensberry rules. . . . The referee shall have the power to stop and decide the contest when so directed by the seconds and the contest committee. . . . "
69. Adams, p. 110.
70. Although Bowen fought as a white and, indeed, boxed at the Olympic Club after Dixon defeated Skelly, he was listed as a mulatto in the official court report in *State v. Olympic Club.*
71. Adams, p. 111.
72. Ibid.
73. Adams, passim; Somers, *New Orleans,* passim; Steven A. Riess, "In the Ring and Out: Professional Boxing in New York, 1896–1920," in Donald Spivey, ed., *Sport in America: New Historical Perspectives* (Westport, Conn.: Greenwood Press), pp. 95–128. Riess amply documents and effectively illustrates the almost continuous presence of big-time professional boxing in New York, despite laws that forbade the sport. While some might argue that New York always was boxing's center, evidence indicates that the designation might be appropriate based on the quantity of fights but not always the quality. There were clear shifts in the struggle for boxing supremacy, and I maintain that consistent hosting or promotion of championship fights, especially in the heavyweight division, was the single most important indicator of dominance.
74. Allen Guttmann, *From Ritual to Record: The Nature of Modern Sports* (New York: Columbia University Press, 1978), pp. 26–27; Somers, *New Orleans,* p. 189.

75. Somers, *New Orleans,* p. 189.
76. Million, "Texas," pp. 152–54.
77. Ibid., p. 155.
78. Ibid.
79. Ibid., pp. 156–57.
80. Ibid., pp. 158–59.
81. Adams, p. 93.; *Attorney General* v. *Fitzsimmons and Corbett,* 35 Amer. Law Reg. 100 (Arkansas), quoted in *State of Ohio* v. *William N. Hobart, et al.,* no. 120, 498, Court of Common Pleas, Hamilton County (1901).
82. In *Ohio* v. *Hobart, et al.,* pp. 16–17.
83. Bert Randolph Sugar, ed., *The Ring Record Book and Encyclopaedia* (New York: Atheneum, 1981), p. 472.
84. *Fitzsimmons* v. *New York State Athletic Commission,* 146 NYS 117 (1914); Randy Roberts, *Jack Dempsey: The Manassa Mauler* (Baton Rouge: Louisiana State University Press, 1979), p. 93; Arnold, pp. 41, 44.
85. Stuart Lake, *Wyatt Earp* (Cambridge, Mass: Riverside Press, 1931), pp. 26–27.
86. Ibid., p. 366.
87. David Wiggins, "Peter Jackson and the Elusive Heavyweight Championship: A Black Athlete's Struggle against the Late Nineteenth Century Color-Line," *Journal of Sport History,* 12 (Summer 1985), p. 149.
88. Lake, p. 638.
89. Ibid., p. 370.
90. Randy Roberts, *Papa Jack: Jack Johnson and the Era of White Hopes* (New York: Free Press, 1983), p. 19.
91. David Pivar, *The Purity Crusade: Sexual Morality and Social Control, 1868–1900* (Westport, Conn: Greenwood Press, 1973), p. 234.
92. *Ohio* v. *Hobart, et al.,* p. 5.
93. Zane Miller, *Boss Cox's Cincinnati: Urban Politics in the Progressive Era* (New York: Oxford University Press, 1968), p. ix.
94. Ibid., pp. 59–67; Don Heinrich Tolzmann, "The Survival of an Ethnic Community: The Cincinnati Germans, 1918 through 1932" (unpublished doctoral dissertation, University of Cincinnati, 1983), pp. 99–100.
95. Stanley Matthews, "Aftermath of a Golden Jubilee," *Historical Society Bulletin* (Cincinnati), 16 (1958), p. 145.
96. Ibid.
97. *Ohio* v. *Hobart, et al.,* p. 47.
98. Ibid., p. 1.
99. Matthews, pp. 146–47.
100. *Ohio* v. *Hobart, et al.,* p. 48.
101. Melvin G. Holli and Peter d'A. Jones, eds., *Biographical Dictionary of American Mayors, 1820–1980: Big City Mayors* (Westport, Conn: Greenwood Press, 1981), pp. 119–20; Matthews, p. 148; *Ohio* v. *Hobart, et al.,* p. 154.
102. *Ohio* v. *Hobart, et al.,* p. 53.

103. Ibid., pp. 160–86.
104. Ibid., p. 184.
105. Ibid., p. 186.
106. Robert Sobel and John Raimo, eds., *Biographical Directory of the Governors of the United States,* vol. 3: 1784–1978 (Westport, Conn: Meckler Books, 1978), p. 1222.
107. *Ohio* v. *Hobart, et al.,* p. 113.
108. Sugar, p. 473.

Chapter 2: Total Onslaught

1. Roberts, *Papa Jack,* p. 16; "A Ring Trophy Awaiting a New Heavyweight Champion," *Literary Digest,* May 4, 1929, p. 70.
2. Abraham Lincoln, "Gettysburg Address," Nov. 19, 1863, reprinted in Theodore B. Dolmatch, ed., *Information Please Almanac: Atlas and Yearbook* (New York: Viking Press, 33rd ed., 1979), p. 576.
3. Cited in W. Manning Marable, "Black Athletes in White Men's Games," *Maryland Historian,* 4 (Fall 1973), pp. 143–44.
4. Ibid.
5. Jack Orr, *The Black Athlete: His Story in American History* (New York: Pyramid Books, 1970), p. 7.
6. Altschuler and La Forse, p. 76; Whorton, p. 163.
7. "Black Fists: Bomber Louis in Good Company as Boxing Champion," *Literary Digest,* July 3, 1937, pp. 34–35; Elliot Gorn, various personal communications (written and oral); Frederick Douglass, *Narrative of the Life of Frederick Douglass: An American Slave* (New York: Signet, 1968, rpt.), pp. 84–89. According to Ann Malone (personal communication), plantation records and unpublished WPA interviews suggest that wrestling (fighting) among slaves was fairly common in Louisiana and/or Texas. She indicates that slavery scholars have found references to wrestling contests in other areas of the South as well. Her own research reveals that slave owners paid a premium for wrestlers, because of their potential value in garnering gambling stakes. As entertainment for masters and slaves, wrestling seemed to have been a valuable component of plantation life.
8. John W. Blassingame, *The Slave Community: Plantation Life in the Antebellum South* (New York: Oxford University Press, 2d rev. ed., 1979), p. 265.
9. Paul Magriel, "Tom Molineaux: Career of an American Negro Boxer in England and Ireland, 1809–18," *Phylon,* 12 (Dec. 1951), pp. 320–36.
10. "Black Fists," pp. 34–35.
11. Magriel, pp. 330–34.
12. Ibid.
13. Benjamin Quarles, "Peter Jackson Speaks of Boxers," *Negro History Bulletin,* 18 (Nov. 1954), pp. 39–40.
14. Ibid.
15. Wiggins, p. 156.

16. Ibid., p. 166.
17. C. Vann Woodward, *The Strange Career of Jim Crow* (New York: Oxford University Press, 3d rev. ed., 1974), pp. 70–71.
18. Rayford Logan, *The Betrayal of the Negro: From Rutherford B. Hayes to Woodrow Wilson* (London: Collier Books, 1965), p. 121.
19. Marable, pp. 143–44.
20. *State* v. *Olympic Club,* p. 191; Dolmatch, pp. 918–19; Grombach, p. 38.
21. Jervis Anderson, "Black Heavies," *American Scholar,* 47 (1977–78), p. 388.
22. Sugar, p. 474.
23. Roberts, *Papa Jack,* p. 49.
24. Ibid., p. 50.
25. Ibid.; Al-Tony Gilmore, *Bad Nigger: The National Impact of Jack Johnson* (Port Washington, N.Y.: Kenniket Press, 1975), pp. 25–26.
26. Roberts, *Papa Jack,* p. 53.
27. Ibid.
28. Quoted in Gilmore, p. 28.
29. Roberts, *Papa Jack,* pp. 63–65.
30. Quoted in Lawrence Levine, *Black Culture and Black Consciousness: Afro-American Folk Thought from Slavery to Freedom* (New York: Oxford University Press, 1977), p. 430.
31. Ibid.
32. Harry W. Clune, "Palookas and Plutocrats," *North American Review,* Jan. 1929, p. 50.
33. *Time,* Jan. 23, 1956, p. 75.
34. Quoted in Levine, p. 430.
35. Gilmore, p. 33.
36. Levine, pp. 430–31.
37. In Lester S. Levy, *Give Me Yesterday: American History in Song, 1890–1920* (Norman: University of Oklahoma Press, 1975), p. 212.
38. Levine, p. 431.
39. Ibid.
40. Roberts, *Papa Jack,* p. 114.
41. Levy, p. 213.
42. Quoted in Levine, p. 431.
43. *Jeffries-Johnson, 1910* (McGraw-Hill Films, 1971).
44. Levine, p. 431.
45. Roberts, *Jack Dempsey,* p. 24.
46. Levine, p. 432.
47. Ibid.
48. Chris Greyvenstein, *The Fighters: A Pictorial History of SA Boxing from 1881* (Cape Town: Don Nelson, 1981), pp. 132–53. According to Greyvenstein, the pioneering white settler population of South Africa had established a distant kinship of sorts between Americans and Boers.

Bound symbolically with the Americans by wars against colonizers and natives, South Africans were more than willing to lend assistance in the defeat of threats to white superiority. When the call came for a successor to Jack Johnson, they joined in against the common foe, contributing Fred Storbeck and Lodewikus van Vuuren (who fought under the name of George Rodel). Storbeck was the first South African fighter to gain international recognition as an amateur; when Jack London's call went out, Storbeck's name frequently appeared in response. Although he never did challenge Johnson and should not have been taken seriously, in 1911 and 1912 he was very much a part of what Greyvenstein called "the undignified scramble" to return the heavyweight title to the white race. Rodel came a bit closer. Born in the small Free State village of Smithfield in 1888, his unbelievable boxing odyssey ended in 1955 in Brooklyn, New York. Along the way he faced the dangerous black fighter Sam McVey, who had lost to Jack Johnson in three brutal battles for the "Negro World Heavyweight Championship." Rodel also fought future champion Jess Willard twice; the second loss destroyed Rodel's chances of ever being a heavyweight contender, much less a great "white hope."

49. Roberts, *Jack Dempsey,* p. 25.
50. Miller, *Boss Cox,* p. 23.
51. Quoted in John Hope Franklin, *From Slavery to Freedom: A History of Negro Americans* (New York: Alfred A. Knopf, 5th ed., 1980), p. 319.
52. Ibid.
53. Roberts, *Jack Dempsey,* p. 25.
54. Ibid., pp. 26–27; Pivar, p. 234.
55. Roberts, *Jack Dempsey,* p. 27.
56. William Tuttle, *Race Riot: Chicago in the Red Summer of 1919* (New York: Atheneum, 1970), pp. 100–101.
57. Roberts, *Papa Jack,* p. 160.
58. Ibid., p. 161.
59. Ibid., p. 201; Gilmore, pp. 135–41.
60. *Weber* v. *Freed,* 36 Sup. Ct. 131, 239 U.S. 325 (1915).
61. Ibid., pp. 131–32.
62. Ibid.
63. Ralph O. Willgus, "Pictorial Representations of Prize Fights," *New York Law Review,* 6 (Jan. 1928), pp. 7–9.
64. Ibid.
65. Ibid., pp. 8–9.
66. U.S. Congress, Senate, Senator Jones of Washington speaking on "Strengthening Anti-Prize Fight Film Law," S. 2734, 68th Cong., 1st Sess., *Congressional Record,* Mar. 3, 1924, p. 3601.
67. "The Fight Over Fight Films," *Literary Digest,* Oct. 29, 1927, p. 16.
68. Levine, p. 431.
69. Gilmore, p. 31.
70. Ibid., p. 34.

71. Quoted in C. Vann Woodward, *The Strange Career of Jim Crow* (New York: Oxford University Press, 2d rev. ed., 1966), p. 114.
72. Ibid., p. 115.

Chapter 3: The Troubled Twenties

1. Peter Filene, *Him/Her/Self* (New York: Harcourt Brace Jovanovich, 1974-75), pp. 93-94; *Who Was Who in America,* vol. 2: 1943-50 (Chicago: A. N. Marquis Co., 1963), p. 179.
2. Filene, p. 107.
3. Ibid.
4. Ibid.
5. Roderick Nash, *The Nervous Generation: American Thought, 1917-1930* (Chicago: Rand McNally and Co., 1973), p. 2.
6. Ibid., p. 127.
7. Ibid.
8. Filene, pp. 93-94.
9. Nash, p. 128.
10. Ibid.
11. United States, World War I training film, RG 111-H, Signal Corps, roll 1180, National Archives, Washington, D.C.
12. Ibid.
13. Roberts, *Jack Dempsey,* p. 52.
14. Despite this widespread myth, there were some who rightly saw the correlation as being subject to exception if not question. Jack Kofoed tells the story of Fred McKay who, because of his poor boxing record, had been considered "yellow and a quitter." Yet in World War I he signed with the Canadian Army, became a company commander, won citations for gallantry in action, and died a hero at Viny Ridge. Kofoed believes that those who jeered McKay in the ring were wrong; the fighter had courage but lacked the proper temperament and instinct to be successful in boxing. See Jack Kofoed, "Stables," *North American Review,* 224 (July 1932), pp. 20-22.
15. H. W. Whicker, "Cauliflower Ears," *North American Review,* 234 (July 1932), pp. 19-20.
16. Ibid., p. 21.
17. Ibid., p. 22.
18. Ibid.
19. Grombach, p. 52.
20. Roberts, *Jack Dempsey,* p. 51.
21. Ibid., pp. 30, 48-49.
22. Ibid., p. 50.
23. Benjamin Rader, "Compensatory Sport Heroes: Ruth, Grange and Dempsey," *Journal of Popular Culture,* 16 (Spring 1983), pp. 18-19.
24. Roberts, *Jack Dempsey,* p. 55.
25. Ibid.

26. Rader, "Compensatory Sport Heroes," p. 11.
27. Sugar, p. 482.
28. Ibid.
29. Rader, "Compensatory Sport Heroes," p. 11.
30. Johann Huizinga, *Homo Ludens: A Study of the Play Element in Culture* (Boston: Beacon Press, 1955), pp. 10–54.
31. Henry F. May, *The End of American Innocence: A Study of the First Years of Our Own Time, 1912–1917* (New York: Alfred A. Knopf, 1959), p. 341.
32. Filene, pp. 93–94.
33. Dorothy Harris, "Comes the Revolution," *Time,* June 26, 1978, p. 54.
34. Filene, pp. 93–94.
35. Million, "Enforceability," p. 153.
36. *People* v. *Floss,* 7 NYS 504 (1889).
37. Charles W. Wilcox, "Consider the Cauliflower: Social Prestige of the Fight Racket," *Scribner's,* Mar. 1930, pp. 446–47.
38. Ibid., p. 448.
39. Ibid.
40. Terhune, p. 87; John Higham, "The Reorientation of American Culture in the 1890's," in John Weiss, ed., *The Origins of Modern Consciousness* (Detroit: Wayne State University Press, 1965), p. 27.
41. Higham, pp. 30–31.
42. Roberts, *Jack Dempsey,* p. 64.
43. Ibid.
44. Ibid.
45. Wilcox, p. 448.
46. Stephanie Twin, ed., *Out of the Bleachers: Writings on Women and Sport* (New York: Feminist Press/McGraw-Hill, 1979), p. xxviii.
47. Marion Marzolf, *Up from the Footnote: A History of Women Journalists* (New York: Communications Arts Books/Hastings House Publishers, 1977), p. 208.
48. "The Contributors' Club: Women Aren't Fans," *Atlantic Monthly,* May 1928, p. 712.
49. Ibid., p. 713.
50. Ibid.
51. Ibid.
52. Ibid., p. 714.
53. Katharine Fullerton Gerould, "Ringside Seats: A Woman at the Big Fight," *Harper's,* Dec. 1926, p. 25.
54. Ibid., pp. 23–26.
55. Ibid.
56. Ibid., p. 25.
57. Mark Edward Lender and James Kirby Martin, *Drinking in America: A History* (New York: Free Press, 1982), p. 64.
58. Ibid., p. 109.

59. Don S. Kirschner, *City and Country: Rural Responses to Urbanization in the 1920s* (Westport, Conn.: Greenwood Publishing, 1970), p. 251.
60. Lender and Martin, p. 109.
61. Ibid., pp. 109–12; Kirschner, pp. 96–110.
62. Lender and Martin, pp. 163–68; see also Pivar, p. 234.
63. Kirschner, p. 251.
64. Ibid.
65. Lender and Martin, p. 130; Jenna Weissman Joselit, *Our Gang: Jewish Crime and the New York Jewish Community, 1900–1940* (Bloomington: Indiana University Press, 1983), p. 86.
66. Joselit, p. 95.
67. Kirschner, pp. 254–55.
68. Lender and Martin, pp. 163–68.
69. Kirschner, p. 131.
70. Ibid., pp. 96–110.
71. Ibid.
72. *Tilelli* v. *Christenberry,* 120 NYS 2d 697 (1953), p. 700.
73. Million, "Enforceability," pp. 152–53.
74. Ibid., p. 156.
75. Sec. 28, chap. 714, Laws of 1921, New York, quoted in *People* v. *Barr,* 225 NYS 346 (1927), p. 349.
76. Roberts, *Jack Dempsey,* p. 95.
77. Ibid.
78. Robert Caro, *The Power Broker: Robert Moses and the Fall of New York* (New York: Vintage Books, 1975), pp. 324–25.
79. "The Cost of the Dempsey-Tunney Fight," *New Republic,* Oct. 6, 1926, p. 181.
80. *Tilelli* v. *Christenberry,* p. 701.
81. Grantland Rice, "Heavyweight Peerage," *Collier's,* June 21, 1930, p. 22.
82. *Fitzsimmons* v. *NYSAC,* p. 117.
83. Ibid.
84. See chapters 1, 6, and the Conclusion for a more detailed look at death, injuries, and crime in relation to the concern for boxing versus the concern for individuals.
85. *Fitzsimmons* v. *NYSAC,* p. 120.
86. Ibid., p. 121.
87. Ibid.
88. Ibid.
89. Ibid., p. 123.
90. Ibid.
91. Logan, p. 124.
92. "The Big Business of Prize Fighting," *Literary Digest,* Oct. 13, 1923, pp. 60–67.

93. Ibid., p. 64.
94. Ibid.
95. "The Commercialized Prize Ring," *Outlook,* Sept. 28, 1927, p. 105.
96. Jack Kofoed, "The Master of Ballyhoo," *North American Review,* Mar. 1929, p. 282.
97. Ibid., p. 282.
98. Stanley Frank, "The Biggest Fight Build-up in History: Louis-Conn Fight," *Saturday Evening Post,* June 15, 1946, p. 21.
99. Ibid.
100. William Cunningham, "No Wonder They Want to Fight," *Collier's,* 74 (Sept. 13, 1924), p. 14; Clune, pp. 49–55.
101. Frank, p. 21.
102. John Tebbel, *The Media in America* (New York: Mentor Books, 1974), p. 392; "Curiosities and Calamities of the Big Tunney-Dempsey Scrap," *Literary Digest,* Oct. 8, 1927, pp. 63–64.
103. Whicker, p. 21.
104. Roberts, *Jack Dempsey,* p. 249.
105. "From Homer to Hearst," *Outlook,* July 18, 1923, pp. 401–2.
106. Ibid.; Stanley Matthews, "Aftermath of a Golden Jubilee," *Cincinnati Historical Society Bulletin,* 16 (1958), pp. 149–50.
107. "From Homer to Hearst," pp. 401–2.
108. "A Hint in the 'World' to the World," *Outlook,* Aug. 8, 1923, p. 531.
109. Ibid.
110. "From Homer to Hearst," pp. 401–2.
111. Roberts, *Jack Dempsey,* p. 188.
112. *New York Times,* Jan. 31, 1953, pp. 8, 12; Joselit, pp. 151–54.
113. *New York Times,* Jan. 31, 1953, pp. 1, 12; Joselit, p. 155.
114. *New York Times,* Jan. 31, 1953, pp. 1, 12.
115. Ibid.
116. Owen White, "Diatribe upon a Manly Theme," *American Mercury,* 8 (May 1926), pp. 76–77.
117. Ibid.
118. Ibid.
119. Ibid., p. 77.
120. Ibid.
121. Grantland Rice, "The King Maker," *Collier's,* Nov. 13, 1926, p. 10.
122. Grantland Rice, "The Golden Fleece," *Collier's,* Sept. 17, 1927, p. 9; Rice, "King Maker," p. 100.
123. "Cost of Dempsey-Tunney Fight," p. 181.
124. "Shadow on the Ring," *Outlook,* Aug. 3, 1927, p. 434.
125. "Fighting against the $2,000,000 Fight," *Literary Digest,* Sept. 4, 1926.
126. Ibid., pp. 56–60.
127. Ibid.

Chapter 4: Chaos Reigns

1. Roberts, *Jack Dempsey,* p. 46.
2. Orr, p. 29; John B. Kennedy, "If Dempsey's Afraid, Let Him Say So" (interview with Harry Wills), *Collier's,* Mar. 10, 1926, pp. 11, 43.
3. "Battling Siki as a Dark Cloud on the Horizon," *Literary Digest,* Oct. 14, 1922, pp. 62–65.
4. Ibid.
5. *Springfield Republican,* quoted in "Battling Siki," p. 62.
6. Ibid.
7. Ibid.
8. "Fight Prize," *Literary Digest,* July 28, 1923, p. 50.
9. "Battling Siki," p. 62.
10. Quoted in Debra Newman, "Meet Our Pariahs: American Attitudes toward Black Troops in France during World War I" (unpublished seminar paper, Howard University, Apr. 1981), p. 5, from remarks made by General Gourard (about the 369th Regiment), RG 120, 11440-A-1 to A-20, May 6, 1918, National Archives, Washington, D.C.
11. *New York Tribune,* quoted in "Battling Siki," p. 65.
12. Roberts, *Jack Dempsey,* p. 142.
13. Kennedy, p. 43.
14. Roberts, *Jack Dempsey,* p. 218.
15. Ibid.
16. Ibid., pp. 137–40.
17. "$2,000,000 Fight," pp. 55–56.
18. *Dempsey v. Chicago Coliseum Club,* 162 N.E. 237 Indiana (1928), p. 237.
19. Terhune, pp. 84–88.
20. Roberts, *Jack Dempsey,* p. 68; John B. Kennedy, "They Call Me a Bum" (interview with Jack Dempsey), *Collier's,* Sept. 12, 1925, p. 9.
21. Roberts, *Jack Dempsey,* p. 68; Kennedy, "Bum," p. 9.
22. Roberts, *Jack Dempsey,* p. 68; John M. Hoberman, *Sport and Political Ideology* (Austin: University of Texas Press, 1984), pp. 19, 61.
23. Sidney H. Small, "She Knew Them All" (interview with Mr. and Mrs. William Shannon), *Sunset,* Oct. 1926, pp. 30–31.
24. Jim Tulley, "Jack Dempsey," *American Mercury,* Aug. 1933, pp. 24–25.
25. Roberts, *Jack Dempsey,* pp. 68, 218.
26. Kennedy, "Bum," p. 9. Dempsey's manager, Jack "Doc" Kearns, apparently physically restrained Dempsey from going into the ring against Joe Jeannette, telling him, "Sit tight, Jack, box Bond or nobody." Dempsey responded, "I'll fight any white man they put on, but I didn't agree to fight a colored boy."
27. "Opposing the Big Prize Fight," *Literary Digest,* Sept. 10, 1927, p. 32; Myron Stearns, "Champion Ex-Champion," *Harper's,* 179 (Sept. 1939), pp. 419–20.
28. Clune, pp. 49–55.
29. Grantland Rice, "Paper Crown," *Collier's,* Aug. 9, 1930, p. 22.

30. Grantland Rice, "King Hunt," *Collier's,* Sept. 15, 1928, p. 18.
31. Clune, p. 50.
32. *New York Times,* July 24, 1930, p. 19.
33. Clune, p. 55.
34. Roberts, *Jack Dempsey,* p. 267.
35. Ronald Story, "The Greening of Sport: Jackson, Dempsey, and Industrial America," *Reviews in American History,* 8 (Sept. 1980), p. 391.
36. Roberts, *Jack Dempsey,* p. 267; Rader, "Compensatory Sport Heroes," pp. 18–20.
37. "No More Foul Finishes," *Literary Digest,* July 12, 1930, p. 33.
38. Grantland Rice, "Meet the Menace: Schmeling, Von Porat, and Paulino," *Collier's,* 82 (May 11, 1929), p. 34.
39. "Fighting for Fighting's Sake Rules the Paris Prize-Ring," *Literary Digest,* 104 (Feb. 1, 1930), pp. 52–53; John B. Kennedy, "Made in Germany, Max Schmeling," *Collier's,* 83 (June 29, 1929), p. 14.
40. "Shadow on the Ring," p. 434.
41. *New York Times,* June 11, 1930, p. 23.
42. Katherine Brush, "Joe Jacobs, World's Champ," *Outlook and Independent,* July 2, 1930, p. 332.
43. Ibid.
44. "No More Foul Finishes," p. 33.
45. "Fair Fouls," *Outlook and Independent,* July 1930, p. 412.
46. Ibid.
47. Ibid.
48. *New York Times,* June 24, 1930, p. 19.
49. Ibid.
50. Jack A. Hiller, "Language, Law, Sports, and Culture: The Transferability or Nontransferability of Words, Lifestyles, and Attitudes through Law," *Valparaiso University Law Review,* 12 (Spring 1978), pp. 444–45.
51. Dennis Brailsford, "Morals and Maulers: The Ethics of Early Pugilism," *Journal of Sport History,* 12 (Summer 1985), p. 127.
52. David Riesman and Reuel Denney, "Football in America: A Study in Culture Diffusion," in David Riesman, ed. *Individualism Reconsidered* (Glencoe, Ill.: Free Press, 1954), pp. 242–57.
53. Ibid.
54. *New York Times,* Jan. 22, 1933, p. 22; Oct. 26, 1934, p. 29; Nov. 2, 1934, p. 32; Sept. 6, 1939, p. 31.
55. Ibid.
56. Daniel S. Morrow, " 'The Black Shame': German Reaction to the French Deployment of Colored Troops in the Occupied Western Zones, 1918–23" (unpublished masters thesis, University of Virginia, 1970), p. 4.
57. Ibid., p. 35; *Volkischer Beobachter,* May 23, 1929, p. a3; June 7, 1929, p. 1.
58. Guttmann, pp. 62–63.
59. *New York Times,* July 14, 1931, p. 31.
60. *Boersen Courier,* quoted in *New York Times,* July 5, 1931, sec. 10, p. 5.

61. "Hoch! Cries Germany as Max and Cilly Win," *Literary Digest*, 60 (July 18, 1931), pp. 38–39.
62. Ibid.
63. Guttman, p. 63.
64. *New York Times*, June 11, 1930, p. 23; "Sharkey, a Surprised Champion, Germany Bitter," *Literary Digest*, 64 (July 2, 1932), pp. 38–39.
65. Rice, "Paper Crown," p. 22; John D. McCallum, *The World Heavyweight Boxing Championships* (Radnor, Pa.: Chilton Book Co., 1974) p. 137; Brush, p. 332.
66. John Kieran, "As the Heavyweights Go, So Goes Boxing," *New York Times*, July 13, 1930, sec. 10, p. 2.
67. *New York Times*, Feb. 22, 1930, p. 8.
68. Ibid.
69. Ibid., June 18, 1930, p. 20.
70. Ibid., June 23, 1930, p. 24; June 25, 1930, p. 23.
71. Ibid., July 14, 1931, p. 30.
72. Sugar, p. 479.
73. McCallum, pp. 162, 171.
74. *New York Times*, Feb. 1, 1930, p. 14.
75. Ibid.
76. Quoted in "Primo, The 'Mammoth Muscle Merchant of Venice,'" *Literary Digest*, Mar. 1, 1930, p. 29.
77. *New York Times*, Jan. 24, 1930, p. 30; Mar. 30, 1930, sec. 10, p. 2.
78. Ibid., June 23, 1930, p. 24; June 25, 1930, p. 25.
79. Ibid., June 24, 1930, p. 28; see also *Madison Square Garden Corporation, Ill.* v. *Carnera,* 52 Feb. 47 (1931), pp. 47–50.
80. *New York Times*, Apr. 28, 1931, p. 35; Apr. 29, 1931, p. 34; May 1, 1931, p. 15.
81. Ibid., May 3, 1931, sec. 10, p. 2.
82. *Madison Square Garden* v. *Carnera*, pp. 47–50.
83. McCallum, p. 154.
84. Sugar, p. 479.
85. "Death among the Heavyweights," *Literary Digest*, Feb. 25, 1933, p. 26.
86. Quoted in "Death among the Heavyweights," p. 26.
87. Ibid.
88. *New York Times*, Feb. 15, 1933, p. 1.
89. "Death among the Heavyweights," p. 26.
90. Ibid.
91. Ibid.
92. McCallum, p. 164.
93. Grombach, p. 62.
94. *Birmingham News*, Feb. 23, 1934, p. 14.
95. Sugar, p. 479; "New Life in Boxing," *Literary Digest*, June 23, 1934, p. 33.
96. "Jack Dempsey Tries on Tex Rickard's Shoes," *Literary Digest*, June 24, 1933, pp. 24–25.

97. Joselit, p. 43.
98. S. Kirson Weinberg and Henry Arond, "The Occupational Culture of the Boxer," *American Journal of Sociology,* Mar. 1952, p. 461.
99. Ibid.; Orr, p. 7.
100. *Charlotte Observer,* Nov. 17, 1934, p. 10; *New York Times,* June 28, 1939, p. 24.
101. *New York Times,* June 28, 1939, p. 24.
102. *Charlotte Observer,* Nov. 17, 1934; June 5, 1938, p. 16.
103. *Birmingham News,* Sept. 25, 1934, p. 11.
104. *New York Times,* Nov. 20, 1935, p. 31.
105. Ibid., June 10, 1934, p. 17.
106. Sugar, p. 480.
107. *New York Times,* Dec. 20, 1934, p. 24.
108. "New Life in Boxing," p. 33.
109. Joseph Moncure March, *The Wild Party, the Set-up, a Certain Wilderness* (Freeport, Maine: Bond Wheelwright Co., rev. ed. 1968), p. 52.
110. Ibid., p. 56.
111. Ibid.
112. Ralph McGill, "The New Type Hero," *Atlanta Constitution,* June 9, 1935, p. 1B.
113. James Harper, "Baseball: America's First National Pastime," in William J. Baker and John M. Carroll, eds., *Sports in Modern America* (St. Louis: River City Publishers, 1981), p. 56.
114. McGill, p. 1B.
115. *Atlanta Constitution,* June 18, 1935, p. 9.
116. Ibid.

Chapter 5: Pugilistic Renaissance

1. John Field and Earl Brown, "Uncle Mike's Racket," *Life,* July 17, 1946, pp. 56–57; interview with Truman Gibson, Chicago, Ill., June 22, 1985.
2. Field and Brown, pp. 56–57.
3. Quoted in John R. Tunis, *The American Way in Sport* (New York: Duell, Sloan, and Pearce, 1958), p. 69.
4. Anthony Edmonds, *Joe Louis* (Grand Rapids, Mich.: Wm. B. Eerdmans, 1973), p. 35.
5. Alexander Young, Jr., "Joe Louis, Symbol" (unpublished doctoral dissertation, University of Maryland, 1968), p. 22.
6. Edmonds, pp. 30–31.
7. Joe Louis, *Joe Louis, My Life* (New York: Harcourt Brace Jovanovich, 1978), pp. 3–33.
8. Young, p. 22.
9. Edmonds, p. 29.
10. Gibson interview; Edmonds, p. 32.
11. Edmonds, pp. 32–33.

12. The Young and Edmonds works cited above are very similar, both relying on essentially the same material. See also Gerald Astor, *Gloves Off: The Joe Louis Story* (London: Pelham, 1975), a popular biography.
13. Quoted in Dewey W. Grantham, Jr., "The South and the Politics of Sectionalism," in *The South and the Sectional Image,* ed. Dewey W. Grantham, Jr. (New York: Harper and Row, 1967), pp. 46-47.
14. Quoted in C. Vann Woodward, "The Search for Southern Identity," in Grantham, *Sectional Image,* pp. 177-78.
15. Guion Griffiths Johnson, "The Ideology of White Supremacy," in Grantham, *Sectional Image,* p. 78.
16. *New York Times,* July 13, 1931, p. 22; "Black Fists," p. 35.
17. James H. Stevenson, "The Attitude of the *Raleigh News and Observer* toward the Negro, 1944-45" (unpublished master's thesis, Howard University, 1948), p. 101.
18. *Birmingham Age-Herald,* Aug. 6, 1936, p. 9.
19. Stevenson, p. 101.
20. *Charlotte Observer,* Aug. 14, 1934, sec. 2, p. 3.
21. Ibid., Dec. 31, 1934, p. 11.
22. *New York Times,* Nov. 28, 1930, p. 31.
23. Ibid.; Rice, "Paper Crown," p. 22.
24. Franklin, *Slavery to Freedom,* p. 422; Edmonds, pp. 34, 38. Mussolini sent members of the Italian Boxing Commission to investigate the defeat of Primo. They found that he had been beaten fairly and that charges of doping and gangster threats were absurd. See *Atlanta Constitution,* Aug. 13, 1934, p. 11.
25. *Charlotte Observer,* Mar. 7, 1934, p. 5; *Birmingham News,* Apr. 26, 1934, p. 7.
26. *Birmingham News,* Apr. 20, 1934, p. 15.
27. Edmonds, p. 38.
28. *Charlotte Observer,* June 20, 1935, p. 17.
29. Edmonds, p. 38; Young, p. 123.
30. *Charlotte Observer,* June 27, 1935, p. 8.
31. Young, p. 124.
32. *Birmingham Age-Herald,* June 4, 1936, p. 10.
33. Ibid.
34. Edmonds, p. 39.
35. Ibid., pp. 34, 38-39.
36. *Atlanta Constitution,* June 28, 1935, p. 17.
37. Ibid.; Edmonds, p. 88.
38. Field and Brown, pp. 56-57.
39. *New York Times,* Sept. 24, 1935, p. 22.
40. Dolmatch, p. 917.
41. *New Orleans Times-Picayune,* Sept. 26, 1935, p. 11.
42. Edmonds, pp. 92-93.
43. *Raleigh News and Observer,* Sept. 26, 1935, p. 4.
44. Ibid.

45. *Atlanta Constitution,* Dec. 10, 1935, p. 14; *Birmingham News,* Jan. 30, 1936, p. 13; Mar. 5, 1936, p. 13; *Charlotte Observer,* Jan. 9, 1936, sec. 2, p. 6; Feb. 26, 1936, sec. 2, p. 1; *Atlanta Constitution,* June 16, 1935, p. 1B; *Charlotte Observer,* Mar. 1, 1936, sec. 2, p. 13. Jake Wade of the *Charlotte Observer,* who was very close to Braddock, released an interview the Associated Press killed because of what it might do to the "white hope" tournament. Wade said: "Everybody knows that Dempsey's 'white hope' tournament is an insult to the legion of friends Jimmy has throughout the country. Everybody knows that when Dempsey was champion he ran away from Wills, eight years. The fact that they didn't need 'white hopes' in Dempsey's day was that he never gave a colored man a chance at the title."

46. John Lardner, "Two White Hopes on Wholewheat," *Newsweek,* Sept. 4, 1939, p. 35.

47. "White Hope Pops Up; Even Tunney and Dempsey Join Experts in Praising Nova," *Newsweek,* Dec. 26, 1938, p. 19.

48. *Charlotte Observer,* Mar. 1, 1936, sec. 2, p. 13.

49. Sugar, p. 481.

50. Richard Mandell, *The Nazi Olympics* (Urbana: University of Illinois Press, 1987, rpt.), p. 71.

51. *Birmingham News,* Sept. 18, 1934, p. 9; *New York Times,* Mar. 14, 1935, p. 26.

52. Adolf Hitler, *Mein Kampf* (New York: Stackpole Sons Publishers, 1939, rpt.), pp. 397–98; Sugar, p. 480.

53. *New York Times,* Oct. 5, 1935, quoted in Richard E. Lapchick, *The Politics of Race and International Sport: The Case of South Africa.* Center on International Race Relations, University of Denver, Studies in Human Rights, no. 1 (Westport, Conn.: Greenwood Press, 1979), p. xvii.

54. *Birmingham News,* Sept. 27, 1934, p. 8; Lapchick, p. xvii.

55. *Jackson* (Miss.) *Clarion Ledger,* Mar. 27, 1935, p. 11.

56. *New Orleans Times-Picayune,* June 21, 1937, p. 12; *Birmingham News,* July 16, 1937, p. 13.

57. Edmonds, p. 76.

58. *New York Times,* July 9, 1935, p. 37.

59. *Birmingham News,* Aug. 5, 1936, p. 11.

60. Edmonds, p. 78.

61. Young, p. 124; I. Q. Gross, "Yussel Jacobs Okays the Nazis," *Nation,* 144 (June 18, 1938), pp. 633–34.

62. Edmonds, p. 76; Art Buchwald, in *Durham Morning Herald,* Apr. 20, 1981, p. 4A.

63. Alexander De Conde, "The South and Isolationism," in Grantham, *Sectional Image,* pp. 124–25. In 1930 about 500,000 native whites of foreign or mixed parentage and 200,000 foreign-born whites lived in the eleven southeastern states. Before 1938 the South did not differ markedly in sentiment from other sections of the country on issues of preparedness and neutrality.

64. *Birmingham News,* June 19, 1936, p. 18.
65. *Charlotte Observer,* Dec. 13, 1935, sec. 2, p. 7; June 24, 1936, sec. 2, p. 6.
66. *Atlanta Constitution,* June 20, 1936, p. 11.
67. Ibid.
68. *New Orleans Times-Picayune,* June 21, 1936, sec. 2, p. 5.
69. *Birmingham News,* Aug. 5, 1936, p. 11.
70. Edmonds, p. 78.
71. Ibid.
72. *Charlotte Observer,* Dec. 14, 1936, sec. 2, p. 5.
73. *Madison Square Garden Corporation* v. *Braddock,* 90F 2d 924 (1937), pp. 924–25.
74. U.S. Department of State, report from American Consul General (Germany) Douglas Jenkins to the Office of the Economic Adviser, Department of State, on financing of a proposed Braddock-Schmeling bout for the world's championship in Berlin, Feb. 1, 1937, RG 59, SA4E3, 862.4066, National Archives, Washington, D.C. (hereafter cited as "Jenkins Report").
75. "Jenkins Report," pp. 3–4; "Braddock Skips Schmeling for Louis and a Bigger Gate," *Literary Digest,* 73 (Feb. 13, 1937), pp. 38–39.
76. "Jenkins Report," pp. 4–5; *Charlotte Observer,* June 4, 1937, sec. 2, p. 8.
77. Chris Mead, *Champion—Joe Louis: Black Hero in White America* (New York: Charles Scribner's Sons, 1985), p. 174.
78. Joe Louis, "Oh, Where Did My Money Go?" *Saturday Evening Post,* Jan. 7, 1956, p. 68.
79. *New York Times,* June 24, 1937, p. 32; June 25, 1937, p. 20.
80. *Madison Square Garden* v. *Braddock,* p. 925.
81. *Charlotte Observer,* June 4, 1937, sec. 8, p. 2.
82. *New York Times,* Mar. 4, 1937, p. 28; *Clarion Ledger,* Mar. 28, 1937, p. 15; *Madison Square Garden* v. *Braddock,* p. 925.
83. Levine, p. 433.
84. Ibid.
85. *Charlotte Observer,* June 19, 1937, sec. 2, p. 5; June 19, 1937, sec. 1, p. 11; *Birmingham Age-Herald,* June 22, 1937, p. 9.
86. *New Orleans Times-Picayune,* June 15, 1937, p. 13; *Birmingham Age-Herald,* June 24, 1937, p. 13.
87. *New Orleans Times-Picayune,* June 24, 1937, pp. 8, 13.
88. *Atlanta Constitution,* June 24, 1937, p. 8. Despite its position, the *Constitution* hoped for a positive impact on youth, as the following indicates: "Joe Louis should not fail these boys. He can, by setting an example of clean living, modesty, honesty, and proper regard for society's customs, lead thousands of young Negro men to a better way of life and thus to better opportunity for legitimate personal improvements and service to their race and to the nation."
89. Jimmy Cannon, "This Prize Fight Racket," *Esquire,* May 1948, p. 392.
90. *Birmingham News,* June 23, 1937, p. 6.
91. *Columbus News Record,* June 23, 1937, quoted in Edmonds, pp. 92–93.

92. Maya Angelou, *I Know Why the Caged Bird Sings* (New York: Random House, 1977), pp. 111–13.
93. Jimmy Carter, *Why Not the Best* (Nashville, Tenn.: Broadman Press, 1974), p. 37.
94. Walter Weare, *Black Business in the New South* (Urbana: University of Illinois Press, 1973), pp. 250–51.
95. Ibid., pp. 251–52.
96. Levine, p. 420.
97. *Atlanta Constitution,* June 26, 1937, p. 8.
98. Ibid.; Sugar, p. 481.
99. Gibson interview.
100. Anthony Edmonds, "Second Louis-Schmeling Fight: Sport, Symbol, and Culture," *Journal of Popular Culture,* Summer 1973, p. 44.
101. Ibid.
102. *New Orleans Times-Picayune,* Aug. 29, 1937, sec. 4, p. 3.
103. Gross, "Yussel Jacobs," pp. 698–99.
104. Ibid.
105. Edmonds, "Second Louis-Schmeling Fight," pp. 45–46.
106. Budd Schulberg, "Sports' Greatest Event," *Esquire,* Jan. 1962, p. 87.
107. *Charlotte Observer,* June 24, 1938, sec. 2 p. 11.
108. Ibid., June 25, 1938, p. 9; *New Orleans Times-Picayune,* June 24, 1938, p. 15; *Atlanta Constitution,* Sept. 22, 1939, p. 21.
109. *Atlanta Constitution,* Sept. 22, 1939, p. 21.
110. *Charlotte Observer,* June 24, 1938, sec. 2, p. 11; letter from John Roxborough to Hugh Wilson, Department of State, July 30, 1938, RG 109, 862.4061, National Archives, Washington, D.C.
111. *Birmingham Age-Herald,* June 24, 1938, p. 15.
112. Ibid.
113. *Birmingham News,* Jan. 26, 1939, p. 18; *New York Times,* Feb. 11, 1939, p. 11.
114. *New York Times,* Apr. 22, 1942, p. 9.
115. Ibid., Mar. 9, 1978, sec. 4, p. 15.
116. *Durham Morning Herald,* Apr. 20, 1981, p. 4A.
117. Ibid.
118. Ibid.
119. Grombach, p. 232.
120. Field and Brown, pp. 56–57; *New York Times,* Jan. 25, 1953, p. 84.
121. Sugar, p. 477; "The Fight Film," *New Republic,* Nov. 2, 1927, p. 286.
122. "The Fight Film," p. 286.
123. "Motion Pictures of Prize Fights," *New York Law Review,* 5 (Nov. 1927), p. 432–33; *New York Times,* July 7, 1931, p. 19.
124. Willgus, p. 9.
125. Ibid.
126. Terrence Hickey, "Television Broadcasts of Boxing Matches," *Marquette Law Review,* 16 (June 1932), p. 261.

127. *New York Times,* June 11, 1939, sec. 9, p. 10; June 14, 1939, p. 28.
128. U.S. Congress, Senate, Senator Warren Barbour speaking on divesting prizefight films of their character as subjects of interstate commerce, S. 2285, 74th Cong., 1st Sess., *Congressional Record,* 1935, p. 3804.
129. U.S. Congress, Senate, Subcommittee of the Committee on Interstate Commerce, hearings on legalizing transportation of prizefight films, S. 2047, 76th Cong., 1st Sess., *Congressional Record,* 1939, p. 3 (hereafter cited as "Fight Film Hearings").
130. Ibid., pp. 38-39.
131. Ibid.
132. *New York Times,* June 14, 1939, p. 28; Oct. 4, 1939, p. 52.
133. Edmonds, p. 89.
134. "Fight Film Hearings," pp. 45-56.
135. *New York Times,* Oct. 4, 1939, p. 52.
136. United States Statutes at Large, 76th Cong., 2d and 3d Sess., 1939-41, LIV, pt. 1, Public Laws Reorganization Plans, chap. 443, public no. 673, p. 686.
137. *New York Times,* Mar. 15, 1941, p. 19.
138. "Fight Film Hearings," pp. 45-56.
139. *New York Times,* Apr. 27, 1939, p. 33.
140. Frank Deford, "The Boxer and the Blonde," *Sports Illustrated,* June 17, 1985, p. 90.
141. Ibid., p. 84.
142. Mead, p. 174.
143. Ibid., p. 91.
144. Gerald N. Grob and George Athan Billias, eds., *Interpretations of American History: Patterns and Perspectives,* vol. 2: Since 1865 (New York: Free Press, 1978, 3d ed.), p. 348.
145. Ibid., p. 347.
146. Paul W. Schroeder, "The Coming of World War II," in Grob and Billias, pp. 362-64.
147. *New York Times,* Dec. 9, 1943, p. 36.
148. Ibid., Dec. 21, 1942, p. 29.
149. *Birmingham News,* Jan. 7, 1942, p. 16; *New Orleans Times-Picayune,* Jan. 7, 1942, p. 12; Grombach, p. 60.
150. *New York Times,* Oct. 7, 1941, p. 31.
151. Ibid., May 29, 1945, p. 11.
152. Ibid., Jan. 7, 1942, p. 26; July 23, 1942, p. 24.
153. Ibid.
154. *Birmingham News,* May 22, 1941, p. 22.
155. Ibid.
156. *New Orleans Times-Picayune,* Jan. 10, 1942, p. 10; *Birmingham News,* Jan. 16, 1942, p. 24; *New Orleans Times-Picayune,* Jan. 7, 1942, p. 12; *Birmingham News,* Mar. 27, 1942, p. 7.
157. Gibson interview.

158. Ibid.
159. *Birmingham News,* Mar. 27, 1942, p. 7.
160. Ibid., Jan. 8, 1942, p. 20.
161. Gibson interview.
162. U.S. Congress, House, Representative O'Toole speaking on fight promotion during the war, 77th Cong., 2d Sess., *Congressional Record,* vol. 88, Sept. 23, 1942, p. 7337.
163. Gibson interview.
164. *Charlotte Observer,* Jan. 10, 1942, sec. 2, p. 5.
165. Young, pp. 50, 156.
166. Neil A. Wynn, *The Afro-American and the Second World War* (London: Paul Elek, 1976), p. 31.
167. Gibson interview.
168. Ibid.
169. Ulysses Lee, *United States Army in World War II, Special Studies: The Employment of Negro Troops* (Washington, D.C.: Office of the Chief of Military History, U.S. Army, 1965), p. 307.
170. Franklin, p. 443.
171. U.S. Department of the Interior, letter from Archibald MacLeish, Director, Office of Facts and Figures, to Harold Ickes, Secretary of the Interior, Apr. 7, 1942, file no. 1-188 (war information), National Archives, Washington, D.C.
172. Alan M. Osur, *Blacks in the Army Air Forces during World War II* (New York: Arno Press, 1980), p. 78.
173. A. Russell Buchanan, *Black Americans in World War II* (Santa Barbara, Calif.: Clio Books, 1977), pp. 46-53.
174. Ibid.
175. Frank Capra, *The Name above the Title: An Autobiography* (New York: Belvedere Publishers, 1971), pp. 376-78.
176. Ibid.
177. *The Negro Soldier* (Frank Capra film, 1943); Thomas Cripps, "Racial Ambiguities in American Propaganda Movies," in *Film and Radio Propaganda in World War II,* ed. K. R. M. Short (Knoxville: University of Tennessee Press, 1983), pp. 128-32.
178. Ibid.
179. Ibid.
180. Lee, p. 327.
181. Wynn, p. 83; Osur, pp. 78-79.
182. Letter to the editor from C. E. Boulware, in *Charlotte Observer,* Feb. 8, 1942, sec. 3, p. 4.
183. Edmonds, pp. 99-100.
184. Young, p. 151; Joe Louis, "My Toughest Fight," *Salute,* Dec. 1947, p. 13.
185. Gibson interview.
186. Levine, p. 433.

Chapter 6: The Unholy Trinity

1. *New York Times,* Jan. 27, 1942, p. 23; Apr. 30, 1942, p. 10; Oct. 17, 1942, p. 9; John Lardner, "Out of the Icebox," *Newsweek,* Jan. 21, 1946, p. 92.
2. Lardner, "Icebox," p. 92.
3. Ibid.; Dolmatch, p. 917.
4. Sugar, p. 515.
5. Roger Burlingame, *Engines of Democracy* (New York: Scribner and Sons, 1940), p. 460.
6. *New York Times,* Mar. 19, 1939, quoted in Horace Newcomb, *TV: The Most Popular Art* (Garden City, N.Y.: Anchor Books, 1974), p. 2.
7. Thomas H. Hutchinson, *Here Is Television: Your Window to the World* (New York: Hastings House, 2d rev. ed., 1950), p. xi.
8. Newcomb, p. 331; George Comstock, *Television in America.* Sage Commontext Series, vol. 1 (Beverly Hills, Calif.: Sage Publications, 1980), pp. 56–57.
9. Hickey, "Television Broadcasts," p. 261; *New York Times,* Mar. 19, 1939, sec. 11, p. 5.
10. *New York Times,* Apr. 27, 1939, p. 33.
11. Ibid., Feb. 27, 1939, sec. 10, p. 12; Nov. 12, 1939, sec. 9, p. 10.
12. T. R. Kennedy, Jr., "Prize Fight via Television," *Science Digest,* June 1941, p. 65; *New York Times,* May 10, 1941, p. 17; Comstock, pp. 13–14.
13. Schulberg, Jan. 1962, p. 87.
14. *New York Times,* June 23, 1946, sec. 2, p. 7.
15. Ibid.
16. "At the Knife and Fork," *New Yorker,* June 29, 1946, pp. 16–17.
17. Ibid.
18. Ibid.
19. Ibid., p. 17; *New York Times,* Dec. 23, 1963, p. 31.
20. David M. Solinger, "Unauthorized Uses of Television Broadcasts," *Columbia Law Review,* 48 (1948), p. 849; Grombach, p. 135.
21. Solinger, p. 849.
22. Ibid., pp. 848–49.
23. *New York Times,* Feb. 13, 1949, p. 33. The networks were now engaged in serious competition over delivery systems and advanced technology. One such encounter came over the color picture breakthrough. NBC and RCA teamed up to defeat a CBS proposal to enter the market with a sequential color system. The former deemed it inferior to the simultaneous system, which was in the preparatory stage. The issue hinged on quality versus speed.
24. Solinger, p. 849.
25. Grombach, p. 135.
26. Solinger, p. 866.
27. *Twentieth Century Sporting Club, Inc.* v. *Transradio Press Service, Inc.,* 165 Misc. 71, 300 NYS 159 (1937).
28. Ibid.
29. *New York Times,* Mar. 7, 1971, sec. 5, p. 3; Mar. 9, 1971, p. 30.

30. *Norman* v. *Century Athletic Club,* 193 Md. 584, 69 A 2d 466, 15 ALR 2d 777 (1949).
31. *Norman* v. *Century Athletic Club,* p. 782–83; *New York Times,* Nov. 12, 1949, p. 24.
32. *New York Times,* Nov. 12, 1949, p. 24.
33. *Ettore* v. *Philco,* 229 Fed. 481, 58 ALR 2d 626 (1956).
34. Ibid., p. 626.
35. Ibid., pp. 637–38.
36. Ibid., p. 642.
37. *United States* v. *International Boxing Club,* 150 F. Supp. 397 (1957), reprinted in U.S. Congress, Senate, Committee on the Judiciary, Subcommittee on Antitrust and Monopoly, hearings on professional boxing, pursuant to S. Res. 238, pt. 2 (Frank Carbo), 86th Cong., 2nd Sess., *Congressional Record,* 1960, pp. 886–87 (hereafter cited as "Carbo Hearings").
38. Ibid.; Barney Nagler, *James Norris and the Decline of Boxing* (New York: Bobbs-Merrill, 1964), pp. 4, 36–38.
39. Cannon, p. 281.
40. "Carbo Hearings," p. 550.
41. Nagler, pp. 37–45; "Carbo Hearings," p. 908.
42. Cannon, p. 281.
43. *International Boxing Club* v. *United States* (1959), cited in "Carbo Hearings," p. 908; *New York Times,* Mar. 8, 1952, p. 18; Mar. 18, 1952, p. 30.
44. *IBC* v. *U.S.,* cited in "Carbo Hearings," p. 909.
45. Ibid.
46. Ibid., p. 910.
47. *New York Times,* Mar. 8, 1952, p. 18; Mar. 18, 1952, p. 30; *IBC* v. *U.S.,* cited in "Carbo Hearings," p. 910.
48. Ibid., p. 911.
49. Gibson interview.
50. "Carbo Hearings," pp. 322–27; Nagler, pp. 88–89.
51. *New York Times,* June 14, 1949, p. 39.
52. "Carbo Hearings," pp. 322–27; *New York Times,* July 15, 1950, p. 8; "The Fight Game," *March of Times Films,* 200 MT 14111, National Archives, Washington, D.C.
53. "Carbo Hearings," pp. 324, 956–78.
54. Roberts, *Jack Dempsey,* p. 37.
55. "Carbo Hearings," pp. 324, 956–78.
56. Ibid., pp. 573, 597, 613.
57. Ibid.
58. Humbert S. Nelli, *The Business of Crime: Italians and Syndicates in the United States* (New York: Oxford University Press, 1976), pp. x–xi, 253.
59. Nelli, p. 253; Estes Kefauver, *Crime in America,* ed. Sidney Shalett (New York: Doubleday and Co., 1951), p. 1.
60. Joseph Bruce Gorman, *Kefauver: Political Biography* (New York: Oxford University Press, 1971), pp. 74–75.

61. *New York Times,* Dec. 20, 1946, p. 48; Jan. 22, 1948, p. 37.
62. Ibid., Dec. 20, 1946, p. 48.
63. Ibid., Feb. 6, 1946, p. 15.
64. Ibid., Jan. 27, 1947, p. 15.
65. Ibid.
66. Ibid., Feb. 8, 1947, pp. 1, 12; Jan. 28, 1947, p. 1.
67. Ibid., Feb. 8, 1947, pp. 1, 12; Jan. 29, 1947, p. 1.
68. Ibid., Feb. 8, 1947, pp. 1, 12.
69. Ibid., Feb. 15, 1947, p. 12; Feb. 18, 1947, p. 32.
70. Ibid., Feb. 20, 1947, p. 33.
71. Ibid.
72. Sugar, p. 560.
73. *New York Times,* Jan. 31, 1947, p. 42.
74. "Carbo Hearings," 1960, p. 292.
75. Ibid., p. 279.
76. Ibid.
77. Ibid.
78. Joselit, pp. 85, 86, 95.
79. *New York Times,* Sept. 27, 1947, p. 19.
80. Ibid., June 24, 1947, p. 27.
81. Ibid., Feb. 13, 1947, p. 33; Feb. 14, 1947, p. 14.
82. Ibid., Jan. 30, 1947, p. 24.
83. Ibid.
84. Field and Brown, pp. 56–57; *New York Times,* Jan. 25, 1953, p. 84.
85. *New York Times,* Jan. 30, 1947, p. 24.
86. Ibid.
87. Ibid.
88. Ibid.
89. *Atlanta Constitution,* Dec. 3, 1947, p. 10.
90. Ibid.
91. "Carbo Hearings," pp. 661–90.
92. Ibid., p. 665.
93. U.S. Congress, Senate, Committee on the Judiciary, Subcommittee on Antitrust and Monopoly, hearings on professional boxing, pertaining to S. Res. 238, 86th Cong., 2d Sess., *Congressional Record,* pt. 1 (Jacob "Jake" LaMotta), 1960, p. 55 (hereafter cited as "LaMotta Hearings.")
94. "Carbo Hearings," pp. 669–73.
95. Ibid.
96. "LaMotta Hearings," p. 116.
97. Ibid., pp. 17, 29.
98. Ibid.
99. Ibid.
100. Ibid., p. 114.
101. *New York Times,* Nov. 19, 1947, p. 39.
102. "LaMotta Hearings," p. 198.

103. *New York Times,* Nov. 19, 1947, p. 39; "LaMotta Hearings," p. 198.
104. "LaMotta Hearings," p. 198.
105. Ibid.
106. Ibid.
107. Ibid., pp. 20, 83; Sugar, p. 516.
108. "LaMotta Hearings," pp. 25, 59.
109. Ibid., pp. 55–70, 154.
110. *New York Times,* Apr. 29, 1964, p. 83; *Advertising Age,* Apr. 16, 1953, p. 11.
111. "Boxing Sponsors Have a Problem," *Advertising Age,* May 4, 1953, pp. 2, 66; Arthur Daley, "Is Boxing on the Ropes?" *New York Times Magazine,* Jan. 31, 1954, p. 22.
112. Daley, p. 22.
113. "Boxing Sponsors," pp. 2, 66; Daley, p. 19.
114. "Boxing Sponsors," pp. 2, 66.
115. *Advertising Age,* May 4, 1953, p. 66.
116. Charles Einstein, "TV Slugs the Boxers," *Harper's,* Aug. 1956, pp. 65–68.
117. J. Fred MacDonald, *Blacks and White TV: Afro-Americans in Television since 1948* (Chicago: Nelson-Hall Publishers, 1983), p. 62.
118. Ibid.
119. Daley, pp. 19–25; "Build-up to a Fight—TV Makes a Difference," *Business Week,* Feb. 27, 1954, p. 109.
120. "Carbo Hearings," p. 287.
121. Ibid., p. 286.
122. Ibid.
123. Ibid., p. 1139.
124. Ibid.
125. U.S. Congress, Senate, Committee on the Judiciary, Subcommittee on Antitrust and Monopoly, hearings on professional boxing, pursuant to S. Res. 52 on S. 1474, 87th Cong. 1st Sess., *Congressional Record,* 1961, p. 1250 (hereafter cited as "Professional Boxing Hearings, 1961").
126. "Carbo Hearings," p. 292.
127. Ibid., p. 572.
128. Ibid., p. 285–87.
129. Ibid., p. 658.
130. Ibid., p. 289.
131. "Professional Boxing Hearings, 1961," p. 1394.
132. *New York Times,* July 3, 1958, p. 32; "Carbo Hearings," pp. 289, 469. After a series of postponements, hearings into Wallman's and Grant's activities continued in 1961. Wallman maintained that he had given money to Grant between 1954 and 1959 but testified that such money "was not given pursuant to any conspiracy or agreement or prearranged plan to influence the said Bertram L. Grant's performance of his duties as a ring official or to influence his decisions as such official in any above stated boxing match." *New York Times,* Sept. 28, 1961, p. 58; Dec. 13, 1961, p. 59.
133. "Carbo Hearings," pp. 608–9.

134. Ibid.
135. Ibid., p. 608.
136. *New York Times,* Jan. 17, 1955, p. 13; Nagler, p. 94.
137. *New York Times,* Dec. 13, 1955, pp. 1, 57.
138. Ibid.
139. Ibid.
140. Ibid.
141. Ibid.
142. "LaMotta Hearings," pp. 48-49.
143. *London Sporting Club* v. *Helfand,* 152 NYS 2d 819 (1956), p. 822.
144. Ibid.
145. *New York Times,* Jan. 8, 1956, sec. 5., pp. 1, 7.
146. Ibid.
147. Ibid., Jan. 11, 1956, p. 38.
148. Ibid., Sept. 23, 1957, p. 20.
149. Ibid.
150. "Carbo Hearings," p. 618.
151. Ibid., pp. 625-26.
152. Gorman, p. 299.
153. *U.S.* v. *IBC,* cited in "Carbo Hearings," pp. 886-90; *New York Times,* June 12, 1951, p. 40.
154. *New York Times,* June 13, 1951, p. 40.
155. Ibid.
156. James P. Dawson, "Video in Theaters Seen as Sports Boon," *New York Times,* June 17, 1951, sec. 5, p. 9.
157. *New York Times,* Sept. 14, 1951, p. 35.
158. Ibid., June 28, 1951, p. 30.
159. Ibid.
160. Ibid.
161. Ibid.; Jack Gould, " 'Eavesdroppers' Hear Maxim-Robinson Title Bout by Listening to Canadian Broadcast," *New York Times,* June 27, 1952, p. 30.
162. *New York Times,* Aug. 11, 1951, p. 14; Mar. 8, 1952, p. 18.
163. Ibid., Mar. 18, 1952, p. 30; Louis, "Where Did My Money Go?" pp. 68-69.
164. Louis, "Where Did My Money Go?" pp. 68-69.
165. *U.S.* v. *IBC,* cited in "Carbo Hearings," p. 876.
166. Ibid.
167. *Federal Baseball Club* v. *National League,* 259 US 200 (1922); *Toolson* v. *New York Yankees,* 346 US 356 (1953); *New York Times,* Feb. 5, 1954, p. 27.
168. Steven R. Rivkin, "Sports Leagues and the Federal Anti-trust Laws," in *Government and the Sports Business,* ed. Roger G. Noll (Washington, D.C.: Brookings Institution, 1974) pp. 387-88; *Northern Pacific Railway Co.* v. *United States,* 356 U.S. 1, at 4 (1958), quoted in Rivkin, p. 387.
169. *New York Times,* Feb. 5, 1954, p. 27.
170. *United States* v. *International Boxing Club,* 348 U.S. 236 (1955).
171. Ibid., p. 244.

172. Ibid.
173. U.S. Congress, Senate, Committee on the Judiciary, report no. 426, to accompany the Professional Sports Act of 1965, S. 950, 89th Cong., 1st Sess., *Congressional Record,* July 16, 1965, pp. 4–11.
174. *U.S.* v. *IBC* (1955), p. 249.
175. Ibid.
176. Ibid., p. 252.
177. Ibid.
178. Ibid., pp. 250–51.
179. Ibid.
180. *New York Times,* Jan. 19, 1930, sec. 10, p. 9.
181. Ibid.
182. *U.S.* v. *IBC* (1955), pp. 248–51.
183. Ibid.
184. *New York Times,* May 15, 1957, p. 45; "Carbo Hearings," p. 282.
185. *U.S.* v. *IBC* (1957), cited in "Carbo Hearings," pp. 886–90.
186. *New York Times,* May 15, 1957, p. 45; "Carbo Hearings," p. 282.
187. *Schine Theaters* v. *United States,* 334 U.S. 110 (1948).
188. Gibson interview.
189. *Schine* v. *U.S.,* pp. 128–29, quoted in *IBC* v. *U.S.,* cited in "Carbo Hearings," p. 915.
190. *U.S.* v. *IBC* (1957), cited in "Carbo Hearings," pp. 899–903; *IBC* v. *U.S.,* cited in "Carbo Hearings," pp. 916–17.
191. *New York Times,* May 15, 1957, p. 45.
192. Ibid.
193. "Carbo Hearings," p. 282.
194. *IBC* v. *U.S.,* cited in "Carbo Hearings," p. 920.
195. *New York Times,* May 15, 1957, p. 45.
196. *IBC* v. *U.S.,* cited in "Carbo Hearings," p. 920.
197. Ibid.
198. "Carbo Hearings," p. 398.
199. Ibid., pp. 397–98.
200. Ibid., pp. 353–606 passim.
201. "Education of a Boy Promoter," *Time,* Sept. 7, 1959, pp. 40–41; *New York Times,* Aug. 9, 1959, sec. 5, p. 3.
202. *New York Times,* July 25, 1958, p. 1.
203. Ibid.
204. James Stewart-Gordon, "Abolish Professional Boxing," *Reader's Digest,* Apr. 1960, pp. 81–82.
205. Stewart-Gordon, pp. 81–82; "Carbo Hearings," pp. 279–80; Nagler, pp. 182–83.
206. Ibid.
207. *Washington Post,* May 31, 1961, quoted in "Professional Boxing Hearings," p. 124.
208. *New York Times,* June 26, 1978, sec. 3, p. 6.

209. Ibid.
210. Michael F. Armstrong, Warren H. Colodner, William O. Purcell, "Report Regarding Alleged Irregularities in the United States Boxing Championships" (New York: Barrett, Smith, Schapiro, Simon, and Armstrong, Aug. 25, 1977), p. 311.
211. U.S. Congress, House, Committee on Interstate and Foreign Commerce, hearings on the Federal Boxing Commission, H.R. 8635, H.R. 8676, H.R. 9140, H.R. 9196, H.R. 9426, H.R. 9633, 89th Cong., 1st Sess., *Congressional Record,* July 6, 7, 8, 1965, p. 172 (hereafter cited as "Federal Boxing Commission Hearings, 1965").
212. *Carbo v. United States,* 314 Fed. 718 (1963), p. 724.
213. Ibid.
214. *Carbo v. U.S.,* pp. 726–27; California State Athletic Commission hearings, May 14, 1959, cited in "Carbo Hearings," pp. 1525–28.
215. Ibid.
216. *Carbo v. U.S.,* p. 728.
217. Ibid.
218. Ibid., pp. 728–29.
219. Ibid.
220. Ibid., p. 729.
221. Ibid.
222. Ibid.
223. California State Athletic Commission hearings, May 14, 1959, transcript of recorded conversation between Bill Daly and Jack Leonard, cited in "Federal Boxing Commission Hearings, 1961," p. 1492; Nagler, p. 222.
224. Ibid.
225. Stewart-Gordon, pp. 84–85; *Carbo v. U.S.,* pp. 730–32.
226. *Carbo v. U.S.,* pp. 730–32.
227. "Professional Boxing Hearings," pp. 1249–50; U.S. Congress, Senate, Committee on Government Operations, report no. 1310, on gambling and organized crime, 87th Cong., 2d Sess., *Congressional Record,* Mar. 28, 1962, p. 1.
228. "Mind and Muscle," *Time,* Oct. 5, 1959, p. 80.
229. *Carbo v. U.S.,* pp. 730–32.
230. Ibid., p. 725.
231. Nagler, pp. 246–49.
232. Ibid., pp. 248–49.
233. *New York Times,* Feb. 2, 1958, p. 32; *Broadcasting Cable Yearbook* (Washington, D.C.: Broadcasting Publications, 1981), p. D-112; *New York Times,* Dec. 23, 1963, p. 31.
234. Ibid.
235. *New York Times,* Dec. 23, 1963, p. 31.
236. James A. Farley, Jr., "My Fight in Defense of Boxing," *Sports Illustrated,* Apr. 23, 1962, pp. 26–27.
237. U.S. Congress, Senate, Committee on the Judiciary, Subcommittee on

Anti-trust and Monopoly, hearings on professional boxing, pursuant to S. Res. 262 on S. 1182, 88th Cong., 2d Sess., *Congressional Record,* 1964, p. 1387 (hereafter cited as "Professional Boxing Hearings, 1964").

238. John Kieran, "Sports of the Times," *New York Times,* June 30, 1930, p. 17.
239. "Carbo Hearings," pp. 847–853.
240. Kieran, p. 17.
241. U.S., Congress, House, joint resolution to establish a National Boxing Commission, H.J. Res. 510, 76th Cong., 3d Sess., *Congressional Record,* 1940, p. 1.
242. Ibid.
243. "Professional Boxing Hearings, 1961," pp. 1249–51.
244. Ibid., p. 1259.
245. Ibid.
246. Ibid.
247. *New York Times,* Mar. 20, 1961, p. 1; Apr. 2, 1964, p. 38; "Professional Boxing Hearings, 1964," p. 1777, 1838.
248. Ibid.
249. *New York Times,* Apr. 1, 1963, pp. 1, 56; Gorman, p. 367.
250. U.S. Congress, House, report no. 593 on bribery and sports, referred to the Committee on the Judiciary, S. 741, 88th Cong., 1st Sess., *Congressional Record,* Oct. 31, 1963, pp. 1–3; USC Title 18, chap. 11, p. 1042.
251. USC Title 18, chap. 11, p. 1042.
252. *Washington Post,* May 31, 1961, cited in "Professional Boxing Hearings, 1961," p. 1246.
253. "LaMotta Hearings," p. 107.
254. Ibid.
255. New York State Athletic Commission, hearings on Sonny Liston, Apr. 27, 1962, p. 107 (hereafter cited as "Liston Hearings"), in "Federal Boxing Commission Hearings, 1965."
256. "Carbo Hearings," pp. 760–67.
257. Ibid., pp. 644–45.
258. Ibid.
259. Ibid., pp. 644–50, 770–71.
260. Ibid.
261. Ibid., p. 645.
262. "Professional Boxing Hearings, 1964," p. 1662.
263. Ibid.
264. "Liston Hearings," pp. 106–7.
265. Ibid.
266. Ibid., p. 107.
267. Sugar, p. 485.
268. "Professional Boxing Hearings, 1964," pp. 1618–1713 passim.
269. Ibid., pp. 760–71.
270. Ibid.
271. Ibid., p. 787.

272. Ibid., p. 1616.
273. Ibid., p. 1635.
274. Ibid., p. 1616.
275. Ibid., pp. 1620, 1647, 1695.
276. "Report of State Attorney Richard E. Gerstein on Investigation of Clay-Liston Heavyweight Championship Fight," cited in "Professional Boxing Hearings, 1964," p. 1845 (hereafter cited as "Gerstein Report").
277. "Professional Boxing Hearings, 1964," p. 1633.
278. "Gerstein Report," p. 1845.
279. Ibid.
280. Ibid.
281. "Professional Boxing Hearings, 1964," pp. 1670–73.
282. "Gerstein Report," p. 1845.
283. Ibid.
284. "Professional Boxing Hearings, 1964," pp. 1670–73.
285. Ibid., p. 1842.
286. Muhammad Ali (with Richard Durham), *The Greatest: My Own Story* (New York: Ballantine Books, 1975), p. 133. The Black Muslims once labeled all whites as devils and considered them unredeemable. Malcolm X personally presented a frightening specter to white America. He had gained his greatest notoriety and condemnation for his reference to President Kennedy's death as a case of "America's chickens come home to roost." Taken out of context, the statement was part of a larger discussion about "the atmosphere of racial hatred and social violence that whites had created in America, a rabid intolerance that had finally struck down the Chief of State himself." See Budd Schulberg, "Chinese Boxes of Muhammad Ali," *Saturday Review,* February 26, 1972, p. 25.
287. Ali, *The Greatest,* p. 115.

Chapter 7: Civil Rights to Rebellion to Reaction

1. Quoted in James T. Patterson, *America in the Twentieth Century: A History* (New York: Harcourt Brace Jovanovich, 1976), p. 371.
2. Ibid.
3. Quoted in George B. Tindall, *America: A Narrative History,* vol. 2 (New York: W. W. Norton, 1984), p. 1228.
4. George C. Herring, *America's Longest War: The United States and Vietnam, 1950–1975* (New York: Alfred A. Knopf, 2d ed., 1986), pp. 45–46. According to Herring, "Had it looked all over the world, the United States could not have chosen a less promising place for an experiment in nation-building. In southern Vietnam, chaos reigned. . . . It had been devastated by nearly fourteen years of war and was held together by enormous French military expenditures that would soon cease. . . . Assuming the premiership in the summer of 1954, the staunchly anti-French Ngo Dinh Diem inherited antiquated institutions patterned on French practices and ill-

suited to the needs of an independent nation—an 'oriental despotism with a French accent'."

5. Schulberg, "Chinese Boxes," p. 23.
6. Albert P. Blaustein and Robert L. Zangrando, eds., *Civil Rights and the Black American: A Documentary History* (New York: Clarion Books, 1970), pp. 420-24.
7. Blaustein and Zangrando, pp. 414-18. Relying specifically on the 1954 *Brown* ruling, the Supreme Court in 1955 declared segregation illegal on public beaches in Maryland and on public golf courses in Georgia.
8. Ibid.
9. Letter from Maury Maverick to H. Boyd Hall, Jan. 3, 1954, NAACP Files, Barker Library of Texas History, University of Texas, Austin.
10. *Harvey* v. *Morgan,* 272 S.W. 2d 621 (1954), p. 621. An unidentified newspaper clipping lists his record as five wins and sixteen losses.
11. Anonymous interview, June 1983, San Antonio, Tex.
12. *Harvey* v. *Morgan,* pp. 621-23.
13. Ibid., pp. 623-24.
14. Ibid., p. 625.
15. *Liberty Annex Corporation* v. *City of Dallas,* 289 S.W. 1067, cited in *Harvey* v. *Morgan,* p. 626; ibid., p. 625.
16. *Sweatt* v. *Painter,* 339 U.S. 629 (1950); letter from H. J. Williams, M.D., president of Corpus Christi branch of the NAACP, to Bill Will, Corpus Christi Park and Recreation Department, June 5, 1954, Barker Library of Texas History, University of Texas, Austin.
17. *New York Times,* Feb. 25, 1955, p. 37.
18. "The Defeated," *Time,* Aug. 5, 1957, p. 37.
19. Sugar, p. 485.
20. *New York Times,* Jan. 24, 1953, p. 20.
21. Ibid., Nov. 22, 1956, p. 35.
22. "Action Program for 1955," New Orleans branch of the NAACP, box 28-97, University of New Orleans Archives, New Orleans, La.
23. *New York Times,* Dec. 3, 1956, p. 19.
24. Ibid.
25. *New Orleans Times-Picayune,* Mar. 29, 1957.
26. Ibid., Apr. 3, 1957.
27. Ibid., Mar. 29, 1957.
28. Ibid., Apr. 1, 1958, pp. 1, 26; Apr. 2, 1958, p. 24; *New York Times,* Apr. 2, 1958, p. 64.
29. *New Orleans Times-Picayune,* Oct. 31, 1957, p. 2.
30. Ibid., Mar. 1, 1928, p. 1.
31. Dan Parker, "Congressman Hebert Gives Us an Honest Fight," *New York Mirror,* May 8, 1958, reprinted in *Congressional Record,* 85th Cong., 2d Sess., May 14, 1958, pp. 4466-67.
32. *New Orleans Item,* Jan. 10, 1958, p. 25.
33. *New York Times,* Nov. 29, 1958, pp. 1, 22; *Dorsey* v. *State Athletic*

Commission, 168 F. Supp. 149 (1958); *State Athletic Commission* v. *Dorsey,* 359 U.S. 533 (1959); *State Athletic Commission* v. *Dorsey,* 360 U.S. 940, 79 S. Ct. 1446 (1960).

34. *New Orleans Item,* Nov. 28, 1958, p. 21; *New York Times,* Nov. 30, 1958, sec. 4, p. 8.
35. *New Orleans Times-Picayune,* Dec. 3, 1958.
36. Lerone Bennett, Jr., "When the Man and the Hour Are Met," in *Martin Luther King, Jr.: A Profile,* ed. C. Eric Lincoln (New York: Hill and Wang, 1970), pp. 12–13.
37. Ibid.
38. In *Gayle* v. *Browder,* 352 U.S. 903 (1956), the Supreme Court ruled that the Montgomery, Alabama, law requiring segregation violated the Constitution. This transportation case overturned *Plessy* v. *Ferguson* (1896) and its separate-but-equal doctrine.
39. "Roar of the Crowd," *Time,* Sept. 23, 1957, pp. 75–76.
40. Jack Scott, *The Athletic Revolution* (New York: Free Press, 1971), pp. 80–81.
41. Howard Cosell, *Cosell* (Chicago: Playboy Press, 1973), pp. 159–64.
42. *New York Times,* July 23, 1963, p. 23.
43. "Jesse Owens on the Olympics," *Black Sports,* Mar. 1976, pp. 46–47.
44. "The Blow That K.O.'d Joe Louis," *U.S. News and World Report,* Jan. 25, 1957, pp. 63–68.
45. *New York Times,* July 23, 1963, p. 23.
46. Schulberg, "Chinese Boxes," p. 23.
47. *New York Times,* July 23, 1963, p. 23.
48. Ibid.
49. Maurice Berube, "Defeat of the Great Black Hope," *Commonweal,* Mar. 26, 1971, p. 54.
50. Ibid.
51. "Budgeted Beakbusting: Louisville Businessman Promotes Heavyweight, Cassius Clay," *Business Week,* Nov. 24, 1962, pp. 30–31.
52. Ali, p. 114; "Professional Boxing Hearings, 1964," p. 1687; "Budgeted Beakbusting," p. 30.
53. Schulberg, "Chinese Boxes," p. 23.
54. Ibid., p. 24.
55. Ali, pp. 130–35.
56. Malcolm X, *The Autobiography of Malcolm X* (New York: Ballantine Books, 1984, rpt.), p. 316.
57. Ali, p. 110.
58. Ibid.
59. Schulberg, "Chinese Boxes," p. 24.
60. Earl Grant, "The Last Days of Malcolm X," in *Malcolm X: The Man and His Times,* ed. John Henrik Clarke (Toronto: Collier Books, 1969), p. 83.
61. *New York Times,* Feb. 28, 1969, p. 22.
62. Malcolm X, p. 238.

63. C. Eric Lincoln, *The Black Muslims in America* (Boston: Beacon Press, 1973), p. xxi.
64. Ibid.
65. Francis Stann, "Win, Lose, or Draw—Unsavory Conclusion Doesn't Help Boxing," in *Congressional Record,* 88th Cong., 2d Sess., Feb. 27, 1964, p. 316.
66. U.S. Congress, Senate, Senator Richard Russell speaking on civil rights and Cassius Clay's boxing title, 88th Cong., 2d Sess., *Congressional Record,* Mar. 24, 1964, pp. 6029–30 (hereafter cited as "Civil Rights and Cassius Clay").
67. U.S. Congress, Senate, Senator Richard Russell speaking on racial propaganda, 88th Cong., 2d Sess., *Congressional Record,* Feb. 24, 1964, pp. 3398–99 (hereafter cited as "Racial Propaganda").
68. Ibid.
69. "Civil Rights and Cassius Clay," p. 6029.
70. Ibid., p. 6030.
71. *New York Times,* Mar. 8, 1964, sec. 5, pp. 1–2; Nov. 28, 1965, sec. 5, p. 10.
72. Cosell, p. 177.
73. Schulberg, "Chinese Boxes," p. 23.
74. Cosell, pp. 165–67.
75. *New York Times,* Mar. 8, 1964, sec. 5, pp. 1–2.
76. Cosell, p. 163; Ali, pp. 149–51.
77. Cosell, p. 222.
78. Ali, p. 191.
79. Cosell, pp. 192–96.
80. Ibid., p. 176.
81. *New York Times,* June 29, 1971, p. 24; Schulberg, "Chinese Boxes," pp. 23–24.
82. Cosell, p. 205.
83. Ali, p. 144.
84. *Revolutionary Worker,* Nov. 30, 1984, p. 8.
85. U.S. Congress, House, Representative Frank Clark speaking on the heavyweight champion, 89th Cong., 2d Sess., *Congressional Record,* Mar. 5, 1966, vol. 112, p. 5880 (hereafter cited as "Heavyweight Champion").
86. Herring, p. 66; Robert Shaplen, *The Lost Revolution* (New York: Harper Colophon Books, 1966), pp. xxi–xxii.
87. Townsend Hoopes, *The Limits of Intervention* (New York: David McKay Company, 1969), pp. 14–21.
88. Charles De Benedetti, "A CIA Analysis of the Anti-Vietnam War Movement: October 1967," *Peace and Change: A Journal of Peace Research,* 9 (Spring 1983), pp. 32–35.
89. Quoted in ibid., p. 29.
90. Ibid., p. 34.
91. James T. Patterson, *America in the Twentieth Century: A History* (New York: Harcourt Brace Jovanovich, 2d ed., 1983), p. 124.

92. Todd Gitlin, *The Whole World Is Watching: Mass Media in the Making and Unmaking of the New Left* (Berkeley: University of California Press, 1980), pp. 9-11.
93. Charles De Benedetti, "On the Significance of Citizen Peace Activism: America, 1961-1975," *Peace and Change: A Journal of Peace Research,* 9 (Summer 1983), p. 14.
94. "Heavyweight Champion," p. 5880.
95. Ali, p. 186.
96. Ibid., pp. 186-87.
97. Ibid.
98. *New York Times,* Nov. 28, 1965, sec. 5, p. 10.
99. Ali, p. 188.
100. "Civil Rights and Cassius Clay," p. 6029; Bob Woodward and Scott Armstrong, *The Brethren* (New York: Avon Books, 1979), p. 158.
101. Woodward and Armstrong, p. 158.
102. Ali, p. 206.
103. U.S. Congress, House, Representative Claude Pepper excerpting from columns on Ali by John Spolski of the *Sanford Herald,* 90th Cong., 1st Sess., *Congressional Record,* Aug. 21, 1967, vol. 93, p. 23357 (hereafter cited as "Spolski Columns on Ali").
104. Ali, p. 206.
105. Frederic Cople Jaher, "White America Views Jack Johnson, Joe Louis, and Muhammad Ali," in Spivey, p. 175.
106. David J. Garrow, *The FBI and Martin Luther King, Jr.* (New York: W. W. Norton and Co., 1981), p. 207.
107. "Spolski Columns on Ali," p. 23357.
108. Jackie Robinson, *I Never Had It Made* (New York: G. P. Putnam's Sons, 1972), pp. 94-98.
109. Although Jabbar became a member of the Hanafi Sect, which found itself at odds with the Nation of Islam, his break with Christianity, his association with third-world causes, and a heightened political awareness clearly indicated the new breed of athlete Ali had in part helped to develop.
110. U.S. Congress, House, Representative George Hansen speaking on blacks in sports, citing "Bleacher Notes" by Joe Richmond (*Idaho State Journal,* May 26, 1968), 90th Cong., 2d Sess., *Congressional Record,* May 23, 1968, vol. 114, p. 15702 (hereafter cited as "Richmond's Bleacher Notes").
111. Quoted in Robert Lipsyte, *Sports World: An American Dream Land* (New York: Quadrangle Books, 1975), p. 12.
112. Ibid., pp. 17-18; Dave Meggyesy, *Out of Their League* (Berkeley, Calif.: Ramparts Press, 1970), pp. 254-56.
113. *New York Times,* Mar. 1, 1968, p. 44.
114. Ibid., May 4, 1970, p. 57; Jaher, p. 175.
115. Herring, p. 187.
116. Gitlin, pp. 205-7; Herring, p. 191.
117. Gitlin, pp. 208-9.

118. Richard N. Current, T. Harry Williams, and Frank Freidel, *American History: A Survey,* vol. 2: Since 1865 (New York: Alfred A. Knopf, 4th ed., 1975), p. 820.
119. Ibid.
120. Gitlin, pp. 187, 191, 210.
121. U.S. Congress, House, Representative James R. Mann speaking on Lt. William L. Calley, Jr. (citing a letter from Robert C. Mardian, assistant attorney general, March 15, 1971), 92d Cong., 1st Sess., *Congressional Record,* Apr. 1, 1971, vol. 117, p. 8980 (hereafter cited as "Calley").
122. *New York Times,* Aug. 20, 1969, p. 56.
123. Ibid., Dec. 12, 1969, p. 102.
124. U.S. Congress, House, Representative Fletcher Thompson speaking on Muhammad Ali and un-American activities, 91st Cong., 1st Sess., *Congressional Record,* Oct. 23, 1969, vol. 115, p. 31249 (hereafter cited as "Ali and Un-American Activities"); *New York Times,* Jan. 30, 1970, p. 37.
125. Quoted in *Revolutionary Worker,* Nov. 30, 1984.
126. "Super Fight: Ali v. Marciano," *Time,* Jan. 19, 1970, p. 95; *New York Times,* Jan. 21, 1970, p. 52.
127. *New York Times,* Jan. 30, 1970, p. 37.
128. Ibid.
129. Ibid.
130. Ibid., May 4, 1970, p. 57; Ali, p. 328.
131. Ali, p. 328.
132. *New York Times,* Sept. 16, 1970, p. 75.
133. Robert H. Brisbane, *Black Activism: Racial Revolution in the United States* (Valley Forge, Pa.: Judson Press, 1974), p. 249.
134. Ali, p. 332.
135. Nathan Hare, "A Study of the Black Fighter," *Black Scholar,* Nov. 1971, pp. 3–4; Grombach, p. 89.
136. Ali, pp. 343–45.
137. Grombach, pp. 164–65.
138. *Ali* v. *Division of State Athletic Commission of the Department of State of New York,* 316 F. Supp. 1246 (1970), p. 1248.
139. Ibid., p. 1249.
140. Ibid.
141. Ibid., pp. 1252–53.
142. Ali, pp. 343–45.
143. *New York Times,* Sept. 28, 1975, sec. 5, p. 2.
144. Ibid., June 29, 1975, sec. 7, p. 9.
145. Ibid., Sept. 28, 1975, sec. 5, p. 2.
146. Ibid.
147. Ibid., Mar. 7, 1971, sec. 5, p. 3.
148. Roberts, *Jack Dempsey,* p. 109.
149. *New York Times,* Mar. 10, 1971, p. 44.
150. As quoted in U.S. Supreme Court decision in *C. M. Clay, Jr. A/K/A*

Muhammad Ali, Petitioner v. *U.S.A. Respondent* (Washington, D.C.: Alderson Reporting Co.), Apr. 19, 1971, p. 30, NA-8-2345, National Archives.

151. *New York Times,* Sept. 28, 1975, sec. 5, p. 2.
152. Cosell, pp. 230–32.
153. Donald Reeves, "The Black Prince," *New York Times,* May 17, 1971, p. 35.
154. *New York Times,* Apr. 1, 1973, sec. 5, p. 5.
155. Ibid.
156. Ibid.
157. "Calley," p. 8980.
158. Ralph Ellison, *Invisible Man* (New York: Signet Books, 1947), pp. 7–8.
159. Letter from Harry R. Gaines to the Clerk of U.S. Supreme Court, Dec. 31, 1970, RG no. 267, 5W2, row 12, compartment 12, shelf F, National Archives, Washington, D.C.
160. Letter from E. Robert Seaver, U.S. Supreme Court clerk, to William S. Watrous, Dec. 15, 1970; letter from Watrous to Seaver, Dec. 21, 1970; letter from Bill Currie, Cox Broadcasting operations manager, Charlotte, N.C., to John F. Davis, U.S. Supreme Court clerk, Nov. 1, 1970, in ibid.
161. Woodward and Armstrong, pp. 154–56.
162. *Welsh* v. *United States,* 398 U.S. 333 (1970); letter from Seaver to Robert Kaufman, Jan. 15, 1971, RG no. 267, National Archives.
163. Woodward and Armstrong, pp. 159–60.
164. Ibid.
165. Ibid.
166. Ibid.
167. Ibid., p. 160.
168. Ibid.
169. Ibid.
170. *Welsh* v. *U.S.,* pp. 336–37; Malcolm X, p. 196; Woodward and Armstrong, pp. 159–60.
171. *Kansas City Times* editorial, June 30, 1971, in *Editorials on File,* 11 (July 1-15, 1971), pp. 866–72. Of the eighteen editorials compiled there, the most virulently anti-Ali was one from the *Detroit News.*
172. *Louisville Times* editorial, June 29, 1971, in *Editorials on File,* p. 868.
173. Sugar, p. 488.
174. U.S. Congress, House, Representative Fortney H. Stark speaking on George Foreman, the heavyweight champion of the world, 93rd Cong., 1st Sess., *Congressional Record,* vol. 119, Jan. 26, 1973, p. 23333 (hereafter cited as "Foreman—Heavyweight Champion").
175. George Foreman, "Don't Knock the American System to Me," *Congressional Record,* 93d Cong., 1st Sess., vol. 119, pt. 2, Feb. 5, 1973, p. 3370; Apr. 12, 1973, p. 12279; May 9, 1973, p. 15103.
176. Ibid.
177. U.S. Congress, House, Representative Frank M. Clark speaking on George Foreman, the twice world's champion, 93d Cong., 1st Sess., *Congressional*

Record, vol. 119, pt. 3, Feb. 5, 1973, p. 3370 (hereafter cited as "Foreman—Twice World's Champion").

178. Ibid., pp. 3370–72.
179. U.S. Congress, House, Representative Yvonne Braithwaite Burke speaking on the philosophy of George Foreman, 93d Cong., 1st Sess., *Congressional Record,* vol. 119, pt. 3, Apr. 16, 1973, p. 12610 (hereafter cited as "Philosophy of Foreman").
180. Sugar, p. 489.
181. Calvin Fentress, "The Champ," *New York Times,* Mar. 1978, reprinted in *Congressional Record,* 95th Cong., 2d Sess., vol. 124, Sept. 19, 1978, p. S15464.
182. U.S. Congress, House, Representative Lester L. Wolff speaking on the future of boxing, including testimonies of witnesses, 91st Cong., 2d Sess., *Congressional Record,* vol. 116, pt. 29, Dec. 2, 1970, p. 39660 (hereafter cited as "Future of Boxing").
183. David Dempsey, "Man in the Middle," *New York Times Magazine,* July 10, 1949, p. 14.
184. Field and Brown, pp. 56–57.
185. *New York Times,* Nov. 26, 1975, p. 87; May 23, 1976, sec. 11, p. 34; Jan. 20, 1977, p. 41.
186. "From Killer to King: Promoter Don King," *Time,* June 30, 1975, pp. 55–56.
187. Donn Rogosin, *Invisible Men: Life in Baseball's Negro Leagues* (New York: Atheneum, 1983), pp. 104–9.
188. "From Killer to King," pp. 55–56.
189. Don Coughlin, "King Already Nets Tidy Sum," *Cleveland Plain Dealer,* Mar. 31, 1974, reprinted in *Congressional Record,* 93d Cong., 2d Sess., vol. 126, pt. 9, Apr. 22, 1974, pp. 11234–35.
190. *New York Times,* Aug. 10, 1975, sec. 5, p. 3.
191. Ibid., Apr. 13, 1976, p. 42.
192. Ibid., Mar. 30, 1974, p. 20.
193. Allen Wiggins, "Jimmy Bivins Fought 'Em All, in Wrong Place, Wrong Time," *Cleveland Plain Dealer,* Mar. 31, 1974, reprinted in *Congressional Record,* 93d Cong., 2d Sess., vol. 120, Apr. 22, 1974, pp. 8369–71.
194. *New York Times,* Mar. 30, 1974, p. 20.
195. Ibid., July 2, 1974, p. 44.
196. Wiggins, "Jimmy Bivins," p. 8371.
197. Dave Nightingale, "Cleveland's King Shocks Boxing's White Establishment," in ibid., p. 11235.
198. Ibid.
199. *New York Times,* Aug. 13, 1974, p. 30.
200. Ibid., Oct. 31, 1974, p. 55.
201. Ibid., p. 58.
202. Ibid., Dec. 22, 1976, p. 21.
203. Tom Dowling, "Come September—in Zaire," *Washington Star,* Mar. 28,

1974, reprinted in *Congressional Record,* 93d Cong., 2d Sess., vol. 126, pt. 9, Apr. 22, 1974, pp. 11235–36.

204. Ibid., p. 11236.
205. Joel Williamson, *The Crucible of Race: Black-White Relations in the American South since Emancipation* (New York: Oxford University Press, 1984), pp. 119–21, 406–7.
206. Norman Mailer, *The Fight* (Boston: Little, Brown and Co., 1975), pp. 118–19.
207. Wiggins, "Jimmy Bivins," p. 8369.
208. *New York Times,* May 8, 1977, sec. 5, p. 5.
209. Ibid.
210. U.S. Federal Communications Commission, letter of admonition to American Broadcasting Companies, Inc., Apr. 25, 1978, FCC 78-287, 94877, pp. 1–5.
211. Ibid.
212. Armstrong et al., p. 311. On April 19, 1977, Michael F. Armstrong, former chief counsel of the Knapp Commission was retained by ABC Sports' outside counsel to investigate the extent of any irregularities in the organization and management of the tournament on the part of any person or entity, including ABC Sports. Prior to the suspension of the tournament, Philip R. Forlenza of Hawkins, Delafield, and Wood, outside counsel to ABC, was involved in matters concerning the U.S. Boxing Commission and in counseling ABC Sports.
213. FCC letter of admonition, p. 8.
214. *New York Times,* May 8, 1977, sec. 5, p. 5.
215. Ibid., July 19, 1978, p. 17; July 28, 1978, p. A19.
216. Ibid.
217. Ibid., July 28, 1978, p. A19.
218. Thomas Hauser, *The Black Lights: Inside the World of Professional Boxing* (New York: McGraw-Hill, 1986), p. 211.
219. N.J. Commission of Investigation, report on Organized Crime in Boxing (Trenton: Government Printer, 1985), pp. 45, 57 (hereafter cited as "Organized Crime in Boxing").
220. Hauser, p. 211.
221. *New York Times,* Nov. 9, 1974, p. 33.
222. Ibid.
223. Ibid., Mar. 25, 1974, p. 46.
224. "Face the Nation," CBS Television, May 2, 1974, transcript in *Congressional Record,* 94th Cong., 2d Sess., vol. 122, pt. 10, May 4, 1976, p. 12372–74.
225. Ibid.
226. *New York Times,* May 8, 1977, sec. 5, p. 5; May 22, 1977, sec. 5, p. 2.
227. Phil Berger, "Ali's Made-for-TV Challenger," *New York Times,* Jan. 29, 1978, sec. 6, p. 30.
228. "The Big Wind," *Time,* June 7, 1954, p. 65.
229. "Nino and the Nanimal," *New Yorker,* Aug. 7, 1954, p. 52.

230. Sugar, pp. 488–89.
231. Martin Ralbovsky, "Now They Can Leave Poor Leon Alone," *Philadelphia Inquirer,* June 25, 1979, sec. C., p. 1.
232. Fentress, p. S15464.
233. U.S. Congress, Senate, Senator Charles Percy speaking on Muhammad Ali's world acclaim, 95th Cong., 2d Sess., *Congressional Record,* vol. 124, no. 146, Sept. 19, 1978, p. S15463 (hereafter cited as "Ali and World Acclaim").
234. Ibid.
235. UCLA Foundation and the World Boxing Council Sports Medicine Foundation, "The Main Event—A Tribute to Muhammad Ali" (Beverly Hills, Calif.: Capitol Press, 1985), p. 3.
236. *Revolutionary Worker,* Nov. 30, 1984, p. 9.
237. Ibid.
238. Ibid., p. 9.
239. Ibid.
240. Russell, "Civil Rights and Cassius Clay," p. 3916.
241. *Rand Daily Mail* (Johannesburg, South Africa), Sept. 22, 1972; *Argus* (Cape Town, South Africa), Sept. 7, 1972.
242. *New York Times,* Oct. 3, 1972, p. 63.
243. *Cape Times* (Cape Town, South Africa), Dec. 3, 1973.
244. *A Survey of Race Relations in South Africa, 1977* (Johannesburg: South African Institute of Race Relations, 1978), p. 558.
245. Andre Odendaal, ed., *Cricket in Isolation: The Politics of Race and Cricket in South Africa* (Cape Town: Andre Odendaal, 1977), p. 269.
246. *New York Times,* Mar. 9, 1978, sec. 4, p. 15.
247. Ibid.
248. Ibid., Mar. 11, 1978, p. 17; Mar. 12, 1978, sec. 5, p. 1.
249. Ibid.
250. Ibid., Mar. 9, 1978, sec. 4, p. 15; Sugar, p. 486.
251. *New York Times,* Jan. 12, 1980, p. 19.
252. Ibid.
253. *Raleigh News and Observer,* Feb. 6, 1980, p. 5A.
254. Perry E. Gianakos, "The Black Muslims: An American Millennialistic Response to Racism and Cultural Deracination," *Centennial Review,* 3 (1979), p. 450.
255. Jaher, pp. 180–82.

Conclusion

1. "Federal Boxing Commission Hearings, 1965," pp. 158–59; *Ohio v. Hobart et al.,* p. 25.
2. Lawrence Perry, "The Gladiators," *Scribner's,* 77 (Jan. 1925), p. 60.
3. Weinberg and Arond, p. 463; Hare, pp. 7–8.
4. Grantland Rice, "Too Proud to Fight," *Collier's,* Aug. 14, 1926, p. 10.

5. Frederick Lewis Allen, *The Big Change 1900–1950* (New York: Bantam Matrix Edition, 1969), pp. 127–28.
6. Arthur Mann, "The Prize-Fighting Racket," *American Mercury,* Aug. 1934, p. 413.
7. Weinberg and Arond, p. 462.
8. Ibid.; Walter Bernstein, "Hit Him on the Horn, Georgie," *New Yorker,* Sept. 16, 1950, p. 70.
9. Thomas Boswell, "The Boxers of Washington," *Washington Post,* Jan. 8, 1978, sec. N, p. 1.
10. Ibid.
11. Tony Kornheiser, "Boxing Booms in the Gyms," *New York Times,* May 9, 1977, p. 33.
12. Robert Lipsyte, "Too Many Hands Often Spoil Boxing Pot of Gold," *New York Times,* Apr. 4, 1965, sec. 5, pp. 1–2.
13. Stewart-Gordon, p. 80.
14. *New Orleans Times-Picayune,* June 23, 1935, sec. 4, p. 5.
15. Len Zinberg, "The World of the Pug," *American Mercury,* Nov. 1951, p. 78.
16. Sugar Ray Robinson, *Sugar Ray* (New York: Signet Book, 1969–70), pp. 266–67.
17. Ibid., p. 267.
18. "The Blow That K.O.'d Joe Louis," p. 63.
19. John Lardner, "The Pathos of Taxes," *Newsweek,* Jan. 16, 1956, p. 73; "The Blow That K.O.'d Joe Louis," p. 63.
20. Edmonds, *Joe Louis,* p. 105; Nagler, p. 81.
21. "The Blow That K.O.'d. Joe Louis," p. 64; Nagler, pp. 76–77.
22. Gerald Astor, *Gloves Off: The Joe Louis Story* (London: Pelham, 1975), p. 270.
23. *Standard Federal Tax Reporter Index* (Chicago: Publisher Commerce Clearing House, 1982), pp. 151–52.
24. Public Law 91–172, 804 (a), amending Internal Revenue Code 1348.
25. Public Law 88–272, 232 (a), amending Internal Revenue Code 1731 *et seq.; New York Times,* May 21, 1964, p. 28; "Federal Boxing Commission Hearings, 1965," p. 173.
26. *Ray S. Robinson,* 44 T.C. 20 (1965).
27. Martha A. Van De Ven and Steven A. Kauffman, "Merits of Incorporating the Athlete," *Tax Advisor,* Aug. 1978, pp. 479–81.
28. "Federal Boxing Commission Hearings, 1965," pp. 61–63.
29. "Executive at Work," *Newsweek,* Feb. 26, 1951, pp. 74–75; John Lardner, "Whiz Kid in the Ring and in Business, Too," *New York Times Magazine,* Feb. 25, 1951, pp. 18–19; Robinson, *Sugar Ray,* pp. 123, 178; *Ray S. Robinson.*
30. *Los Angeles Times,* Jan. 9, 1976, sec. 1, p. 27.
31. Louis, "Where Did My Money Go?," pp. 69–70; Lardner, "Pathos," p. 73; "The Blow That K.O.'d Joe Louis," pp. 63–68.
32. Mann, p. 413.

33. *Houston Chronicle,* Aug. 12, 1985, sec. 3, p. 3.
34. Hare, p. 7.
35. *On the Waterfront* (Columbia Pictures, 1954).
36. Hare, p. 7; Weinberg and Arond, p. 468.
37. U.S. Congress, House, Representative Lester L. Wolff introducing testimonies at a hearing on boxing, 91st Cong., 2d Sess., *Congressional Record,* vol. 116, pt. 29, Dec. 1, 1970, pp. 39437–38 (hereafter cited as "Boxing Testimonies").
38. Dave Anderson, "The Most Thing Is, I Love to Fight," *New York Times,* Mar. 18, 1976, p. 53.
39. Dave Anderson, "People Who Need People Don't Retire," *New York Times,* June 25, 1975, p. 35.
40. U.S. Congress, House, Subcommittee on Labor Standards of the Committee on Education and Labor, hearings on the Federal Boxing Board, pursuant to H.R. 2726, 96th Cong., 1st Sess., *Congressional Record,* 1979, p. 111 (hereafter cited as "Federal Boxing Board Hearings, 1979").
41. Hare, pp. 7–8.
42. "Federal Boxing Board Hearings, 1979," pp. 146–47.
43. Massachusetts, report on the examination of the accounts of the Boxers' Fund Board, Sept. 15, 1976–Sept. 15, 1977, no. 78-9-5-15, pp. 4–5, State Library, Boston.
44. "Federal Boxing Board Hearings, 1979," pp. 146–47.
45. Ibid., p. 39.
46. David B. Wilson, "America a Nation of Losers?" *Houston Chronicle,* May 10, 1986, sec. 1, p. 26.
47. Farley, p. 26.
48. *Rosenwieg v. State,* 171 NYS ed. 912, 5 AD 2d 293 (1959), pp. 914–16.
49. Ibid.
50. In Edward F. Carroll, Jr., "Punch Drunk," *Readers Digest,* Feb. 1937 (condensed from the *American Journal of the Medical Sciences,* May 1936), pp. 56–58.
51. "Punchy: Prizefighters Walk on Their Heels after Getting Numerous Hooks to Chin," *Literary Digest,* Apr. 10, 1937, p. 39.
52. Jay Stuller, "The Toughest Job in Sports," *Playboy,* May 1980, p. 165.
53. Ibid., p. 260.
54. J. A. N. Corsellis, C. J. Bruton, and Dorothy Freeman-Browne, "The Aftermath of Boxing," *Psychological Medicine,* 3 (Sept. 1973), pp. 270–303 passim.
55. Stuller, p. 262.
56. Ibid.
57. Patrick Malone, "Death for Many Athletes an Ominous Handmaiden," *Philadelphia Inquirer,* June 16, 1980, sec. C, pp. 1, 6.
58. Thomas Gorman, "Death in the Ring," *Hygenia,* June 1949, pp. 385, 420–21.
59. Carroll, pp. 55–57.

60. Arthur H. Steinhaus, "Boxing—Legalized Murder," *Look,* Jan. 3, 1950, pp. 34–39.
61. Perry, p. 63.
62. *New York Times,* May 24, 1962, p. 42; interview with Dr. David Loiselle, June 17, 1980, Chapel Hill, N.C.; *Houston Chronicle,* June 16, 1986, sec. 7, p. 1.
63. Corsellis et al., pp. 275–78.
64. Ibid.; Marvin Petal, "Manly Art of Self-Defense: Legalized Murder or Healthy Outlet," *New York Times,* May 12, 1974, sec. 5, p. 2.
65. Ibid., p. 303.
66. David Noonan, "Boxing and the Brain," *New York Times Magazine,* June 12, 1983, pp. 40, 58.
67. Ibid.
68. George Lundberg, "Boxing Should Be Banned in Civilized Countries," *JAMA,* 249 (Jan. 14, 1983), p. 250.
69. American Medical Association, Council on Scientific Affairs, "Brain Injury in Boxing," *JAMA,* 249 (Jan. 14, 1983), pp. 256–57.
70. Ibid.
71. *Houston Post,* June 24, 1983, p. 4C; *Chronicle of Higher Education,* July 20, 1983, p. 7.
72. *Houston Chronicle,* May 9, 1986, sec. 1, p. 8;
73. Ralph Wiley, "Then All the Joy Turned to Sorrow," *Sports Illustrated,* Nov. 22, 1982, p. 33.
74. J. I. Maguire and W. E. Benson, "Retinal Injury and Detachment in Boxers," *JAMA,* 255 (May 9, 1986), p. 2453.
75. Ibid.
76. Russell Patterson, "On Boxing and Liberty," *JAMA,* 255 (May 9, 1986), pp. 2481–82; Wally Tokarz, "Safety Issue Dominates Conference on Boxing," *American Medical News,* Mar. 11, 1983.
77. James J. Kilpatrick, "Boxing: An Uncivilized Activity," Universal Press syndicated column, ca. 1982.
78. New Jersey Commission of Investigation, Interim Report and Recommendations on the Inadequate Regulation of Boxing (Trenton: State Printing Office, 1984), pp. 12–17 (hereafter cited as "Inadequate Regulation of Boxing").
79. "A Boxer Beats a Bruiser," *Outlook,* Oct. 6, 1926, p. 167.
80. Seymour Feshbach, "The Stimulating versus Cathartic Effects of a Vicarious Aggressive Activity," *Journal of Abnormal Psychology,* 63 (1961), p. 381–85.
81. Leonard Berkowitz, *Aggression: A Social Psychological Analysis* (New York: McGraw Hill, 1962), p. 242.
82. Ibid., pp. 219–20.
83. Ibid., pp. 242–43.
84. B. F. Husman, "Aggression in Boxers and Wrestlers as Measured by

Projective Techniques," *American Association of Health and Physical Education Research Quarterly,* 26 (1955), pp. 421-25.

85. Husman, p. 422; Berkowitz, p. 204.
86. "Benny Leonard Disagrees with Bertrand Russell on Boxing," *Literary Digest,* Mar. 17, 1928, p. 56.
87. Quoted in Norman Cousins, "Who Killed Benny Paret?" *Saturday Review,* May 5, 1962, p. 14.
88. Ibid.
89. "A Ring Requiem," *Commonweal,* Apr. 21, 1962, p. 73.
90. "Inadequate Regulation of Boxing," passim.
91. Ibid., pp. 1-2.
92. Ibid., pp. 67-70.
93. Ibid., p. 19.
94. Ibid., p. 2.
95. Ibid.
96. "Organized Crime in Boxing," pp. 1-3.
97. Ibid., pp. 2-3.
98. Ibid., pp. 106-9.
99. Ibid., pp. 80-82, 111-12.
100. Ibid., p. 111.
101. Ibid., p. 45.
102. Ibid., pp. 55-72, 91.
103. Ibid., p. 2.
104. Ibid., pp. 55-72.
105. Ibid., pp. 118-26.
106. Ibid., p. 126.
107. Ibid., p. 3.
108. "The Cost of the Dempsey-Tunney Fight," pp. 181-82.

Index

A Note on the Author

Jeffrey T. Sammons is an assistant professor of history, director of Afro-American studies, and Henry Rutgers Fellow at Rutgers University–Camden. A native of Bridgeton, New Jersey, he was educated at Rutgers University, Tufts University, and the University of North Carolina at Chapel Hill. He is the author of several scholarly articles and is currently writing a book on South Africa.